OpenStack Cloud Computing Cookbook

Third Edition

Over 110 effective recipes to help you build and operate OpenStack cloud computing, storage, networking, and automation

Kevin Jackson

Cody Bunch

Egle Sigler

[PACKT] PUBLISHING

open source

community experience distilled

BIRMINGHAM - MUMBAI

OpenStack Cloud Computing Cookbook
Third Edition

First published: September 2012

Second edition: October 2013

Third edition: August 2015

Production reference: 1170815

Published by Packt Publishing Ltd.
Livery Place
35 Livery Street
Birmingham B3 2PB, UK.

ISBN 978-1-78217-478-3

www.packtpub.com

Credits

Authors
Kevin Jackson
Cody Bunch
Egle Sigler

Reviewers
Chris Beatty
Walter Bentley
Victoria Martinez de la Cruz
Stefan Lenz
Andy McCrae
Melissa Palmer
Sriram Rajan

Commissioning Editor
Kartikey Pandey

Acquisition Editor
Indrajit Das

Content Development Editor
Akashdeep Kundu

Technical Editors
Naveenkumar Jain
Narsimha Pai

Copy Editors
Roshni Banerjee
Trishya Hajare

Project Coordinator
Milton Dsouza

Proofreader
Safis Editing

Indexer
Hemangini Bari

Graphics
Sheetal Aute

Production Coordinator
Nitesh Thakur

Cover Work
Nitesh Thakur

Foreword

At CERN, the European Organization for Nuclear Research, physicists and engineers are probing the fundamental structure of the universe. They use the world's largest and most complex scientific instruments to study the basic constituents of matter—the fundamental particles. The particles are made to collide together at close to the speed of light. The process gives clues to physicists about how the particles interact and provides insights into the fundamental laws of nature.

The Large Hadron Collider (LHC) is the world's largest and most powerful particle accelerator. The LHC consists of a 27-kilometer ring of superconducting magnets with a number of accelerating structures to boost the energy of the particles along the way. Inside the accelerator, two high-energy particle beams travel at close to the speed of light, before they are made to collide. This produces 27 petabytes of data every year, which is recorded and analyzed by thousands of computers in the CERN data centre.

With an upgrade to the LHC in 2015 to nearly double the collision energy, it was clear that further computing resources were needed. To provide the additional capacity and be more responsive to the users, a new approach was needed. In 2012, a small team at CERN started looking at OpenStack, a piece of open source software, to create computing clouds. It was a very promising technology with an enthusiastic community but a significant level of complexity. Along with the code being very new, those were very early days for the documentation and training. We wanted to educate people rapidly to start the project and so looked for guides to make the new administrators productive. This was when we encountered the first edition of the book, *OpenStack Cloud Computing Cookbook*. It became the standard document for newcomers in the team to understand the concepts, set up their first clouds, and then start work on the CERN cloud.

As the cloud evolved and the OpenStack technology matured, we continued to use this guide, even as the members of the team rotated, building small clouds to try out new concepts and investigate the flexibility of cloud computing.

Over the years, I have frequently met Kevin, Cody and Ėgle at the OpenStack summits that give the community an opportunity to meet and exchange experiences. With OpenStack evolving so rapidly, it also gives an opportunity to get the latest editions of the cookbook, which they have continued to keep up to date.

The CERN cloud is now in production across two data centers in Geneva and Budapest, with over 3,000 servers running tens of thousands of virtual machines. With new staff members joining frequently, we continue to use the cookbook as a key part of the team's training and look forward to the updates in the latest edition.

Tim Bell

Infrastructure Manager, CERN

About the Authors

Kevin Jackson is married and has three children. He is an experienced IT professional working with business and enterprises of all sizes at Rackspace as an OpenStack and private cloud specialist. Kevin has been working with OpenStack since early 2011 and has extensive experience of various flavors of Linux, Unix, and hosting environments. Kevin can be found on Twitter at `@itarchitectkev`.

Kevin authored the first edition and coauthored the second edition of the *OpenStack Cloud Computing Cookbook, Packt Publishing*. Kevin also coauthored OpenStack Foundation's *OpenStack Architecture Design Guide* during a 5-day book sprint in California.

I'd like to thank Cody for stepping up to the plate again to go through the pain and anguish to get another edition of the book out. Also thanks, of course, go to Egle, whom we somehow commandeered to help get this out the door bigger and better than before. We have a whole bunch of tech reviewers from across the globe too who have helped keep us within reach of our goals, so thanks for keeping it real.

I'd also like to thank my family, although I'm not sure they have realized I wrote another one. I think I may have just about gotten away with this one unscathed.

Finally, I'd like to thank Rackspace for giving me the opportunity and support to pursue such endeavors and the many people I bug now for answers to stupid questions.

Cody Bunch is a principal architect in the Rackspace Private Cloud group based out of San Antonio, Texas. Cody has been working with OpenStack since early 2012, coauthored the second edition of this book and also coauthored *OpenStack Security Guide*. Cody has extensive experience with virtualized and cloud environments in various-sized enterprises and hosting environments. Cody can be found on Twitter at `@cody_bunch`.

I'd like to thank Kevin for coming along on this crazy ride, yet again. I would also like to thank Egle, who jumped into the fray and has gone above and beyond to make this book more awesome than the last one. This book would not be possible without the wonderful reviewers, as well as the folks at Packt who stepped up their game between editions.

Next up, and likely much more important, to thank are my kids and loving wife. Without their support, well, I'm not entirely sure this edition would have made it out the door. Also, on the time, understanding, and support list is my employer, Rackspace.

I'd like to thank the writers, publisher, reviewers, and employer. While this is a small army of folks who help with the writing and publishing of this edition, I think it would be super amiss if I didn't thank the awesome-tastic OpenStack community for whom we wrote this. Y'all provide not just the support, technical guidance, and such, but also the "why" behind putting another volume out in the market. Thanks!

Egle Sigler is an OpenStack Foundation board member and a principal architect in the Rackspace Private Cloud group based out of San Antonio, Texas. Egle holds an M.S. degree in computer science. She started her career as a software developer and still has a soft spot for all the people who write, test, and deploy code, since she has had the chance to do all of those tasks throughout her career. Egle dreams about a day when writing, testing, and deploying code will be a seamless and easy process—bug and frustration free for all. Egle believes that knowledge should be shared and has tried to do this by writing this book, giving talks and workshops at conferences, and blogging. Egle can be found on Twitter at `@eglute`.

She has coauthored *DevOps for VMware Administrators* (VMware Press Technology).

I would like to thank my husband, my love, and my technical advisor for his constant and unwavering support while writing, traveling, installing, and troubleshooting. For some reason, it is always the networking that needs troubleshooting.

I ask for forgiveness from my friends and family, who didn't get to talk to me very much while I was working on this book.

OpenStack developers, quality engineers, operators, users, and documentation writers, thank you for making OpenStack better each day!

Kevin and Cody, thank you for bringing me along on this adventure! I cannot believe how much quality work was already put into this book, as well as into the Vagrant environment scripts. Technical reviewers, thank you for volunteering hundreds of hours to review everything. Reviewers and editors from Packt, thank you for your prompt communication and constant feedback. Rackers, thank you for your advice and guidance. Lastly, thanks to Rackspace for supporting my writing endeavors.

About the Reviewers

Chris Beatty is a seasoned IT professional with a varied background in systems administration and infrastructure architecture. He is currently working for Rackspace, helping enterprise customers design and run high-performant hosted solutions.

> I'd like to thank my wife and children for giving me the time to review this book, as well as my colleagues for asking me to help out!!

Walter Bentley is a Rackspace private cloud solutions architect. He is a new Racker with a diverse background in production systems administration and solutions architecture. He brings over 17 years of experience across numerous industries, such as online marketing, financial, insurance, aviation, the food industry, and education. In the past, he has always been the requestor, consumer, and advisor to companies to use technologies such as OpenStack. Now, he is a promoter of the OpenStack technology and a cloud educator.

> I would like to sincerely thank the authors for allowing me to be part of this great publication and opportunity.

Victoria Martinez de la Cruz is a licentiate in computer sciences from the Computer Sciences and Engineering department of Universidad Nacional del Sur in Bahia Blanca, Argentina. During her last years in college, she got started with OpenStack through the GNOME Outreachy and Google Summer of Code internships. She is currently a software engineer at Red Hat and a core member of OpenStack's Trove and Zaqar projects. Her main interests are operative systems, networks, and databases. She is FOSS passionate and loves to help newcomers to get involved with open source projects. Victoria can be contacted at `victoria@vmartinezdelacruz.com`.

> I would like to thank the authors and publishers of *OpenStack Cookbook Third Edition* for giving me the opportunity to join as a technical reviewer; it was a great experience!

Stefan Lenz works for BMW in Munich. He is a manager of the data center and cloud services division in BMW's global IT organization. In this role, he is responsible for the delivery of compute, storage, and network services for BMW worldwide.

He holds a PhD in nuclear physics from Erlangen University in Germany and has worked as a postdoctoral associate at Yale university, doing nuclear research on high-performance computers. He worked as a consultant for high-performance computing in the German automotive industry before becoming an IT architect for high-performance computers and engineering IT at BMW. From 2002 to 2014, he worked in several initiatives and projects to consolidate and globalize BMW's IT organization.

He is married, lives in Munich, and likes to ski, hike, and bike in the Alps. Together with his wife, he has written six books on hiking, mountain bike tours, and the Camino de Santiago in Spain. You can contact him on Twitter as `@stefan_km_lenz` or via his website `www.serverfabrik.de`.

> During the summer of 2014, I spent long hours in my private computer lab in the basement of our house, learning the basics of Openstack. My guide on that journey was the first edition of *OpenStack Cookbook*. I'd like to thank the authors, who have helped me a lot. I would also like to thank my wife for her support, her patience, and for donating two old computers from her own business to my lab.

Andy McCrae is a software developer at Rackspace working within the Rackspace Private Cloud team. Andy began his career in 2007 as a Linux system administrator for Rackspace after completing master's of engineering (MEng), majoring in computer science at University College London (UCL).

Andy specializes in Swift (Object Storage) and Ansible. Andy was the core contributor to OpenStack-Chef and is now working on the os-ansible-deployment community projects within OpenStack.

Recently, Andy spoke at the Vancouver OpenStack Summit on managing logging within an OpenStack environment.

Melissa Palmer is a systems engineer and architect and a virtualization, infrastructure, and OpenStack enthusiast. She has bachelor's and master's of engineering degrees focused on electrical engineering and secure networked systems design. As a strong advocate of the community, Melissa is a VMUG member and has been featured on panel discussions and podcasts for IT architecture and community programs. She is also the creative director of the Virtual Design Master challenge located at `http://virtualdesignmaster.com`. Melissa enjoys cooking, writing, and attending rocket launches in her free time. You can find Melissa on Twitter at `@vMiss33` or on her blog at `http://vMiss.net`.

Sriram Rajan is a principal engineer at Rackspace, where he is responsible for designing solutions for its customers and assists them with their automation needs. Prior to Rackspace, he worked as a systems programmer at Texas State University, from where he also earned his master's degree in computer science. He has more than a decade of professional experience working with Linux systems, networks, programming, and security. In his nonprofessional life, he spends time traveling, working on home automation, watching cricket, programming for fun, and discussing technology.

www.PacktPub.com

Support files, eBooks, discount offers, and more

For support files and downloads related to your book, please visit www.PacktPub.com.

Did you know that Packt offers eBook versions of every book published, with PDF and ePub files available? You can upgrade to the eBook version at www.PacktPub.com and as a print book customer, you are entitled to a discount on the eBook copy. Get in touch with us at service@packtpub.com for more details.

At www.PacktPub.com, you can also read a collection of free technical articles, sign up for a range of free newsletters and receive exclusive discounts and offers on Packt books and eBooks.

https://www2.packtpub.com/books/subscription/packtlib

Do you need instant solutions to your IT questions? PacktLib is Packt's online digital book library. Here, you can search, access, and read Packt's entire library of books.

Why Subscribe?

- Fully searchable across every book published by Packt
- Copy and paste, print, and bookmark content
- On demand and accessible via a web browser

Free Access for Packt account holders

If you have an account with Packt at www.PacktPub.com, you can use this to access PacktLib today and view 9 entirely free books. Simply use your login credentials for immediate access.

Table of Contents

Preface

OpenStack is open source software for building public and private clouds. It is now a global success and is developed and supported by thousands of people around the globe; backed by leading players in the cloud space today. This book is specifically designed to quickly help you get up to speed with OpenStack and give you the confidence and understanding to roll it out into your own data centers. From test installations of OpenStack running under VirtualBox to automated installation recipes that help you scale out production environments, this book covers a wide range of topics that help you install and configure a private cloud. This book will show you the following:

- How to install and configure all the core components of OpenStack to run an environment that can be managed and operated just like Rackspace, HP Helion, and other cloud environments
- How to master the complete private cloud stack; from scaling out Compute resources to managing object storage services for highly redundant, highly available storages
- Practical, real-world examples of each service built upon in each chapter, allowing you to progress with the confidence that they will work in your own environments

The *OpenStack Cloud Computing Cookbook* gives you clear, step-by-step instructions to install and run your own private cloud successfully. It is full of practical and applicable recipes that enable you to use the latest capabilities of OpenStack and implement them.

What this book covers

Chapter 1, Keystone – OpenStack Identity Service, takes you through the installation and configuration of Keystone, which underpins all of the other OpenStack services.

Chapter 2, Glance – OpenStack Image Service, teaches you how to install, configure, and use the Image service within an OpenStack environment.

Chapter 3, Neutron – OpenStack Networking, helps you install and configure OpenStack networking, including new features such as DVR.

Chapter 4, Nova – OpenStack Compute, teaches you how to set up and use OpenStack Compute along with examples to get you started by running OpenStack Compute within a VirtualBox environment.

Chapter 5, Swift – OpenStack Object Storage, teaches you how to configure and use OpenStack Object Storage along with examples showing this service running within a VirtualBox environment.

Chapter 6, Using OpenStack Object Storage, teaches you how to use the storage service to store and retrieve files and objects.

Chapter 7, Administering OpenStack Object Storage, takes you through how to use tools and techniques that can be used to run OpenStack Storage within data centers.

Chapter 8, Cinder – OpenStack Block Storage, teaches you how to install and configure the persistent block storage service for use, by using instances running in an OpenStack Compute environment.

Chapter 9, More OpenStack, explores other features of OpenStack such as Neutron's LBaaS and FWaaS services, Ceilometer, and Heat.

Chapter 10, Using the OpenStack Dashboard, teaches you how to install and use the web user interface to perform tasks such as creating users, modifying security groups, and launching instances.

Chapter 11, Production OpenStack, shows you how to use Ansible for automated installations and introduces you to tools and techniques for making OpenStack services resilient and highly available.

What you need for this book

To use this book, you will need access to computers or servers that have hardware virtualization capabilities. In a typical small starter installation of OpenStack, you will need a Controller host, Network host, and Compute host. To run Swift, we provide the steps to create a multi-node environment consisting of a proxy server and five storage nodes.

To set up the lab environment, you will install and use Oracle's VirtualBox and Vagrant. You can access details of how to set up your computer using VirtualBox and Vagrant by visiting `http://bit.ly/OpenStackCoobookSandbox`.

There are additional recipes to get you started with the lab environment, and these are available at `http://www.openstackcookbook.com`. Refer to this website for information on the installation of supporting software such as MariaDB/MySQL. More information can be found at `http://bit.ly/OpenStackCookbookPreReqs`.

To fully utilize the automated Ansible scripts in *Chapter 11, Production OpenStack*, it is assumed that the reader has access to six physical servers.

Who this book is for

This book is aimed at system administrators and technical architects moving from a virtualized environment to cloud environments; who are familiar with cloud computing platforms. Knowledge of virtualization and managing Linux environments is expected. Prior knowledge or experience of OpenStack is not required, although beneficial.

Conventions

In this book, you will find a number of styles of text that distinguish between different kinds of information. Here are some examples of these styles, and an explanation of their meaning.

Code words in text, database table names, folder names, filenames, file extensions, pathnames, dummy URLs, user input, and Twitter handles are shown as follows: "Controlling OpenStack Object Storage services is achieved using the tool called `swift-init`."

A block of code is set as follows:

```
account-server: bind_port = 6000
container-server: bind_port = 6001
object-server: bind_port = 6002
```

When we wish to draw your attention to a particular part of a code block, the relevant lines or items are set in bold:

```
[swift-hash]
# Random unique string used on all nodes
swift_hash_path_prefix=a4rUmUIgJYXpKhbh
swift_hash_path_suffix=NESuuUEqc6OXwy6X
```

Any command-line input or output is written as follows:

```
sudo swift-init all start
sudo swift-init all stop
sudo swift-init all restart
```

New terms and **important words** are shown in bold. Words that you see on the screen, in menus or dialog boxes for example, appear in the text like this: "An important field is the **Common Name** field."

Warnings or important notes appear in a box like this.

Tips and tricks appear like this.

Reader feedback

Feedback from our readers is always welcome. Let us know what you think about this book—what you liked or may have disliked. Reader feedback is important for us to develop titles that you really get the most out of.

To send us general feedback, simply send an e-mail to `feedback@packtpub.com`, and mention the book title via the subject of your message.

If there is a topic that you have expertise in and you are interested in either writing or contributing to a book, see our author guide on `www.packtpub.com/authors`.

Customer support

Now that you are the proud owner of a Packt book, we have a number of things to help you to get the most from your purchase.

Downloading the example code

You can download the example code files for this book at `https://github.com/OpenStackCookbook/OpenStackCookbook`. All the support files are available here.

Downloading the color images of this book

We also provide you with a PDF file that has color images of the screenshots/diagrams used in this book. The color images will help you better understand the changes in the output. You can download this file from: `http://www.packtpub.com/sites/default/files/downloads/47830S_ColoredImages.pdf`.

Errata

Although we have taken every care to ensure the accuracy of our content, mistakes do happen. If you find a mistake in one of our books—maybe a mistake in the text or the code—we would be grateful if you would report this to us. By doing so, you can save other readers from frustration and help us improve subsequent versions of this book. If you find any errata, please report them by visiting `http://www.packtpub.com/submit-errata`, selecting your book, clicking on the **errata submission form** link, and entering the details of your errata. Once your errata are verified, your submission will be accepted and the errata will be uploaded on our website, or added to any list of existing errata, under the Errata section of that title. Any existing errata can be viewed by selecting your title from `http://www.packtpub.com/support`.

Piracy

Piracy of copyright material on the Internet is an ongoing problem across all media. At Packt, we take the protection of our copyright and licenses very seriously. If you come across any illegal copies of our works, in any form, on the Internet, please provide us with the location address or website name immediately so that we can pursue a remedy.

Please contact us at `copyright@packtpub.com` with a link to the suspected pirated material.

We appreciate your help in protecting our authors, and our ability to bring you valuable content.

Questions

You can contact us at `questions@packtpub.com` if you are having a problem with any aspect of the book, and we will do our best to address it.

1
Keystone – OpenStack Identity Service

In this chapter, we will cover:

- Installing the OpenStack Identity Service
- Configuring OpenStack Identity for SSL communication
- Creating tenants in Keystone
- Configuring roles in Keystone
- Adding users to Keystone
- Defining service endpoints
- Creating the service tenant and service users
- Configuring OpenStack Identity for LDAP Integration

Introduction

The OpenStack Identity service, known as **Keystone**, provides services for authenticating and managing user accounts and role information for our OpenStack cloud environment. It is a crucial service that underpins the authentication and verification between all of our OpenStack cloud services and is the first service that needs to be installed within an OpenStack environment. The OpenStack Identity service authenticates users and tenants by sending a validated authorization token between all OpenStack services. This token is used for authentication and verification so that you can use that service, such as OpenStack Storage and Compute. Therefore, configuration of the OpenStack Identity service must be completed first, consisting of creating appropriate roles for users and services, tenants, the user accounts, and the service API endpoints that make up our cloud infrastructure.

In Keystone, we have the concepts of **tenants**, **roles** and **users**. A tenant is like a project and has resources such as users, images, and instances, as well as networks in it that are only known to that particular project. A user can belong to one or more tenants and is able to switch between these projects to gain access to those resources. Users within a tenant can have various roles assigned. In the most basic scenario, a user can be assigned either the role of *admin* or just be a *member*. When a user has *admin* privileges within a tenant, they are able to utilize features that can affect the tenant (such as modifying external networks), whereas a normal user is assigned the *member* role, which is generally assigned to perform user-related roles, such as spinning up instances, creating volumes, and creating tenant only networks.

Installing the OpenStack Identity Service

We will be performing an installation and configuration of the OpenStack Identity service, known as Keystone, using the Ubuntu Cloud Archive. Once configured, connecting to our OpenStack cloud environment will be performed through our new OpenStack Identity service.

The backend datastore for our OpenStack Identity service will be a MariaDB database. The environment we will be installing is shown in the following figure. In this chapter, we will be concentrating on the Controller host.

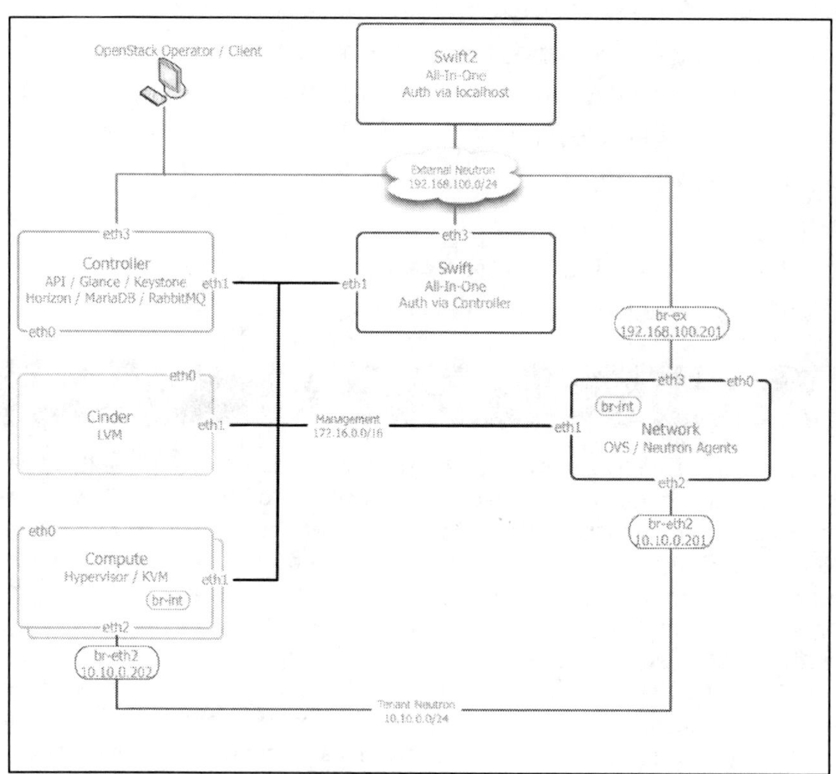

Getting ready

To ensure that we're running the Ubuntu Cloud Archive, we must first configure our Ubuntu 14.04 installation to use this service. For more information, visit `http://bit.ly/OpenStackCookbookCloudArchive`.

All of the steps can be found at `http://www.openstackcookbook.com/`.

We will configure Keystone to use MariaDB as the database backend, so this needs to be installed prior to installing Keystone.

If MariaDB is not installed, visit `http://bit.ly/OpenStackCookbookPreReqs` for instructions on how to do this.

Ensure that you have a suitable server available for installation of the OpenStack Identity service components. If you are using the accompanying Vagrant environment, as described in the *Preface*, this will be the `controller` node.

Make sure that you are logged in to the `controller` node and ensure that it has Internet access to allow us to install the required packages in our environment for running Keystone. If you created this node with Vagrant, you can execute the following command:

```
vagrant ssh controller
```

The instructions here assume that the `controller` node has two IP addresses. It will have a front-facing IP address, 192.168.100.200, and a backside IP address, 172.16.0.200, (which is also the address of the MariaDB server). The reason it has two addresses is that internal data will communicate over the backside IP address (for example, database traffic), and any Keystone traffic will traverse the front.

How to do it...

Carry out the following instructions to install the OpenStack Identity service:

1. Installation of the OpenStack Identity service is done by specifying the Keystone package in Ubuntu, and we do this as follows:

   ```
   sudo apt-get update
   sudo apt-get install ntp keystone python-keyring
   ```

2. Once installed, we need to configure the backend database store, so we first create the `keystone` database in MariaDB. We do this as follows (here, we have a user in MariaDB called `root` with the password `openstack`, which can create databases):

```
MYSQL_ROOT_PASS=openstack
mysql -uroot -p$MYSQL_ROOT_PASS -e "CREATE DATABASE \
    keystone;"
```

3. It is good practice to create a user that is specific to our OpenStack Identity service, so we create a Keystone user in the database as follows:

```
MYSQL_KEYSTONE_PASS=openstack
mysql -uroot -p$MYSQL_ROOT_PASS -e "GRANT ALL PRIVILEGES ON \
keystone.* TO 'keystone'@'localhost' IDENTIFIED BY \
'$MYSQL_KEYSTONE_PASS';"
mysql -uroot -p$MYSQL_ROOT_PASS -e "GRANT ALL PRIVILEGES ON \
keystone.* TO 'keystone'@'%' IDENTIFIED BY \
'$MYSQL_KEYSTONE_PASS';"
```

4. We then need to configure the OpenStack Identity service by editing the `/etc/keystone/keystone.conf` file to have the following content:

```
[DEFAULT]
admin_token = ADMIN
log_dir=/var/log/keystone

[database]
connection = mysql://keystone:openstack@172.16.0.200/keystone

[extra_headers]
Distribution = Ubuntu
use_syslog = True
syslog_log_facility = LOG_LOCAL0
```

5. We can now restart the `keystone` service to pick up these changes:

```
sudo stop keystone
sudo start keystone
```

6. With `keystone` started, we can now populate the `keystone` database with the required tables by issuing the following command:

```
sudo keystone-manage db_sync
```

Congratulations! We have now installed the OpenStack Identity service and it is ready for use in our OpenStack environment.

How it works...

A convenient way to install the OpenStack Identity service in our OpenStack environment is by using the Ubuntu packages. Once installed, we configure our MariaDB database server with a `keystone` database and set up the `keystone.conf` configuration file with the corresponding values. After starting the Keystone service, running the `keystone-manage db_sync` command populates the `keystone` database with the appropriate tables ready for us to add in the required users, roles, and tenants required in our OpenStack environment.

Configuring OpenStack Identity for SSL communication

One of the many updates to this book will be a more hardened all-around approach. To that end, we begin by enabling SSL communication for services with Keystone by default. It is important to note that we will be doing this via self-signed certificates to illustrate how to configure the services. It is strongly recommended that you acquire the appropriate certificates from a **Certificate Authority** (**CA**) for deployment in production.

Getting ready

Ensure that you are logged in to the `controller` node and that it has Internet access to allow us to install the required packages in our environment for running Keystone. If you created this node with Vagrant, you can execute the following command:

```
vagrant ssh controller
```

How to do it...

Carry out the following instructions to configure the Keystone service:

1. Before we can configure Keystone to use SSL, we need to generate the required OpenSSL Certificates. To do so, log in to the server that is running Keystone and issue the following commands:

   ```
   sudo apt-get install python-keystoneclient
   ```

   ```
   keystone-manage ssl_setup --keystone-user keystone \
       --keystone-group keystone
   ```

The command `keystone-manage ssl_setup` is not intended for production use. This is a convenient tool for creating self-signed certificates for Keystone.

2. Once our certificates are generated, we can use them when communicating with our Keystone service. We can refer to the generated CA file for our other services by placing this in an accessible place. To do so, issue the following commands:

   ```
   sudo cp /etc/keystone/ssl/certs/ca.pem /etc/ssl/certs/ca.pem
   sudo c_rehash /etc/ssl/certs/ca.pem
   ```

3. We also take the same CA and CA Key file to use on our client, so copy these where you will be running the relevant `python-*client` tools. In our Vagrant environment, we can copy this to our host as follows:

   ```
   sudo cp /etc/keystone/ssl/certs/ca.pem /vagrant/ca.pem
   sudo cp /etc/keystone/ssl/certs/cakey.pem /vagrant/cakey.pem
   ```

4. We then need to edit the Keystone configuration file `/etc/keystone/keystone.conf` to include the following section:

   ```
   [ssl]
   enable = True
   certfile = /etc/keystone/ssl/certs/keystone.pem
   keyfile = /etc/keystone/ssl/private/keystonekey.pem
   ca_certs = /etc/keystone/ssl/certs/ca.pem
   cert_subject=/C=US/ST=Unset/L=Unset/O=Unset/CN=192.168.100.200
   ca_key = /etc/keystone/ssl/certs/cakey.pem
   ```

5. Finally, restart the Keystone service:

   ```
   sudo stop keystone
   sudo start keystone
   ```

How it works...

The OpenStack services normally intercommunicate via standard HTTP requests. This provides a large degree of flexibility, but it comes at the cost of all communication happening in plain text. By adding SSL certificates and changing Keystone's configuration, all communication with Keystone will now be encrypted via HTTPS.

Creating tenants in Keystone

A tenant in OpenStack is a project, and the two terms are generally used interchangeably. Users can't be created without having a tenant assigned to them, so these must be created first. For this section, we will create a tenant called **cookbook** for our users.

Getting ready

We will be using the `keystone` client to operate Keystone. If the `python-keystoneclient` tool isn't available, follow the steps described at `http://bit.ly/OpenStackCookbookClientInstall`.

Ensure that we have our environment set correctly to access our OpenStack environment for administrative purposes:

```
export OS_TENANT_NAME=cookbook
export OS_USERNAME=admin
export OS_PASSWORD=openstack
export OS_AUTH_URL=https://192.168.100.200:5000/v2.0/
export OS_NO_CACHE=1
export OS_KEY=/vagrant/cakey.pem
export OS_CACERT=/vagrant/ca.pem
```

You can use the `controller` node if no other machines are available on your network, as this has the `python-keystoneclient` and the relevant access to the OpenStack environment. If you are using the Vagrant environment issue the following command to get access to the Controller:

```
vagrant ssh controller
```

How to do it...

To create a tenant in our OpenStack environment, perform the following steps:

1. We start by creating a tenant called cookbook:

```
keystone tenant-create \
    --name cookbook \
    --description "Default Cookbook Tenant" \
    --enabled true
```

This will produce output similar to:

```
+-------------+----------------------------------+
|   Property  |              Value               |
+-------------+----------------------------------+
| description |      Default Cookbook Tenant     |
|   enabled   |               True               |
|      id     | fba7b31689714d1ab39a751bc9483efd |
|     name    |             cookbook             |
+-------------+----------------------------------+
```

2. We also need an `admin` tenant so that when we create users in this tenant, they have access to our complete environment. We do this in the same way as in the previous step:

```
keystone tenant-create \
    --name admin \
    --description "Admin Tenant" \
    --enabled true
```

How it works...

Creation of the tenants is achieved by using the `keystone` client, specifying the `tenant-create` option with the following syntax:

```
keystone tenant-create \
    --name tenant_name \
    --description "A description" \
    --enabled true
```

The `tenant_name` is an arbitrary string and must not contain spaces. On creation of the tenant, this returns an ID associated with it that we use when adding users to this tenant. To see a list of tenants and the associated IDs in our environment, we can issue the following command:

```
keystone tenant-list
```

Configuring roles in Keystone

Roles are the permissions given to users within a tenant. Here, we will configure two roles: an `admin` role that allows for the administration of our environment, and a `member role` that is given to ordinary users who will be using the cloud environment.

Getting ready

We will be using the `keystone` client to operate Keystone. If the `python-keystoneclient` tool isn't available, follow the steps described at `http://bit.ly/OpenStackCookbookClientInstall`.

Ensure that we have our environment set correctly to access our OpenStack environment for administrative purposes:

```
export OS_TENANT_NAME=cookbook
export OS_USERNAME=admin
export OS_PASSWORD=openstack
export OS_AUTH_URL=https://192.168.100.200:5000/v2.0/
export OS_NO_CACHE=1
export OS_KEY=/vagrant/cakey.pem
export OS_CACERT=/vagrant/ca.pem
```

You can use the `controller` node if no other machines are available on your network, as this has the `python-keystoneclient` and the relevant access to the OpenStack environment. If you are using the Vagrant environment, issue the following command to get access to the Controller:

`vagrant ssh controller`

How to do it...

To create the required roles in our OpenStack environment, perform the following steps:

1. Create the `admin` role as follows:

   ```
   # admin role
   keystone role-create --name admin
   ```

   You will get an output like this:

   ```
   +----------+----------------------------------+
   | Property |              Value               |
   +----------+----------------------------------+
   |    id    | 625b81ae9f024366bbe023a62ab8a18d |
   |   name   |              admin               |
   +----------+----------------------------------+
   ```

2. To create the `Member role`, we repeat the step and specify the `Member role`:

```
# Member role
keystone role-create --name Member
```

How it works...

Creation of the roles is simply achieved by using the `keystone` client and specifying the `role-create` option with the following syntax:

```
keystone role-create --name role_name
```

The `role_name` attribute can't be arbitrary for `admin` and `Member roles`. The `admin` role has been set by default in `/etc/keystone/policy.json` as having administrative rights:

```
{
    "admin_required": [["role:admin"], ["is_admin:1"]]
}
```

The `Member role` is also configured by default in the OpenStack Dashboard, Horizon, for a non-admin user created through the web interface.

On creation of the role, the ID associated with is returned, and we can use it when assigning roles to users. To see a list of roles and the associated IDs in our environment, we can issue the following command:

```
keystone role-list
```

Adding users to Keystone

Adding users to the OpenStack Identity service requires that the user has a tenant that they can exist in and there is a defined role that can be assigned to them. For this section, we will create two users. The first user will be named `admin` and will have the `admin` role assigned to them in the `cookbook` tenant. The second user will be named `demo` and will have the `Member` role assigned to them in the same `cookbook` tenant.

Getting ready

We will be using the `keystone client` to operate Keystone. If the `python-keystoneclient` tool isn't available, follow the steps described at `http://bit.ly/OpenStackCookbookClientInstall`.

Ensure that we have our environment set correctly to access our OpenStack environment for administrative purposes:

```
export OS_TENANT_NAME=cookbook
export OS_USERNAME=admin
export OS_PASSWORD=openstack
export OS_AUTH_URL=https://192.168.100.200:5000/v2.0/
export OS_NO_CACHE=1
export OS_KEY=/vagrant/cakey.pem
export OS_CACERT=/vagrant/ca.pem
```

You can use the `controller` node if no other machines are available on your network, as this has the `python-keystoneclient` and the relevant access to the OpenStack environment. If you are using the Vagrant environment, issue the following command to get access to the Controller:

```
vagrant ssh controller
```

How to do it...

To create the required users in our OpenStack environment, perform the following steps:

1. To create a user in the `cookbook` tenant, we first need to get the `cookbook` tenant ID. To do this, issue the following command, which we conveniently store in a variable named `TENANT_ID` with the `tenant-list` option:

   ```
   TENANT_ID=$(keystone tenant-list \
       | awk '/\ cookbook\ / {print $2}')
   ```

2. Now that we have the tenant ID, the `admin` user in the `cookbook` tenant is created using the `user-create` option and a password is chosen for the user:

   ```
   PASSWORD=openstack
   keystone user-create \
       --name admin \
       --tenant_id $TENANT_ID \
       --pass $PASSWORD \
       --email root@localhost \
       --enabled true
   ```

The preceding code will produce the following output:

```
+----------+-----------------------------------+
| Property |               Value               |
+----------+-----------------------------------+
|  email   |          root@localhost           |
| enabled  |               True                |
|    id    | 2e23d0673e8a4deabe7c0fb70dfcb9f2  |
|   name   |               admin               |
| tenantId | 14e34722ac7b4fe298886371ec17cf40  |
| username |               admin               |
+----------+-----------------------------------+
```

3. As we are creating the `admin` user, which we are assigning the admin role, we need the admin role ID. We pick out the ID of the `admin` role and conveniently store it in a variable to use it when assigning the role to the user with the `role-list` option:

```
ROLE_ID=$(keystone role-list \
    | awk '/\ admin\ / {print $2}')
```

4. To assign the role to our user, we need to use the user ID that was returned when we created that user. To get this, we can list the users and pick out the ID for that particular user with the following user-list option:

```
USER_ID=$(keystone user-list \
    | awk '/\ admin\ / {print $2}')
```

5. With the tenant ID, user ID, and an appropriate role ID available, we can assign that role to the user with the following user-role-add option:

```
keystone user-role-add \
    --user $USER_ID \
    --role $ROLE_ID \
    --tenant_id $TENANT_ID
```

Note that there is no output produced on successfully running this command.

6. The `admin` user also needs to be in the `admin` tenant for us to be able to administer the complete environment. To do this, we need to get the `admin` tenant ID and then repeat the previous step using this new tenant ID:

```
ADMIN_TENANT_ID=$(keystone tenant-list \
    | awk '/\ admin\ / {print $2}')
keystone user-role-add \
    --user $USER_ID \
    --role $ROLE_ID \
    --tenant_id $ADMIN_TENANT_ID
```

7. To create the `demo` user in the `cookbook` tenant with the `Member role` assigned, we repeat the process defined in steps 1 to 5:

```
# Get the cookbook tenant ID
TENANT_ID=$(keystone tenant-list \
    | awk '/\ cookbook\ / {print $2}')

# Create the user
PASSWORD=openstack
keystone user-create \
    --name demo \
    --tenant_id $TENANT_ID \
    --pass $PASSWORD \
    --email demo@localhost \
    --enabled true

# Get the Member role ID
ROLE_ID=$(keystone role-list \
    | awk '/\ Member\ / {print $2}')

# Get the demo user ID
USER_ID=$(keystone user-list \
    | awk '/\ demo\ / {print $2}')
```

```
# Assign the Member role to the demo user in cookbook
keystone user-role-add \
    --user $USER_ID \
    --role $ROLE_ID \
    --tenant_id $TENANT_ID
```

How it works...

Adding users in the OpenStack Identity service involves a number of steps and dependencies. First, a tenant is required for the user to be part of. Once the tenant exists, the user can be added. At this point, the user has no role associated, so the final step is to designate the role to this user, such as `Member` or `admin`.

Use the following syntax to create a user with the `user-create` option:

```
keystone user-create \
    --name user_name \
    --tenant_id TENANT_ID \
    --pass PASSWORD \
    --email email_address \
    --enabled true
```

The `user_name` attribute is an arbitrary name but cannot contain any spaces. A `password` attribute must be present. In the previous examples, these were set to `openstack`. The `email_address` attribute must also be present.

To assign a role to a user with the `user-role-add` option, use the following syntax:

```
keystone user-role-add \
    --user USER_ID \
    --role ROLE_ID \
    --tenant_id TENANT_ID
```

This means that we need to have the ID of the user, the ID of the role, and the ID of the tenant in order to assign roles to users. These IDs can be found using the following commands:

```
keystone tenant-list
keystone user-list
keystone role-list
```

Defining service endpoints

Each of the services in our cloud environment runs on a particular URL and port—these are the endpoint addresses for our services. When a client communicates with our OpenStack environment that runs the OpenStack Identity service, it is this service that returns the endpoint URLs that the user can use in an OpenStack environment. To enable this feature, we must define these endpoints. In a cloud environment, we can define multiple regions. Regions can be thought of as different datacenters, which would imply that they would have different URLs or IP addresses. Under the OpenStack Identity service, we can define these URL endpoints separately for each region. As we only have a single environment, we will reference this as `RegionOne`.

Getting ready

We will be using the `keystone` command line client to operate Keystone. If the `python-keystoneclient` tool isn't available, follow the steps described at `http://bit.ly/OpenStackCookbookClientInstall`.

Ensure that we have our environment set correctly to access our OpenStack environment for administrative purposes:

```
export OS_TENANT_NAME=cookbook
export OS_USERNAME=admin
export OS_PASSWORD=openstack
export OS_AUTH_URL=https://192.168.100.200:5000/v2.0/
export OS_NO_CACHE=1
export OS_KEY=/vagrant/cakey.pem
export OS_CACERT=/vagrant/ca.pem
```

You can use the `controller` node if no other machines are available on your network, as this has the `python-keystoneclient` and has the relevant access to the OpenStack environment. If you are using the Vagrant environment, issue the following command to get access to the Controller:

`vagrant ssh controller`

How to do it...

Defining the services and their endpoints in the OpenStack Identity service involves running the `keystone` client command. Although we might not have all services currently running in our environment, we will be configuring them within the OpenStack Identity service for future use. To define endpoints for services in our OpenStack environment, carry out the following steps:

1. We can now define the actual services that the OpenStack Identity service needs to know about in our environment:

```
# OpenStack Compute Nova API Endpoint
keystone service-create \
    --name nova \
    --type compute \
    --description 'OpenStack Compute Service'
# OpenStack Compute EC2 API Endpoint
keystone service-create \
    --name ec2 \
    --type ec2 \
    --description 'EC2 Service'

# Glance Image Service Endpoint
keystone service-create \
    --name glance \
    --type image \
    --description 'OpenStack Image Service'

# Keystone Identity Service Endpoint
keystone service-create \
    --name keystone \
    --type identity \
    --description 'OpenStack Identity Service'

# Neutron Networking Service Endpoint
keystone service-create \
    --name network \
```

```
    --type network \
    --description 'OpenStack Network Service'

#Cinder Block Storage Endpoint
keystone service-create \
    --name volume \
    --type volume \
    --description 'Volume Service'
```

2. After we have done this, we can add in the service endpoint URLs that these services run on. To do this, we need the ID that was returned for each of the service endpoints created in the previous step. The ID is then used as a parameter when specifying the endpoint URLS for that service.

> The OpenStack Identity service can be configured to service requests on three URLs: a public facing URL (that the end users use), an administration URL (that users with administrative access can use that might have a different URL), and an internal URL (that is appropriate when presenting the services on either side of a firewall to the public URL).

3. For the following services, we will configure separate public, admin, and internal service URLs to provide appropriate separation for our environment. The public endpoint in the accompanying lab environment will be the nominated public interface IP of our controller, which is 192.168.100.200. The internal endpoint will be 172.16.0.200. The `admin` endpoint will also be the public IP of 192.168.100.200. To do this run the following commands:

```
# OpenStack Compute Nova API
NOVA_SERVICE_ID=$(keystone service-list \
    | awk '/\ nova\ / {print $2}')

PUBLIC_ENDPOINT=192.168.100.200
ADMIN_ENDPOINT=192.168.100.200
INT_ENDPOINT=172.16.0.200

PUBLIC="http://$PUBLIC_ENDPOINT:8774/v2/\$(tenant_id)s"
ADMIN="http://$ADMIN_ENDPOINT:8774/v2/\$(tenant_id)s"
INTERNAL="http://$INT_ENDPOINT:8774/v2/\$(tenant_id)s"
```

```
keystone endpoint-create \
    --region RegionOne \
    --service_id $NOVA_SERVICE_ID \
    --publicurl $PUBLIC \
    --adminurl $ADMIN \
    --internalurl $INTERNAL
```

You will get output similar to what is shown below:

```
+-------------+----------------------------------------------+
|   Property  |                     Value                    |
+-------------+----------------------------------------------+
|   adminurl  | http://192.168.100.200:8774/v2/$(tenant_id)s  |
|      id     |        87b59c5ce8314d8b9029bf1efd5044d7       |
| internalurl |   http://172.16.0.100:8774/v2/$(tenant_id)s   |
|  publicurl  |   http://192.168.100.200:8774/v2/$(tenant_id)s |
|    region   |                  RegionOne                    |
|  service_id |        a3529dcbeab44d479d1f258ae6d202b4       |
+-------------+----------------------------------------------+
```

4. We continue to define the rest of our service endpoints, as shown in the following steps:

```
# OpenStack Compute EC2 API
EC2_SERVICE_ID=$(keystone service-list \
    | awk '/\ ec2\ / {print $2}')

PUBLIC="http://$PUBLIC_ENDPOINT:8773/services/Cloud"
ADMIN="http://$ADMIN_ENDPOINT:8773/services/Admin"
INTERNAL="http://$INT_ENDPOINT:8773/services/Cloud"

keystone endpoint-create \
    --region RegionOne \
    --service_id $EC2_SERVICE_ID \
    --publicurl $PUBLIC \
    --adminurl $ADMIN \
    --internalurl $INTERNAL

# Glance Image Service
```

```
GLANCE_SERVICE_ID=$(keystone service-list \
    | awk '/\ glance\ / {print $2}')

PUBLIC="http://$PUBLIC_ENDPOINT:9292/v1"
ADMIN="http://$ADMIN_ENDPOINT:9292/v1"
INTERNAL="http://$INT_ENDPOINT:9292/v1"

keystone endpoint-create \
    --region RegionOne \
    --service_id $GLANCE_SERVICE_ID \
    --publicurl $PUBLIC \
    --adminurl $ADMIN \
    --internalurl $INTERNAL


# Keystone OpenStack Identity Service
# Note we're using SSL HTTPS here
KEYSTONE_SERVICE_ID=$(keystone service-list \
    | awk '/\ keystone\ / {print $2}')

PUBLIC="https://$PUBLIC_ENDPOINT:5000/v2.0"
ADMIN="https://$ADMIN_ENDPOINT:35357/v2.0"
INTERNAL="https://$INT_ENDPOINT:5000/v2.0"

keystone endpoint-create \
    --region RegionOne \
    --service_id $KEYSTONE_SERVICE_ID \
    --publicurl $PUBLIC \
    --adminurl $ADMIN \
    --internalurl $INTERNAL


# Neutron Networking Service
```

```
NEUTRON_SERVICE_ID=$(keystone service-list \
    | awk '/\ network\ / {print $2}')

PUBLIC="http://$PUBLIC_ENDPOINT:9696"
ADMIN="http://$ADMIN_ENDPOINT:9696"
INTERNAL="http://$INT_ENDPOINT:9696"

keystone endpoint-create \
    --region RegionOne \
    --service_id $NEUTRON_SERVICE_ID  \
    --publicurl $PUBLIC \
    --adminurl $ADMIN \
    --internalurl $INTERNAL

#Cinder Block Storage Service
CINDER_SERVICE_ID=$(keystone service-list \
    | awk '/\ volume\ / {print $2}')

PUBLIC="http://$PUBLIC_ENDPOINT:8776/v1/%(tenant_id)s"
ADMIN=$PUBLIC
INTERNAL=$PUBLIC

keystone endpoint-create \
    --region RegionOne \
    --service_id $CINDER_SERVICE_ID  \
    --publicurl $PUBLIC \
    --adminurl $ADMIN \
    --internalurl $INTERNAL
```

How it works...

Configuring the services and endpoints within the OpenStack Identity service is done with the `keystone` client command.

We first add the service definitions using the `keystone` client and the `service-create` option with the following syntax:

```
keystone service-create \
    --name service_name \
    --type service_type \
    --description 'description'
```

In the `service_name` is an arbitrary name or label defining our service of a particular type. We refer to the name when defining the endpoint to fetch the ID of the service.

The `type` option can be one of the following: `compute`, `object-store`, `image-service`, `network`, and `identity-service`. Note that we haven't configured the OpenStack Object Storage service (`type object-store`) at this stage, as this is covered in later recipes in the book.

The `description` field is again an arbitrary field describing the service.

Once we have added in our service definitions, we can tell OpenStack Identity service from where these services run by defining the endpoints using the `keystone` client and the `endpoint-create` option. The syntax is as follows:

```
keystone endpoint-create \
    --region region_name \
    --service_id service_id \
    --publicurl public_url \
    --adminurl admin_url \
    --internalurl internal_url
```

Here, `service_id` is the ID of the service when we created the service definitions in the first step. The list of our services and IDs can be obtained by running the following command:

```
keystone service-list
```

As OpenStack is designed for global deployments, a region defines a physical datacenter or a geographical area that comprises of multiple connected datacenters. For our purpose, we define just a single region—RegionOne. This is an arbitrary name that we can reference when specifying what runs in what datacenter/area and we carry the region name through to when we configure our client for use with these regions.

All of our services can be configured to run on three different URLs, as follows, depending on how we want to configure our OpenStack cloud environment:

- `public_url`: This parameter is the URL that end users would connect on. In a public cloud environment, this would be a public URL that resolves to a public IP address.
- `admin_url`: This parameter is a restricted address for conducting administration. In a public deployment, you would keep this separate from the `public_url` by presenting the service you are configuring on a different, restricted URL. Some services have a different URI for the admin service, so this is configured using this attribute.
- `internal_url`: This parameter would be the IP or URL that existed only within the private local area network. The reason for this is that you can connect to services from your cloud environment internally without connecting over a public IP address space, which could incur data charges for traversing the Internet. It is also potentially more secure and less complex to do so.

Once the initial `keystone` database has been set up, after running the initial `keystone-manage db_sync` command on the OpenStack Identity service server, administration can be done remotely using the `keystone` client.

Creating the service tenant and service users

Now that the service endpoints are created, we can configure them so that our other OpenStack services can utilize them. To do this, each service is configured with a username and password within a special `service` tenant. Configuring each service to have its own username and password allows for greater security, troubleshooting, and auditing within our environment. When setting up a service to use the OpenStack Identity service for authentication and authorization, we specify these details in their relevant configuration file. Each service itself has to authenticate with `keystone` in order for it to be available within OpenStack. Configuration of that service is then done using these credentials. For example, for `glance`, we specify the following lines in `/etc/glance/glance-registry.conf`, when used with OpenStack Identity service, which matches what we created previously:

```
[keystone_authtoken]
identity_uri = https://192.168.100.200:35357
admin_tenant_name = service
admin_user = glance
admin_password = glance
insecure = True
```

The use of `insecure = True` here is only required as self-signed certificates are used throughout this book. In production, we would use issued certificates and omit this option in our configs.

Getting ready

We will be using the `keystone` client to operate Keystone. If the `python-keystoneclient` tool isn't available, follow the steps described at `http://bit.ly/OpenStackCookbookClientInstall`.

Ensure that we have our environment set correctly to access our OpenStack environment for administrative purposes:

```
export OS_TENANT_NAME=cookbook
export OS_USERNAME=admin
export OS_PASSWORD=openstack
export OS_AUTH_URL=https://192.168.100.200:5000/v2.0/
export OS_NO_CACHE=1
export OS_KEY=/vagrant/cakey.pem
export OS_CACERT=/vagrant/ca.pem
```

You can use the `controller` node if no other machines are available on your network, as this has the `python-keystoneclient` and the relevant access to the OpenStack environment. If you are using the Vagrant environment, issue the following command to get access to the Controller:

```
vagrant ssh controller
```

How to do it...

To configure an appropriate `service` tenant, carry out the following steps:

1. Create the `service` tenant as follows:

   ```
   keystone tenant-create \
       --name service \
       --description "Service Tenant" \
       --enabled true
   ```

This produces output similar to what is shown as follows:

```
+-------------+----------------------------------+
|   Property  |              Value               |
+-------------+----------------------------------+
| description |          Service Tenant          |
|   enabled   |               True               |
|      id     | 8e77d9c13e884bf4809077722003bba0 |
|     name    |             service              |
+-------------+----------------------------------+
```

2. Record the ID of the service tenant so that we can assign service users to this ID:

```
SERVICE_TENANT_ID=$(keystone tenant-list \
    | awk '/\ service\ / {print $2}')
```

3. For each of the services in this section, we will create the user accounts to be named the same as the services and set the password to be the same as the service name too. For example, we will add a user called `nova` with a password `nova` in the `service` tenant by using the user-create option:

```
keystone user-create \
    --name nova \
    --pass nova \
    --tenant_id $SERVICE_TENANT_ID \
    --email nova@localhost \
    --enabled true
```

The preceding code will produce an output similar to what is shown here:

```
+----------+----------------------------------+
| Property |              Value               |
+----------+----------------------------------+
|  email   |          nova@localhost          |
| enabled  |               True               |
|    id    | 50ea356a4b6f4cb7a9fa22c1fb08549b |
|   name   |               nova               |
| tenantId | 42e5c284de244e3190e12cc44fbbbe62 |
| username |               nova               |
+----------+----------------------------------+
```

4. We then repeat this for each of our other services that will use OpenStack Identity service:

```
keystone user-create \
    --name glance \
    --pass glance \
    --tenant_id $SERVICE_TENANT_ID \
    --email glance@localhost \
    --enabled true

keystone user-create \
    --name keystone \
    --pass keystone \
    --tenant_id $SERVICE_TENANT_ID \
    --email keystone@localhost \
    --enabled true

keystone user-create \
    --name neutron \
    --pass neutron \
    --tenant_id $SERVICE_TENANT_ID \
    --email neutron@localhost \
    --enabled true

keystone user-create \
    --name cinder \
    --pass cinder \
    --tenant_id $SERVICE_TENANT_ID \
    --email cinder@localhost \
    --enabled true
```

5. We can now assign these users the `admin` role in the `service` tenant. To do this, we use the `user-role-add` option after retrieving the user ID of the `nova` user. For example, to add the admin role to the `nova` user in the `service` tenant, we use the following code:

```
# Get the nova user id
NOVA_USER_ID=$(keystone user-list \
    | awk '/\ nova\ / {print $2}')

# Get the admin role id
ADMIN_ROLE_ID=$(keystone role-list \
    | awk '/\ admin\ / {print $2}')

# Assign the nova user the admin role in service tenant
keystone user-role-add \
    --user $NOVA_USER_ID \
    --role $ADMIN_ROLE_ID \
    --tenant_id $SERVICE_TENANT_ID
```

6. We then repeat this for our other service users, `glance`, `keystone`, `neutron`, and `cinder`:

```
# Get the glance user id
GLANCE_USER_ID=$(keystone user-list \
    | awk '/\ glance\ / {print $2}')

# Assign the glance user the admin role in service tenant
keystone user-role-add \
    --user $GLANCE_USER_ID \
    --role $ADMIN_ROLE_ID \
    --tenant_id $SERVICE_TENANT_ID
# Get the keystone user id
KEYSTONE_USER_ID=$(keystone user-list \
    | awk '/\ keystone\ / {print $2}')

# Assign the keystone user the admin role in service tenant
keystone user-role-add \
    --user $KEYSTONE_USER_ID \
```

```
        --role $ADMIN_ROLE_ID \
        --tenant_id $SERVICE_TENANT_ID

    # Get the cinder user id
    NEUTRON_USER_ID=$(keystone user-list \
        | awk '/\ neutron \ / {print $2}')

    # Assign the neutron user the admin role in service tenant
    keystone user-role-add \
        --user $NEUTRON_USER_ID \
        --role $ADMIN_ROLE_ID \
        --tenant_id $SERVICE_TENANT_ID

    # Get the cinder user id
    CINDER_USER_ID=$(keystone user-list \
        | awk '/\ cinder \ / {print $2}')

    # Assign the cinder user the admin role in service tenant
    keystone user-role-add \
        --user $CINDER_USER_ID \
        --role $ADMIN_ROLE_ID \
        --tenant_id $SERVICE_TENANT_ID
```

How it works...

Creation of the `service` tenant, which is populated with the services required to run OpenStack, is no different from creating any other users on our system that require the `admin` role. We create the usernames and passwords and ensure that they exist in the `service` tenant with the `admin` role assigned to each user. We then use these credentials when configuring the services to authenticate with the OpenStack Identity service.

Downloading the example code

You can download the example code files for this book at `https://github.com/OpenStackCookbook/OpenStackCookbook`. All the support files are available here.

Configuring OpenStack Identity for LDAP Integration

The OpenStack Identity service that we have built so far provides you with a functional, but isolated, set up for your OpenStack environment. This is a useful setup for Proof of Concept and lab environments. However, it is likely that you will need to integrate OpenStack with your existing authentication system. OpenStack Identity provides a pluggable authentication back end for this, with LDAP being the most widely used.

Getting ready

We will be using the `keystone` client to operate Keystone. If the `python-keystoneclient` tool isn't available, follow the steps described at `http://bit.ly/OpenStackCookbookClientInstall`.

Ensure that we have our environment set correctly to access our OpenStack environment for administrative purposes:

```
export OS_TENANT_NAME=cookbook
export OS_USERNAME=admin
export OS_PASSWORD=openstack
export OS_AUTH_URL=https://192.168.100.200:5000/v2.0/
export OS_NO_CACHE=1
export OS_KEY=/vagrant/cakey.pem
export OS_CACERT=/vagrant/ca.pem
```

You can use the `controller` node if no other machines are available on your network, as this has the `python-keystoneclient` and the relevant access to the OpenStack environment. If you are using the Vagrant environment, issue the following command to get access to the Controller:

```
vagrant ssh controller
```

Additionally, to connect to an external LDAP service, you will need to possess the hostname or IP address of the LDAP server and have appropriate access to the server. You will also need to have the LDAP path information for an `admin` user, and for the Organizational Units that contain the Users, Roles, and Tenants.

We have provided a sample OpenLDAP server that is prepopulated with the required values as part of this book's supplementary materials, and instructions on how to use it located on our book blog at `http://bit.ly/OpenStackCookbookLDAP`

How to do it...

To configure OpenStack Identity to communicate with LDAP, perform the following steps:

1. Using your favorite editor, enable LDAP authentication in the `keystone.conf` file:

```
[identity]
driver=keystone.identity.backends.ldap.Identity
```

2. Next, create the `ldap` section and add the URL to your existing LDAP server:

```
[ldap]
url = ldap://openldap
```

3. On the following lines, specify the LDAP path for the `admin` user you will use, along with its password and the *suffix*, or where you would like Keystone to begin searching LDAP:

```
user = cn=admin,dc=cook,dc=book
password = openstack
suffix = cn=cook,cn=book
```

4. In the same `[ldap]` section, we tell Keystone four pieces of information about how to find users. `user_tree_dn` specifies which OU within the LDAP tree to search for users. `user_objectclass` specifies how a user is represented within LDAP. `user_id_attribute` tells Keystone which property of the user to use as a username. Similarly, `user_mail_attribute` tells Keystone where to find the user's e-mail address. The code is as follows:

```
user_tree_dn = ou=Users,dc=cook,dc=book
user_objectclass = inetOrgPerson
user_id_attribute = cn
user_mail_attribute = mail
```

5. Next, add the same details for Tenants and Roles:

```
tenant_tree_dn = ou=Projects,dc=cook,dc=book
tenant_objectclass = groupOfNames
tenant_id_attribute = cn
tenant_desc_attribute = description

role_tree_dn = ou=Roles,dc=cook,dc=book
role_objectclass = organizationalRole
role_id_attribute = cn
role_member_attribute = roleOccupant
```

6. Save the file and restart `keystone`:

```
sudo stop keystone
sudo start keystone
```

How it works...

The OpenStack Identity service, like other OpenStack services, is based on plugins. In its default state, Keystone will store and access all user identity and authentication data from a SQL database. However, when integrating OpenStack into an existing environment, this is not always the most desirable or secure method. To accommodate this, we changed the identity back end to LDAP. This allows for integration with OpenLDAP, Active Directory, and many others. However, when configuring the backend, you need to pay special attention to the LDAP paths.

Where are the entries for the services catalog? These are still stored in Keystone's SQL database, as they aren't specifically related to user identity or authentication.

2

Glance – OpenStack Image Service

In this chapter, we will cover the following recipes:

- Installing OpenStack Image Service
- Configuring OpenStack Image Service with OpenStack Identity Service
- Configuring OpenStack Image Service with OpenStack Object Storage
- Managing images with OpenStack Image Service
- Registering a remotely stored image
- Sharing images among tenants
- Viewing shared images
- Using image metadata
- Migrating a VMware image
- Creating an OpenStack image

Introduction

OpenStack Image Service, also known as Glance, is a service that allows you to register, discover, and retrieve virtual machine images for use in our OpenStack environment. Images made available through OpenStack Image Service can be stored in a variety of backend locations, from local filesystem storage to distributed filesystems, such as OpenStack Object Storage.

In this chapter we will be concentrating on the Controller host as shown below:

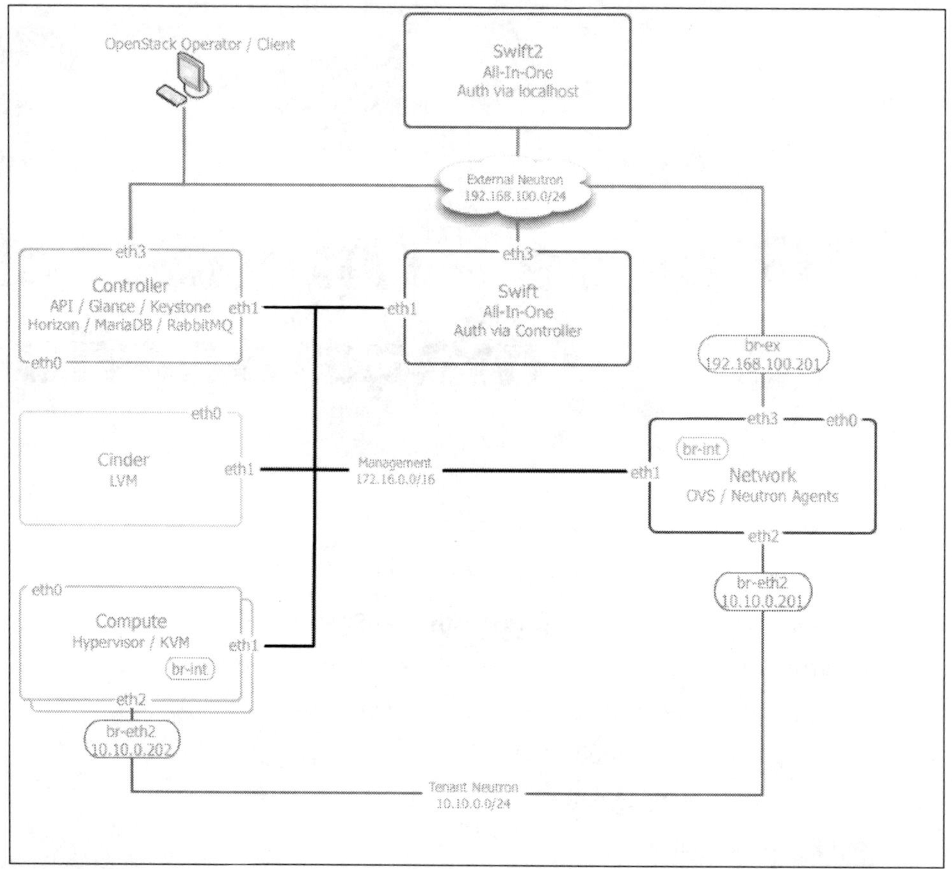

Installing OpenStack Image Service

Installation of the latest OpenStack Image Service is simply achieved by using the packages provided from the Ubuntu Cloud Archive repositories, which have been packaged for our Ubuntu 14.04 LTS GNU/Linux installation.

Getting ready

To begin with, ensure you're logged in to our OpenStack Controller host where OpenStack Image Service will be installed.

To log in to our OpenStack Controller host that was created using Vagrant, issue the following command:

```
vagrant ssh controller
```

Ensure that our Ubuntu 14.04 LTS release is using the Ubuntu Cloud Archive that has the packages required for the Juno release. For more information, visit `http://bit.ly/OpenStackCookbookCloudArchive`.

[All of the steps can be found at `http://www.openstackcookbook.com/`.]

We will configure Glance to use MariaDB as the database backend, so this needs to be installed prior to installing Glance.

[If MariaDB is not installed, visit `http://bit.ly/OpenStackCookbookInstallMariaDB` for instructions on how to do this.]

We will also need to have RabbitMQ installed as our message queue service, so this needs to also be installed prior to installing Glance.

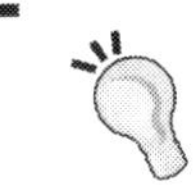

[If RabbitMQ is not installed, visit `http://bit.ly/OpenStackCookbookInstallRabbitMQ` for instructions on how to do this.]

The instructions in this section assume the `controller` node has two IP addresses. It will have a front-facing IP address 192.168.100.200 and a backside IP address 172.16.0.200 (which is also the address of the MariaDB server). It has two addresses because the internal data will communicate over the backside IP address (for example, database traffic) and any Glance traffic will traverse the front.

How to do it...

Carry out the following steps to install OpenStack Image Service:

1. Installation of OpenStack Image Service is done by specifying the glance package in Ubuntu:

   ```
   sudo apt-get update
   sudo apt-get install ntp glance python-keyring
   ```

2. Once installed, we need to configure the backend database store, so we first create the `glance` database in MariaDB. We do this as follows:

```
MYSQL_ROOT_PASS=openstack
mysql -uroot -p$MYSQL_ROOT_PASS -e "CREATE DATABASE \
    glance;"
```

   We have a user called root in MariaDB with the password openstack, which is able to create databases.

3. It is a good practice to create a user that is specific to our OpenStack Image service, so we create a `glance` user in the database as follows:

```
MYSQL_GLANCE_PASS=openstack
mysql -uroot -p$MYSQL_ROOT_PASS -e "GRANT ALL PRIVILEGES ON \
glance.* TO 'glance'@'localhost' IDENTIFIED BY \
'$MYSQL_KEYSTONE_PASS';"
mysql -uroot -p$MYSQL_ROOT_PASS -e "GRANT ALL PRIVILEGES ON \
glance.* TO 'glance'@'%' IDENTIFIED BY '$MYSQL_GLANCE_PASS';"
```

4. We can now configure OpenStack Image Service to use this database by editing the `/etc/glance/glance-registry.conf` and `/etc/glance/glance-api.conf` files and changing the `sql_connection` line to match the database credentials. We do this by ensuring the following lines are in the files:

```
[database]
backend = sqlalchemy
connection = mysql://glance:openstack@172.16.0.200/glance
```

5. We configure OpenStack Image Service to use RabbitMQ by ensuring the following lines are present in `/etc/glance/glance-registry.conf`:

```
rabbit_host = localhost
rabbit_port = 5672
rabbit_use_ssl = false
rabbit_userid = guest
rabbit_password = guest
rabbit_virtual_host = /
rabbit_notification_exchange = glance
rabbit_notification_topic = notifications
rabbit_durable_queues = False
```

6. We can now restart the `glance-registry` service:

```
sudo stop glance-registry
sudo start glance-registry
```

7. Restart the `glance-api` service:

```
sudo stop glance-api
sudo start glance-api
```

8. The `glance` database is version controlled under Ubuntu 14.04 to allow the upgrade and downgrade of the service. We first set the version control to be `0` by issuing the following command:

```
sudo glance-manage db_version_control 0
```

9. We now sync the database to ensure the correct table structure is present. We do this by issuing the following command:

```
sudo glance-manage db_sync
```

Congratulations! We now have OpenStack Image service installed and ready for use in our OpenStack environment.

How it works...

OpenStack Image Service is split into two running services: `glance-api` and `glance-registry`. It is the `glance-registry` service that connects to the database backend. The first step is to create our `glance` database and the `glance` user, so it can perform operations on the `glance` database that we have created.

Once this is done, we modify the `/etc/glance/glance-registry.conf` and `/etc/glance/glance-api.conf` files so that `glance` knows where to find and connect to our MySQL database. This is provided by the standard `SQLAlchemy` connection string that has the following syntax:

```
sql_connection = mysql://USER:PASSWORD@HOST/DBNAME
```

See also

- *Chapter 1, Keystone – OpenStack Identity Service*

Configuring OpenStack Image Service with OpenStack Identity Service

Configuring OpenStack Image Service to use OpenStack Identity Service is required to allow our OpenStack Compute to operate correctly.

Getting ready

To begin with, ensure you're logged in to our OpenStack Controller host or the host that is running OpenStack Image Service. If the OpenStack Identity Service is not installed, carry out the steps in the *Installing the OpenStack Identity Service* recipe of *Chapter 1, Keystone – OpenStack Identity Service*. We also require that the Glance service user and endpoints have been set up. See the Defining Service Endpoints and *Creating the service tenant and service users* recipes of *Chapter 1, Keystone – OpenStack Identity Service*.

To log in to our OpenStack Controller host that was created using Vagrant, issue the following command:

```
vagrant ssh controller
```

How to do it...

To configure OpenStack Image Service to use OpenStack Identity Service, carry out the following steps:

1. We first edit the `/etc/glance/glance-api.conf` file to tell OpenStack Image Service to utilize OpenStack Identity Service by adding a `[keystone_authtoken]` section. Note that we are using `insecure = True` in the configuration because we are using `self-signed certificates`. In production, it is expected that issued certificates are used and they don't require this parameter. The code is as follows:

```
[keystone_authtoken]
auth_uri = https://192.168.100.200:35357/v2.0/
identity_uri = https://192.168.100.200:5000
admin_tenant_name = service
admin_user = glance
admin_password = glance
insecure = True
```

2. We repeat this process for the `/etc/glance/glance-registry.conf` file, configuring the `glance` service user in the `[keystone_authtoken]` section. We are using `insecure = True` here because our example used self-signed certificates. The code is as follows:

   ```
   [keystone_authtoken]
   auth_uri = https://192.168.100.200:35357/v2.0/
   identity_uri = https://192.168.100.200:5000
   admin_tenant_name = service
   admin_user = glance
   admin_password = glance
   insecure = True
   ```

3. Finally, we restart the two services to pick up the changes:

   ```
   sudo restart glance-api
   sudo restart glance-registry
   ```

How it works...

OpenStack Image Service runs two services: `glance-api`, which is the service that our clients and services talk to, and the `glance-registry` service that manages the objects on the disk and database registry. Both of these services need to have matching credentials that were defined previously in OpenStack Identity Service in their configuration files in order to allow a user to authenticate with the service successfully.

Configuring OpenStack Image Service with OpenStack Object Storage

By default, images are stored as files in the `/var/lib/glance/images/` directory. However, OpenStack Image Service can be configured to use OpenStack Object Storage (Swift) for storing images, as well as other backend storage such as Ceph and GlusterFS. In this recipe, we will go through the steps required to configure OpenStack Image service (Glance) to use Object Storage service (Swift).

Getting ready

To begin with, ensure you're logged in to our OpenStack Controller host or the host that is running OpenStack Image Service.

To log in to our OpenStack Controller host that was created using Vagrant, issue the following command:

```
vagrant ssh controller
```

How to do it...

To configure OpenStack Image Service to use OpenStack Object Storage, carry out the following steps:

1. We first edit the `/etc/glance/glance-api.conf` file to notify Glance that we will use Swift instead of the default filesystem by editing the following line under the [DEFAULT] section:

   ```
   [DEFAULT]
   default_store = swift
   ```

2. We then edit the `[glance_store]` section in the same file to configure Swift:

   ```
   [glance_store]
   stores = glance.store.filesystem.Store,
            glance.store.http.Store,
            glance.store.swift.Store
   swift_store_auth_version = 2
   swift_store_auth_address = https://192.168.100.200:5000/v2.0/
   swift_store_user = service:glance
   swift_store_key = glance
   swift_store_container = glance
   swift_store_create_container_on_put = True
   swift_store_large_object_size = 5120
   swift_store_large_object_chunk_size = 200
   swift_enable_snet = False
   swift_store_auth_insecure = True
   ```

We are using `swift_store_auth_insecure = True` because we are using self-signed certificates for our SSL Keystone implementation. Adjust this to suit your environment.

3. Then, we restart the two OpenStack Image Service processes to pick up the changes:

```
sudo restart glance-api
sudo restart glance-registry
```

How it works...

OpenStack Image Service can be configured to use several different backend for storing images, such as Ceph, OpenStack Object Storage, and raw disk. Once Object Storage is configured as a backend, images will be uploaded to Swift instead of being stored locally. Check *Chapter 5, Swift - OpenStack Object Storage* on configuring and using Object Storage.

Managing images with OpenStack Image Service

Uploading and managing images within OpenStack Storage is achieved using the `glance` command-line tool. This tool allows us to upload, remove, and change information about the stored images for use within our OpenStack environment.

Getting ready

To begin with, ensure that you are either logged in to an Ubuntu client where we can run the `glance` tool, or on our OpenStack Controller where OpenStack Image Service is running directly. If the Glance client isn't installed, this can be installed using the following commands:

```
sudo apt-get update
sudo apt-get install python-glanceclient
```

Ensure that you have your environment variables set up correctly with our `admin` user and password, as created in the previous chapter:

```
export OS_TENANT_NAME=cookbook
export OS_USERNAME=admin
export OS_PASSWORD=openstack
export OS_AUTH_URL=https://192.168.100.200:5000/v2.0/
export OS_NO_CACHE=1
export OS_KEY=/vagrant/cakey.pem
export OS_CACERT=/vagrant/ca.pem
```

How to do it...

We can upload and view images in our OpenStack Image Service in a number of ways. Carry out the following steps to upload and show details of our uploaded images.

Uploading Ubuntu images

Ubuntu provides images that can easily be added to our OpenStack environment, as follows:

1. We download an Ubuntu cloud image from `http://uec-images.ubuntu.com`, as follows:

   ```
   wget https://cloud-images.ubuntu.com/trusty/current/trusty-server-cloudimg-amd64-disk1.img
   ```

2. We then upload our cloud image:

   ```
   glance image-create \
       --name='Ubuntu 14.04 x86_64 Server' \
       --disk-format=qcow2 \
       --container-format=bare \
       --is-public True < \
       trusty-server-cloudimg-amd64-disk1.img
   ```

   You will see an output like this:

   ```
   +------------------+--------------------------------------+
   | Property         | Value                                |
   +------------------+--------------------------------------+
   | checksum         | d03071f4d387dfb976e29f00ff397496     |
   | container_format | bare                                 |
   | created_at       | 2015-01-09T09:31:35                  |
   | deleted          | False                                |
   | deleted_at       | None                                 |
   | disk_format      | qcow2                                |
   | id               | 18584bff-2c12-4c2d-85f6-59771073c936 |
   | is_public        | False                                |
   | min_disk         | 0                                    |
   | min_ram          | 0                                    |
   | name             | Ubuntu 14.04 x86_64 Server           |
   | owner            | 45c787efeaec42aa9cab522711bf5f4d     |
   | protected        | False                                |
   | size             | 256180736                            |
   | status           | active                               |
   | updated_at       | 2015-01-09T09:31:37                  |
   | virtual_size     | None                                 |
   +------------------+--------------------------------------+
   ```

Listing images

To list the images in our OpenStack Image Service repository, we use the Glance client to interrogate the Image Service directly, or use the Nova client that is used to manage our OpenStack environment. This is covered in *Chapter 4, Nova – OpenStack Compute*.

To list the images available to our user using the Glance client, we issue the following command:

```
glance image-list
```

The preceding command produces a result like this:

```
+--------------------------------------+---------------------------+-------------+------------------+-----------+--------+
| ID                                   | Name                      | Disk Format | Container Format | Size      | Status |
+--------------------------------------+---------------------------+-------------+------------------+-----------+--------+
| fc1ec7e2-f9ef-4afa-9634-993e370a26c0 | cirros-image              | qcow2       | bare             | 9761280   | active |
| db02ab51-f9a1-4e38-8c3d-22b367962154 | trusty-image              | qcow2       | bare             | 256115200 | active |
| 18584bff-2c12-4c2d-85f6-59771073c936 | Ubuntu 14.04 x86_64 Server | qcow2      | bare             | 256180736 | active |
+--------------------------------------+---------------------------+-------------+------------------+-----------+--------+
```

Viewing image details

We can view further details of our images in the repository. To show further details of any image, issue the following command:

```
glance image-show IMAGE_ID
```

Consider the following example:

```
glance image-show 18584bff-2c12-4c2d-85f6-59771073c936
```

This returns the same details as when we uploaded our image (shown on the previous page).

Deleting images

There will be times when you will need to remove images from being able to be called within your OpenStack cloud environment. You can delete images where you have permission to do so:

1. To delete an image, issue the following command:

   ```
   glance image-delete IMAGE_ID
   ```

2. Consider the following example:

   ```
   glance image-delete 794dca52-5fcd-4216-ac8e-7655cdc88852
   ```

3. OpenStack Image Service will not produce any output when you successfully delete an image. You can verify this with the `glance image-list` command.

Making private images public

When you upload an image, they get entered into OpenStack Image Service as private, by default. If an image is uploaded this way but you want to make it public, you perform the following steps in OpenStack Image Service:

1. First, list and view the image(s) that you want to make public. In this case, we will choose our first uploaded image:

   ```
   glance image-show IMAGE_ID
   ```

   Consider the following example:

   ```
   glance image-show 18584bff-2c12-4c2d-85f6-59771073c936
   ```

   This produces results somewhat similar to what is shown here:

   ```
   +------------------+--------------------------------------+
   | Property         | Value                                |
   +------------------+--------------------------------------+
   | checksum         | d03071f4d387dfb976e29f00ff397496     |
   | container_format | bare                                 |
   | created_at       | 2015-01-09T09:31:35                  |
   | deleted          | False                                |
   | deleted_at       | None                                 |
   | disk_format      | qcow2                                |
   | id               | 18584bff-2c12-4c2d-85f6-59771073c936 |
   | is_public        | False                                |
   | min_disk         | 0                                    |
   | min_ram          | 0                                    |
   | name             | Ubuntu 14.04 x86_64 Server           |
   | owner            | 45c787efeaec42aa9cab522711bf5f4d     |
   | protected        | False                                |
   | size             | 256180736                            |
   | status           | active                               |
   | updated_at       | 2015-01-09T09:31:37                  |
   | virtual_size     | None                                 |
   +------------------+--------------------------------------+
   ```

2. We can now convert this to a public image that is available to all the users of our cloud environment with the following command:

   ```
   glance image-update 18584bff-2c12-4c2d-85f6-59771073c936 \
       --is-public True
   ```

3. List the available public images as follows:

   ```
   glance image-show 18584bff-2c12-4c2d-85f6-59771073c936
   ```

We will now see the following output:

```
+-------------------+--------------------------------------+
| Property          | Value                                |
+-------------------+--------------------------------------+
| checksum          | d03071f4d387dfb976e29f00ff397496     |
| container_format  | bare                                 |
| created_at        | 2015-01-09T09:31:35                  |
| deleted           | False                                |
| deleted_at        | None                                 |
| disk_format       | qcow2                                |
| id                | 18584bff-2c12-4c2d-85f6-59771073c936 |
| is_public         | True                                 |
| min_disk          | 0                                    |
| min_ram           | 0                                    |
| name              | Ubuntu 14.04 x86_64 Server           |
| owner             | 45c787efeaec42aa9cab522711bf5f4d     |
| protected         | False                                |
| size              | 256180736                            |
| status            | active                               |
| updated_at        | 2015-01-09T09:41:21                  |
| virtual_size      | None                                 |
+-------------------+--------------------------------------+
```

How it works

OpenStack Image Service is a very flexible system for managing images in our private cloud environment. It allows us to modify many aspects of our OpenStack Image Service registry—adding new images, deleting them, updating information, such as the name that is used so that end users can easily identify them, and making private images public or vice-versa.

To do all this, we use the `glance` tool from any connected client.

Registering a remotely stored image

OpenStack Image Service provides a mechanism to remotely add an image that is stored at an externally accessible location. This allows for a convenient method of adding images we might want to on our private cloud that have been uploaded to an external third-party server.

Getting ready

To begin with, ensure you are logged in to our Ubuntu client where we can run the `glance` tool. This can be installed using the following command:

```
sudo apt-get update
sudo apt-get install python-glanceclient
```

Ensure that you have your environment variable set up correctly with our `admin` user and password, as created in the previous chapter:

```
export OS_TENANT_NAME=cookbook
export OS_USERNAME=admin
export OS_PASSWORD=openstack
export OS_AUTH_URL=https://192.168.100.200:5000/v2.0/
export OS_NO_CACHE=1
export OS_KEY=/vagrant/cakey.pem
export OS_CACERT=/vagrant/ca.pem
```

How to do it...

Carry out the following steps to remotely store an image in our OpenStack Image Service:

1. To register a remote virtual image into our environment, we add a location parameter instead of streaming the image through a pipe on our `glance` command line:

   ```
   glance image-create \
       --name='Ubuntu 12.04 x86_64 Server' \
       --disk-format=qcow2 \
       --container-format=bare \
       --public \
       --location http://webserver/precise-server-cloudimg-amd64-
   disk1.img
   ```

2. The preceding step returns information similar to what you can see here, which is then stored in our OpenStack Image Service:

```
+------------------+--------------------------------------+
| Property         | Value                                |
+------------------+--------------------------------------+
| container_format | bare                                 |
| created_at       | 2015-01-09T09:47:45                  |
| deleted          | False                                |
| disk_format      | qcow2                                |
| id               | b03eb63b-e58c-4743-8dee-320b3b30fa3e |
| is_public        | False                                |
| min_disk         | 0                                    |
| min_ram          | 0                                    |
| name             | Ubuntu 12.04 x86_64 Server           |
| owner            | 45c787efeaec42aa9cab522711bf5f4d     |
| protected        | False                                |
| size             | 262865408                            |
| status           | active                               |
| updated_at       | 2015-01-09T09:47:45                  |
+------------------+--------------------------------------+
```

How it works...

Using the `glance` tool to specify remote images directly provides a quick and convenient way to add images to our OpenStack Image Service repository. The way this happens is with the `location` parameter. We add in our usual meta information to accompany this, as we would with a locally-specified image.

Sharing images among tenants

When an image is private, it is only available to the tenant to which that image was uploaded. OpenStack Image Service provides a mechanism whereby these private images can be shared between different tenants. This allows greater control over images that need to exist for different tenants without making them public for all tenants.

Getting ready

To begin with, ensure you are logged in to our Ubuntu client where we can run the `glance` tool. This can be installed using the following command:

```
sudo apt-get update
sudo apt-get install glance-client
```

Ensure that you have your environment variable set up correctly with our admin user and password, as created in the previous chapter:

```
export OS_TENANT_NAME=cookbook
export OS_USERNAME=admin
export OS_PASSWORD=openstack
export OS_AUTH_URL=https://192.168.100.200:5000/v2.0/
export OS_NO_CACHE=1
export OS_KEY=/vagrant/cakey.pem
export OS_CACERT=/vagrant/ca.pem
```

How to do it...

Carry out the following steps to share a private image in our cookbook tenant to another tenant:

1. We first get the tenant ID of the tenant that is able to use our image. We do this as follows:

   ```
   keystone tenant-list
   ```

2. We then list our images as follows:

   ```
   glance image-list
   ```

3. From our cookbook tenant with ID `45c787efeaec42aa9cab522711bf5f4d` and an image with ID `18584bff-2c12-4c2d-85f6-59771073c936`, we would share the image as follows:

   ```
   glance member-create \
       18584bff-2c12-4c2d-85f6-59771073c93 \
       45c787efeaec42aa9cab522711bf5f4d
   ```

How it works...

The `member-create` option for the `glance` command allows us to share images with other tenants. The syntax is as follows:

```
glance [--can-share] member-create image-id tenant-id
```

The preceding command comes with an optional extra parameter, `--can-share`, that gives permission to that tenant to share the image.

Viewing shared images

We can view what images have been shared for a particular tenant when someone has used the `member-create` option. This allows us to manage and control which users have what type of access to images in our OpenStack environment.

Getting ready

To begin with, ensure that you are logged in to our Ubuntu client where we can run the `glance` tool. This can be installed using the following command:

```
sudo apt-get update
sudo apt-get install python-glanceclient
```

Ensure that you have your environment variable set up correctly with our `admin` user and password, as created in the previous chapter:

```
export OS_TENANT_NAME=cookbook
export OS_USERNAME=admin
export OS_PASSWORD=openstack
export OS_AUTH_URL=https://192.168.100.200:5000/v2.0/
export OS_NO_CACHE=1
export OS_KEY=/vagrant/cakey.pem
export OS_CACERT=/vagrant/ca.pem
```

How to do it...

Carry out the following steps to view the images that have been shared for a particular tenant:

1. We first get the tenant ID of the tenant we want to view. We do this as follows:

   ```
   keystone tenant-list
   ```

2. We can now list the images that have been shared with that tenant ID as follows:

   ```
   glance member-list --tenant-id \
       45c787efeaec42aa9cab522711bf5f4d
   ```

   This produces the following output:

   ```
   +--------------------------------------+----------------------------------+-----------+
   | Image ID                             | Member ID                        | Can Share |
   +--------------------------------------+----------------------------------+-----------+
   | 18584bff-2c12-4c2d-85f6-59771073c936 | 45c787efeaec42aa9cab522711bf5f4d |           |
   +--------------------------------------+----------------------------------+-----------+
   ```

How it works...

The `member-list` option in the `glance` command allows us to view which images have been shared with other tenants. The syntax is as follows:

```
glance member-list --image-id IMAGE_ID
glance member-list --tenant-id TENANT_ID
```

Using image metadata

We can set arbitrary metadata to help describe images and how they are associated to other OpenStack components. This specific data that is set during image creation or updated at a later time can be used to enable specific functionality in other OpenStack services or to simply allow a custom description of the images.

Getting ready

To begin with, ensure you are logged in to our Ubuntu client where we can run the `glance` tool. This can be installed using the following command:

```
sudo apt-get update
sudo apt-get install python-glanceclient
```

Ensure that you have your environment variable set up correctly with our `admin` user and password, as created in the previous chapter:

```
export OS_TENANT_NAME=cookbook
export OS_USERNAME=admin
export OS_PASSWORD=openstack
export OS_AUTH_URL=https://192.168.100.200:5000/v2.0/
export OS_NO_CACHE=1
export OS_KEY=/vagrant/cakey.pem
export OS_CACERT=/vagrant/ca.pem
```

How to do it...

Image metadata can be added, updated, and deleted, as well as used for host scheduling.

Updating image properties

Carry out the following steps to update the metadata on the image:

1. We first get the image ID for which we want to update metadata. We do this as follows:

   ```
   glance image-list
   ```

2. Add metadata to the image and set the `image_state` and `os_distro` properties:

   ```
   glance image-update db02ab51-f9a1-4e38-8c3d-22b367962154
       --property image_state=available \
       --property os_distro=ubuntu
   ```

3. We get the following output:

```
+--------------------------+--------------------------------------+
| Property                 | Value                                |
+--------------------------+--------------------------------------+
| Property 'image_state'   | available                            |
| Property 'os_distro'     | ubuntu                               |
| checksum                 | 4a992ed9b91ddea133201cd45f127156     |
| container_format         | bare                                 |
| created_at               | 2015-01-09T05:34:09                  |
| deleted                  | False                                |
| deleted_at               | None                                 |
| disk_format              | qcow2                                |
| id                       | db02ab51-f9a1-4e38-8c3d-22b367962154 |
| is_public                | False                                |
| min_disk                 | 0                                    |
| min_ram                  | 0                                    |
| name                     | trusty-image                         |
| owner                    | 45c787efeaec42aa9cab522711bf5f4d     |
| protected                | False                                |
| size                     | 256115200                            |
| status                   | active                               |
| updated_at               | 2015-01-09T10:06:11                  |
| virtual_size             | None                                 |
+--------------------------+--------------------------------------+
```

Deleting all image properties

Carry out the following steps to delete image properties:

1. We first get the image ID for which we want to delete metadata. We do this as follows:

   ```
   glance image-list
   ```

2. To remove all the metadata, enter the following command:

   ```
   glance image-update db02ab51-f9a1-4e38-8c3d-22b367962154 \
   --purge-props
   ```

Deleting specific image properties

Carry out the following steps to delete image properties:

1. We first get the image ID for which we want to delete metadata. We do this as follows:

```
glance image-list
```

2. To remove specific metadata, we need to specify which properties to keep during the update. In this example, we will remove the `image_state` property and any others that might have been set, but we keep the `os_distro` property. Note that user-added properties are removed if not specified. The code is as follows:

```
glance image-update db02ab51-f9a1-4e38-8c3d-22b367962154 \
--purge-props --property os_distro=ubuntu
```

Using metadata for host scheduling

Metadata can be used to determine the scheduling of hosts. For example, if you have hosts with different hypervisor types, you can specify properties to identify on which hypervisor the image may be deployed. Carry out the following steps to enable scheduling based on image metadata:

1. We first need to edit the `/etc/nova/nova.conf` file to update the scheduler property:

```
# Scheduler
scheduler_default_filters=ImagePropertiesFilter
```

While scheduling is inherently an OpenStack compute function, we are including this section with Glance for completeness.

2. Restart `nova` scheduler:

```
sudo stop nova-scheduler
sudo start nova-scheduler
```

3. Get the image ID for which we want to update metadata:

```
glance image-list
```

4. Set `architecture` and `hypervisor` type properties, both `kvm` and `qemu` will have the `qemu` hypervisor type:

```
glance image-update db02ab51-f9a1-4e38-8c3d-22b367962154 \
    --property architecture=arm \
    --property hypervisor_type=qemu
```

How it works...

The `glance image-update` option in the `glance` command allows us to add, modify, and remove custom image properties. The syntax is as follows:

```
glance image-create [other options] --property <key=value>
glance image-update IMAGE_ID --property <key=value>
```

See also

- *Chapter 4, Nova – OpenStack Compute*

Migrating a VMware image

We can migrate a VMware based image, `vmdk`, to other disk image formats. This can be achieved using an image conversion utility. This same utility can be used to verify that the conversion worked properly. Once the image has been converted, it can be uploaded to OpenStack Image Service.

Getting ready

To begin with, ensure you are logged in to our Ubuntu client where we will be doing the image conversion. Make sure you have `qemu-util` installed; if not, you may install it using the following:

```
sudo apt-get install qemu-utils
```

How to do it...

Carry out the following steps to convert a VMDK image to the QCOW2 format:

1. Verify the image using the following command:

   ```
   qemu-img info custom-iso-1415990568-disk1.vmdk
   ```

2. You will get the following output:

   ```
   image: custom-iso-1415990568-disk1.vmdk
   file format: vmdk
   virtual size: 39G (41943040000 bytes)
   disk size: 2.7G
   cluster_size: 65536
   ```

```
Format specific information:
    cid: 2481477841
    parent cid: 4294967295
    create type: monolithicSparse
    extents:
        [0]:
            virtual size: 41943040000
            filename: custom-iso-1415990568-disk1.vmdk
            cluster size: 65536
            format:
```

3. Convert the image using the following command:

   ```
   qemu-img convert -f vmdk -O qcow2 -c \
   -p custom-iso-1415990568-disk1.vmdk \
   custom-iso-1415990568-disk1.qcow2
   ```

   Here, `-f` is the input disk image format, `-O` is the output format, `-c` target should be compressed QCOW format only), and `-p` show progress.

4. Verify the converted image as follows and it should show that the images are identical if all went as expected:

   ```
   qemu-img compare -s -f vmdk \
   -F qcow2  custom-iso-1415990568-disk1.vmdk \
   custom-iso-1415990568-disk1.qcow2
   Images are identical.
   ```

How it works...

The `qemu-img convert` command-line tool works on multiple formats, including VMDK. Conversion to VMDK or other desired formats would work as well. Since the QCOW format supports image compression, it can be useful to get a smaller image which then can grow.

Creating an OpenStack image

We can now create our custom OpenStack image, however, it is advisable to do so outside of our OpenStack installation. Also, you need to make sure that you do not have VirtualBox, Fusion, or similar virtualization technology, running on the system where you will be creating your image. We will be creating a KVM-based, CentOS image.

Getting ready

To begin with, ensure you are logged in to a Linux system that is not your OpenStack environment.

On Ubuntu, install the `kvm/qemu` and `libvirt` libraries:

```
sudo apt-get install qemu-kvm libvirt-bin virt-manager
```

Start the `libvirt-bin` service with the following command:

```
sudo start libvirt-bin
```

On CentOS or RHEL:

```
sudo yum groupinstall "Virtualization" "Virtualization Platform"
sudo chkconfig libvirtd on
sudo service libvirtd start
```

On Fedora:

```
sudo yum groupinstall "Virtualization" "Virtualization Platform"
sudo systemctl enable libvirtd
sudo systemctl start libvirtd
```

Ideally, you will also need a VNC client, though our example could be done without using one.

How to do it...

Carry out the following steps to create a custom image:

1. Create a `kickstart` file called `openstack.txt`:

```
install
text
url --url http://mirror.rackspace.com/CentOS/6.6/os/x86_64/
lang en_US.UTF-8
keyboard us
network --onboot yes --bootproto dhcp --noipv6
timezone --utc America/Chicago
zerombr
clearpart --all --initlabel
```

```
bootloader --location=mbr --append="crashkernel=auto rhgb quiet"
part / --fstype=ext4 --size=1024 --grow
authconfig --enableshadow --passalgo=sha512
rootpw openstack
firewall --disable
selinux --disabled
skipx
shutdown
%packages
@core
openssh-server
openssh-clients
wget
curl
git
man
vim
ntp
%end
%post
%end
```

2. Execute the following command:

```
sudo virt-install --virt-type kvm --name centos-6.6 --ram 1024 \
--location=http://mirror.rackspace.com/CentOS/6.6/os/x86_64/ \
--disk path=/tmp/centos-6.6-vm.img,size=5 \
--network network=default --graphics vnc,listen=0.0.0.0 \
--noautoconsole --os-type=linux --os-variant=rhel6 \
--initrd-inject=centos-6.6-x86_64-openstack.txt \
--extra-args="noverifyssl  console=tty0 console=ttyS0,115200 \
ks=file:/centos-6.6-x86_64-openstack.txt "
```

3. You should see something similar to the following output:

```
Starting install...

Retrieving file .treeinfo...
|  728 B     00:00 ...

Retrieving file vmlinuz...
| 7.9 MB     00:00 ...

Retrieving file initrd.img...
|  66 MB     00:00 ...
```

```
Creating domain...
|      0 B     00:01
Domain installation still in progress. You can reconnect to the
console to complete the installation process.
```

4. Verify that the image creation was completed by using VNC. The `VNC server` will be running by default on `host:5900`:

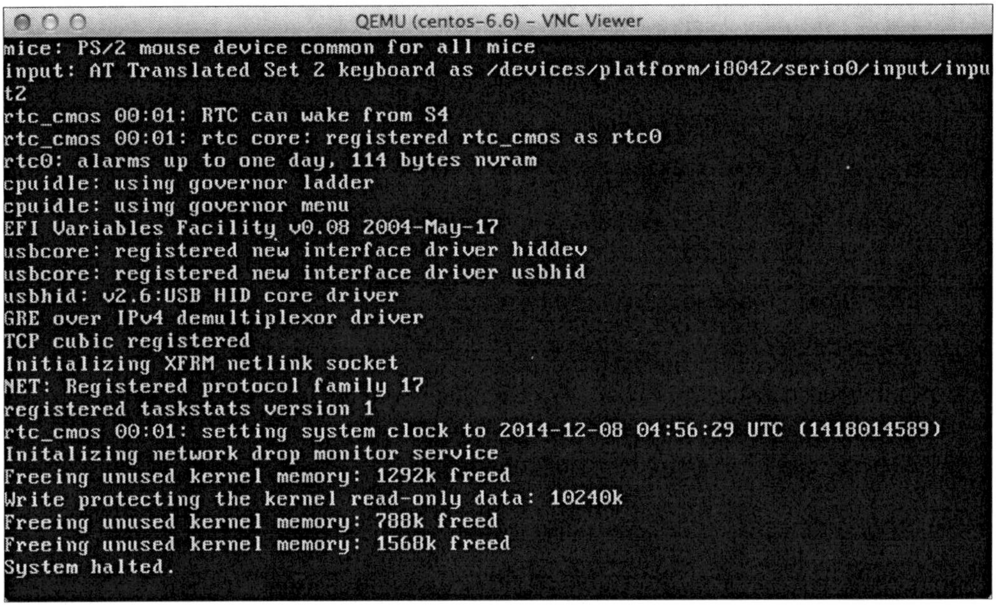

```
QEMU (centos-6.6) - VNC Viewer
mice: PS/2 mouse device common for all mice
input: AT Translated Set 2 keyboard as /devices/platform/i8042/serio0/input/inpu
t2
rtc_cmos 00:01: RTC can wake from S4
rtc_cmos 00:01: rtc core: registered rtc_cmos as rtc0
rtc0: alarms up to one day, 114 bytes nvram
cpuidle: using governor ladder
cpuidle: using governor menu
EFI Variables Facility v0.08 2004-May-17
usbcore: registered new interface driver hiddev
usbcore: registered new interface driver usbhid
usbhid: v2.6:USB HID core driver
GRE over IPv4 demultiplexor driver
TCP cubic registered
Initializing XFRM netlink socket
NET: Registered protocol family 17
registered taskstats version 1
rtc_cmos 00:01: setting system clock to 2014-12-08 04:56:29 UTC (1418014589)
Initalizing network drop monitor service
Freeing unused kernel memory: 1292k freed
Write protecting the kernel read-only data: 10240k
Freeing unused kernel memory: 788k freed
Freeing unused kernel memory: 1568k freed
System halted.
```

If you do not have access to a VNC client, or for some reason cannot use it, wait for 10 minutes (a rough estimate) and proceed to the next step. We will assume things worked.

5. List the running VMs in `virsh` with the following commands:

```
sudo virsh list --all
 Id    Name                           State
----------------------------------------------------
 62    centos-6.6                     running
```

6. Stop (destroy) the VM with the following command:

```
sudo virsh destroy centos-6.6
Domain centos-6.6 destroyed
```

7. Start the VM with the following commands:

```
sudo virsh start centos-6.6
Domain centos-6.6 started
```

8. Log in to the VM console as `root` user with the password `openstack`. To escape from the console session, press *Ctrl* +].

```
sudo virsh console centos-6.6
Connected to domain centos-6.6
Escape character is ^]
```

Now, let's exit by clicking *Enter*:

```
CentOS release 6.6 (Final)
Kernel 2.6.32-504.el6.x86_64 on an x86_64

localhost.localdomain login: root
Password:
```

9. In the guest, install the `cloud-init` package with the following commands:

```
sudo yum install http://dl.fedoraproject.org/pub/epel/6Server/
x86_64/epel-release-6-8.noarch.rpm

sudo yum install cloud-init cloud-utils cloud-utils-growpart
```

10. Change guest's cloud `config file /etc/cloud/cloud.cfg` with the following commands:

```
rm /etc/cloud/cloud.cfg
vi /etc/cloud/cloud.cfg
```

11. Paste the following:

```
users:
 - default

disable_root: 1
ssh_pwauth:   0

locale_configfile: /etc/sysconfig/i18n
mount_default_fields: [~, ~, 'auto', 'defaults,nofail', '0', '2']
resize_rootfs_tmp: /dev
ssh_deletekeys:   0
```

```
ssh_genkeytypes:  ~
syslog_fix_perms: ~

cloud_init_modules:
 - bootcmd
 - write-files
 - resizefs
 - set_hostname
 - update_hostname
 - update_etc_hosts
 - rsyslog
 - users-groups
 - ssh

cloud_config_modules:
 - mounts
 - locale
 - set-passwords
 - timezone
 - puppet
 - chef
 - salt-minion
 - mcollective
 - disable-ec2-metadata
 - runcmd

cloud_final_modules:
 - rightscale_userdata
 - scripts-per-once
 - scripts-per-boot
 - scripts-per-instance
 - scripts-user
 - ssh-authkey-fingerprints
 - keys-to-console
 - phone-home
 - final-message

system_info:
  distro: rhel
  default_user:
    name: centos
    lock_passwd: True
    shell: /bin/bash
```

```
    sudo: ["ALL=(ALL) NOPASSWD: ALL"]
  paths:
    cloud_dir: /var/lib/cloud
    templates_dir: /etc/cloud/templates
  ssh_svcname: sshd
```

12. Make sure the guest can communicate with the metadata service with the following command:

    sudo echo "NOZEROCONF=yes" >> /etc/sysconfig/network

13. Remove persistent rules with the following command:

    sudo rm -f /etc/udev/rules.d/70-persistent-net.rules

14. Remove machine-specific MAC address and UUID. Edit the `/etc/sysconfig/network-scripts/ifcfg-eth0` file and remove lines starting with `HWADDR` and `UUID`:

    sudo sed -i '/HWADDR/d' /etc/sysconfig/network-scripts/ifcfg-eth0

    sudo sed -i '/UUID/d' /etc/sysconfig/network-scripts/ifcfg-eth0

15. After making the changes, the `/etc/sysconfig/network-scripts/ifcfg-eth0` file should look like this:

    ```
    DEVICE="eth0"
    BOOTPROTO="dhcp"
    IPV6INIT="no"
    MTU="1500"
    NM_CONTROLLED="yes"
    ONBOOT="yes"
    TYPE="Ethernet"
    ```

16. Clean up the `yum`, `logs`, `temporary` files, and history with the following commands:

    sudo yum clean all

    sudo rm -rf /var/log/*

    sudo rm -rf /tmp/*

    sudo history -c

17. Shutdown the guest with the following command:

    sudo shutdown -h now

18. Compress the newly created image with the following command:

```
sudo qemu-img convert -c /tmp/centos-6.6-vm.img \
-O qcow2 /tmp/centos-6.6.img
```

19. Upload the image to Glance with the following command:

```
glance image-create --name centos-6.6 \
--disk-format=qcow2 --container-format=bare --file /tmp/centos-
6.6.img
```

How it works...

The `qemu-img convert` command-line tool works on multiple formats, including VMDK. Conversion to VMDK or other desired formats would work as well. Since the QCOW format supports image compression, it can be useful to get a smaller image that can grow later.

3

Neutron – OpenStack Networking

In this chapter, we will cover the following recipes:

- Installing Neutron and Open vSwitch on a dedicated network node
- Configuring Neutron and Open vSwitch
- Installing and configuring the Neutron API service
- Creating a tenant Neutron network
- Deleting a Neutron network
- Creating an external Floating IP Neutron network
- Using Neutron networks for different purposes
- Configuring Distributed Virtual Routers
- Using Distributed Virtual Routers

Introduction

OpenStack Networking is the **Software Defined Networking** (**SDN**) component of OpenStack and its project name is Neutron. With SDN, we can describe complex networks in a secure multitenant environment that overcomes the issues often associated with the Flat and VLAN OpenStack networks. In OpenStack, SDN is a pluggable architecture, which means we are able to plug in and control various switches, firewalls, and load balancers and achieve various functions such as Firewall-as-a-Service. All this is defined in software to give you fine-grained control over your complete cloud infrastructure.

OpenStack Networking is a replacement for the networking component that is available with OpenStack Compute itself: nova-network. While nova-network is still seen as more robust and available for use, many people are deploying OpenStack Networking in production. Nova-network is expected to be deprecated in an upcoming release of OpenStack.

The following figure shows the OpenStack architecture as described in this chapter.

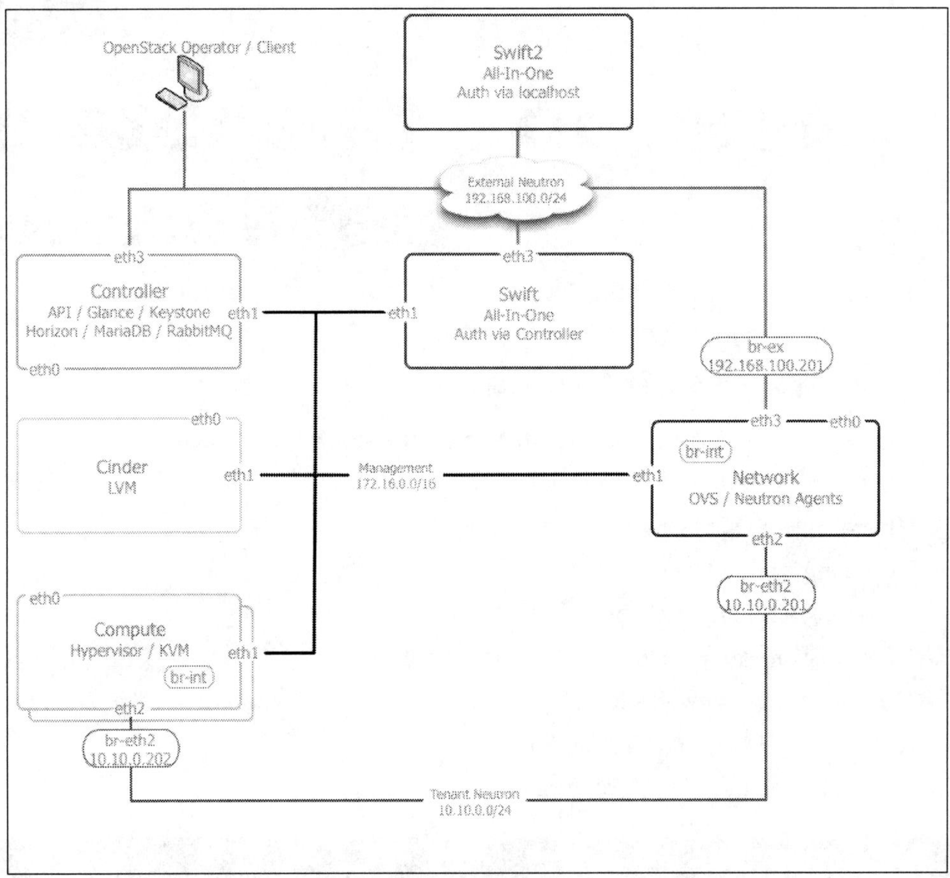

In this environment, we have a **Controller**, a **Network** host, and one or more **Compute** hosts. The hosts are all running Ubuntu 14.04 and have a number of network cards installed as shown in the figure. For the purpose of this chapter, we reference the virtual environment that accompanies the text and as such an interface `eth0` is dedicated to the out-of-band management for the environment itself. Therefore, it remains unassigned. As you begin to work with OpenStack in a production environment, the networking requirements will likely vary, and will need to change the interface assignments.

For consistency of network configuration, each interface has a dedicated network associated with it. This is described in the following table:

Interface	Subnet	Purpose
eth1	172.16.0.0/16	This is the management network. This network is for internal traffic between OpenStack services.
eth2	10.10.0.0/24	This is the tenant Neutron network. This network has the tunnel endpoints that OpenStack uses when creating software-defined networks based on VXLAN or GRE. VLAN networks will also traverse this interface if configured.
eth3	192.168.100.0/24	This is the Public and External Neutron network. Our client PCs connect to this network and it will become the Floating IP network so we can route traffic from our client PCs to our instances.

Installing Neutron and Open vSwitch on a dedicated network node

To create a SDN layer in OpenStack, we first need to install the software on our `network` node. This node will utilize Open vSwitch as our switch that we can use and control when defining our networks. **Open vSwitch** (**OVS**) is a production-quality, multilayer switch. In this section, we are going to configure the `network` node and we will use `eth2` for creating Neutron tenant networks and `eth3` for creating an externally routable network.

Getting ready...

Ensure that you have a suitable server available for installation of the OpenStack network components. If you are using the accompanying Vagrant environment, this will be the `network` node that we will be using.

Ensure that you are logged in to the `network` node and that it has Internet access to allow us to install the required packages in our environment for running OVS and Neutron. If you created this node with Vagrant, you can execute the following command:

```
vagrant ssh network
```

Neutron requires access to a database and message queue. Check that the pre requisites have been installed by following the instructions at `http://bit.ly/OpenStackCookbookPreReqs`.

How to do it...

To configure our OpenStack network node, carry out the following steps:

1. When we started our `network` node, using vagrant, we had to assign the third and fourth interfaces (`eth2` and `eth3`) an IP address. We no longer want an IP assigned to this physical interface, but we still want this under the control of Neutron and OVS. We will then move their corresponding addresses to a bridge. These bridges are shown in the preceding figure as `br-eth2` and `br-ex`.
2. Use the following commands to remove these IPs from our interfaces on the Network virtual machine created by Vagrant:

```
sudo ifconfig eth2 down
sudo ifconfig eth2 0.0.0.0 up
sudo ip link set eth2 promisc on

sudo ifconfig eth3 down
sudo ifconfig eth3 0.0.0.0 up
sudo ip link set eth3 promisc on
```

> If you are in a virtual environment, you need to ensure that your virtualization software is configured to allow VMs to enter promiscuous mode. Your virtualization software vendor documentation will provide guidance on how to do this.
>
> On a physical server running Ubuntu, we configure this in our `/etc/network/interfaces` file as follows:

```
auto eth2
iface eth2 inet manual
  up ip link set $IFACE up
  down ip link set $IFACE down
auto eth3
iface eth3 inet manual
  up ip link set $IFACE up
  down ip link set $IFACE down
```

3. We then update the packages installed on the node using the following commands:

```
sudo apt-get update
sudo apt-get upgrade
```

4. Next, we install the kernel headers package as the installation will compile some new kernel modules:

   ```
   sudo apt-get install linux-headers-`uname -r`
   ```

5. We need to install some supporting applications and utilities using the following commands:

   ```
   sudo apt-get install vlan bridge-utils dnsmasq-base \
     dnsmasq-utils ipset python-mysqldb ntp
   ```

6. We are now ready to install Open vSwitch:

   ```
   sudo apt-get install openvswitch-switch \
     openvswitch-datapath-dkms
   ```

7. After this has installed and configured some kernel modules, we can start our OVS service with the following command:

   ```
   sudo service openvswitch-switch start
   ```

8. Now we will proceed to install the Neutron components that run on this node: the Neutron DHCP Agent, the Neutron L3 Agent, the Neutron OVS Plugin, and the Neutron ML2 Plugin. The commands are as follows:

   ```
   sudo apt-get install neutron-dhcp-agent \
     neutron-l3-agent neutron-plugin-openvswitch-agent \
     neutron-plugin-ml2
   ```

How it works...

We have completed the installation of the packages on a new node in our environment that runs the software networking components of our SDN environment. This includes the OVS service through the ML2 Neutron plugin system and various Neutron components that interact with this. While we have used OVS in our example, there are many vendor plugins that include Nicira and Cisco UCS/Nexus among others. More details on the plugins that Neutron supports can be found at `https://wiki.openstack.org/wiki/Neutron`.

First, we configured our interface on this switch node that will serve as our tenant Neutron and External networks. The External network in OpenStack terms is often referred to as the Provider Network. On a physical server in a datacenter, this externally bridged interface (`br-ex`) will be connected to the network that routes to the rest of our physical servers. The assignment of this network is described in the recipe *Creating an external Floating IP Neutron network*. Both of the interfaces used by Neutron are created without an IP address so that our OpenStack environment can control this by bridging new networks to it. We assign IP addresses to the bridges themselves to create tunnels between these IP endpoints that have overlay networks created on them. It is these networks created within the tunnels that our instances get attached to in OpenStack.

A number of packages were installed on this `network` node. The list of packages that we specify for installation (excluding dependencies) is as follows:

Operating System	`linux-headers-`uname -r``

Generic Networking Components	`vlan`
	`bridge-utils`
	`dnsmasq-base`
	`dnsmasq-utils`

Open vSwitch	`openvswitch-switch` `openvswitch-agent`

Neutron	`neutron-dhcp-agent`
	`neutron-l3-agent`
	`neutron-plugin-ml2`
	`neutron-plugin-openvswitch`
	`neutron-plugin-openvswitch-agent`

Configuring Neutron and Open vSwitch

Configuration of OVS and Neutron involves running OVS commands to configure the software switch and a number of configuration files for Neutron. For this section, we are configuring the `network` node. We will be using `eth2` for creating Neutron tenant networks and `eth3` for creating an externally routable network.

Getting ready

Ensure that you have a suitable server available for installation of the OpenStack network components. If you are using the accompanying Vagrant environment, this will be the `network` node that we will be using.

Ensure that you are logged in to the `network` node and it has the required packages in our environment for running OVS and Neutron. If you created this node with Vagrant, you can execute the following command:

```
vagrant ssh network
```

How to do it...

To configure OVS and Neutron on our OpenStack network node, carry out the following steps:

1. With the installation of the required packages complete, we can now configure our environment. To do this, we first configure our OVS switch service. We need to configure a bridge that we will call `br-int`. This is the integration bridge that glues our bridges together within our SDN environment. The command is as follows:

   ```
   sudo ovs-vsctl add-br br-int
   ```

2. We now configure the Neutron Tenant tunnel network bridge, which will allow us to create GRE and VXLAN tunnels between our Compute hosts and `network` node to give us our Neutron network functionality within OpenStack. This interface is `eth2` so we need to configure a bridge called `br-eth2` within OVS as follows:

   ```
   sudo ovs-vsctl add-br br-eth2
   sudo ovs-vsctl add-port br-eth2 eth2
   ```

3. We now assign the IP address that was previously assigned to our `eth3` interface to this bridge:

   ```
   sudo ifconfig br-eth2 10.10.0.201 netmask 255.255.255.0
   ```

> This address is on the network that we will use to create the GRE and VXLAN Neutron tunnel mesh networks. Instances within OpenStack will attach to the OpenStack created networks encapsulated on this network. We assigned this range as `10.10.0.0/24`, as described in the `vagrant` file:
>
> ```
> network_config.vm.network :hostonly, "10.10.0.201",
> :netmask => "255.255.255.0"
> ```

4. Next add an external bridge that is used on our external network. This will be used to route traffic to/from the outside of our environment and onto our SDN network:

   ```
   sudo ovs-vsctl add-br br-ex
   sudo ovs-vsctl add-port br-ex eth3
   ```

5. We now assign the IP address that was previously assigned to our `eth3` interface to this bridge:

   ```
   sudo ifconfig br-ex 192.168.100.201 netmask 255.255.255.0
   ```

> This address is on the network that we will use to access instances within OpenStack. We assigned this range as 192.168.100.0/24, as described in the `vagrant` file:
>
> ```
> network_config.vm.network :hostonly,
> "192.168.100.201", :netmask => "255.255.255.0"
> ```

6. We need to ensure that we have set the following in `/etc/sysctl.conf`:

```
net.ipv4.ip_forward=1
net.ipv4.conf.all.rp_filter=0
net.ipv4.conf.default.rp_filter=0
```

7. To pick up these system changes in this file, run the following command:

```
sysctl -p
```

8. We now need to configure the backend database store, so we first create the `neutron` database in `MariaDB`. We do this as follows (where we have a user in MariaDB called `root`, with password `openstack`, that is able to create databases):

```
MYSQL_ROOT_PASS=openstack
mysql -uroot -p$MYSQL_ROOT_PASS -e "CREATE DATABASE \
    neutron;"
```

9. It is good practice to create a user that is specific to our OpenStack Networking service, so we create a `neutron` user in the database as follows:

```
MYSQL_NEUTRON_PASS=openstack
mysql -uroot -p$MYSQL_ROOT_PASS -e "GRANT ALL PRIVILEGES ON \
neutron.* TO 'neutron'@'localhost' IDENTIFIED BY \
'$MYSQL_KEYSTONE_PASS';"
mysql -uroot -p$MYSQL_ROOT_PASS -e "GRANT ALL PRIVILEGES ON \
neutron.* TO 'neutron'@'%' IDENTIFIED BY '$MYSQL_NEUTRON_PASS';"
```

10. Next we will edit the Neutron configuration files. There are a number of these to edit on our `network` node. The first is the `/etc/neutron/neutron.conf` file. Edit this file and insert the following content:

```
[DEFAULT]
verbose = True
debug = True
state_path = /var/lib/neutron
lock_path = $state_path/lock
log_dir = /var/log/neutron
```

```
use_syslog = True
syslog_log_facility = LOG_LOCAL0

bind_host = 0.0.0.0
bind_port = 9696

# Plugin
core_plugin = ml2
service_plugins = router
allow_overlapping_ips = True

# auth
auth_strategy = keystone

# RPC configuration options. Defined in rpc __init__
# The messaging module to use, defaults to kombu.
rpc_backend = neutron.openstack.common.rpc.impl_kombu

rabbit_host = 172.16.0.200
rabbit_password = guest
rabbit_port = 5672
rabbit_userid = guest
rabbit_virtual_host = /
rabbit_ha_queues = false

# ===== Notification System Options ==========
notification_driver = neutron.openstack.common.notifier.rpc_
notifier

[agent]
root_helper = sudo

[keystone_authtoken]
auth_uri = https://192.168.100.200:35357/v2.0/
identity_uri = https://192.168.100.200:5000
admin_tenant_name = service
admin_user = neutron
admin_password = neutron
insecure = True

[database]
connection = mysql://neutron:openstack@172.16.0.200/neutron
```

As we are using self-signed SSL certificates, we set `insecure = True`. In a production environment, you will want to obtain proper SSL certificates and set `insecure = False`.

11. After this, we edit the `/etc/neutron/l3_agent.ini` file with the following content:

```
[DEFAULT]
interface_driver = neutron.agent.linux.interface.
OVSInterfaceDriver
use_namespaces = True
```

12. Locate the `/etc/neutron/dhcp_agent.ini` file and insert the following content:

```
[DEFAULT]
interface_driver = neutron.agent.linux.interface.
OVSInterfaceDriver
dhcp_driver = neutron.agent.linux.dhcp.Dnsmasq
use_namespaces = True
dnsmasq_config_file = /etc/neutron/dnsmasq-neutron.conf
```

13. Create a file called `/etc/neutron/dnsmasq-neutron.conf` and add in the following content to alter the **maximum transmission unit** (**MTU**) of our Neutron Tenant interface of our guests:

```
# To allow tunneling bytes to be appended
dhcp-option-force=26,1400
```

14. After this, we edit the `/etc/neutron/metadata_agent.ini` file to insert the following content:

```
[DEFAULT]
auth_url = https://192.168.100.200:5000/v2.0
auth_region = RegionOne
admin_tenant_name = service
admin_user = neutron
admin_password = neutron
nova_metadata_ip = 172.16.0.200
metadata_proxy_shared_secret = foo
auth_insecure = True
```

15. The last Neutron service file we need to edit is the `/etc/neutron/plugins/ml2/ml2_conf.ini` file. Insert the following content:

```
[ml2]
type_drivers = gre,vxlan
tenant_network_types = vxlan
mechanism_drivers = openvswitch

[ml2_type_gre]
tunnel_id_ranges = 1:1000

[ml2_type_vxlan]
vxlan_group =
vni_ranges = 1:1000

[vxlan]
enable_vxlan = True
vxlan_group =
local_ip = 10.10.0.201
l2_population = True

[agent]
tunnel_types = vxlan
vxlan_udp_port = 4789

[ovs]
local_ip = 10.10.0.201
tunnel_type = vxlan
enable_tunneling = True
[securitygroup]
firewall_driver = neutron.agent.linux.iptables_firewall.
OVSHybridIptablesFirewallDriver
enable_security_group = True
```

16. With our environment and switch configured, we can restart the relevant services to pick up the changes:

```
sudo service neutron-plugin-openvswitch-agent restart
sudo service neutron-dhcp-agent restart
sudo service neutron-l3-agent restart
sudo service neutron-metadata-agent restart
```

How it works...

We completed the configuration of a new node in our environment that runs the software networking components of our SDN environment.

Once we installed our applications and service dependencies and started the services, we configured our environment by assigning a bridge that acts as the integration bridge that internally bridges our instances with the rest of the network. It also connects bridges to our interfaces on the Tenant and Provider networks.

We then edit a number of files to get Neutron up-and-running in our environment. The first is the `/etc/neutron/neutron.conf` file. This is the main configuration file for our Neutron services. In this file, we define how Neutron is configured and what components, features, and plugins should be used.

In the `/etc/neutron/l3_agent.ini` file, we specify that we are allowing tenants to create overlapping IP ranges (`use_namespaces = True`). This means that Tenant A users can create and use a private IP CIDR that also exists within Tenant B. We also specify that we are to use OVS to provide L3 routing capabilities.

The `/etc/neutron/dhcp_agent.ini` file specifies that we are going to use Dnsmasq as the service for DHCP within our environment. We also reference the `/etc/neutron/dnsmasq-neutron.conf` file, which allows us to pass extra options to Dnsmasq when it starts up processes for that network. We do this so we can specify an MTU of 1400 that gets set on the instance network interfaces. This is because the default of 1500 conflicts with the extra bytes that tunneling adds to the packets and its inability to handle fragmentation. By lowering the MTU, all the normal IP information plus the extra tunneling information can be transmitted at once without fragmentation.

The `/etc/neutron/metadata_agent.ini` file notifies Neutron and our instances where to find the metadata service. It points to our `controller` node and ultimately the nova API service. Here, we set a secret key as described in the `metadata_proxy_shared_secret = foo` line that matches the same random keyword that we will eventually configure in `/etc/nova/nova.conf` on our `controller` node: `neutron_metadata_proxy_shared_secret=foo`.

The last configuration file, `/etc/neutron/plugins/ml2/ml2_conf.ini`, configures the L2 plugins within our environment and describes our L2 capabilities. The configuration options are as follows:

```
[ml2]
type_drivers = gre,vxlan
tenant_network_types = vxlan
mechanism_drivers = openvswitch
```

We're configuring our networking type to be either **Generic Routing Encapsulation** (**GRE**) or **Virtual eXtensible LAN** (**VXLAN**) tunnels. This allows our SDN environment to capture a wide range of protocols over the tunnels we create.

We specify that VXLAN tunnels are to be created when a non-admin user creates their own private Neutron networks. An admin user is able to specify GRE as an option on the command line:

```
[ml2_type_gre]
tunnel_id_ranges = 1:1000
```

This specifies that, when a user specifies a private Neutron tenant network without specifying an ID range for a GRE network, an ID is taken from this range. OpenStack ensures that each tunnel created is unique. The code is as follows:

```
[ml2_type_vxlan]
vxlan_group =
vni_ranges = 1:1000

[vxlan]
enable_vxlan = True
vxlan_group =
local_ip = 10.10.0.201
[agent]
tunnel_types = vxlan
vxlan_udp_port = 4789
```

The preceding sections describe our VXLAN options. In the same way as for GRE, we have an endpoint IP that is the IP assigned to the interface that we want tunneled traffic to flow over, and we specify the valid `vxlan` IDs to use within our environment. The code is as follows:

```
[ovs]
local_ip = 10.10.0.201
tunnel_type = gre
enable_tunneling = True
```

The preceding section describes the options to pass to OVS, and details our tunnel configuration. Its endpoint address is `10.10.0.201` and we're specifying the tunnel type GRE to be used. The code is as follows:

```
[securitygroup]
firewall_driver = neutron.agent.linux.iptables_firewall.
OVSHybridIptablesFirewallDriver
enable_security_group = True
```

The preceding code tells Neutron to use `IPtables` rules when creating security groups.

Note that we have added a line to our keystone reference lines that says `insecure = True`. This is because our environment uses self-signed certificates and would cause SSL errors that are ignored with this setting.

Installing and configuring the Neutron API service

The Neutron service provides an API for our services to access and define our software-defined networking. In our environment, we install the Neutron service on our `controller` node alongside our other API services such as **Glance** and **Keystone**.

Getting ready

Ensure you have a suitable server available for installation of the OpenStack network components. If you are using the accompanying Vagrant environment, this will be the `controller` node that we will be using.

Ensure you are logged in to the `controller` node. If you created this node with Vagrant, you can execute the following command:

```
vagrant ssh controller
```

Neutron requires access to a database and message queue. Check that the pre requisites have been installed by following the instructions at `http://bit.ly/OpenStackCookbookPreReqs`.

How to do it...

To configure our OpenStack Controller node for Neutron, carry out the following steps:

1. First update the packages installed on the node:

   ```
   sudo apt-get update
   sudo apt-get upgrade
   ```

2. We are now ready to install the Neutron service and the ML2 plugin using the following commands:

   ```
   sudo apt-get install neutron-server \
     neutron-plugin-ml2 ntp
   ```

3. Next we will edit the Neutron configuration files. As we are just providing the Neutron API service, we first need to configure the service in the `/etc/neutron/neutron.conf` file. Edit this file to insert the following contents that match the configuration found on our *network* node:

```
[DEFAULT]
verbose = True
debug = True
state_path = /var/lib/neutron
lock_path = $state_path/lock
log_dir = /var/log/neutron
use_syslog = True
syslog_log_facility = LOG_LOCAL0

bind_host = 0.0.0.0
bind_port = 9696
# Plugin
core_plugin = ml2
service_plugins = router
allow_overlapping_ips = True

# auth
auth_strategy = keystone

# RPC configuration options. Defined in rpc __init__
# The messaging module to use, defaults to kombu.
rpc_backend = neutron.openstack.common.rpc.impl_kombu

rabbit_host = 172.16.0.200
rabbit_password = guest
rabbit_port = 5672
rabbit_userid = guest
rabbit_virtual_host = /
rabbit_ha_queues = false

# ===== Notification System Options ==========
notification_driver = neutron.openstack.common.notifier.rpc_
notifier

# ======== neutron nova interactions ==========
notify_nova_on_port_status_changes = True
notify_nova_on_port_data_changes = True
nova_url = http://172.16.0.200:8774/v2
nova_region_name = RegionOne
```

```
nova_admin_username = nova
nova_admin_tenant_name = service
nova_admin_password = nova
nova_admin_auth_url = https://192.168.100.200:35357/v2.0
nova_ca_certificates_file = /etc/ssl/certs/ca.pem
[agent]
root_helper = sudo

[keystone_authtoken]
auth_uri = https://192.168.100.200:35357/v2.0/
identity_uri = https://192.168.100.200:5000
admin_tenant_name = service
admin_user = neutron
admin_password = neutron
insecure = True

[database]
connection = mysql://neutron:openstack@172.16.0.200/neutron
```

4. We then need to edit the `/etc/neutron/plugins/ml2/ml2_conf.ini` file to have the following content that matches the network node's configuration for consistency (except the `local_ip` option):

```
[ml2]
type_drivers = gre,vxlan
tenant_network_types = vxlan
mechanism_drivers = openvswitch

[ml2_type_gre]
tunnel_id_ranges = 1:1000

[ml2_type_vxlan]
vxlan_group =
vni_ranges = 1:1000

[vxlan]
enable_vxlan = True
vxlan_group =
local_ip =
[agent]
tunnel_types = vxlan
vxlan_udp_port = 4789
```

```
[securitygroup]
firewall_driver = neutron.agent.linux.iptables_firewall.
OVSHybridIptablesFirewallDriver
enable_security_group = True
```

5. After these files have been configured correctly, we run the following command to ensure our Neutron database is at the correct level for the version of OpenStack we are using:

   ```
   sudo neutron-db-manage \
     --config-file /etc/neutron/neutron.conf \
     --config-file /etc/neutron/plugins/ml2/ml2_conf.ini \
     upgrade juno
   ```

6. At this stage, we configure Nova to use Neutron. Nova component installation is covered in the next chapter, but it is shown here for your convenience. After the Nova components have been installed, configure the `/etc/nova/nova.conf` file to tell the OpenStack Compute components to utilize Neutron. Add the following lines under [Default] in our `/etc/nova/nova.conf` file:

   ```
   # Network settings
   network_api_class=nova.network.neutronv2.api.API
   neutron_url=http://172.16.0.200:9696/
   neutron_auth_strategy=keystone
   neutron_admin_tenant_name=service
   neutron_admin_username=neutron
   neutron_admin_password=neutron
   neutron_admin_auth_url=https://192.168.100.200:35357/v2.0
   neutron_ca_certificates_file=/etc/ssl/certs/ca.pem
   libvirt_vif_driver=nova.virt.libvirt.vif.
   LibvirtHybridOVSBridgeDriver
   linuxnet_interface_driver=nova.network.linux_net.
   LinuxOVSInterfaceDriver
   firewall_driver=nova.virt.libvirt.firewall.IptablesFirewallDriver
   service_neutron_metadata_proxy=true
   neutron_metadata_proxy_shared_secret=foo
   ```

7. Using the following command, restart our Neutron services running on this node to pick up the changes:

   ```
   sudo service neutron-server restart
   ```

8. When Nova has been installed, restart the Nova services running on this node to pick up the changes in the `/etc/nova/nova.conf` file:

   ```
   ls /etc/init/nova-* | cut -d '/' -f4 | cut -d '.' -f1 | while read
   S; do sudo stop $S; sudo start $S; done
   ```

How it works...

Configuring our Neutron API service on the `controller` node is very straightforward with the right information at hand. We install a couple of required packages.

Use the following commands to install the Neutron package:

`neutron-server`

`neutron-plugin-ml2`

Once the Neutron package is installed, we configure the `/etc/neutron/neutron.conf` file that matches our network node `config`, with only one new section: the neutron nova interaction section. Here, we ensure correct settings to allow nova to interoperate with Neutron. We also configure the ML2 plugin file that also matches our network node, but we can omit the OVS section because it is surplus on our `controller` node.

We then run a command to ensure that our Neutron database has the correct rows and columns for use with the OpenStack Juno release.

Finally, we configure `/etc/nova/nova.conf`, which is the most important configuration file for our OpenStack Compute services:

- `network_api_class=nova.network.neutronv2.api.API`: This tells our OpenStack Compute service to use Neutron Networking.
- `neutron_url=http://172.16.0.200:9696/`: This is address of our Neutron Server API (running on our `controller` node).
- `neutron_auth_strategy=keystone`: This tells Neutron to utilize the OpenStack Identity and Authentication service, Keystone.
- `neutron_admin_tenant_name=service`: This is the name of the service tenant in Keystone.
- `neutron_admin_username=neutron`: This is the username that Neutron uses for authentication in Keystone.
- `neutron_admin_password=neutron`: This is the password that Neutron uses to authenticate with in Keystone.
- `neutron_admin_auth_url=https://172.16.0.200:35357/v2.0`: This is the address of our Keystone service.
- `neutron_ca_certificates_file = /etc/ssl/certs/ca.pem`: This references the Certificate Authority file that we generated in *Chapter 1, Keystone – OpenStack Identity Service*, to allow our SSL calls to Keystone to work correctly without setting an insecure flag.
- `libvirt_vif_driver=nova.virt.libvirt.vif.LibvirtHybridOVSBridgeDriver`: This tells Libvirt to use the OVS Bridge driver.

- `linuxnet_interface_driver=nova.network.linux_net.LinuxOVSInterfaceDriver`: This is the driver used to create Ethernet devices on our Linux hosts.
- `firewall_driver=nova.virt.libvirt.firewall.IptablesFirewallDriver`: This is the driver that is used to manage the firewalls.
- `service_neutron_metadata_proxy=true`: This allows us to utilize the metadata proxy service that passes requests from Neutron to the Nova API service.
- `foo`: This is the random key we set in order to utilize the proxy service. It must match on all nodes running this service to ensure a level of security when passing proxy requests.

  ```
  neutron_metadata_proxy_shared_secret=foo
  ```

See Also

- *Chapter 4, Nova – OpenStack Compute*

Creating a tenant Neutron network

Now that we have our OpenStack Network services running, we can use these to create networks within our OpenStack environment. Networks are created for each tenant and we can use these to connect to our VMs. Neutron networks can either be private or shared. When a Neutron network is private, only the operators and instances of that tenant can utilize these networks. When they are marked as shared, all instances can attach to this shared network so it is important to utilize this shared network feature carefully to ensure security between tenants. When using shared networks, we implement Security Group rules to ensure the traffic flow matches our security requirements.

Getting ready

Ensure you have a suitable client available for using Neutron. If you are using the accompanying Vagrant environment, you can use the `controller` node. This has the `python-neutronclient` package that provides the `neutron` command-line client.

If you created this node with Vagrant, you can execute the following command:

```
vagrant ssh controller
```

Ensure you have the following credentials set (adjust the path to your certificates and key file to match your environment if not using the Vagrant environment):

```
export OS_TENANT_NAME=cookbook
export OS_USERNAME=admin
export OS_PASSWORD=openstack
export OS_AUTH_URL=https://192.168.100.200:5000/v2.0/
export OS_NO_CACHE=1
export OS_KEY=/vagrant/cakey.pem
export OS_CACERT=/vagrant/ca.pem
```

At this stage, Keystone should be installed and configured correctly. See the Installing the OpenStack Identity Service recipe in *Chapter 1, Keystone – OpenStack Identity Service*, for more information.

How to do it...

To create a private Neutron network for a particular tenant, follow these steps:

1. We first need to get the tenant id that we can reference when creating the network information for that particular tenant. To do so, issue the following command:

   ```
   TENANT_ID=$(keystone tenant-list \
     | awk '/\ cookbook\ / {print $2}')
   ```

2. We then use this value to create the layer 2 network for this tenant:

   ```
   neutron net-create \
     --tenant-id ${TENANT_ID} \
     cookbook_network_1
   ```

3. With the network in place, we now allocate a subnet to this network using the CIDR format (10.200.0.0/24):

   ```
   neutron subnet-create \
     --tenant-id ${TENANT_ID} \
     --name cookbook_subnet_1 \
     cookbook_network_1 \
     10.200.0.0/24
   ```

4. We will now create a router on this network that we can use to act as the default gateway for our instances. Adding routers is optional—they are a design consideration, allowing you to route from one network that we create to another. This option avoids multihoming instances with multiple interfaces and networks. This router will be used to allow us to assign an IP from our physical host range that provides access to our instances:

   ```
   neutron router-create \
     --tenant-id ${TENANT_ID} \
     cookbook_router_1
   ```

5. We add this `router` to our subnet:

   ```
   neutron router-interface-add \
     cookbook_router_1 \
     cookbook_subnet_1
   ```

How it works...

We created a network with a defined subnet that our VMs utilize when they start up. To create a `network`, the following syntax is used:

```
neutron net-create \
  --tenant-id TENANT_ID \
  NAME_OF_NETWORK
```

To create a subnet, the following syntax is used:

```
neutron subnet-create \
  --tenant-id TENANT_ID \
  --name NAME_OF_SUBNET \
  NAME_OF_NETWORK \
  CIDR
```

Routers are optional on networks and the function is to route traffic from one subnet to another. In a Neutron SDN, this is no different. Layer 3 (L3) Routers allow you to configure gateways and routes to other networks on-demand. If we only require our instances to communicate between each other on the same subnet, there is no need to have a router because there will be no other network that needs to be routed to or from. The syntax to create routers is as follows:

```
neutron router-create \
  --tenant-id TENANT_ID \
  NAME_OF_ROUTER
```

The syntax to add the router to our Subnet (used to allow routes from one network (physical or software-defined)) is as follows:

```
neutron router-interface-add \
  ROUTER_NAME \
  SUBNET_NAME
```

We can then add further subnets using the preceding syntax to this router and allow traffic to flow between instances on different OpenStack Neutron-created subnets.

Deleting a Neutron network

The steps to remove a Neutron network are similar to the set of steps we followed to create the network.

Getting ready

Ensure that you have a suitable client available for using Neutron. If you are using the accompanying Vagrant environment, you can use the `controller` node. This has the `python-neutronclient` package that provides the `neutron` command-line client.

If you created this node with Vagrant, you can execute the following command:

```
vagrant ssh controller
```

Ensure you have the following credentials set (adjust the path to your certificates and key file to match your environment if not using the Vagrant environment):

```
export OS_TENANT_NAME=cookbook
export OS_USERNAME=admin
export OS_PASSWORD=openstack
export OS_AUTH_URL=https://192.168.100.200:5000/v2.0/
export OS_NO_CACHE=1
export OS_KEY=/vagrant/cakey.pem
export OS_CACERT=/vagrant/ca.pem
```

How to do it...

To delete a Neutron network for a particular tenant, follow these steps:

1. List the networks with the following command:

   ```
   neutron net-list
   ```

You will get the following output:

id	name	subnets
5b738491-4368-4e56-adaa-f4bdb0ef9dd9	cookbook_network_1	6436a0dc-1537-4010-8981-ccbf34fa35ee 10.200.0.0/24

2. To list the subnets, issue the following command:

```
neutron subnet-list
```

You will get the following output:

id	name	cidr	allocation_pools
6436a0dc-1537-4010-8981-ccbf34fa35ee	cookbook_subnet_1	10.200.0.0/24	{"start": "10.200.0.2", "end": "10.200.0.254"}

3. To delete a network and subnets, ensure that there are no instances and services using the networks and subnets you are about to delete. To check which ports are connected to your network, query the port list in Neutron using the following command:

```
neutron port-list
```

You will get the following output:

id	name	mac_address	fixed_ips
0ecefb17-f126-4205-9c86-6708316d2346		fa:16:3e:e2:73:4c	{"subnet_id": "6436a0dc-1537-4010-8981-ccbf34fa35ee", "ip_address": "10.200.0.1"}
8d007e1e-fd9e-4eb4-8f94-144bff91ac96		fa:16:3e:91:66:fc	{"subnet_id": "6436a0dc-1537-4010-8981-ccbf34fa35ee", "ip_address": "10.200.0.3"}

4. You can also look at the running instances and the networks that they are attached to by issuing the following command:

```
nova list
```

You will get the following output:

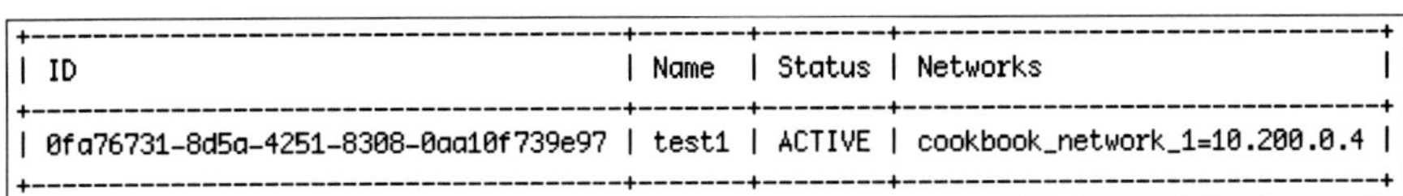

ID	Name	Status	Networks
0fa76731-8d5a-4251-8308-0aa10f739e97	test1	ACTIVE	cookbook_network_1=10.200.0.4

You can see that we have a `cookbook_network_1` instance on the network that we want to delete.

5. You need to delete any instances that are running on this network, for example:

```
nova delete test1
```

6. Now that you have stopped the instances that you want to remove, you can remove any router interfaces attached to this network with the following commands:

```
ROUTER_ID=$(neutron router-list \
  | awk '/\ cookbook_router_1\ / {print $2}')

SUBNET_ID=$(neutron subnet-list \
  | awk '/\ cookbook_subnet_1\ / {print $2}')

neutron router-interface-delete \
  ${ROUTER_ID} \
  ${SUBNET_ID}
```

7. With the router interface removed, you can proceed to delete the subnet with the following command:

```
neutron subnet-delete cookbook_subnet_1
```

8. With the subnet removed, you can delete the network with the following command:

```
neutron net-delete cookbook_network_1
```

How it works...

In the preceding steps, we performed a series of steps to remove a network. This involves first removing any (virtual) devices attached to this network such as instances and routers, removing the subnet that has been attached to that network, and removing the underlying network itself. Let's see the net list:

- To list a nework, use the following command:

```
neutron net-list
```

- To list a subnet, use the following command:

```
neutron subnet-list
```

- The following command lists used Neutron Ports:

```
neutron port-list
```

- To remove a router interface from a subnet, use the following syntax:

```
neutron router-interface-delete \
  ROUTER_ID \
  SUBNET_ID
```

- To remove a subnet, use the following syntax:

```
neutron subnet-delete NAME_OF_SUBNET
```

- To remove a network, use the following syntax:

```
neutron subnet-delete NAME_OF_NETWORK
```

Creating an external floating IP Neutron network

In Neutron, it is easy to create many private networks that allow communication between your instances. To allow access from your client to these, though, we must create a router on the provider network (an external network) that is routed into our OpenStack environment. This provider network allows us to allocate floating addresses to our instances.

Getting ready

Ensure that you have a suitable client available for using Neutron. If you are using the accompanying Vagrant environment, you can use the `controller` node. This has the `python-neutronclient` package installed that provides the `neutron` command-line client.

If you created this node with Vagrant, you can execute the following command:

```
vagrant ssh controller
```

Ensure you have the following credentials set (adjust the path to your certificates and key file to match your environment if not using the Vagrant environment):

```
export OS_TENANT_NAME=cookbook
export OS_USERNAME=admin
export OS_PASSWORD=openstack
export OS_AUTH_URL=https://192.168.100.200:5000/v2.0/
export OS_NO_CACHE=1
export OS_KEY=/vagrant/cakey.pem
export OS_CACERT=/vagrant/ca.pem
```

How to do it...

To create an external router on our Neutron network for a particular tenant, we need to have tenant admin privileges. We will first create a public network in our `admin` tenant and then attach this to a tenant's router that requires external access to our instances. This will be achieved by assigning of a floating IP to the instance.

Once our environment has been set correctly with `admin` privileges, follow these steps:

1. We first need to get the service tenant ID that we can reference when creating the public shared network. To do so, issue the following command:

   ```
   ADMIN_TENANT_ID=$(keystone tenant-list \
     | awk '/\ service\ / {print $2}')
   ```

> The use of the `service` tenant is not a strict requirement. We are referring to a tenant outside all our private tenants that is under the control of our admin user only.

2. We can now create a new public network, which we will call `floatingNet`, to provide our external routing capability. To do this, we issue the following commands:

   ```
   neutron net-create \
     --tenant-id ${ADMIN_TENANT_ID} \
     --router:external=True \
     floatingNet
   ```

3. We then create our external/floating range on this network. In this example, this external subnet is `192.168.100.0/24`. To do this, we specify a n address range that we will manually assign to instances as floating address, ensuring that the allocation pool (the list of allowed IPs) does not conflict with any IPs used currently in our physical environment:

   ```
   neutron subnet-create \
     --tenant-id ${ADMIN_TENANT_ID} \
     --name floatingSubnet \
     --allocation-pool \
       start=192.168.100.10,end=192.168.100.20 \
     --enable_dhcp=False \
     floatingNet \
     192.168.100.0/24
   ```

4. We now need to set a gateway on our Cookbook router (described in step 4 of the *Creating a tenant Neutron network* recipe) to this floating network using the following commands:

   ```
   neutron router-gateway-set \
     cookbook_router_1 \
     floatingNet
   ```

5. With the networking elements complete, we can now utilize this floating network. To do so, we assign a floating IP to our running instance, so first we need to see what IP has been assigned to our instance on the `cookbook_network_1` network by issuing a `nova list` command:

   ```
   nova list
   ```

   You will get the following output:

   ```
   +--------------------------------------+-------+--------+------------------------+
   | ID                                   | Name  | Status | Networks               |
   +--------------------------------------+-------+--------+------------------------+
   | 9f8dff28-41fc-4f9f-a41f-a858abebc529 | test1 | ACTIVE | cookbookNet=10.200.0.2 |
   +--------------------------------------+-------+--------+------------------------+
   ```

6. We also gather some information about the routers and Neutron network ports used in our environment. To collect information about our `cookbook_router_1` network, issue the following command:

   ```
   neutron router-show cookbook_router_1
   ```

   You will get the following output. The information we need is the router ID and the Network ID:

   ```
   +-----------------------+--------------------------------------------------------+
   | Field                 | Value                                                  |
   +-----------------------+--------------------------------------------------------+
   | admin_state_up        | True                                                   |
   | external_gateway_info | {"network_id": "213fedde-ae5e-4396-9754-cb757cba25ea"} |
   | id                    | f0a5c988-6eb2-4593-8b15-90896fd55d3a                   |
   | name                  | cookbookRouter                                         |
   | routes                |                                                        |
   | status                | ACTIVE                                                 |
   | tenant_id             | d856d921d02d4ded8f590e30a5392254                       |
   +-----------------------+--------------------------------------------------------+
   ```

7. To assign a `floating` IP to the instance attached to this port, we issue the following command that first creates a new `floating` IP available for our use from the `floatingNet` network:

   ```
   neutron floatingip-create \
     --tenant-id ${ADMIN_TENANT_ID} \
     floatingNet
   ```

You will get the following output:

```
Created a new floatingip:
+---------------------+--------------------------------------+
| Field               | Value                                |
+---------------------+--------------------------------------+
| fixed_ip_address    |                                      |
| floating_ip_address | 192.168.100.11                       |
| floating_network_id | 2c7d13ff-f634-4d46-8165-a7c989d974b0 |
| id                  | 48e2ca77-af4d-44b3-8c10-b6574d94d6ce |
| port_id             |                                      |
| router_id           |                                      |
| status              | DOWN                                 |
| tenant_id           | 210ef2a4890a4064ba646beb1e84ae1f     |
+---------------------+--------------------------------------+
```

8. We assign this floating IP to the port that our instance is attached to. This information can be found by interrogating the list of ports in use on the router:

   **neutron port-list **

   --router_id=e63fe19d-7628-4180-994d-72035f770d77

   You will get the following output and the information you need matches the IP address listed in the `nova list` command. In this case, we need the port ID matching the IP address `10.200.0.2`, as this is assigned to our instance:

```
+--------------------------------------+------+-------------------+----------------------------------------------------------------------------------------+
| id                                   | name | mac_address       | fixed_ips                                                                              |
+--------------------------------------+------+-------------------+----------------------------------------------------------------------------------------+
| 41ea7756-9521-4ba2-a885-1aca70a96ddc |      | fa:16:3e:b4:b4:a4 | {"subnet_id": "a2580694-d5f4-41b4-9ede-f5212d86deba", "ip_address": "192.168.100.10"} |
| 5f1f68a4-2af2-4528-934d-f7f52ac5b3d3 |      | fa:16:3e:a3:2b:6f | {"subnet_id": "e88b3347-db4d-40c9-abf2-27762dfbb6a9", "ip_address": "10.200.0.2"}     |
| 85f1f3ad-4285-42aa-a15e-45620f065fa4 |      | fa:16:3e:33:35:16 | {"subnet_id": "e88b3347-db4d-40c9-abf2-27762dfbb6a9", "ip_address": "10.200.0.3"}     |
| c8a2fa53-7aa8-459e-9233-2ec180049c3c |      | fa:16:3e:90:80:6c | {"subnet_id": "e88b3347-db4d-40c9-abf2-27762dfbb6a9", "ip_address": "10.200.0.1"}     |
+--------------------------------------+------+-------------------+----------------------------------------------------------------------------------------+
```

9. In the preceding output, the instance with the IP address 10.200.0.2 is attached to port ID `3e5a298b-5ca8-4484-b473-fa71410fd31c`. When we created the `floating` IP, this had an ID of `48e2ca77-af4d-44b3-8c10-b6574d94d6ce`. We associate this floating IP ID with the instance port ID to assign the floating IP to the instance using the following commands:

   **neutron floatingip-associate **

   **48e2ca77-af4d-44b3-8c10-b6574d94d6ce **

   3e5a298b-5ca8-4484-b473-fa71410fd31c

   You will get the message `Associated floating IP 48e2ca77-af4d-44b3-8c10-b6574d94d6ce` when successful.

You can view a list of available `floating` IP addresses and IDs with the `neutron floatingip-list` command.

10. We are now able to access our instance using the assigned Floating IP address of `192.168.100.11`, which had limited access from our network node:

```
+--------------------------------------+-------+--------+---------------------------------------+
| ID                                   | Name  | Status | Networks                              |
+--------------------------------------+-------+--------+---------------------------------------+
| 9f8dff28-41fc-4f9f-a41f-a858abebc529 | test1 | ACTIVE | cookbookNet=10.200.0.2, 192.168.100.11 |
+--------------------------------------+-------+--------+---------------------------------------+
```

How it works...

We have created a network that allows us to assign floating addresses to our instances. This subnet is routable from the rest of the network outside OpenStack, or a public address space directly on the Internet. To do this, we first create a network in an admin tenant that can have a gateway set by using the `--router:external=True` flag to our `neutron net-create` command:

```
neutron net-create \
  --tenant-id ADMIN_TENANT_ID \
  --router:external=True \
  NAME_OF_EXTERNAL_NETWORK
```

As we will be configuring addresses manually to allow us to assign floating IP addresses to instances, we specify a subnet where we define the range of IP addresses but disable DHCP:

```
neutron subnet-create \
  --tenant-id ADMIN_TENANT_ID \
  --name NAME_OF_SUBNET \
  --allocation-pool start=IP_RANGE_START,end=IP_RANGE_END \
  --enable_dhcp=False \
 EXTERNAL_NETWORK_NAME \
  SUBNET_CIDR
```

We assign a router gateway to the network by issuing the following command on an existing router on our network. This router then provides the appropriate NAT when we assign this to an instance on the private network connected to that router:

```
neutron router-gateway-set \
  ROUTER_NAME \
  EXTERNAL_NETWORK_NAME
```

Once configured, we can now allocate a floating IP address from this new range to our running instance. To do this, we run the following command:

```
nova list
```

Get the IP address of our running instance using the following command:

```
neutron router-show ROUTER_NAME
```

To get the ports in use on our router, use the following command:

```
neutron port-list \
  --router_id=ROUTER_ID
```

To create a floating IP for our use from our external network, use the following command (note the tenant ID doesn't have to be the admin tenant as used in the example):

```
neutron floatingip-create \
  --tenant-id=TENANT_ID \
  EXTERNAL_NETWORK_NAME
```

To associate the Floating IP to the instance, we use the port ID associated with the instance (as shown in the port listing on our router):

```
neutron floatingip-associate \
  FLOATING_IP_ID \
  VM_PORT_ON_ROUTER
```

At this point, we can access this instance from our physical network on this floating IP address.

Using Neutron networks for different purposes

In Neutron, it is easy to create many private networks that allow communication between your instances. Sometimes, you might require certain features of a particular network such as when utilizing a dedicated 10G interface; creating a VLAN network to operate with a physical network device, for example, a load balancer; or a SQL Server cluster. With Neutron's SDN, an administrator can set up networks to cater for these purposes.

The following figure shows an example environment with another interface that we can use within Neutron. The physical SQL servers in this environment could be on a Subnet of `192.168.200.0/24` on `VLAN 200`. To use to this network from within OpenStack, we can specify another interface, `eth4`, that will be used to connect OpenStack Virtual instances to physical servers using this same subnet and VLAN.

The network on `eth4` can be configured for a number of different VLANs as you would expect on this type of network.

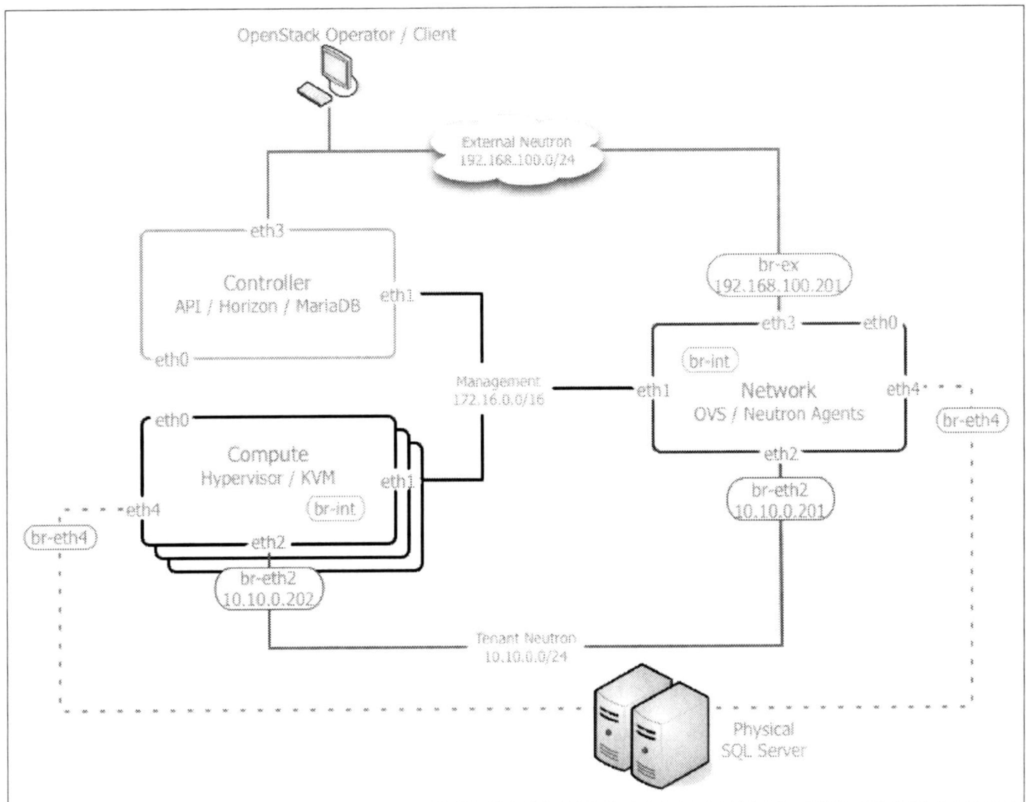

Getting ready

Ensure that you are logged in to both the *Network* and *Compute* nodes, as we will be configuring a new interface for use with OpenStack Networking on each. If you created these nodes with Vagrant, you can execute the following command:

```
vagrant ssh network
vagrant ssh compute
```

As we will be utilizing the Neutron client too, log in to the controller node (or a suitable computer that has the `python-neutronclient` available). If you created these nodes with Vagrant, you can execute the following command:

```
vagrant ssh controller
```

Ensure that you have set the following credentials (adjust the path to your certificates and key file to match your environment if not using the Vagrant environment):

```
export OS_TENANT_NAME=cookbook
export OS_USERNAME=admin
export OS_PASSWORD=openstack
export OS_AUTH_URL=https://192.168.100.200:5000/v2.0/
export OS_NO_CACHE=1
export OS_KEY=/vagrant/cakey.pem
export OS_CACERT=/vagrant/ca.pem
```

How to do it...

An example environment might have a tenant Neutron network configured such that the tunneling occurs over 1G interfaces; in our environment, this could be our `eth2` bridge, `br-eth2`. The environment can also utilize any number of network interfaces that might route to different devices or be cabled up to different segments of the network. In OpenStack networking, we create new bridges that Neutron knows about that an administrator can use when creating networks.

As an administrator of the tenant, carry out the following instructions to set up this new interface bridge and specify a Neutron network, of type VLAN, that allows us to communicate with the physical servers on 192.168.200.0/24:

1. We first configure this new interface on both the *network* and *compute* nodes:

   ```
   sudo ifconfig eth4 down
   sudo ifconfig eth4 0.0.0.0 up
   sudo ip link set eth4 promisc on
   ```

On a physical server running Ubuntu, we would configure this in our `/etc/network/interfaces` file as follows:

```
auto eth4
iface eth4 inet manual
  up ip link set $IFACE up
  down ip link set $IFACE down
```

2. We then create a new bridge in OVS that includes the new `eth4` interface. We do this on all Compute and network nodes in our environment using the following commands:

   ```
   sudo ovs-vsctl add-br br-eth4
   sudo ovs-vsctl add-port br-eth4 eth4
   ```

3. As we are using VLANs for this example, we need to configure our ML2 Plugin configuration to be aware of the interface(s) used for VLAN networks. To do so, edit the `/etc/neutron/plugins/ml2/ml2_conf.ini` file so it has the following content:

   ```
   [ml2]
   type_drivers = gre,vxlan,vlan
   tenant_network_types = vxlan
   mechanism_drivers = openvswitch,l2population

   [ml2_type_gre]
   tunnel_id_ranges = 1:1000

   [ml2_type_vxlan]
   vxlan_group =
   vni_ranges = 1:1000

   [vxlan]
   enable_vxlan = True
   vxlan_group =
   local_ip = 10.10.0.202

   [agent]
   tunnel_types = vxlan
   vxlan_udp_port = 4789

   [ml2_type_vlan]
   network_vlan_ranges = physnet4:100:300

   [ovs]
   bridge_mappings = physnet4:br-eth4
   [securitygroup]
   firewall_driver = neutron.agent.linux.iptables_firewall.
   OVSHybridIptablesFirewallDriver
   enable_security_group = True
   ```

4. We can use the new bridge (via `bridge_mappings` of `physnet4`) when creating a VLAN network. In this example, the SQL servers exist on the subnet 192.168.200.0/24 with VLAN ID 200. To create a Neutron network with these details, we use the following commands:

```
neutron net-create sqlServerNet \
    --provider:physical_network=physnet4 \
    --provider:network_type=vlan \
    --provider:segmentation_id=200 \
    --shared
```

5. We can now use this network to create the subnet details. To do this, we will use a segment of the subnet 192.168.200.0/24 for use by OpenStack by restricting the DHCP range to avoid conflict with any physical servers already on that subnet. To do so, we issue the following commands:

```
neutron subnet-create sqlServerNet 192.168.200.0/24 \
    --name sqlServerSubnet \
    --allocation-pool start=192.168.200.201,end=192.168.200.240 \
    --gateway 192.168.200.1
```

We can now spin up OpenStack instances using this network, defined as sqlServerNet on the subnet 192.168.200.0/24, that can communicate with physical servers on the same subnet.

How it works...

We created another interface bridge on our Compute and network nodes that we can then use when creating VLAN Neutron networks. By using VLAN networks in this way with OpenStack, we can set up communication between our OpenStack Compute cloud environment and physical servers on that same Subnet and VLAN.

To do this, we ensured that our new `eth4` interface was set to promiscuous mode and we created a bridge called `br-eth4` within OVS. This bridge is then referenced in the `/etc/neutron/plugins/ml2/ml2_conf.ini` file within the `[ovs]` section, as shown here:

```
[ovs]
bridge_mappings = physnet4:br-eth4
```

We assign a mapping between that bridge and a name we can use on the neutron command line when specifying it for use, as shown in the following `neutron net-create` command:

```
neutron net-create sqlServerNet \
    --provider:physical_network=physnet4 \
    --provider:network_type=vlan \
    --provider:segmentation_id=200 \
    --shared
```

As you can see, we also specify that we are creating a network of type `vlan` and we are assigning the VLAN ID 200.

Finally, as we are creating this as an admin user, the `--shared` flag allows us to ensure that this network is available to all tenants.

With this network in place, we assign the relevant subnet associated with the VLAN and restrict the DHCP range to avoid conflict with the other part of this subnet. We do this within the neutron subnet-create command by specifying the –allocation-pool flag as shown here:

```
neutron subnet-create sqlServerNet 192.168.200.0/24 \
    --name sqlServerSubnet \
    --allocation-pool start=192.168.200.201,end=192.168.200.240 \
    --gateway 192.168.200.1
```

We only allow OpenStack to spin up instances between the IP addresses 192.168.200.201 and 192.168.200.240.

Configuring Distributed Virtual Routers

The OpenStack Juno release comes with a feature that brings closer parity with the legacy nova-network called **Distributed Virtual Routers** (**DVR**). This feature allows L3 Routers to be distributed across our Compute hosts, in the same way as the nova-network feature, and thus provide high availability of this important routing feature. The result is that each instance attaches to the router located on the Compute host, rather than a central point on the network nodes. This is an acceptable HA failure scenario; if a Compute host fails (and therefore that router), it only affects the instances running on that Compute host.

The following figure shows the environment used in this chapter, but our Compute hosts are now running the L3 Agent. We also utilize the `eth3` interface and the external bridge, `br-ex`, to our Compute host. This interface wasn't needed in a Legacy L3 Router environment but, for a DVR-enabled Compute host, we are adding in the capabilities that previously existed only on our network node. Overall, the result is similar to a network node with additional Compute/Hypervisor functionality.

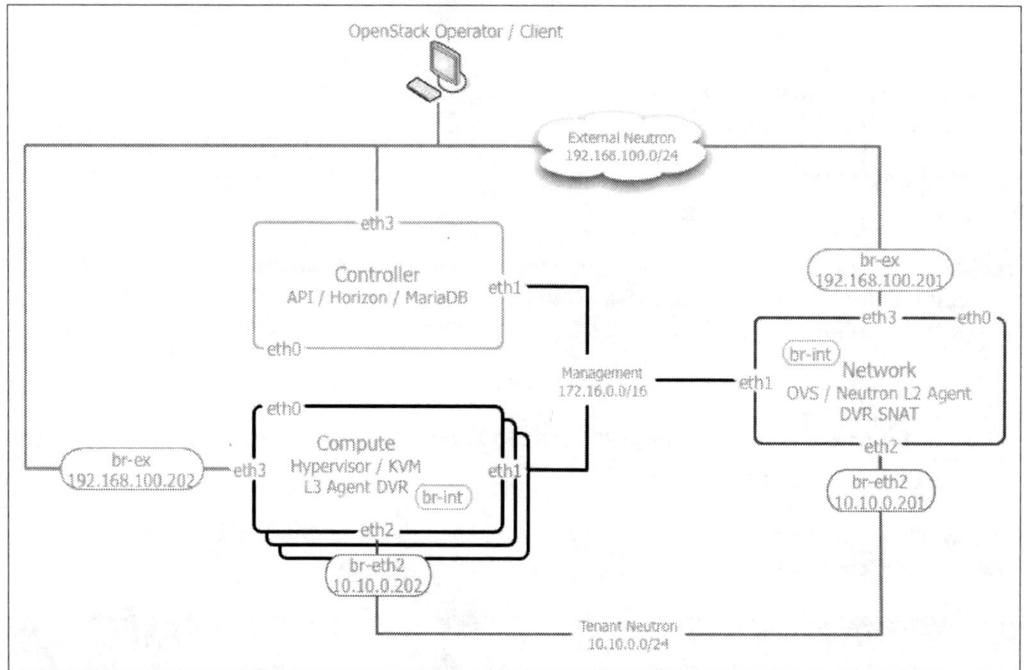

Getting ready

To demonstrate the features of DVR, we naturally require more than one Compute host in our environment. Ensure that you have a second Compute host that has been configured for Neutron networking. Complete installation instructions for Compute hosts can be found in the next chapter.

If you are using the accompanying Vagrant environment, ensure that the second compute host, `compute2`, is running in our environment. Edit the `Vagrant` file, to ensure that `compute2` is available.

Ensure that you are logged in to the `network`, `compute`, `compute2`, and `controller` nodes as we will be configuring configuration files for DVR on all of these nodes. If you created these nodes with Vagrant, you can execute the following commands in separate shells:

```
vagrant ssh controller
vagrant ssh network
vagrant ssh compute
vagrant ssh compute2
```

How to do it...

To set up DVR, we make small adjustments in a number of Neutron configuration files in our environment. These are described in the following sections.

Network node

1. Edit the `/etc/neutron/neutron.conf` file and specify that we are to use distributed routers by adding the following lines to the configuration in the `[DEFAULT]` section:

   ```
   router_distributed = True
   ```

2. Ensure that the `/etc/neutron/l3_agent.ini` file has the following content in the `[DEFAULT]` section:

   ```
   [DEFAULT]
   interface_driver = neutron.agent.linux.interface.
   OVSInterfaceDriver
   use_namespaces = True
   agent_mode = dvr_snat
   external_network_bridge = br-ex
   ```

3. Edit the `/etc/neutron/plugins/ml2/ml2_conf.ini` file to make sure it has the following content:

   ```
   [ml2]
   type_drivers = gre,vxlan,vlan,flat
   tenant_network_types = vxlan
   mechanism_drivers = openvswitch,l2population

   [ml2_type_gre]
   tunnel_id_ranges = 1:1000
   ```

```
[ml2_type_vxlan]
vni_ranges = 1:1000

[vxlan]
enable_vxlan = True
local_ip = 10.10.0.201
l2_population = True

[agent]
tunnel_types = vxlan
l2_population = True
enable_distributed_routing = True
arp_responder = True

[ovs]
local_ip = 10.10.0.201
tunnel_type = vxlan
enable_tunneling = True
l2_population = True
enable_distributed_routing = True
tunnel_bridge = br-tun

[securitygroup]
firewall_driver neutron.agent.linux.iptables_firewall.
OVSHybridIptablesFirewallDriver
enable_security_group = True
```

4. Restart your Neutron services on the `network` node using the following commands:

   ```
   sudo service neutron-plugin-openvswitch-agent restart
   sudo service neutron-l3-agent restart
   ```

The Controller Node

We can now configure the Neutron service on the controller node:

1. Edit the `/etc/neutron/neutron.conf` file to specify that we will use distributed routers by adding the following lines to the configuration in the `[DEFAULT]` section:

   ```
   router_distributed = True
   ```

2. Restart your Neutron API service to pick up this change using the following command:

   ```
   sudo neutron-server restart
   ```

Compute nodes

For the Compute nodes, we need to add in an extra service because these nodes will be routing most of the Neutron traffic instead of the `network` node:

1. Add the following packages:

```
sudo apt-get install neutron-plugin-ml2 \
    neutron-plugin-openvswitch-agent \
    neutron-l3-agent \
    neutron-metadata-agent
```

2. Ensure that you have an external bridge that is used on our external network. This will be used to route traffic to/from the outside of our environment and onto our SDN network:

```
sudo ifconfig eth3 down
sudo ifconfig eth3 0.0.0.0 up
sudo ip link eth3 promisc on
sudo ovs-vsctl add-br br-ex
sudo ovs-vsctl add-port br-ex eth3
```

3. Assign the IP address that was previously assigned to our `eth3` interface to this bridge:

```
sudo ifconfig br-ex 192.168.100.202 netmask 255.255.255.0
```

This address is on the network that we will use to access instances within OpenStack. We assigned this range as 192.168.100.0/24, as described in the `vagrant` file:

```
network_config.vm.network :hostonly,
"192.168.100.201", :netmask => "255.255.255.0"
```

4. Edit the `/etc/neutron/l3_agent.ini` file so it has the following content:

```
[DEFAULT]
interface_driver = neutron.agent.linux.interface.
OVSInterfaceDriver
use_namespaces = True
agent_mode = dvr
external_network_bridge = br-ex
```

5. Edit the /etc/neutron/metadata_agent.ini file so it has the following content:

```
[DEFAULT]
auth_url = https://192.168.100.200:5000/v2.0
auth_region = RegionOne
admin_tenant_name = service
admin_user = neutron
admin_password = neutron
nova_metadata_ip = 172.16.0.200
auth_insecure = True
metadata_proxy_shared_secret = foo
```

6. Ensure that the /etc/neutron/plugins/ml2/ml2_conf.ini file has the following content:

```
[ml2]
type_drivers = gre,vxlan,vlan,flat
tenant_network_types = vxlan
mechanism_drivers = openvswitch,l2population

[ml2_type_gre]
tunnel_id_ranges = 1:1000

[ml2_type_vxlan]
vni_ranges = 1:1000

[vxlan]
enable_vxlan = True
local_ip = 10.10.0.202
l2_population = True

[agent]
tunnel_types = vxlan
l2_population = True
enable_distributed_routing = True
arp_responder = True

[ovs]
local_ip = 10.10.0.202
tunnel_type = vxlan
enable_tunneling = True
l2_population = True
enable_distributed_routing = True
tunnel_bridge = br-tun
```

```
[securitygroup]
firewall_driver neutron.agent.linux.iptables_firewall.
OVSHybridIptablesFirewallDriver
enable_security_group = True
```

7. Stop and start the Neutron L3 Agent service using the following commands:

```
sudo stop neutron-l3-agent
sudo start neutron-l3-agent
sudo stop neutron-plugin-openvswitch-agent
sudo start neutron-plugin-openvswitch-agent
sudo stop neutron-metadata-agent
sudo start neutron-metadata-agent
```

How it works...

We modified a typical Neutron installation to add DVR capabilities. This moves L2 Plugin and L3 Agents to our Compute hosts so that instances running on that Compute host utilize that L3 router agent as their router, rather than an L3 router running centrally on the `network` nodes. We are performing steps similar to the ones we used to set up a `network` node, but replicating these steps on our Compute hosts. This makes sense as we're adding in routing capabilities that were previously possessed only by our Network host in Legacy L3 Routing mode.

The key steps were as follows:

- Modify the `network` node's `/etc/neutron/l3_agent.ini` to include the following content:

  ```
  [DEFAULT]
  agent_mode = dvr_snat
  ```

- Modify the `network` node's `/etc/neutron/plugins/ml2/ml2_conf.ini` file to include the following lines:

  ```
  [DEFAULT]
  mechanism_drivers = openvswitch,l2population

  [agent]
  tunnel_types = vxlan
  l2_population = True
  enable_distributed_routing = True
  arp_responder = True
  ```

```
[ovs]
l2_population = True
enable_distributed_routing = True
```

- On the Controller node, edit the `/etc/neutron/neutron.conf` file that sets the default mode of created routers so they are always distributed:

```
[DEFAULT]
router_distributed = True
```

- On the Compute nodes, install the following packages:

  neutron-plugin-ml2

  neutron-plugin-openvswitch-agent

  neutron-l3-agent

  neutron-metadata-agent

- Ensure that the external interface, `eth3`, is enabled. This is then set up as a br-ex bridge that Neutron can use for External routed networks.
- These packages were configured on our Computes to match our `network` node, with one key difference in the `/etc/neutron/l3_agent.ini` file (on a `network` node only, this line reads `agent_mode = dvr_snat`):

```
[DEFAULT]
agent_mode = dvr
```

Using Distributed Virtual Routers

When we create Neutron routers in DVR mode, the routers are created on our Compute nodes instead of the `network` node. This allows for a much more distributed layout of routing, and prevents bottlenecks through our `network` nodes. In normal operation, the process of creating and deleting routers behaves in the same way as for the Legacy mode, but understanding and troubleshooting them is a little different.

Getting ready

Ensure that you have a suitable client available for using Neutron. If you are using the accompanying Vagrant environment, you can use the `controller` node. This has the `python-neutronclient` package that provides the neutron command-line client.

If you created this node with Vagrant, you can execute the following command:

```
vagrant ssh controller
```

Ensure that you have the following credentials set (adjust the path to your certificates and key file to match your environment if not using the Vagrant environment):

```
export OS_TENANT_NAME=cookbook
export OS_USERNAME=admin
export OS_PASSWORD=openstack
export OS_AUTH_URL=https://192.168.100.200:5000/v2.0/
export OS_NO_CACHE=1
export OS_KEY=/vagrant/cakey.pem
export OS_CACERT=/vagrant/ca.pem
```

How to do it...

In this section, we will create and view the details of a DVR mode router and see how these present themselves to our Compute hosts. The steps are as follows:

1. First, create a router using the following command:

   ```
   neutron router-create cookbook_router_1
   ```

   You will get the following output:

   ```
   Created a new router:
   +-----------------------+--------------------------------------+
   | Field                 | Value                                |
   +-----------------------+--------------------------------------+
   | admin_state_up        | True                                 |
   | distributed           | True                                 |
   | external_gateway_info |                                      |
   | ha                    | False                                |
   | id                    | 93953489-f5a2-42c9-9230-3d8d8c8a2e95 |
   | name                  | cookbook_router_1                    |
   | routes                |                                      |
   | status                | ACTIVE                               |
   | tenant_id             | 5481d8e9091f49dca2a72b9e223e1f40     |
   +-----------------------+--------------------------------------+
   ```

   As you can see in the output, a new `distributed` field is shown that is set to `True`.

2. We can attach any of our networks to this router as we did before:

   ```
   neutron router-interface-add \
     cookbook_router_1 \
     cookbook_subnet_1
   ```

3. We still haven't seen any difference yet between this router and any Legacy routers. To locate this router, we can use the following command:

   ```
   neutron l3-agent-list-hosting-router cookbook_router_1
   ```

You will get the following output:

```
+--------------------------------------+---------+----------------+-------+
| id                                   | host    | admin_state_up | alive |
+--------------------------------------+---------+----------------+-------+
| 0d38b23b-855d-4a11-9765-b97fdb57f2d7 | compute | True           | :-)   |
+--------------------------------------+---------+----------------+-------+
```

In the output, you can see that the router is available on our Compute host and not our `network` node.

4. In Legacy L3 Routing mode, when we troubleshoot the Namespace of the router, we had Namespaces of the form `qrouter-{netuuid}` on our `network` node. In DVR, we have this as well as a new `fip-{extent-uuid}` namespace that we can use to troubleshoot Floating IP assignments. On the Compute host, issue the following command:

   ```
   ip netns list
   ```

   You will get the following output:

   ```
   fip-ca2fc700-b5e2-4c8b-9fa4-6a80f1174360
   qrouter-93953489-f5a2-42c9-9230-3d8d8c8a2e95
   ```

5. We can then use this Namespace to test connectivity to any instances that have a Floating IP assigned. Assume we have 192.168.100.11 assigned to an instance running on our Compute host:

   ```
   ip netns exec fip-ca2fc700-b5e2-4c8b-9fa4-6a80f1174360 ping
   192.168.100.11
   ```

   You will get the following output:

   ```
   PING 192.168.100.11 (192.168.100.11) 56(84) bytes of data.
   64 bytes from 192.168.100.11: icmp_seq=1 ttl=63 time=6.31 ms
   64 bytes from 192.168.100.11: icmp_seq=2 ttl=63 time=1.51 ms
   64 bytes from 192.168.100.11: icmp_seq=3 ttl=63 time=1.13 ms
   64 bytes from 192.168.100.11: icmp_seq=4 ttl=63 time=0.475 ms
   ^C
   --- 192.168.100.11 ping statistics ---
   4 packets transmitted, 4 received, 0% packet loss, time 3005ms
   rtt min/avg/max/mdev = 0.475/2.359/6.313/2.312 ms
   ```

How it works...

We discussed a few steps to highlight the difference when running routers in distributed mode. By default, due to the setting in distributed `/etc/neutron/neutron.conf` where we set `router_distributed = True`, any routers we normally create will be created on our distributed Compute hosts. To troubleshoot them, we can connect to our Compute hosts and view the namespaces created.

4
Nova – OpenStack Compute

In this chapter, we will cover:

- Installing OpenStack Compute controller services
- Installing OpenStack Compute packages
- Configuring database Services
- Configuring OpenStack Compute
- Configuring OpenStack Compute with OpenStack Identity Service
- Stopping and starting Nova services
- Installation of command-line tools on Ubuntu
- Using the command-line tools with HTTPS
- Checking OpenStack Compute Services
- Using OpenStack Compute
- Managing security groups
- Creating and managing key pairs
- Launching our first cloud instance
- Fixing a broken instance deployment
- Terminating your instances
- Using live migration
- Working with nova-schedulers
- Creating flavors
- Defining host aggregates

- Launching instances in specific Availability Zones
- Launching instances on specific Compute hosts
- Removing Nova nodes from a cluster

Introduction

OpenStack Compute, also known as Nova, is the compute component of the open source cloud operating system, OpenStack. It is the component that allows you to run multiple instances of multiple types across any number of hosts that run the OpenStack Compute service, allowing you to create a highly scalable and redundant cloud environment. The open source project strives to be hardware and hypervisor agnostic. OpenStack Compute powers some of the biggest compute clouds such as the Rackspace Open Cloud.

This chapter gets you to speed up quickly by giving you the information you need to provide a cloud environment. At the end of this chapter, you will be able to create and access virtual machines using the OpenStack tools. The following figure shows the OpenStack architecture we are working with in this chapter:

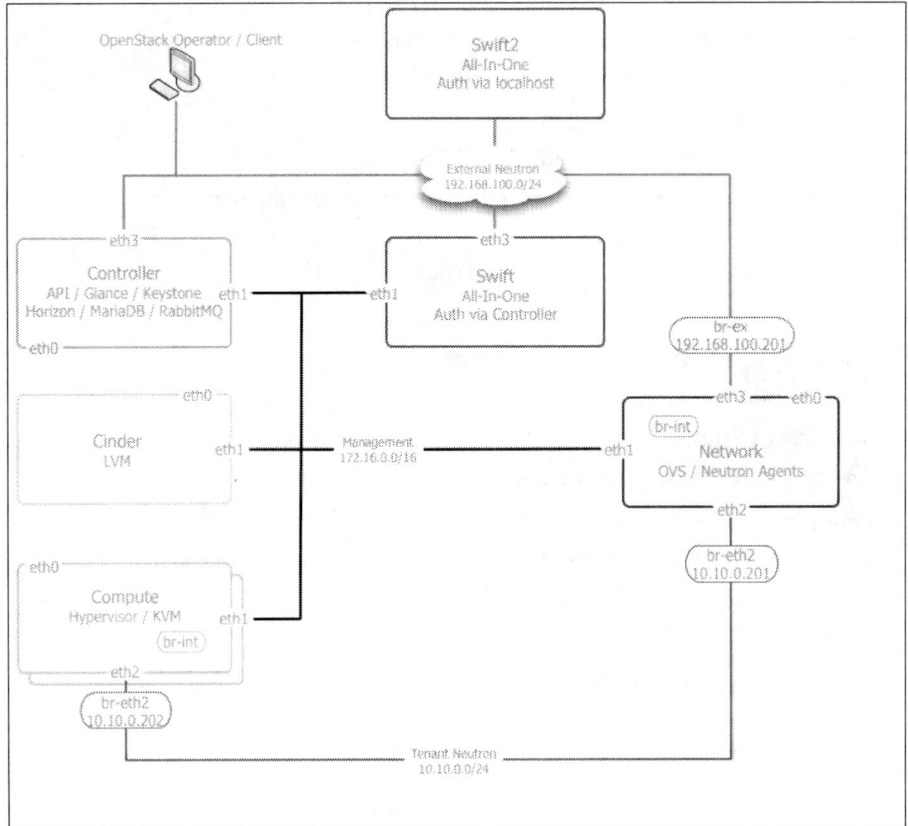

We are specifically working with the **Compute** block of the figure.

Installing OpenStack Compute controller services

Before we create a server to run the OpenStack Compute services to run our instances, there are some final services that need be installed on the `controller` node where the OpenStack Identity and Image services are running. Separating out controller services from the Compute nodes allows us to scale our OpenStack environment resources horizontally in the controller and Compute services.

To do this, we will install some further packages to our `controller` node that we created in *Chapter 1, Keystone – OpenStack Identity Service*; *Chapter 2, Glance – OpenStack Image Service*; and *Chapter 3, Neutron - OpenStack Networking*, currently running Keystone and Glance. The services are as follows:

- `nova-scheduler`: This scheduler picks the server for fulfilling the request to run the instance.
- `nova-api`: This is service requests OpenStack to operate the services within it. For example, you make a call to this service to start up a new Nova instance.
- `nova-conductor`: This is a new service introduced in the Grizzly release to remove direct database calls by the Compute service.
- `nova-objectstore`: This is a file storage service.
- `nova-common`: Common Python libraries that underpin all of the OpenStack environment.
- `nova-cert`: This is the Nova certificate management service that is used for authentication to Nova.
- `ntp`: Network Time Protocol is essential in a multi-node environment; the nodes must have the same time (tolerance is within 5 seconds and outside of this you get unpredictable results).

Getting ready

Ensure that you are logged in to the OpenStack controller node. If you used Vagrant to create this, as described in *Chapter 1, Keystone – OpenStack Identity Service*, we can access this with the following command:

```
vagrant ssh controller
```

How to do it...

Installation of OpenStack under Ubuntu 14.04 is simply achieved using the `apt-get` tool, as the OpenStack packages are available from the Ubuntu Cloud Archive repositories.

We can install the required packages with the following command:

```
sudo apt-get update
sudo apt-get install nova-api \
    nova-conductor nova-scheduler nova-objectstore
```

How it works...

Installation of OpenStack Compute controller packages from the Ubuntu Cloud Archive package repository represents a very straightforward and well-understood way of getting the latest OpenStack onto our Ubuntu server. This adds a greater level of certainty around stability and upgrade paths by not deviating away from the main archives.

Installing OpenStack Compute packages

Now that we have a machine for running OpenStack Compute, we can install the appropriate packages that will allow us to spawn its own virtual machine instances.

To do this, we will create a machine that runs all the appropriate services for running OpenStack Nova. The services are as follows:

- `nova-compute`: This is the main package for running the virtual machine instances.
- `nova-api-metadata`: This is the Nova API metadata frontend. It is used when we are running a multihost nova network in our environment, so our compute instances can download metadata.
- `nova-compute-qemu`: This provides QEMU services on our compute host. It is only required where hardware virtualization assistance isn't available (as required to run OpenStack under VirtualBox).

Getting ready

Ensure that you are logged in to the server that you will install as the Openstack Compute node. This should be a server running Ubuntu 14.04 LTS, and it should have networking configured, as shown in the figure in the *Introduction* section of this chapter.

How to do it...

Once logged in to the node where you plan to install the OpenStack Compute services, proceed with the following steps:

1. We can install the required packages with the following command:

```
sudo apt-get update
sudo apt-get install nova-compute \
    nova-api-metadata nova-compute-qemu
```

Refer to the recipe *Configuring Ubuntu Cloud Archive* in *Chapter 1, Keystone – OpenStack Identity Service*, for instructions on setting up the Ubuntu Cloud Archive repository on this server.

Once the installation is complete, we need to install and configure `ntp` as follows:

```
sudo apt-get install ntp
```

2. NTP is important in any multinode environment. In the OpenStack environment, it is a requirement that server times are kept in sync. To do this, we edit `/etc/ntp.conf` with the following contents:

```
# Replace ntp.ubuntu.com with an NTP server on your network
server ntp.ubuntu.com
server 127.127.1.0
fudge 127.127.1.0 stratum 10
```

3. Once NTP has been configured correctly, we restart the service to pick up the change:

```
sudo service ntp restart
```

How it works...

Installation of OpenStack Compute from the Ubuntu Cloud Archive package repository represents a very straightforward and well-understood way of getting the latest OpenStack onto our Ubuntu server. This adds a greater level of certainty around stability and upgrade paths by not deviating away from the main archives.

There's more...

There are various ways to install OpenStack, from source code building to installation from packages, but this represents the easiest and most consistent method available. There are also alternative releases of OpenStack available. By using the Ubuntu Cloud Archive, we are able to use various releases on our Ubuntu 14.04 LTS platform.

Using an alternative release

If you wish to optionally deviate from stable releases, it is appropriate when you are helping develop or debug OpenStack or require functionality that is not available in the current release. To enable different releases, you add different **Personal Package Archives** (**PPA**) to your system. To view the OpenStack PPAs, visit `http://wiki.openstack.org/PPAs`. To use them, we first install a prerequisite tool that allows us to easily add PPAs to our system, as follows:

```
sudo apt-get update
sudo apt-get install software-properties-common python-software-
properties
```

To use a particular release of PPA, for example, `Kilo`, we issue the following command:

```
sudo add-apt-repository cloud-archive:kilo
```

Configuring database services

OpenStack supports a number of database backends—an internal SQLite database (the default), MySQL, and Postgres. SQLite is used only for testing and is not supported and should not be used in a production environment. Ultimately, the choice of using MySQL or PostgreSQL is down to the experience of the database staff. As discussed at the beginning of this book, we will be using MariaDB.

Getting ready

We will configure our OpenStack controller services to use MariaDB as the database backend, so this needs to be installed prior to configuring our OpenStack Compute environment.

> For instructions on setting up MariaDB,
> follow the recipe on our companion website:
> `http://bit.ly/OpenStackCookbookPreReqs.`
> To configure MariaDB for high availability, refer to *Installing the MariaDB Galera cluster* of *Chapter 11, Production OpenStack*.

If you are not already logged into the OpenStack Controller, `ssh` into it now.

How to do it...

To use OpenStack Compute (Nova), we first need to ensure that our backend database has the required nova database. To create this, perform the following steps on our controller host running MySQL:

1. With MySQL running, we configure an appropriate database user called `nova` and privileges for use by OpenStack Compute:

```
MYSQL_ROOT_PASS=openstack

mysql -uroot -p$MYSQL_ROOT_PASS -e 'CREATE DATABASE nova;'

MYSQL_NOVA_PASS=openstack

mysql -uroot -p${MYSQL_ROOT_PASSWORD} \
    -e "GRANT ALL PRIVILEGES ON nova.* TO 'nova'@'%' IDENTIFIED BY
'${MYSQL_NOVA_PASSWORD}';"
mysql -uroot -p${MYSQL_ROOT_PASSWORD} \
    -e "GRANT ALL PRIVILEGES ON nova.* TO 'nova'@'localhost'
IDENTIFIED BY '${MYSQL_NOVA_PASSWORD}';"
```

2. We now simply reference our MySQL server in our `/etc/nova/nova.conf` file to use MySQL by adding in the `sql_connection` flag:

```
sql_connection=mysql://nova:openstack@192.168.100.200/nova
```

How it works...

MySQL is an essential service to OpenStack as a number of services rely on it. Configuring MySQL appropriately ensures your servers operate smoothly. We added in a database called nova that will eventually be populated by tables and data from the OpenStack Compute services, and granted all privileges to the nova database user so that user can use it. Finally, we configured our OpenStack.

Compute installation to specify these details so they can use the nova database.

See also

- The *Installing the MariaDB Galera cluster* recipe in *Chapter 11, Production OpenStack*

Configuring OpenStack Compute

The `/etc/nova/nova.conf` file is a very important file and is referred to many times in this book. This file informs each OpenStack Compute service how to run and what to connect to in order to present OpenStack to our end users. This file will be replicated amongst our nodes as our environment grows.

The same `/etc/nova/nova.conf` file is used on all of our OpenStack Compute service nodes. Create this once and copy to all other nodes in our environment.

Getting ready

We will be configuring the `/etc/nova/nova.conf` file on both the Controller host and Compute host.

If you are using the Vagrant environment provided with this book, log in to our OpenStack Controller and Compute hosts using the following commands:

```
vagrant ssh controller
vagrant ssh compute-01
```

How to do it...

To run our sandbox environment, we will configure OpenStack Compute so that it is accessible from our underlying host computer. We will have the API service (the service our client tools talk to) listen on our public interface and configure the rest of the services to run on the correct ports. The complete `nova.conf` file, as used by the sandbox environment, is laid out next and an explanation of each line (known as flags) follows:

1. First, we amend the `/etc/nova/nova.conf` file to have the following contents:

```
[DEFAULT]
dhcpbridge_flagfile=/etc/nova/nova.conf
dhcpbridge=/usr/bin/nova-dhcpbridge
logdir=/var/log/nova
state_path=/var/lib/nova
lock_path=/var/lock/nova
root_wrap_config=/etc/nova/rootwrap.conf
verbose=True

use_syslog = True
syslog_log_facility = LOG_LOCAL0

api_paste_config=/etc/nova/api-paste.ini
enabled_apis=ec2,osapi_compute,metadata

# Libvirt and Virtualization
libvirt_use_virtio_for_bridges=True
connection_type=libvirt
libvirt_type=qemu

# Messaging
rabbit_host=192.168.100.200

# EC2 API Flags
ec2_host=192.168.100.200
ec2_dmz_host=192.168.100.200
ec2_private_dns_show_ip=True

# Network settings
network_api_class=nova.network.neutronv2.api.API
neutron_url=http://192.168.100.200:9696
neutron_auth_strategy=keystone
neutron_admin_tenant_name=service
neutron_admin_username=neutron
```

```
neutron_admin_password=neutron
neutron_admin_auth_url=https://192.168.100.200:5000/v2.0
libvirt_vif_driver=nova.virt.libvirt.vif.
LibvirtHybridOVSBridgeDriver
linuxnet_interface_driver=nova.network.linux_net.
LinuxOVSInterfaceDriver
#firewall_driver=nova.virt.libvirt.firewall.IptablesFirewallDriver
security_group_api=neutron
firewall_driver=nova.virt.firewall.NoopFirewallDriver
neutron_ca_certificates_file=/etc/ssl/certs/ca.pem

service_neutron_metadata_proxy=true
neutron_metadata_proxy_shared_secret=foo

#Metadata
#metadata_host = 192.168.100.200
#metadata_listen = 192.168.100.200
#metadata_listen_port = 8775

# Cinder #
volume_driver=nova.volume.driver.ISCSIDriver
volume_api_class=nova.volume.cinder.API
iscsi_helper=tgtadm
iscsi_ip_address=172.16.0.200

# Images
image_service=nova.image.glance.GlanceImageService
glance_api_servers=192.168.100.200:9292

# Scheduler
scheduler_default_filters=AllHostsFilter

# Auth
auth_strategy=keystone
keystone_ec2_url=https://192.168.100.200:5000/v2.0/ec2tokens

# NoVNC
novnc_enabled=true
novncproxy_host=192.168.100.200
novncproxy_base_url=http://192.168.100.200:6080/vnc_auto.html
novncproxy_port=6080

xvpvncproxy_port=6081
```

```
xvpvncproxy_host=192.168.100.200
xvpvncproxy_base_url=http://192.168.100.200:6081/console

vncserver_proxyclient_address=192.168.100.200
vncserver_listen=0.0.0.0

# Database
[database]
sql_connection=mysql://nova:openstack@192.168.100.200/nova

[keystone_authtoken]
auth_host = 192.168.100.200
auth_port = 35357
auth_protocol = https
admin_tenant_name = service
admin_user = nova
admin_password = nova
insecure = True
```

2. Repeat the first step and create the file `/etc/nova/nova.conf` on each Compute host.
3. Back on the Controller host, issue a command that ensures that the database has the correct tables schema installed and initial data populated with the right information:

```
sudo nova-manage db sync
```

There is no output when this command runs successfully.

How it works...

The `/etc/nova/nova.conf` file is an important file in our OpenStack Compute environment and the same file is used on all `compute` and `controller` nodes. We create this once and then we ensure this is present on all of our nodes. The following flags are present in our `/etc/nova/nova.conf` configuration file:

- `dhcpbridge_flagfile=`: This is the location of the configuration (`flag`) file for the `dhcpbridge` service.
- `dhcpbridge=`: This is the location of the `dhcpbridge` service.

- `logdir=/var/log/nova`: It writes all service logs here. This area will be written to as root user.
- `state_path=/var/lib/nova`: This is an area on your host where Nova will maintain various states about the running service.
- `lock_path=/var/lock/nova`: This is the location where the nova will write its lock files.
- `root_wrap_config=/etc/nova/rootwrap.conf`: This specifies a helper script configuration to allow the OpenStack Compute services to obtain specific root privileges.
- `verbose`: This sets whether more information should be displayed in the logs or not.
- `use_syslog`: This send logs to `syslog` logging facility.
- `syslog_log_facility`: This indicates which log facility to use. We configure the same one, LOG_LOCAL0, for all services. For production use, we recommend separate ones for different services.
- `api_paste_config`: This is the location of the paste file containing the `paste.deploy` configuration for the `nova-api` service.
- `enabled_apis`: This specifies which APIs are enabled by default.
- `connection_type=libvirt`: This specifies the connection to use `libvirt`.
- `libvirt_use_virtio_for_bridges`: This uses the `virtio` driver for bridges.
- `libvirt_type=qemu`: This sets the virtualization mode. `qemu` is a software virtualization that runs under VirtualBox. Other options include `kvm` and `xen`.
- `sql_connection=mysql://nova:openstack@192.168.100.200/nova`: This is our SQL connection line created in the previous section. It denotes the `user:password@HostAddress/database` name (in our case, nova).
- `rabbit_host=192.168.100.200`: This tells OpenStack services where to find the `rabbitmq` message queue service.
- `ec2_host=192.168.100.200`: This denotes the external IP address of the `nova-api` service.
- `ec2_dmz_host=192.168.100.200`: This denotes the internal IP address of the `nova-api` service.
- `ec2_private_dns_show_ip`: This returns the IP address for the private hostname if set to `true`, and it returns the hostname if set to `false`.
- `network_api_class`: This sets the full name of network API class to use.
- `neutron_url`: This sets the API for Neutron (networking) service.
- `neutron_auth_strategy`: This sets the authentication strategy to be used. We are using Keystone.

- `neutron_admin_tenant_name`: This sets the tenant to be used when authenticating to neutron service.
- `neutron_admin_username`: This sets the user name for authenticating to neutron service.
- `neutron_admin_password`: This sets the password for authenticating to neutron service.
- `neutron_admin_auth_url`: This indicates the neutron authentication end point.
- `libvirt_vif_driver`: This sets `VIF` plugin to be used with nova security filtering.
- `linuxnet_interface_driver`: This sets the driver to create Ethernet devices.
- `security_group_api`: This sets the class name of the security API.
- `firewall_driver`: This sets the firewall driver.
- `neutron_ca_certificates_file`: This sets a certificate file to be used for SSL validation.
- `service_neutron_metadata_proxy`: This indicates the Compute node to be used for metadata proxy.
- `neutron_metadata_proxy_shared_secret`: This sets the secret to be used for metadata proxy.
- `volume_driver`: This sets the full class name for the volume driver class.
- `volume_api_class`: This sets the full class name of the volume API class to be used.
- `iscsi_helper`: This specifies that we are using the `tgtadm` daemon as our iSCSI target `user-land` tool.
- `iscsi_ip_address`: This specifies the iSCSI IP address.
- `image_service`: This specifies that we'll be using Glance in order to manage our images for this installation.
- `glance_api_servers`: This specifies the server that is running the Glance Imaging service.
- `scheduler_default_filters`: This specifies that the scheduler can send requests to all compute hosts.
- `auth_strategy`: This specifies that we will be using Keystone for all authentication.
- `keystone_ec2_url`: This specifies the Keystone `ec2` URL.
- `novnc_enabled`: We are enabled `noVNC` client for our compute instances. This provides VNC through a web browser.
- `novncproxy_host`: This specifies the `noVNC` proxy IP.
- `novncproxy_base_url`: This specifies `noVNC` base URL.

- `novncproxy_port`: This specifies `noVNC` proxy port.
- `xvpvncproxy_port`: This specifies the nova XVP VNC console proxy port.
- `xvpvncproxy_host`: This specifies the nova XVP VNC IP.
- `xvpvncproxy_base_url`: This specifies the nova XVP VNC console URL.
- `vncserver_proxyclient_address`: This specifies the VNC server proxy client address.
- `vncserver_listen`: This indicates where the VNC server is listening.
- `auth_host`: This sets the Keystone address.
- `auth_port`: This sets the Keystone port.
- `auth_protocol`: This sets the authentication protocol. We are using HTTPS.
- `admin_tenant_name`: This sets the tenant name for authentication.
- `admin_user`: This sets the user name for Compute services to authenticate to Keystone.
- `admin_password`: This sets the password for authenticating to Keystone.

After changing configuration options, we will need to restart the Nova services. We will show you how to do so in the *Stopping and starting Nova services* recipe.

There's more...

There are a wide variety of options that are available for configuring OpenStack Compute. These will be explored in more detail in later chapters as the `nova.conf` file underpins most of OpenStack Compute services.

See also

- You can find a description of each flag at the OpenStack website at `http://docs.openstack.org/juno/config-reference/content/list-of-compute-config-options.html`

Configuring OpenStack Compute with OpenStack Identity Service

With OpenStack Identity Service (Keystone) installed and configured, we now need to tell our OpenStack Compute Service (Nova) that it can be used to authenticate users and services.

> The following steps are repeated on all Controller and Compute hosts in our environment.

Getting ready

To begin with, ensure that you're logged in to our OpenStack compute and Controller hosts. If you did this through Vagrant, you can log in with the following commands in separate shells:

```
vagrant ssh controller
vagrant ssh compute-01
```

How to do it...

Configuring the authentication mechanism in our OpenStack Compute sandbox environment is achieved with the following steps:

1. We first ensure that our OpenStack Compute host has the required `python-keystone` package installed, if this host is a standalone compute host:

   ```
   sudo apt-get update
   sudo apt-get install python-keystone
   ```

2. Configuration of the OpenStack Compute service to use the OpenStack Identity Service is then done by filling in the `[default]` and `[keystone_authtoken]` sections of the `/etc/nova/nova.conf` file with the details that we created for the Nova service user in the recipe *Creating the service tenant and service users* in *Chapter 1, Keystone – OpenStack Identity Service*. The code is as follows:

   ```
   [DEFAULT]
   api_paste_config=/etc/nova/api-paste.ini
   auth_strategy=keystone
   keystone_ec2_url=https://192.168.100.200:5000/v2.0/ec2tokens
   ```

```
[keystone_authtoken]
admin_tenant_name = service
admin_user = nova
admin_password = nova
identity_uri = https://192.168.100.200:35357/
insecure = True
```

3. With the `nova.conf` file configured correctly, we edit `/etc/nova/api-paste.ini` and set `keystone` as the authentication mechanism by adding in the following lines under the `[filter:keystonecontext]` and `[filter:authtoken]` sections:

```
[filter:keystonecontext]
paste.filter_factory = nova.api.auth:NovaKeystoneContext.factory

[filter:authtoken]
paste.filter_factory = keystonemiddleware.auth_token:filter_
factory
```

4. With OpenStack Identity service running, we can restart our OpenStack Compute services to pick up this authentication change, as follows:

```
ls /etc/init/nova-* | cut -d '/' -f4 | cut -d '.' -f1 | while read
S; do sudo stop $S; sudo start $S; done
```

How it works...

Configuration of OpenStack Compute to use OpenStack Identity Service is done on all hosts in our environment running OpenStack Compute (Nova) services (for example, the Controller and Compute hosts). This first involves editing `/etc/nova/nova.conf` file, and adding the credentials and Keystone details.

We then configure the `/etc/nova/api-paste.ini` file and fill the `[filter:keystonecontext]` and `[filter:authtoken]` parts of the file with details of the `keystone factory`.

Stopping and starting nova services

Now that we have configured our OpenStack Compute installation, it's time to start our services so that they're running on both of our OpenStack Compute virtual machines (Controller and Compute), ready for us to launch our own private cloud instances.

Getting ready

If you haven't done so already, `ssh` to our OpenStack controller and OpenStack Compute virtual machines. If you created these using Vagrant, you can log in to these using the following commands in separate shells:

```
vagrant ssh controller
vagrant ssh compute-01
```

This ensures that we can access our virtual machines, as we will need access to spin up instances from your personal computer. Let's see the OpenStack services that we have running as part of our sandbox environments.

Controller

The following are the services:

- `nova-api`
- `nova-objectstore`
- `nova-scheduler`
- `nova-conductor`
- `nova-cert`
- `nova-novncproxy`
- `nova-consoleauth`

Compute

The following are the services:

- `nova-compute`
- `nova-api-metadata`
- `nova-novncproxy`
- `libvirt-bin`

How to do it...

Carry out the following steps to stop the OpenStack Compute services that we have running:

1. As part of the package installation, the OpenStack Compute services start up by default. So, the first thing to do is to stop them, as shown here.

   On the `controller` node, use the following commands:

   ```
   sudo stop nova-api
   sudo stop nova-scheduler
   ```

```
sudo stop nova-objectstore
sudo stop nova-conductor
sudo stop nova-cert
sudo stop nova-novncproxy
sudo stop nova-consoleauth
```

On the Compute node, use the following commands:

```
sudo stop nova-compute
sudo stop nova-api-metadata
sudo stop nova-novcnproxy
```

To stop all of the OpenStack Compute services, use the following command:

```
ls /etc/init/nova-* | cut -d '/' -f4 | cut -d '.' -f1
| while read S; do sudo stop $S; done
```

2. There is also the `libvirt` service we installed, which can be stopped in the same way:

   ```
   sudo stop libvirt-bin
   ```

   Carry out the following steps to start the OpenStack Compute services:

3. You can start the OpenStack Compute services in the same way that you stopped them.

   On the `controller` node, use the following commands:

   ```
   sudo start nova-api
   sudo start nova-scheduler
   sudo start nova-objectstore
   sudo start nova-conductor
   sudo start nova-cert
   sudo start nova-novncproxy
   sudo start nova-consoleauth
   ```

   On the Compute node, use the following commands:

   ```
   sudo start nova-compute
   sudo start nova-network
   sudo start nova-api-metadata
   sudo start nova-novcnproxy
   ```

To start all of the OpenStack Compute services, use the following command:

```
ls /etc/init/nova-* | cut -d '/' -f4 | cut -d '.' -f1 | while read S; do sudo start $S; done
```

4. There is also the `libvirt` service we installed that can be stopped in the same way:

```
sudo start libvirt-bin
```

How it works...

Stopping and starting OpenStack Compute services under Ubuntu are controlled using upstart scripts. This allows us to simply control the running services by the start and stop commands, followed by the service we wish to control.

Installation of command-line tools on Ubuntu

Management of OpenStack Compute from the command line is achieved using the `nova client`. The `nova client` tool uses the OpenStack Compute API and the OS-API. Understanding this tool is invaluable in comparison to understanding the flexibility and power of cloud environments, as it will allow you to create powerful scripts to manage your cloud.

Getting ready

The tools will be installed on your host computer if it's running Ubuntu, which is the easiest way to get hold of the `nova client` packages that are ready to manage your cloud environment.

How to do it...

The `nova client` packages are conveniently available from the Ubuntu repositories. If the host PC isn't running Ubuntu, creating an Ubuntu virtual machine alongside our OpenStack Compute virtual machine is a convenient way to get access to these tools.

As a normal user on our Ubuntu machine, type the following commands:

```
sudo apt-get update
sudo apt-get install python-novaclient
```

How it works...

Using `nova client` on Ubuntu is a very natural way of managing our OpenStack cloud environment. Installation is very straightforward as these are provided as part of standard Ubuntu packaging.

See also

- More information can be found at http://bit.ly/OpenStackCookbookClientInstall

Using the command-line tools with HTTPS

When OpenStack Identity endpoint is configured to use HTTPs, using the command-line tools with OpenStack Compute will require specifying SSL certificates for validation.

Getting ready

The tools will be installed on your host computer if it's running Ubuntu, which is the easiest way to get hold of the nova client packages ready to manage your cloud environment. If using our Vagrant lab environment, self-signed certificates are installed and set up for using with HTTPS endpoints. We recommend that you use certificates issued by a trusted **Certificate Authority** (**CA**) for your production environment.

How to do it...

The `nova client` packages are conveniently available from the Ubuntu repositories. SSL certificates are already installed and configured for use by Keystone for validation.

1. As a normal user on our Ubuntu machine, type the following commands:

   ```
   sudo apt-get update
   sudo apt-get install python-novaclient
   ```

2. After installing the command-line tools, set up your environment credentials. You will need to use your OpenStack cluster's SSL certificates. Adjust the path to your certificates and key file to match your environment, if not using the Vagrant environment:

   ```
   export OS_TENANT_NAME=cookbook
   export OS_USERNAME=admin
   export OS_PASSWORD=openstack
   ```

```
export OS_AUTH_URL=https://192.168.100.200:5000/v2.0/
export OS_NO_CACHE=1
export OS_KEY=/vagrant/cakey.pem
export OS_CACERT=/vagrant/ca.pem
```

Note that we have set up the `OS_KEY` environment variable points to our private key. The `OS_CACERT` variable points to the CA bundle file to use in verifying a TLS (`https`) server certificate.

3. For troubleshooting certificate or connectivity issues, you can use the `--insecure` flag to bypass SSL validation. When using this flag with the `nova` command-line client, your server's certificate will not be verified against any certificate authorities.

Note that the `--insecure` flag is very useful for troubleshooting connectivity issues. It also bypasses all certificate validation—they may as well not even be enabled.

How it works...

Using `nova client` on Ubuntu is a very natural way to manage our OpenStack cloud environment. However, if your authentication endpoints are setup to use HTTPS, you will need to point your command-line client to the certificates installed on your system. Adding environment variables to point to certificates will automatically validate against them.

Checking OpenStack Compute services

Now that we have OpenStack Compute installed, we need to ensure what we have configured is what we expect. OpenStack Compute provides tools to check various parts of our environment. We'll also use common system commands to check whether the other underlying services that support our OpenStack Compute environment are running as expected.

Getting ready

Log in to the OpenStack `controller` node. If you used Vagrant to create this node, log in to it using the following command:

```
vagrant ssh controller
```

How to do it...

To check whether the OpenStack Compute services are running, we invoke the `nova-manage` tool and ask it various questions of the environment as follows:

1. To check whether the OpenStack Compute hosts are running OK, use the following command:

   ```
   sudo nova-manage service list
   ```

   You will see the following output:

   ```
   Binary           Host                                Zone             Status     State Updated_At
   nova-scheduler   controller                          internal         enabled    :-)   2015-01-28 04:25:16
   nova-consoleauth controller                          internal         enabled    :-)   2015-01-28 04:25:19
   nova-cert        controller                          internal         enabled    :-)   2015-01-28 04:25:19
   nova-conductor   controller                          internal         enabled    :-)   2015-01-28 04:25:15
   nova-consoleauth compute-01                          internal         enabled    :-)   2015-01-28 04:25:16
   nova-compute     compute-01                          nova             enabled    :-)   2015-01-28 04:25:20
   nova-consoleauth compute-02                          internal         enabled    :-)   2015-01-28 04:25:18
   nova-compute     compute-02                          nova             enabled    :-)   2015-01-28 04:25:15
   ```

   The :-) icons are indicative that everything is fine.

2. If you see `XXX` where the `:-)` icon should be, then you have a problem.

   ```
   Binary           Host                                Zone             Status     State Updated_At
   nova-scheduler   controller                          internal         enabled    :-)   2015-01-28 05:26:38
   nova-consoleauth controller                          internal         enabled    :-)   2015-01-28 05:26:42
   nova-cert        controller                          internal         enabled    :-)   2015-01-28 05:26:41
   nova-conductor   controller                          internal         enabled    :-)   2015-01-28 05:26:46
   nova-consoleauth compute-01                          internal         enabled    :-)   2015-01-28 05:26:38
   nova-compute     compute-01                          nova             enabled    XXX   2015-01-28 05:25:41
   nova-consoleauth compute-02                          internal         enabled    :-)   2015-01-28 05:26:40
   nova-compute     compute-02                          nova             enabled    :-)   2015-01-28 05:26:46
   ```

   If you do see XXX, then the answer will be in the logs at `/var/log/nova/`.

> If you get intermittent `XXX` and `:-)` icons for a service, first check whether the clocks are in sync.

3. Glance doesn't have a tool to check, so we can use some system commands instead:

   ```
   ps -ef | grep glance
   netstat -ant | grep 9292.*LISTEN
   ```

   These should return process information for Glance to show it is running and `9292` is the default port that should be open in the `LISTEN` mode on your server ready for use.

4. Other services that you should check are as follows:

 - Check `rabbitmq` with the following command:

   `sudo rabbitmqctl status`

 - Here is an example output from `rabbitmqctl` when everything is running OK:

```
Status of node rabbit@controller ...

[{pid,26086},
 {running_applications,[{rabbit,"RabbitMQ","3.2.4"},
                        {os_mon,"CPO  CXC 138 46","2.2.14"},
                        {mnesia,"MNESIA  CXC 138 12","4.11"},
                        {xmerl,"XML parser","1.3.5"},
                        {sasl,"SASL  CXC 138 11","2.3.4"},
                        {stdlib,"ERTS  CXC 138 10","1.19.4"},
                        {kernel,"ERTS  CXC 138 10","2.16.4"}]},
 {os,{unix,linux}},
 {erlang_version,"Erlang R16B03 (erts-5.10.4) [source] [64-bit] [smp:2:2] [async-threads:30] [kernel-
poll:true]\n"},
 {memory,[{total,128095000},
          {connection_procs,3760040},
          {queue_procs,1981200},
          {plugins,0},
          {other_proc,13575624},
          {mnesia,355808},
          {mgmt_db,0},
          {msg_index,84024},
          {other_ets,918776},
          {binary,86007184},
          {code,16522377},
          {atom,594537},
          {other_system,4295430}]},
 {vm_memory_high_watermark,0.4},
 {vm_memory_limit,1303538892},
 {disk_free_limit,50000000},
 {disk_free,34748444672},
 {file_descriptors,[{total_limit,924},
                    {total_used,88},
                    {sockets_limit,829},
                    {sockets_used,86}]},
 {processes,[{limit,1048576},{used,1013}]},
 {run_queue,0},
 {uptime,90276}]
...done.
```

 - You can check NTP with the following command:

   `ntpq -p`

 - It should return output about contacting NTP servers, as shown here:

```
     remote           refid      st t when poll reach   delay   offset  jitter
==============================================================================
*yurizoku.tk     209.51.161.238   2 u  104 1024  377   46.426    2.183   1.889
-propjet.latt.ne 187.253.153.32   2 u   56 1024  377   47.226    5.163   1.253
+juniperberry.ca 192.93.2.20      2 u  395 1024  377  113.354    2.171   1.618
```

- You can check the MySQL database server with the following command:

```
MYSQL_ROOT_PASS=openstack
mysqladmin -uroot -p{$MYSQL_ROOT_PASS} status
```

- This will return some basic statistics about MySQL, if it is running:

```
Uptime: 91271  Threads: 21  Questions: 762166  Slow queries: 0  Opens: 1745  Flush tables: 1  Open tables: 
332  Queries per second avg: 8.350
```

How it works...

We have used some basic commands that communicate with OpenStack Compute and other services to show they are running. This elementary level of troubleshooting ensures you have the system running as expected:

- `sudo nova-manage service list`: This lists Nova services and their respective statuses
- `ps -ef | grep glance`: This lists the running Glance services
- `netstat -ant | grep 9292.*LISTEN`: This allows you to check whether the glance daemon is listening on the network
- `sudo rabbitmqctl status`: This allows you to validate that the rabbitMQ services are running
- `ntpq -p`: This confirms whether NTP is functional and connecting to the configured remote servers
- `mysqladmin -uroot -p{$MYSQL_ROOT_PASS} status`: This returns basic information about the MySQL process

Using OpenStack Compute

OpenStack Identity Service underpins all of the OpenStack services. With OpenStack Image Service configured to use OpenStack Identity Service, the OpenStack Compute environment can now be used.

Getting ready

To begin with, log in to an Ubuntu client and ensure that Nova client is available. If it isn't, it can be installed as follows:

```
sudo apt-get update
sudo apt-get python-novaclient
```

How to do it...

To use OpenStack Identity Service as the authentication mechanism in our OpenStack environment, we need to set our environment variables accordingly. For our demo user, this is achieved as follows:

1. With the Nova client installed, we use them by configuring our environment with the appropriate environment variables. We do this as follows:

```
export OS_TENANT_NAME=cookbook
export OS_USERNAME=admin
export OS_PASSWORD=openstack
export OS_AUTH_URL=https://192.168.100.200:5000/v2.0/
export OS_NO_CACHE=1
export OS_KEY=/vagrant/cakey.pem
export OS_CACERT=/vagrant/ca.pem
```

Add these to a file called `novarc` in your home area. We can then source these credentials each time by simply executing the following command:

```
novarc
```

Note that if the user credential environment variables have been set in a shell that has the `SERVICE_TOKEN` and `SERVICE_ENDPOINT` environment variables. These will override our user credentials set in this step. Remove the `SERVICE_TOKEN` and `SERVICE_ENDPOINT` variables before continuing.

2. To access any Linux instances that we launch, we must create a key pair that allows us to access our cloud instance. Key pairs are SSH private and public key combinations that together allow you to access a resource. You keep the private portion safe, but you're able to give the public key to anyone or any computer without fear or compromise to your security. However, only your private portion will match enabling you to be authorized. Cloud instances rely on key pairs for access. We create a key pair using Nova client with the following commands:

```
nova keypair-add demo > demo.pem
chmod 0600 *.pem
```

3. We can test that this is successful by issuing some nova commands, for example:

```
nova list
nova credentials
```

How it works...

Configuring our environment to use OpenStack Identity Service for authentication for Nova client, so that we can launch our instances, involves manually creating an environment resource file with the appropriate environment variables in.

Our environment passes on our username, password, and tenant to OpenStack Identity Service for authentication and passes back—behind the scenes—an appropriate token that validates our user. This allows us to seamlessly spin up instances within our tenancy (project) of cookbook.

Managing security groups

Security groups are firewalls for your instances, and they're mandatory in our cloud environment. The firewall actually exists on our OpenStack Compute host that is running the instance, and not as `iptables` rules within the running instance itself. They allow us to protect our hosts by restricting or allowing access to specified service ports, and also protect our instances from other users' instances running on the same hosts. Security groups are the only way to separate a tenant's instances from another user's instances in another tenant when VLAN or tunnel separation isn't available, or in instances where the flat networking model is in use.

Getting ready

To begin with, ensure that you're logged in to a client that has access to the Nova client tools. These packages can be installed using the following commands:

```
sudo apt-get update
sudo apt-get install python-novaclient
```

And ensure you have set the following credentials:

```
export OS_TENANT_NAME=cookbook
export OS_USERNAME=admin
export OS_PASSWORD=openstack
export OS_AUTH_URL=https://192.168.100.200:5000/v2.0/
export OS_NO_CACHE=1
export OS_KEY=/vagrant/cakey.pem
export OS_CACERT=/vagrant/ca.pem
```

How to do it...

The following sections describe how to create and modify security groups in our OpenStack environment.

Creating security groups

To create a security group that opens TCP port `80` and port `443` on our instances using Nova client, grouping that under a security group called webserver, we run the following commands:

```
nova secgroup-create webserver "Web Server Access"
nova secgroup-add-rule webserver tcp 80 80 0.0.0.0/0
nova secgroup-add-rule webserver tcp 443 443 0.0.0.0/0
```

The reason we specified a new group, instead of assigning these to the default group, is that we might not want to open up our web server to everyone, which would happen every time we spin up a new instance. Putting it into its own security group allows us to open up access to our instance to port `80` by simply specifying this security group when we launch an instance.

For example, we specify the `--security_groups` option when we boot an instance:

```
nova boot myInstance \
    --image 0e2f43a8-e614-48ff-92bd-be0c68da19f4
    --flavor 2 \
    --key_name demo \
    --security_groups default,webserver
```

Removing a rule from a security group

To remove a rule from a security group, we run the `nova secgroup-delete` command. For example, suppose we want to remove the HTTPS rule from our `webserver` group. To do this by using a Nova client, we run the following command:

```
nova secgroup-delete-rule webserver tcp 443 443 0.0.0.0/0
```

Deleting a security group

To delete a security group, for example, `webserver`, we run the following command:

```
nova secgroup-delete webserver
```

How it works...

Creation of a security group is done in just two steps. We add a group using the `nova secgroup-create` command. Following the creation of a security group, we can define rules in that group using the `nova secgroup-add-rule` command. With this command, we can specify the destination ports that we can open up on our instances and the networks that are allowed access.

Defining groups and rules using Nova client

The `nova secgroup-create` command has the following syntax:

```
nova secgroup-create group_name "description"
```

The `nova secgroup-add-rule` command has the following basic syntax:

```
nova secgroup-add-rule group_name protocol port_from port_to source
```

Removing rules from a security group is done using the `nova secgroup-delete-rule` command and is analogous to the `nova secgroup-add-rule` command. Removing a security group altogether is done using the `nova secgroup-delete` command and is analogous to the `nova secgroup-create` command.

Creating and managing key pairs

SSH key pairs consist of two elements—a public key and a private key. Key pairs are used for access to our Linux hosts via SSH. The public portion of our key pair is injected into our instance at boot-time through a service known as `cloud-init`. It can perform many tasks, one of which is managing this public key pair injection. Only this specific combination of the public and private key will allow us access to our instances.

Getting ready

To begin with, ensure that you are logged in to your Ubuntu client that has access to the Nova client tools. This can be installed using the following commands:

```
sudo apt-get update
sudo apt-get install python-novaclient
```

Ensure you have set the following credentials:

```
export OS_TENANT_NAME=cookbook
export OS_USERNAME=admin
export OS_PASSWORD=openstack
```

```
export OS_AUTH_URL=https://192.168.100.200:5000/v2.0/
export OS_NO_CACHE=1
export OS_KEY=/vagrant/cakey.pem
export OS_CACERT=/vagrant/ca.pem
```

How to do it...

To create a key pair, we use the `nova keypair-add` command. We name the key accordingly, and we will subsequently refer to it when launching instances. The output of the command is the SSH private key that we will use to access a shell on our instance:

1. First create the key pair as follows:

   ```
   nova keypair-add demokey > demokey
   ```

2. Then, protect the private key output so that only our logged in user account can read it:

   ```
   chmod 0600 demokey
   ```

This preceding command has generated a key pair and stored the public portion within our database, at the heart of our OpenStack environment. The private portion has been written to a file on our client, which we will protect by making sure that only our user can access this file.

When we want to use this new key under Nova client, this looks as follows, using the `nova boot` command:

```
nova boot myInstance \
    --image 0e2f43a8-e614-48ff-92bd-be0c68da19f4 \
    --flavor 2 --key_name demokey
```

When we want to run the `ssh` instance, we specify the private key on the `ssh` command line with the `-i` option:

```
ssh ubuntu@172.16.1.1 -i demokey
```

As with most things in Unix, the values and files specified are case sensitive.

Listing and deleting key pairs using Nova client

To list and delete key pairs using Nova client, carry out the set of commands in the following sections.

Listing the key pairs

To list the key pairs in our project using Nova client, we simply run the nova `keypair-list` command, as follows:

```
nova keypair-list
```

The preceding command brings back a list of key pairs in our project, for example:

```
+---------+-------------------------------------------------+
| Name    | Fingerprint                                     |
+---------+-------------------------------------------------+
| demokey | 77:ad:94:d6:8b:c6:d8:45:85:55:22:2b:ad:b3:22:e9 |
+---------+-------------------------------------------------+
```

Deleting the key pairs

To delete a key pair from our project, we simply specify the name of the key as an option to the `nova keypair-delete` tool:

- To delete the `myKey` key pair, we use the following command:

  ```
  nova keypair-delete demokey
  ```

- We can verify this by listing the keys available, using the following command:

  ```
  nova keypair-list
  ```

Deleting key pairs is an irreversible action. Deleting a key pair to a running instance will prevent you from accessing that instance.

How it works...

Key pairs are important in our cloud environment as most Linux images don't allow access to a command-line prompt using usernames and passwords. An exception to this is the Cirros image, which comes with a default username `cirros` and password `cubswin:)`.

The Cirros image is a cut down image that is used for troubleshooting and testing OpenStack environments. Images like Ubuntu only allow access using key pairs.

Creation of a key pair allows us SSH access to our instance and it is carried out using the `nova keypair-add` command. This stores the public key in our backend database store that will be injected into the `.ssh/authorized_keys` file on our cloud instance, as a part of the cloud instance's `boot/cloud init` script. We can then use the private key that gets generated to access the system by specifying this on the `ssh` command line with the `-i` option.

We can, of course, also remove keys from our project, and we do this to prevent further access by that particular key pair. The command `nova keypair-delete` does this for us, and we can verify which keys are available in our project by running the `nova keypair-list` commands.

Launching our first cloud instance

Now that we have a running OpenStack Compute environment and a machine image to use, it's now time to spin up our first cloud instance! Let's see how we can use the information from the `nova image-list` and `nova flavor-list` commands to reference this on the command line to launch the instance that we want.

Getting ready

The following steps are to be carried out on our `network` node under the user that has access to our OpenStack Compute credentials (as created in the *Installation of command-line tools on network* recipe).

Ensure you are logged in to the `network` node and that it has Internet access to allow us to install the required packages in our environment for running OVS and Neutron. If you created this node with Vagrant, you can execute the following command:

```
vagrant ssh network
```

Before we spin up our first instance, we must create the default security settings that define the access rights. We do this only once (or when we need to adjust these) using the nova `secgroup-add-rule` command under Nova client. The following set of commands gives us SSH access (`port 22`) from any IP address and also allows us to ping the instance to help with troubleshooting. Note the default group and its rules are always applied if no security group is mentioned on the command line.

The steps are as follows:

1. With the Nova client installed, we use them by configuring our environment with the appropriate environment variables:

   ```
   export OS_TENANT_NAME=cookbook
   export OS_USERNAME=admin
   export OS_PASSWORD=openstack
   export OS_AUTH_URL=https://192.168.100.200:5000/v2.0/
   export OS_NO_CACHE=1
   export OS_KEY=/vagrant/cakey.pem
   export OS_CACERT=/vagrant/ca.pem
   ```

Add these to a file called `novarc` in your home area. We can then source these credentials in each time by simply executing the `source novarc` command.

2. Using Nova client, we can simply add the appropriate rules using the following commands:

```
nova secgroup-add-rule default tcp 22 22 0.0.0.0/0
nova secgroup-add-rule default icmp -1 -1 0.0.0.0/0
```

If there are no images available yet, follow the steps of the recipe *Managing images with OpenStack Image Service* in *Chapter 2, Glance – OpenStack Image Service*.

How to do it...

Now that our environment is set up correctly, we carry out the following steps to launch our first instance:

1. List the images available by executing the following command:

```
nova image-list
```

This should produce an output like this:

ID	Name	Status	Server
43f974b7-1f74-4305-8354-0ac0c3efe68d	cirros-image	ACTIVE	
5bfb4a6d-da77-4502-ba52-2e8e40597e96	trusty-image	ACTIVE	

2. Then, we get the available image flavors (think of them as sizes) by executing the following command:

```
nova flavor-list
```

Available flavors for our OpenStack installation will be listed like this:

ID	Name	Memory_MB	Disk	Ephemeral	Swap	VCPUs	RXTX_Factor	Is_Public
1	m1.tiny	512	0	0		1	1.0	True
2	m1.small	2048	20	0		1	1.0	True
3	m1.medium	4096	40	0		2	1.0	True
4	m1.large	8192	80	0		4	1.0	True
5	m1.xlarge	16384	160	0		8	1.0	True

We can specify flavor either by its ID or name.

3. Since our lab environment is configured to with two networks, we will need to choose to which network to attach our instance. First, list the available networks using the following command:

   ```
   neutron net-list
   ```

   The available networks will be displayed like this:

```
+--------------------------------------+--------------------+------------------------------------------------------+
| id                                   | name               | subnets                                              |
+--------------------------------------+--------------------+------------------------------------------------------+
| 0375e772-b021-425c-bc17-5a3263247fb8 | cookbook_network_1 | 37ca3149-ee6b-4288-b074-03a4e1635b7c 10.200.0.0/24   |
| 706c9118-68d9-4751-932c-3dc94ec6f4ed | ext_net            | 889c1ef7-09af-48d2-85bf-6971446e2eb7 192.168.100.0/24 |
+--------------------------------------+--------------------+------------------------------------------------------+
```

4. To launch our instance, we need to specify image, flavor, network, and key name information we got earlier on the command line. To launch an instance using Nova client tools, we issue the following command using the UUID of our image that is named `trusty-image` and `cookbook_network_1`:

   ```
   nova boot myInstance \
       --image 5bfb4a6d-da77-4502-ba52-2e8e40597e96 \
       --flavor 2 \
       --nic net-id=0375e772-b021-425c-bc17-5a3263247fb8 \
       --key_name demokey
   ```

   You should see output like the following screenshot when you launch an instance:

```
+--------------------------------------+------------------------------------------------------------+
| Property                             | Value                                                      |
+--------------------------------------+------------------------------------------------------------+
| OS-DCF:diskConfig                    | MANUAL                                                     |
| OS-EXT-AZ:availability_zone          | nova                                                       |
| OS-EXT-SRV-ATTR:host                 | -                                                          |
| OS-EXT-SRV-ATTR:hypervisor_hostname  | -                                                          |
| OS-EXT-SRV-ATTR:instance_name        | instance-00000002                                          |
| OS-EXT-STS:power_state               | 0                                                          |
| OS-EXT-STS:task_state                | scheduling                                                 |
| OS-EXT-STS:vm_state                  | building                                                   |
| OS-SRV-USG:launched_at               | -                                                          |
| OS-SRV-USG:terminated_at             | -                                                          |
| accessIPv4                           |                                                            |
| accessIPv6                           |                                                            |
| adminPass                            | MgkrXAVjbpM8                                               |
| config_drive                         |                                                            |
| created                              | 2015-01-29T06:12:21Z                                       |
| flavor                               | m1.small (2)                                               |
| hostId                               |                                                            |
| id                                   | 5971ab77-9d91-40d8-9961-d86da0945f26                       |
| image                                | trusty-image (5bfb4a6d-da77-4502-ba52-2e8e40597e96)        |
| key_name                             | demokey                                                    |
| metadata                             | {}                                                         |
| name                                 | myInstance                                                 |
| os-extended-volumes:volumes_attached | []                                                         |
| progress                             | 0                                                          |
| security_groups                      | default                                                    |
| status                               | BUILD                                                      |
| tenant_id                            | e99b80a0de78451f91c97beef5b2c2d5                           |
| updated                              | 2015-01-29T06:12:21Z                                       |
| user_id                              | 183fd6a93d7e4a65aa513bdb4fa9850e                           |
+--------------------------------------+------------------------------------------------------------+
```

5. This will take a few brief moments to spin up. To check the status of your instances, issue the following commands:

   nova list

   nova show 5971ab77-9d91-40d8-9961-d86da0945f26

6. The preceding commands will give an output similar to the output of the previous command lines. However, this time it has created the instance, it is now running, and it has IP addresses assigned to it:

```
+--------------------------------------+----------------------------------------------------------------+
| Property                             | Value                                                          |
+--------------------------------------+----------------------------------------------------------------+
| OS-DCF:diskConfig                    | MANUAL                                                         |
| OS-EXT-AZ:availability_zone          | nova                                                           |
| OS-EXT-SRV-ATTR:host                 | compute-02                                                     |
| OS-EXT-SRV-ATTR:hypervisor_hostname  | compute-02.cook.book                                           |
| OS-EXT-SRV-ATTR:instance_name        | instance-00000002                                              |
| OS-EXT-STS:power_state               | 1                                                              |
| OS-EXT-STS:task_state                | -                                                              |
| OS-EXT-STS:vm_state                  | active                                                         |
| OS-SRV-USG:launched_at               | 2015-01-29T06:12:47.000000                                     |
| OS-SRV-USG:terminated_at             | -                                                              |
| accessIPv4                           |                                                                |
| accessIPv6                           |                                                                |
| config_drive                         |                                                                |
| cookbook_network_1 network           | 10.200.0.5                                                     |
| created                              | 2015-01-29T06:12:21Z                                           |
| flavor                               | m1.small (2)                                                   |
| hostId                               | c8b5ccd18b4c6930917d8e6a4b26e4ebf3722f9e6d2515a72991e1ef       |
| id                                   | 5971ab77-9d91-40d8-9961-d86da0945f26                           |
| image                                | trusty-image (5bfb4a6d-da77-4502-ba52-2e8e40597e96)            |
| key_name                             | demokey                                                        |
| metadata                             | {}                                                             |
| name                                 | myInstance                                                     |
| os-extended-volumes:volumes_attached | []                                                             |
| progress                             | 0                                                              |
| security_groups                      | default                                                        |
| status                               | ACTIVE                                                         |
| tenant_id                            | e99b80a0de78451f91c97beef5b2c2d5                               |
| updated                              | 2015-01-29T06:12:47Z                                           |
| user_id                              | 183fd6a93d7e4a65aa513bdb4fa9850e                               |
+--------------------------------------+----------------------------------------------------------------+
```

7. After a short while, you will be able to connect to this instance. If you are using the Vagrant environment, from the `network` node, you will be able to connect to the instance using network space and SSH private key. First, get a list of network spaces using the following command:

   ip netns

   This will show the following example output:

   qdhcp-0375e772-b021-425c-bc17-5a3263247fb8

Now, connect to the instance using the following command:

```
sudo ip netns exec \
   qdhcp-0375e772-b021-425c-bc17-5a3263247fb8 \
   ssh -i demokey ubuntu@10.200.0.5
```

The default user that ships with the Ubuntu cloud images is `ubuntu`.

Congratulations! We have successfully launched and connected to our first OpenStack cloud instance.

How it works...

After creating the default security settings, we made a note of our machine image identifier, UUID value, and then called a tool from Nova client to launch our instance. Part of that command line refers to the *key pair* to use. We then connect to the instance using the private key as part of that *key pair* generated.

How does the cloud instance know what key to use? As part of the boot scripts for this image, it makes a call back to the `meta-server`, which is a function of the `nova-api` and `nova-api-metadata` services. The `meta-server` provides a go-between that bridges our instance and the real world that the Cloud `init` boot process can call. In this case, it downloads a script to inject our private key into the Ubuntu user's `.ssh/authorized_keys` file. We can modify which scripts are called during this boot process, and this will be covered later on.

When a cloud instance is launched, it generates a number of useful metrics and details about that instance. This is presented by the `nova list` and `nova show` commands. The `nova list` command shows a convenient short version listing the ID, name, status, and IP addresses of our instance.

The type of instance we chose was specified as an ID of `2` when using the `nova boot` command. The instance types supported can be listed by running the following command:

```
nova flavor-list
```

These flavors (specification of instances) are summarized as follows:

Type of instance	Memory	VCPUS	Storage	Version
`m1.tiny`	512 MB	1	1 GB	32-bit and 64-bit
`m1.small`	2048 MB	1	20 GB	32-bit and 64-bit
`m1.medium`	4096 MB	2	40 GB	64-bit only
`m1.large`	8192 MB	4	80 GB	64-bit only
`m1.xlarge`	16384 MB	8	160 GB	64-bit only

Fixing a broken instance deployment

When deploying an instance, sometimes an error occurs and deployment fails. If this happens with a new deployment, usually it is simplest to delete the failed instance and deploy again. However, if you must fix the broken instance, there is a `nova rescue` command that will help you. This section explains how to use the `nova rescue` command to fix broken instances.

Getting ready

If you are using the Vagrant environment, these steps are to be carried out on our network node under the user that has access to our OpenStack Compute credentials (as created in the *Installation of command-line tools on network* recipe).

Ensure that you are logged onto the `network` node and that it has Internet access to allow us to install the required packages in our environment for running OVS and Neutron. If you created this node with Vagrant, you can execute the following command:

```
vagrant ssh network
```

How to do it...

From our `network` machine, list the running instances to identify the instance you want to fix using the following steps:

1. We first identify the instance that we want to fix by issuing the following command from our client:

   ```
   nova list
   ```

2. To set instance in a `rescue` mode, we can either specify the name of our instance or use the UUID:

```
nova rescue myInstance
nova rescue 6f41bb91-0f4f-41e5-90c3-7ee1f9c39e5a
```

The preceding commands will give you a temporary root password:

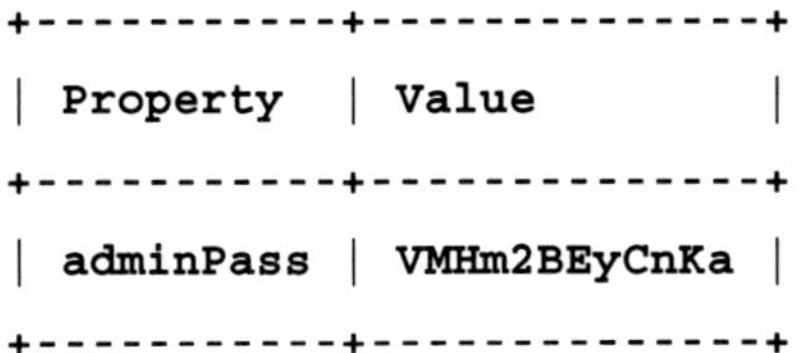

```
+-----------+-------------+
| Property  | Value       |
+-----------+-------------+
| adminPass | VMHm2BEyCnKa |
+-----------+-------------+
```

However, if the instance was created with a nova key, you will still need to use the key rather than the password to log in. The instance will be set in the `RESCUE` status now.

3. To log in to the node, first get a list of network spaces:

```
ip netns
```

The preceding command gives the following example output:

```
qdhcp-0375e772-b021-425c-bc17-5a3263247fb8
```

Connect to the instance using the following commands:

```
sudo ip netns exec \
  qdhcp-0375e772-b021-425c-bc17-5a3263247fb8 \
  ssh -i demokey ubuntu@10.200.0.5
```

This will allow you to repair the instance.

4. After repairing the instance, restart the server from the normal boot disk again:

```
nova unrescue myInstance
```

How it works...

We identify a server that needs rescuing via the `nova list` command. Then, we use either the server name or the server ID to set the server in `rescue` mode using the `nova rescue` command. This reboots the server into a rescue mode, which starts the machine from the initial image and attaches the current boot disk as a secondary. After repairing the server, we need to set it back to `ACTIVE` status and reboot by using the `nova unrescue` command.

Terminating your instances

Cloud environments are designed to be dynamic and this implies that cloud instances are being spun up and terminated as required. Terminating a cloud instance is easy, but it is equally important to understand some basic concepts of cloud instances.

Cloud instances such as the instance we have used are not persistent. This means that the data and work you do on that instance only exists for the time that it is running. A cloud instance can be rebooted, but once it has been terminated, all data is lost.

To ensure no loss of data, the OpenStack Block Storage service Cinder provides a persistent data store functionality that allows you to attach a volume to it that doesn't get destroyed on termination. It allows you to attach it to running instances. A volume is like a USB drive attached to your instance. For more information, go to *Chapter 8, Cinder – OpenStack Block Storage*.

How to do it...

From our Ubuntu machine, list the running instances to identify the instance you want to terminate:

1. We first identify the instance that we want to terminate by issuing the following command from our client:

   ```
   nova list
   ```

2. To terminate an instance, we can either specify the name of our instance or use the UUID:

   ```
   nova delete myInstance
   nova delete 6f41bb91-0f4f-41e5-90c3-7ee1f9c39e5a
   ```

   You can re-run `nova` list again to ensure your instance is terminated.

Of the two methods, named and UUID, the `UUID` method is preferable as it allows you to avoid ambiguity. Further, the named commands may return unexpected results if multiple items exist with the same name. This is not the case with UUID.

How it works...

We simply identify the instance we wish to terminate by its UUID or by name when using `nova list`. Once identified, we can specify this as the instance to terminate using `nova delete`. Once terminated, that instance no longer exists—it has been destroyed. So if you had any data in there, it will be deleted along with the instance.

Using live migration

OpenStack Nova supports live migration of VM-based instances between compute hosts. This is useful during maintenance and cluster balancing operations. To use live migration, you must first add a node to your Nova cluster.

Getting ready

Let's assume that you have more than one host running the Nova Compute services, as described in the *Configuring OpenStack Compute* section. If that is not the case, you will need to configure a second host before continuing. The destination host also needs to be remotely accessible and have resources available to run the instance(s) that will be migrated.

Checking network connectivity

To successfully complete live migration, both hosts must be able to communicate with each other by hostname. You can validate this by logging in to each host and pinging the other:

```
$ ping compute-02
PING compute-02.book (192.168.100.203) 56(84) bytes of data.
64 bytes from compute-02.book (192.168.100.203): icmp_seq=1 ttl=64
time=2.14 ms
64 bytes from compute-02.book (192.168.100.203): icmp_seq=2 ttl=64
time=0.599 ms
$ ping compute-01
PING compute-01.book (192.168.100.202) 56(84) bytes of data.
64 bytes from compute-01.book (192.168.100.202): icmp_seq=1 ttl=64
time=1.29 ms
64 bytes from compute-01.book (192.168.100.202): icmp_seq=2 ttl=64
time=0.389 ms
```

Ensuring resources

Live migration is also dependent on the remote host having available resources for the workload. This can be done by logging into a host with the `nova` command-line utilities and using the following `nova` commands:

```
$ nova host-describe compute-02
+------------+-----------+----+----------+--------+
| HOST       | PROJECT   | cpu | memory_mb | disk_gb |
+------------+-----------+----+----------+--------+
| compute-02 | (total)   | 2  | 3107     | 37     |
| compute-02 | (used_now) | 0  | 512      | 0      |
| compute-02 | (used_max) | 0  | 0        | 0      |
+------------+-----------+----+----------+--------+
```

The first line shows the total resources available on the host. In this case, there are two vCPU, 3 GB memory, and 37 GB disk. To find out what is available on the host, subtract the values from the `used_now` row from the total row. In our case, the only change is that there are 512 MB of RAM in use, leaving 2.5 GB available for migrations.

How to do it...

If you are not already logged into a host with the Nova command-line utilities, you will need to be before proceeding. To migrate a VM-based instance between nodes, run the following commands:

```
export OS_TENANT_NAME=cookbook
export OS_USERNAME=admin
export OS_PASSWORD=openstack
export OS_AUTH_URL=https://192.168.100.200:5000/v2.0/

nova live-migration --block-migrate <UUID> compute-02
```

How it works...

Live migration is an essential feature that enables OpenStack operators and administrators to perform maintenance of the underlying cloud infrastructure without affecting the consumers of said cloud. Additionally, the OpenStack administrator can use telemetry data from Ceilometer and make live-migration decisions to balance workloads across the OpenStack cloud.

Live-migration in OpenStack is handled by the `libvirt` drivers. Specifically, when you issue the `nova live-migration` command, OpenStack compute creates a connection from `libvirtd` on one compute host to the same process on the remote host. Once this connection is established, depending on the parameters you specified, the memory state of the instance is synchronized and control is transferred. In our example, we specified the additional `--block-migrate` parameter, which handles the movement of the instance's disk files in the absence of shared storage.

Working with nova-schedulers

When you launch an instance with OpenStack, the job of the nova-schedulers is to determine which Compute Host (hypervisor) the instance will be created on. The scheduler can be configured to make some basic decisions, such as whether or not RAM exists or not to run the instance and whether enough cores are available. It can also be configured to be more complex and make decisions based on environmental factors and metadata, so that instances can be grouped together on hosts or spread across different hosts to ensure a level of stability in the event of a compute host failure.

Getting ready

Ensure that you are logged in to the OpenStack `controller` node. If you used Vagrant to create this, we can access this with the following command:

```
vagrant ssh controller
```

How to do it...

Let's modify the `/etc/nova/nova.conf` file to enable all the scheduler filters discussed:

1. Add the following lines to the [Default] section of the `/etc/nova/nova.conf` file on the Controller:

```
scheduler_driver=nova.scheduler.multi.MultiScheduler
scheduler_driver_task_period = 60
scheduler_driver = nova.scheduler.filter_scheduler.FilterScheduler
scheduler_available_filters = nova.scheduler.filters.all_filters
scheduler_default_filters = RetryFilter, AvailabilityZoneFilter,
    RamFilter, ComputeFilter, ComputeCapabilitiesFilter,
    ImagePropertiesFilter, ServerGroupAntiAffinityFilter
    ServerGroupAffinityFilter
```

2. Restart the `nova-scheduler` service to pick up the change:

```
sudo service nova-scheduler restart
```

How it works...

You can modify the `nova.conf` file to expose additional features of the nova-scheduler to be used in our environment. In this example, the default scheduler enabled with OpenStack Juno will consider scheduling an instance to a host, if the host meets all of the following criteria:

- `RetryFilter`: This will retry each host (in the first instance, implies the host hasn't been requested before)
- `AvailabilityZoneFilter`: This specifies that the host is in the request availability zone (the default is nova)
- `RamFilter`: This specifies that the Compute host has enough RAM available
- `ComputeFilter`: This specifies that the Compute host is available to service the request
- `ComputeCapabilitiesFilter`: This specifies that the Compute host satisfies any extra specs associated with the instance type requested
- `ImagePropertiesFilter`: This specifies that the image (and associated properties) requested can run on the particular host
- `ServerGroupAntiAffinityFilter`: If requested, whether the instance should run on a different host to another instance in the same group
- `ServerGroupAffinityFilter`: If requested, whether the instance should run on hosts belonging to the same instance group

There's more...

There are a number of schedulers available for a wide variety of scenarios. For more information, visit `http://docs.openstack.org/juno/config-reference/content/section_compute-scheduler.html`.

Creating flavors

Flavors describe the size of the instance specified. They describe the number of cores (virtual CPUs), amount of RAM, and size of allocated local or ephemeral disk resource available to an instance. The standard flavors are usually `m1.tiny`, `m1.small`, `m1.large` and `m1.xlarge`. A user specifies these either on the command line or through the Horizon interface.

Getting ready

Ensure you are logged in to an Ubuntu host that has access to our OpenStack environment on the 192.168.100.0/24 public network. This host will be used to run client tools against the OpenStack environment created. If you are using the accompanying Vagrant environment, as described in the `Preface`, you can use the `controller` node. This node has the `python-novaclient` package that provides the `swift` command-line client.

If you created this node with Vagrant, you can execute the following command:

```
vagrant ssh controller
```

Ensure you have set the following credentials (adjust the path to your certificates and key file to match your environment if not using the Vagrant environment):

```
export OS_TENANT_NAME=cookbook
export OS_USERNAME=admin
export OS_PASSWORD=openstack
export OS_AUTH_URL=https://192.168.100.200:5000/v2.0/
export OS_NO_CACHE=1
export OS_KEY=/vagrant/cakey.pem
export OS_CACERT=/vagrant/ca.pem
```

How to do it...

To create a new flavor that specifies 2 vCPU, 16 GB RAM, and 30 GB disk, carry out the following steps:

1. We run the following commands:

   ```
   nova flavor-create m1.javaserver
       49 16384 30 2
       --is-public=true
   ```

   The preceding commands produce an output like this:

```
+----+---------------+-----------+------+-----------+------+-------+-------------+-----------+
| ID | Name          | Memory_MB | Disk | Ephemeral | Swap | VCPUs | RXTX_Factor | Is_Public |
+----+---------------+-----------+------+-----------+------+-------+-------------+-----------+
| 49 | m1.javaserver | 16384     | 30   | 0         |      | 2     | 1.0         | True      |
+----+---------------+-----------+------+-----------+------+-------+-------------+-----------+
```

2. We can now list the flavors available with the following command:

   ```
   nova flavor-list
   ```

   The preceding command produces an output like this:

```
+----+---------------+-----------+------+-----------+------+-------+-------------+-----------+
| ID | Name          | Memory_MB | Disk | Ephemeral | Swap | VCPUs | RXTX_Factor | Is_Public |
+----+---------------+-----------+------+-----------+------+-------+-------------+-----------+
| 1  | m1.tiny       | 512       | 0    | 0         |      | 1     | 1.0         | True      |
| 2  | m1.small      | 2048      | 20   | 0         |      | 1     | 1.0         | True      |
| 3  | m1.medium     | 4096      | 40   | 0         |      | 2     | 1.0         | True      |
| 4  | m1.large      | 8192      | 80   | 0         |      | 4     | 1.0         | True      |
| 49 | m1.javaserver | 16384     | 30   | 0         |      | 2     | 1.0         | True      |
| 5  | m1.xlarge     | 16384     | 160  | 0         |      | 8     | 1.0         | True      |
+----+---------------+-----------+------+-----------+------+-------+-------------+-----------+
```

How it works...

Create new flavors using the following syntax:

```
nova flavor-create $FLAVOR_NAME
    $FLAVOR_ID $RAM $DISK $CPU
    --is-public={true|false}
    --ephemeral $EPHEMERAL_SIZE_GB
    --swap $SWAP_SIZE_GB
    --rxtx-factor $FACTOR
```

The `nova flavor-create` command doesn't automatically update flavor IDs; therefore, you must specify this and ensure that this is unique. We then specify the amount of RAM, disk and CPU for that flavor. Here are a few extra options:

- `--is-public=true|false`: This specifies whether the flavor exists only within the current tenant, or it is available to all tenants. Only an administrator can specify this. The default value is `true`.
- `--ephemeral $EPHEMERAL_SIZE_GB`: This allows you to specify a secondary ephemeral disk.
- `--swap $SWAP_SIZE_GB`: This specifies an additional swap partition associated with the instance.
- `--rxtx-factor`: This specifies the bandwidth factor of the flavor compared to other flavors. This defaults to `1`. A factor of `0.5` specifies the bandwidth capacity to be half available.

Defining host aggregates

Host aggregates allow us to logically group hardware and create partitions in our deployment. Host aggregates are often used to group same specification hardware together, such as Compute hosts that have a certain type of hardware such as SSDs available. We can then define extra pieces of information associated with that grouping of hardware (known as metadata), which is exposed to a user when launching instances. For example, we can launch an instance and specify that we want it to run on compute hosts that have SSDs. By supplying this extra information, the compute hosts that understand this metadata will request that the instance be launched on that hardware.

Compute hosts can also belong to more than one host aggregate. This allows for greater flexibility when defining the partitions by allowing compute hosts to be organized in multiple ways. The following diagram shows an example of using host aggregate to define groups of Compute resource. Only an administrator can create host aggregates:

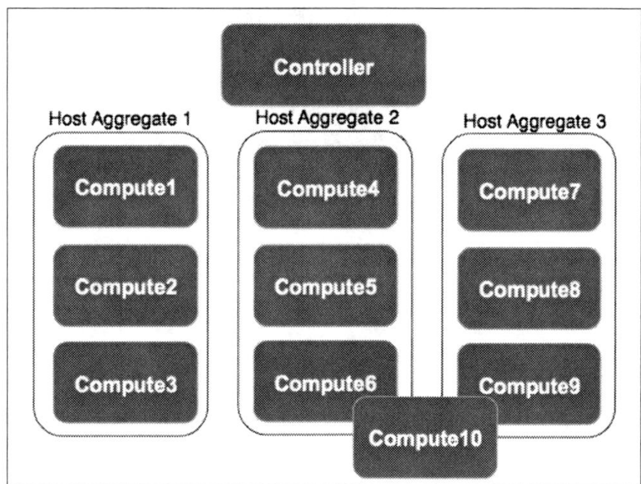

Getting ready

Ensure that you are logged onto an Ubuntu host that has access to our OpenStack environment on the `192.168.100.0/24` public network. This host will be used to run client tools against the OpenStack environment created. If you are using the accompanying Vagrant environment, as described in the *Preface*, you can use the `controller` node. This node has the `python-novaclient` package installed that provides the `swift` command-line client.

If you created this node with Vagrant, you can execute the following command:

vagrant ssh controller

Ensure you have set the following credentials (adjust the path to your certificates and key file to match your environment if not using the Vagrant environment):

```
export OS_TENANT_NAME=cookbook
export OS_USERNAME=admin
export OS_PASSWORD=openstack
export OS_AUTH_URL=https://192.168.100.200:5000/v2.0/
export OS_NO_CACHE=1
export OS_KEY=/vagrant/cakey.pem
export OS_CACERT=/vagrant/ca.pem
```

How to do it...

To create a host aggregate called `TestAggregate` that consists of a compute host called `compute-02`, carry out the following steps:

1. We first create the host aggregate, using the following command:

   nova aggregate-create TestAggregate

   This produces the following output:

   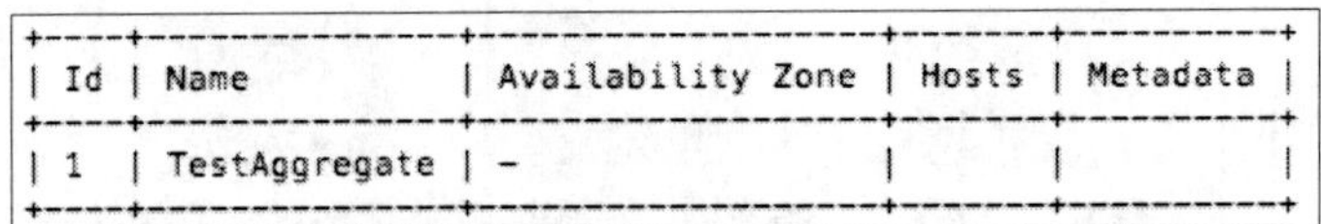

Id	Name	Availability Zone	Hosts	Metadata
1	TestAggregate	-		

2. To find out the specific hostname we should use for our host aggregate, issue the following command:

   nova host-list

The preceding command will result in the following output:

```
+------------+-------------+----------+
| host_name  | service     | zone     |
+------------+-------------+----------+
| controller | scheduler   | internal |
| controller | cert        | internal |
| controller | consoleauth | internal |
| controller | conductor   | internal |
| compute-01 | consoleauth | internal |
| compute-01 | compute     | nova     |
| compute-02 | consoleauth | internal |
| compute-02 | compute     | nova     |
+------------+-------------+----------+
```

3. With the host aggregate created and name of our host recorded, we can simply add our hosts to this aggregate as follows:

   nova aggregate-add-host TestAggregate compute-02

   This will give the following output if it was successful:

```
Host compute-02 has been successfully added for aggregate 1
+----+---------------+-------------------+--------------+----------+
| Id | Name          | Availability Zone | Hosts        | Metadata |
+----+---------------+-------------------+--------------+----------+
| 1  | TestAggregate | -                 | 'compute-02' |          |
+----+---------------+-------------------+--------------+----------+
```

4. We can list the available host aggregates in our environment by issuing the following command:

   nova aggregate-list

   This will give the following output:

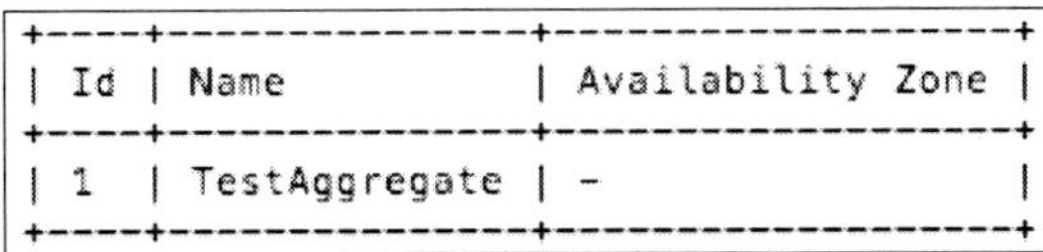

```
+----+---------------+-------------------+
| Id | Name          | Availability Zone |
+----+---------------+-------------------+
| 1  | TestAggregate | -                 |
+----+---------------+-------------------+
```

5. We can get further information about an aggregate, such as which hosts are in the aggregate, any metadata associated with it, and whether or not any availability zones are associated with it, by issuing the following command:

   nova aggregate-details TestAggregate

This will give the following details:

```
+----+---------------+-------------------+---------------+----------+
| Id | Name          | Availability Zone | Hosts         | Metadata |
+----+---------------+-------------------+---------------+----------+
| 1  | TestAggregate | -                 | 'compute-02'  |          |
+----+---------------+-------------------+---------------+----------+
```

6. To define metadata for a host aggregate such that we can later use this extra metadata information to direct our instances to be launched on a host in this group, use the following command:

   nova aggregate-set-metadata TestAggregate highspec=true

   This sets the information `highspec=true`, which will be used later on. The command produces the following output:

```
Metadata has been successfully updated for aggregate 1.
+----+---------------+-------------------+---------------+-----------------+
| Id | Name          | Availability Zone | Hosts         | Metadata        |
+----+---------------+-------------------+---------------+-----------------+
| 1  | TestAggregate | -                 | 'compute-02'  | 'highspec=true' |
+----+---------------+-------------------+---------------+-----------------+
```

7. We can then expose this metadata through the flavors used to launch the instances. To demonstrate this, we will create a flavor called `m1.highspec` and set the metadata on this to match the metadata for our host aggregate. Use the following commands to create a new flavor called `m1.highspec`:

   nova flavor-create

   m1.highspec

   50 2048 20 2

   --is-public=true

8. We can set extra information on this flavor to match the metadata set on the `TestAggregate` aggregate with the following command:

   nova flavor-key m1.highspec set highspec=true

9. We can then view the details of this flavor with the following command:

   nova flavor-show m1.highspec

This will give you the following output:

```
+----------------------------+----------------------+
| Property                   | Value                |
+----------------------------+----------------------+
| OS-FLV-DISABLED:disabled   | False                |
| OS-FLV-EXT-DATA:ephemeral  | 0                    |
| disk                       | 20                   |
| extra_specs                | {"highspec": "true"} |
| id                         | 50                   |
| name                       | m1.highspec          |
| os-flavor-access:is_public | True                 |
| ram                        | 2048                 |
| rxtx_factor                | 1.0                  |
| swap                       |                      |
| vcpus                      | 2                    |
+----------------------------+----------------------+
```

We can specify this flavor when launching an instance. This will automatically schedule to one of the instances in the `TestAggregate` aggregate, which will be `compute-02` in this example.

How it works...

Host Aggregates allow an administrator to define compute resources in a way that is transparent to the end user but group them logically according to their purpose. When metadata is added to an aggregate that matches a flavor's metadata, and when that flavor is used to launch an instance, the instance will be scheduled to run on the compute hosts that have been assigned that to that aggregate.

Launching instances in specific Availability Zones

Availability zones are logical separations of compute resources, representing groups of hypervisors that a user will be able to select when requesting to launch an instance. If no availability zones have been created, the default called **nova** will be used. When an instance is launched in most default cases, the scheduler determines which host will run it within that zone. As a user of the OpenStack cloud, you can specify which availability zone to use if more than one is available. This can help you create more resilient applications. By allowing an instance to be spun up in two separate places, we are protecting ourselves against the failure of a complete zone.

Getting ready

Ensure you are logged onto an Ubuntu host that has access to our OpenStack environment on the 192.168.100.0/24 public network. This host will be used to run client tools against the OpenStack environment created. If you are using the accompanying Vagrant environment, as described in the Preface, you can use the `controller` node. This node has the `python-novaclient` package that provides the `nova` command-line client.

If you created this node with Vagrant, you can execute the following command:

```
vagrant ssh controller
```

Ensure you have set the following credentials (adjust the path to your certificates and key file to match your environment if not using the Vagrant environment):

```
export OS_TENANT_NAME=cookbook
export OS_USERNAME=admin
export OS_PASSWORD=openstack
export OS_AUTH_URL=https://192.168.100.200:5000/v2.0/
export OS_NO_CACHE=1
export OS_KEY=/vagrant/cakey.pem
export OS_CACERT=/vagrant/ca.pem
```

How to do it...

1. To launch an instance into a specific availability zone, we use the following syntax:

   ```
   nova boot
       --flavor $FLAVOR
       --image $IMAGE
       --availability-zone $AZ
       $INSTANCE_NAME
   ```

2. The name of the `$AZ` comes from `nova hypervisor-list`. We use the complete name listed as shown:

   To launch an instance called `myInstance` onto `compute-02`, issue the following command:

   ```
   nova hypervisor-list
   ```

This will give you the following output:

```
+----+---------------------+
| ID | Hypervisor hostname  |
+----+---------------------+
| 1  | compute-01.cook.book |
| 2  | compute-02.cook.book |
+----+---------------------+
```

3. We then boot this onto `compute-02` using the following commands:

```
nova boot
    --flavor 1
    --image trusty-image
    --availability-zone nova:compute-02.cook.book
    MyInstance
```

Note that OpenStack can successfully launch an instance to a specific host only if there are enough cores and RAM available, as well as still satisfying quota counts. You will be presented with an error saying no more hosts available if the resources are not available.

How it works...

To launch an instance into a specific availability zone, we use the following flag to our nova boot command line:-

```
-availability-zone $NAME_OF_ZONE
```

The name of the zone comes from the following command:

```
nova availability-zone-list
```

This command lists the Zones available in our environment.

Launching instances on specific Compute hosts

When an instance is launched, in most cases, the scheduler determines which host will run it. There are times, however, when it is good to be able to directly assign an instance to a host, for example, when helping to troubleshoot or perhaps when the orchestration is managing resource allocation.

Getting ready

Ensure you are logged in to an Ubuntu host that has access to our OpenStack environment on the `192.168.100.0/24` public network. This host will be used to run client tools against the OpenStack environment created. If you are using the accompanying Vagrant environment, as described in the Preface, you can use the `controller` node. This node has the `python-novaclient` package that provides the `nova` command-line client.

If you created this node with Vagrant, you can execute the following command:

```
vagrant ssh controller
```

Ensure that you have set the following credentials (adjust the path to your certificates and key file to match your environment if not using the Vagrant environment):

```
export OS_TENANT_NAME=cookbook
export OS_USERNAME=admin
export OS_PASSWORD=openstack
export OS_AUTH_URL=https://192.168.100.200:5000/v2.0/
export OS_NO_CACHE=1
export OS_KEY=/vagrant/cakey.pem
export OS_CACERT=/vagrant/ca.pem
```

How to do it...

1. To launch an instance onto a specific host, we use the following syntax:

   ```
   nova boot
       --flavor $FLAVOR
       --image $IMAGE
       --availability-zone nova:$HYPERVISOR_NAME
       $INSTANCE_NAME
   ```

   The name of the `$HYPERVISOR_NAME` comes from nova hypervisor-list. We use the complete hypervisor name as shown.

2. To launch an instance called `myInstance` onto `compute-02`, issue the following command:

   ```
   nova hypervisor-list
   ```

   This will give you the following output:

   ```
   +----+---------------------+
   | ID | Hypervisor hostname |
   +----+---------------------+
   | 1  | compute-01.cook.book |
   | 2  | compute-02.cook.book |
   +----+---------------------+
   ```

3. We then boot this onto `compute-02` using the following commands:

   ```
   nova boot
       --flavor 1
       --image trusty-image
       --availability-zone nova:compute-02.cook.book
       myInstance
   ```

Note that OpenStack can successfully launch an instance to a specific host only if there are enough cores and RAM available, as well as still satisfying quota counts. You will be presented with an error saying no more hosts available if the resources are not available.

How it works...

To launch an instance onto a specific compute host, we use the following flag to our nova boot command line:

```
--availability-zone nova:$HYPERVISOR_NAME
```

The name of the hypervisor can be obtained using the following command:

```
nova hypervisor-list
```

The preceding command lists the Compute hosts available in our environment.

Removing Nova nodes from a cluster

Sometimes, you may need to remove a compute node from a cluster for troubleshooting or maintenance reasons. You should be careful while doing so, since it could negatively affect running VMs. Before getting started, make sure you have enough resources in your compute cluster to migrate running VMs to other compute nodes before removing the node.

Getting ready

Ensure you are logged in to an Ubuntu host that has access to our OpenStack environment on the `192.168.100.0/24` public network. This host will be used to run client tools against the OpenStack environment created. If you are using the accompanying Vagrant environment, as described in the *Preface*, you can use the `controller` node. This node has the `python-novaclient` package that provides the `nova` command-line client.

If you created this node with Vagrant, you can execute the following command:

```
vagrant ssh controller
```

Ensure that you have set the following credentials (adjust the path to your certificates and key file to match your environment if not using the Vagrant environment):

```
export OS_TENANT_NAME=cookbook
export OS_USERNAME=admin
export OS_PASSWORD=openstack
export OS_AUTH_URL=https://192.168.100.200:5000/v2.0/
export OS_NO_CACHE=1
export OS_KEY=/vagrant/cakey.pem
export OS_CACERT=/vagrant/ca.pem
```

How to do it...

We will use `nova` command-line client to disable services and migrate the VMs.

1. Determine which `nova` services you want to stop by using the `nova service-list` command:

   ```
   nova service-list
   ```

This will give you the following output:

```
+----+------------------+------------+----------+---------+-------+----------------------------+-----------------+
| Id | Binary           | Host       | Zone     | Status  | State | Updated_at                 | Disabled Reason |
+----+------------------+------------+----------+---------+-------+----------------------------+-----------------+
| 1  | nova-scheduler   | controller | internal | enabled | up    | 2015-02-09T05:16:34.000000 | -               |
| 2  | nova-consoleauth | controller | internal | enabled | up    | 2015-02-09T05:16:41.000000 | -               |
| 3  | nova-cert        | controller | internal | enabled | up    | 2015-02-09T05:16:40.000000 | -               |
| 4  | nova-conductor   | controller | internal | enabled | up    | 2015-02-09T05:16:43.000000 | -               |
| 5  | nova-consoleauth | compute-01 | internal | enabled | up    | 2015-02-09T05:16:37.000000 | -               |
| 6  | nova-compute     | compute-01 | nova     | enabled | up    | 2015-02-09T05:16:37.000000 | -               |
| 7  | nova-consoleauth | compute-02 | internal | enabled | up    | 2015-02-09T05:16:40.000000 | -               |
| 8  | nova-compute     | compute-02 | nova     | enabled | up    | 2015-02-09T05:16:43.000000 | -               |
+----+------------------+------------+----------+---------+-------+----------------------------+-----------------+
```

2. We will need the list of all of the VMs running on `compute-01`. To get the list, search by hostname using the following command:

   ```
   nova list --host compute-01
   ```

   In our case, we have only one VM, `test1`:

```
+--------------------------------------+-------+--------+------------+-------------+------------------------------+
| ID                                   | Name  | Status | Task State | Power State | Networks                     |
+--------------------------------------+-------+--------+------------+-------------+------------------------------+
| 5ee8002a-c658-4a33-8ddd-11af50b2e18c | test1 | ACTIVE | -          | Running     | cookbook_network_1=10.200.0.6 |
+--------------------------------------+-------+--------+------------+-------------+------------------------------+
```

3. We then need to disable `compute-01` with the following command:

   ```
   nova service-disable compute-01 nova-compute
   ```

   The preceding command will give you the following output:

   ```
   +------------+--------------+----------+
   | Host       | Binary       | Status   |
   +------------+--------------+----------+
   | compute-01 | nova-compute | disabled |
   +------------+--------------+----------+
   ```

4. Now, when we check running services with the `nova service-list` command, we will see that `compute-01` is disabled:

```
+----+------------------+------------+----------+----------+-------+----------------------------+-----------------+
| Id | Binary           | Host       | Zone     | Status   | State | Updated_at                 | Disabled Reason |
+----+------------------+------------+----------+----------+-------+----------------------------+-----------------+
| 1  | nova-scheduler   | controller | internal | enabled  | up    | 2015-02-09T05:16:34.000000 | -               |
| 2  | nova-consoleauth | controller | internal | enabled  | up    | 2015-02-09T05:16:41.000000 | -               |
| 3  | nova-cert        | controller | internal | enabled  | up    | 2015-02-09T05:16:40.000000 | -               |
| 4  | nova-conductor   | controller | internal | enabled  | up    | 2015-02-09T05:16:43.000000 | -               |
| 5  | nova-consoleauth | compute-01 | internal | enabled  | up    | 2015-02-09T05:16:37.000000 | -               |
| 6  | nova-compute     | compute-01 | nova     | disabled | up    | 2015-02-09T05:16:40.000000 | -               |
| 7  | nova-consoleauth | compute-02 | internal | enabled  | up    | 2015-02-09T05:16:40.000000 | -               |
| 8  | nova-compute     | compute-02 | nova     | enabled  | up    | 2015-02-09T05:16:43.000000 | -               |
+----+------------------+------------+----------+----------+-------+----------------------------+-----------------+
```

> Note that even though compute nodes are disabled, it does not mean that they are not running. VMs could still be running on them, and if so, they should be migrated.

5. We now need to migrate all VMs running on the `compute-01` node. We need to use the `nova migrate` command on each VM:

   `nova migrate test1`

   There is no output for this command. In our case, we have only one VM `test1` that we will migrate. If you have other VMs that need to be migrated, migrate them as well.

6. Check the status of the VM being migrated by using the `nova show` command:

   `nova show test1`

7. While the VM is being migrated, you should see the following output:

```
+--------------------------------------+-------------------------------------------------------------------+
| Property                             | Value                                                             |
+--------------------------------------+-------------------------------------------------------------------+
| OS-DCF:diskConfig                    | MANUAL                                                            |
| OS-EXT-AZ:availability_zone          | nova                                                              |
| OS-EXT-SRV-ATTR:host                 | compute-01                                                        |
| OS-EXT-SRV-ATTR:hypervisor_hostname  | compute-01.cook.book                                              |
| OS-EXT-SRV-ATTR:instance_name        | instance-00000004                                                 |
| OS-EXT-STS:power_state               | 1                                                                 |
| OS-EXT-STS:task_state                | resize_migrating                                                  |
| OS-EXT-STS:vm_state                  | active                                                            |
| OS-SRV-USG:launched_at               | 2015-02-02T08:06:45.000000                                        |
| OS-SRV-USG:terminated_at             | -                                                                 |
| accessIPv4                           |                                                                   |
| accessIPv6                           |                                                                   |
| config_drive                         |                                                                   |
| cookbook_network_1 network           | 10.200.0.6                                                        |
| created                              | 2015-02-02T08:06:37Z                                              |
| flavor                               | m1.tiny (1)                                                       |
| hostId                               | 80e19db4c2ee0ac10520eedbd960227393fa6467b300bf4db039d738          |
| id                                   | 5ee8002a-c658-4a33-8ddd-11af50b2e18c                              |
| image                                | trusty-image (5bfb4a6d-da77-4502-ba52-2e8e40597e96)               |
| key_name                             | demokey                                                           |
| metadata                             | {}                                                                |
| name                                 | test1                                                             |
| os-extended-volumes:volumes_attached | []                                                                |
| progress                             | 0                                                                 |
| security_groups                      | default                                                           |
| status                               | RESIZE                                                            |
| tenant_id                            | e99b80a0de78451f91c97beef5b2c2d5                                  |
| updated                              | 2015-02-09T04:36:23Z                                              |
| user_id                              | 183fd6a93d7e4a65aa513bdb4fa9850e                                  |
+--------------------------------------+-------------------------------------------------------------------+
```

   We will wait until the VM is in the `VERIFY_RESIZE` status before proceeding to the next step.

8. Verify that the VM migrated successfully and confirm resize with the nova `resize-confirm` command:

   `nova resize-confirm test1`

The `compute-01` is now disabled and contains no VMs. We can now power it off or perform maintenance on the node.

How it works...

To remove a compute node from the cluster, we first need to make sure that there are enough resources in the rest of the cluster for VMs running on that node. Then, we need to disable the node with the `nova service-disable` command.

Disable the Compute node by issuing the `nova service-disable $SERVICE nova-compute` command. After disabling the node, we need to migrate all VMs running on the disabled node to other compute nodes. The `nova migrate` command will migrate the VM to other nodes with sufficient resources.

5
Swift – OpenStack Object Storage

In this chapter, we will cover the following recipes:

- Configuring Swift services and users in Keystone
- Installing OpenStack Object Storage - proxy server
- Configuring OpenStack Object Storage - proxy server
- Installing OpenStack Object Storage services - storage nodes
- Configuring physical storage for use with Swift
- Configuring Object Storage replication
- Configuring OpenStack Object Storage - storage services
- Making the Object Storage rings
- Stopping and starting OpenStack Object Storage
- Setting up SSL access

Introduction

OpenStack Object Storage, also known as **Swift**, is the service that allows massively scalable and highly redundant storage on commodity hardware. This service is implemented by Rackspace as cloud files and is also analogous to Amazon's S3 storage service. It is managed in a similar way under OpenStack. With OpenStack Object Storage, we can store many objects of virtually unlimited size—restricted by the available hardware—and grow our environment as needed in order to accommodate our storage. The highly redundant nature of OpenStack Object Storage is ideal for archiving data (such as logs) as well as providing a storage system that OpenStack Compute can use for virtual machine instance templates.

In this chapter, we will set up a multi-node environment consisting of a single Swift proxy server and five Swift storage nodes with a single extra disk at `/dev/sdb1` where the object storage will be written. The authentication and authorization will be handled by Keystone. The data stored in Swift will be replicated three times. This means that a file of size 1 GB will actually use 3 GB of space across our cluster. It will replicate this data by spreading them across the five nodes (any three of the five nodes will have the data stored), so any failure of a node vastly reduces the amount of time to recover. This guarantees that quorum is maintained regardless of which node failed. This is considered the minimum recommended architecture for any Swift installation.

Typical reference architecture is shown in the following diagram and shows the proxy servers sitting behind a Load Balancer:

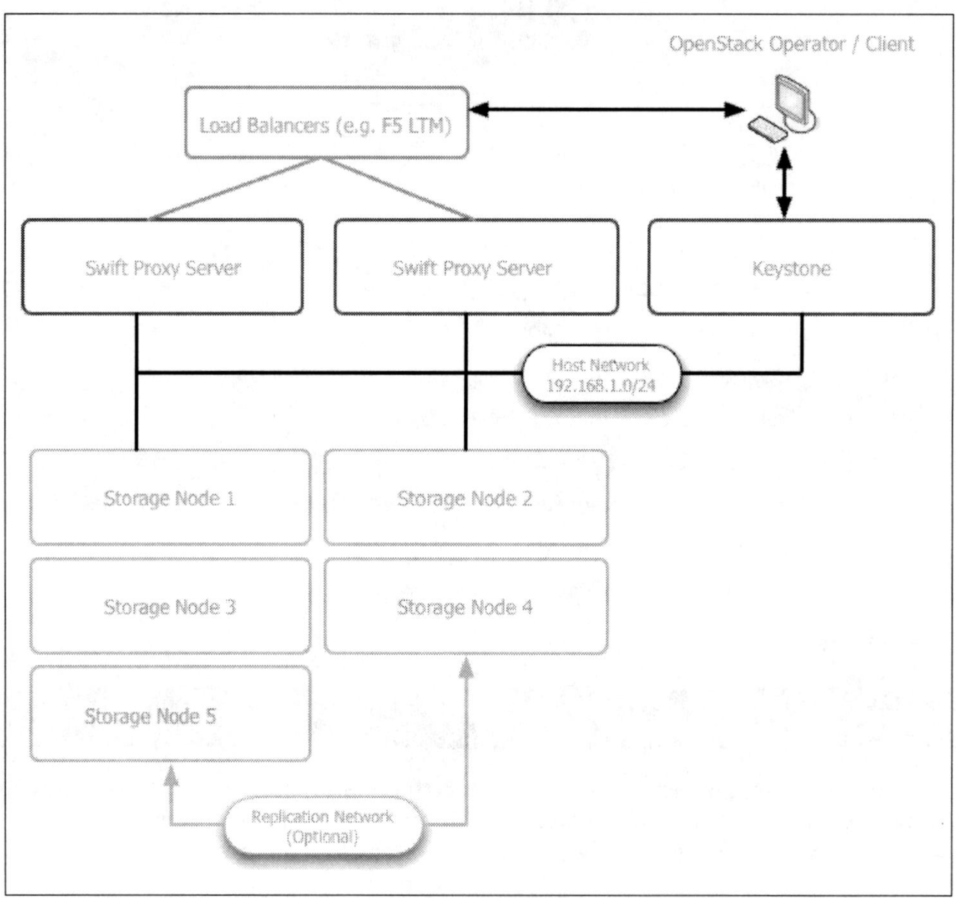

For the multi-node Swift installation that accompanies this chapter, visit `http://bit.ly/OpenStackCookbookSwift`.

Configuring Swift services and users in Keystone

Configuring our OpenStack Object Storage environment in Keystone follows the familiar pattern of defining the service, the endpoint, and creating an appropriate user in the service `tenant`. These details will then be used to configure the storage services later in the chapter.

In this environment, we are defining the address and ports of the proxy server. In the test environment, the proxy server's IP addresses are `192.168.100.209` (public) and `172.16.0.209` (internal/management). In production, this would be a Load-Balanced pool address.

Getting ready

Ensure that you are logged in to the `controller` node or an appropriate client that has access to the `controller` node to configure `keystone`. If this was created using the Vagrant environment, you can issue the following command:

```
vagrant ssh controller
```

How to do it...

Configure Keystone for use by Swift by carrying out the following steps:

1. To do this, we use the Keystone client and configure it for use by an administrator by setting the following environment variables:

```
export ENDPOINT=192.168.100.200
export SERVICE_TOKEN=ADMIN
export SERVICE_ENDPOINT=https://${ENDPOINT}:35357/v2.0
export OS_KEY=/vagrant/cakey.pem
export OS_CACERT=/vagrant/ca.pem
```

2. We can now define the `swift` service in Keystone as follows:

```
# Configure the OpenStack Object Storage Endpoint
keystone service-create \
    --name swift \
    --type object-store \
    --description 'OpenStack Object Storage Service'
```

3. We define the endpoint as follows. Here, we are setting public endpoint to be our public network, `192.168.100.0/24`, and internal and admin URLs on the management network, `172.16.0.0/16`:

```
# Service Endpoint URLs
SWIFT_SERVICE_ID=$(keystone service-list \
     | awk '/\ swift\ / {print $2}')

PUBLIC_URL="http://192.168.100.209:8080/v1/AUTH_\$(tenant_i
d)s"
ADMIN_URL="http://172.16.0.209:8080/v1"
INTERNAL_URL=="http://172.16.0.209:8080/v1/AUTH_\$(tenant_i
d)s"

keystone endpoint-create --region RegionOne \
    --service_id $SWIFT_SERVICE_ID \
    --publicurl $PUBLIC_URL \
    --adminurl $ADMIN_URL \
    --internalurl $INTERNAL_URL
```

4. With the endpoints configured to point to our OpenStack Object Storage server, we can now set up the `swift` user so that our proxy server can authenticate with the OpenStack identity server:

```
# Get the service tenant ID
SERVICE_TENANT_ID=$(keystone tenant-list \
    | awk '/\ service\ / {print $2}')

# Create the swift user with password swift
keystone user-create \
    --name swift \
    --pass swift \
    --tenant_id $SERVICE_TENANT_ID \
    --email swift@localhost \
    --enabled true
```

```
# Get the swift user id
USER_ID=$(keystone user-list \
    | awk '/\ swift\ / {print $2}')

# Get the admin role id
ROLE_ID=$(keystone role-list \
    | awk '/\ admin\ / {print $2}')

# Assign the swift user admin role in service tenant
keystone user-role-add \
    --user $USER_ID \
    --role $ROLE_ID \
    --tenant_id $SERVICE_TENANT_ID
```

How it works...

To use Swift, we will be authenticating through Keystone and, as a result, Swift also needs entries in Keystone to function. We first define the service as we do for any service in OpenStack. In this case, Swift is the `object-store` type. Then, we define the endpoints. Swift will utilize two networks—a front-facing network labeled as `public` (referring to the network the API requests from the client would traverse) and an internal network for intercommunication between the services. Finally, we create the `service` tenant user. In this case, we are using `swift` as the username, and we are also setting `swift` as the password. In production, you would choose a much stronger, randomly generated password for this purpose. Like any other OpenStack service, this user is given the `admin` role in the `service` tenant.

Installing OpenStack Object Storage services – proxy server

Clients connect to OpenStack Object Storage via the Swift proxy servers. This allows us to scale out our OpenStack Object Storage environment as needed, without affecting the frontend to which the clients connect. The proxy servers have the following packages installed:

- `swift`: These are the underlying common files shared among other the OpenStack Object Storage packages, including the Swift client
- `swift-proxy`: This is the proxy service responsible for providing access to the OpenStack Object Storage nodes
- `memcached`: This is a high-performance memory object caching system
- `python-swiftclient`: This is the Swift client for accessing the OpenStack Object Storage environment using the **Command-line Interface** (**CLI**)

- `python-keystoneclient`: These are the clients, as well as libraries allowing the services to communicate with Keystone
- `python-webob`: This is the Python module providing **Web Service Gateway Interface** (**WSGI**) request and response objects
- `curl`: This is the command-line tool for accessing web resources

More than one proxy server can be used for Swift. In fact, in production environments, at least two are required, and they would be placed behind a Load Balancer. Repeat these steps for all the proxy servers you have in your environment.

Getting ready

Ensure that you are logged in to the `swift-proxy` nodes. If you created this with `vagrant`, you can access this node by issuing the following command:

```
vagrant ssh swift-proxy
```

Ensure that NTP is installed across all hosts in the OpenStack Object Storage environment. For more information, visit `http://bit.ly/OpenStackCookbookPreReqs`.

How to do it...

Installation of the OpenStack Object Storage proxy server and associated packages in Ubuntu 14.04 is simply achieved using the familiar `apt-get` tool, as the OpenStack packages available from the official Ubuntu repositories. To install the packages required on each storage node, execute the following steps:

1. We can install all of the OpenStack Object Storage packages used on a storage node as follows:

   ```
   sudo apt-get update
   sudo apt-get install swift swift-proxy memcached \
       python-keystoneclient python-swiftclient \
       curl python-webob
   ```

2. We then create a number of directories that will be used by Swift, and set the appropriate permissions:

   ```
   # Create signing directory and set owner to swift
   mkdir /var/swift-signing
   ```

```
chown -R swift /var/swift-signing

# Create cache directory and set owner to swift
mkdir -p /var/cache/swift
chown -R swift:swift /var/cache/swift

# Create config directory and set owner to swift
mkdir -p /etc/swift
chown -R swift:swift /etc/swift
```

Repeat this installation on each of the storage nodes in the environment.

How it works...

Installation of the Swift proxy server from the main Ubuntu package repository represents a straightforward and well-understood way of getting OpenStack onto our Ubuntu server. This adds a greater level of certainty around stability and upgrade paths by not deviating away from the main archives.

Configuring OpenStack Object Storage – proxy server

Clients connect to OpenStack Object Storage via the proxy servers. This allows us to scale out our OpenStack Object Storage environment as needed, without affecting the frontend to which the clients connect. Configuration of the Swift proxy service is simply done by editing the `/etc/swift/proxy-server.conf` file.

Getting ready

Ensure that you are logged in to the `swift-proxy` nodes. If you created this with `vagrant`, you can access this node by issuing the following command:

```
vagrant ssh swift-proxy
```

How to do it...

To configure the OpenStack Object Storage proxy server, carry out the following steps:

1. We first create the `/etc/swift/proxy-server.conf` file with the following content:

```
[DEFAULT]
bind_port = 8080
user = swift
swift_dir = /etc/swift
log_level = DEBUG

[pipeline:main]
# Order of execution of modules defined as follows
pipeline = catch_errors healthcheck cache authtoken
keystone proxy-server

[app:proxy-server]
use = egg:swift#proxy
allow_account_management = true
account_autocreate = true
set log_name = swift-proxy
set log_facility = LOG_LOCAL0
set log_level = INFO
set access_log_name = swift-proxy
set access_log_facility = SYSLOG
set access_log_level = INFO
set log_headers = True

[filter:healthcheck]
use = egg:swift#healthcheck

[filter:catch_errors]
use = egg:swift#catch_errors

[filter:cache]
use = egg:swift#memcache
set log_name = cache
```

```
[filter:authtoken]
paste.filter_factory =
keystoneclient.middleware.auth_token:filter_factory

# Delaying the auth decision is required to support token-
less
# usage for anonymous referrers ('.r:*').
delay_auth_decision = true

# auth_* settings refer to the Keystone server
auth_uri = https://192.168.100.200:35357/v2.0/
identity_uri = https://192.168.100.200:5000
insecure = True     # using self-signed certs

# the service tenant and swift username and password
created in Keystone
admin_tenant_name = service
admin_user = swift
admin_password = swift

signing_dir = /var/swift-signing

[filter:keystone]
use = egg:swift#keystoneauth
operator_roles = admin, Member
```

2. We also create a new file called `/etc/swift/swift.conf` that must be present on all servers in our environment. We will copy this same file with exactly the same content to all servers (proxy servers and storage nodes):

```
[swift-hash]
# Random unique string used on all nodes
swift_hash_path_prefix=a4rUmUIgJYXpKhbh
swift_hash_path_suffix=NESuuUEqc6OXwy6X
```

How it works...

The contents of the `/etc/swift/proxy-server.conf` file define how the OpenStack Object Storage proxy server is configured.

For our purposes, we will run our proxy on port `8080` as the user `swift`, and it will log to `syslog` using the log level of `INFO` (this is the default logging level).

The `[filter:authtoken]` and `[filter:keystone]` sections connect our OpenStack Object Storage proxy to `keystone` running on our `controller` virtual machine. The contents of `[filter:authtoken]` take the same syntax as our other OpenStack services when configuring to `keystone`.

The `/etc/swift/swift.conf` file is not unique to the proxy server. This file must be present on all of our Swift servers and have exactly the same contents. This will be replicated onto the storage nodes when we configure the services on them.

See also

- There are more complex options and features described in the following file that is installed when you install OpenStack Swift `/usr/share/doc/swift-proxy/proxy-server.conf-sample`.

Installing OpenStack Object Storage services – storage nodes

The storage nodes run a number of OpenStack Object Storage services. These services and libraries can be installed using `apt`, and they are listed as follows:

- `swift`: These are the underlying common files shared among other OpenStack Object Storage packages, including the Swift client
- `swift-account`: This is the account service for accessing OpenStack Object Storage
- `swift-object`: This is the package responsible for object storage and the orchestration of `rsync`
- `swift-container`: This is the package for the OpenStack Object Storage container server
- `rsyncd`: This is the file replication daemon for replicating our objects across our storage nodes
- `python-keystoneclient`: These are the clients, as well as libraries, allowing services to communicate with Keystone
- `python-webob`: This is the Python module providing WSGI requests and response objects

Getting ready

Ensure that you are logged in to the `swift` storage nodes. If you created these nodes with `vagrant`, you will carry out these actions on all five storage nodes. You can access each by issuing the following commands:

```
vagrant ssh swift-01
vagrant ssh swift-02
vagrant ssh swift-03
vagrant ssh swift-04
vagrant ssh swift-05
```

Ensure that NTP is installed across all hosts in the OpenStack Object Storage environment. Follow the instructions at `http://bit.ly/OpenStackCookbookPreReqs` for more information.

How to do it...

Installation of OpenStack Object Storage node services in Ubuntu 14.04 is achieved using the familiar `apt-get` tool, as the OpenStack packages are available from the official Ubuntu repositories. To install the required packages on each storage node, execute the following steps:

1. We can install all of the OpenStack Object Storage packages used on a storage node as follows:

   ```
   sudo apt-get update
   sudo apt-get install swift swift-account \
       swift-container swift-object python-webob \
       python-keystoneclient rsync
   ```

2. We then create a number of directories that will be used by Swift and set the appropriate permissions by running the following commands:

   ```
   # Create signing directory and set owner to swift
   mkdir /var/swift-signing
   chown -R swift /var/swift-signing
   ```

```
# Create cache directory & set owner to swift
mkdir -p /var/cache/swift
chown -R swift:swift /var/cache/swift

# Create config directory and set owner to swift
mkdir -p /etc/swift
chown -R swift:swift /etc/swift
```

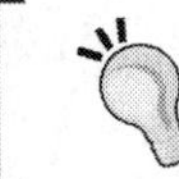

Repeat this installation on each of the storage nodes in the environment.

How it works...

Installation of the services required for running OpenStack Object Storage nodes from the main Ubuntu package repository represents a straightforward and well-understood way of getting OpenStack onto our Ubuntu server. This adds a greater level of certainty around stability and upgrade paths by not deviating away from the main archives.

Configuring physical storage for use with Swift

OpenStack Object Storage, Swift, has relatively simple architecture. It uses proxy servers at the frontend that pass the data to an allocated storage node. The storage nodes can use as many disks as you have available—whether it is one extra disk or a **Just a Bunch Of Disks** (**JBOD**) full of drives. In this recipe, the accompanying virtual environment consists of five storage nodes-each with an extra disk/partition, `/dev/sdb1`, mounted as `/srv/node/sdb1`, which is where the data will be written. This recipe will describe the process in ensuring these drives are configured correctly for use with Swift.

Getting ready

Ensure that you are logged onto the `swift` storage nodes. If you created these nodes with `vagrant`, you will carry out these actions on all five storage nodes. You can access each by issuing the following commands:

```
vagrant ssh swift-01
vagrant ssh swift-02
```

```
vagrant ssh swift-03
vagrant ssh swift-04
vagrant ssh swift-05
```

How to do it...

To configure our OpenStack Object Storage disks for use with Swift, carry out the following steps on all five of our storage nodes. Repeat all the steps until each node has been configured correctly:

1. First, ensure that the tools required to prepare our disk are installed on our storage nodes. The `parted` tool is usually available, but `XFS` isn't installed by default. Install both as follows:

   ```
   sudo apt-get update
   sudo apt-get install parted xfsprogs
   ```

2. Then, we prepare our extra disk, seen as `/dev/sdb`, under our Linux installation using a tool called `parted`. Execute the following commands to create a new partition that uses the whole disk:

   ```
   sudo parted /dev/sdb mklabel msdos
   NUM_CYLINDERS=$(sudo parted /dev/sdb unit cyl print \
       | awk '/Disk.*cyl/ {print $3}')
   sudo parted mkpart primary 0cyl $NUM_CYLINDERS
   ```

3. To get Linux to see this new partition without rebooting, run `partprobe` to reread the disk layout:

   ```
   sudo partprobe
   ```

4. Once completed, we can create our filesystem on the partition `/dev/sdb1`. For this, we will use the `XFS` filesystem as follows:

   ```
   sudo mkfs.xfs -i size=1024 /dev/sdb1
   ```

5. We can now create the required mount point and set up `fstab` to allow us to mount this new area:

   ```
   sudo mkdir /srv/node/sdb1
   ```

6. Then, edit `/etc/fstab` to add in the following contents:

   ```
   /dev/sdb1 /srv/node/sdb1 xfs
     noatime,nodiratime,nobarrier,logbufs=8 0 0
   ```

7. We can now mount this area as follows:

```
sudo mount /srv/node/sdb1
```

8. Ensure that this area is writeable by the Swift user and group:

```
sudo chown -R swift:swift /srv/node
```

Repeat the preceding steps on all Swift storage nodes.

How it works...

We first created a new partition on our extra disk using `parted` and formatted it with the `XFS` filesystem. XFS is very good at handling large objects and has the necessary extended attributes (`xattr`) required for the objects in this filesystem. The commands used in step 1 utilize the entire disk for use by Swift, which is denoted by making a partition that starts from cylinder 0 and goes up to the last cylinder of the disk.

Any filesystem can be used for OpenStack Object Storage, provided it supports `xattr`, which is by far the most widely used and supported is XFS.

Once created, we mounted this area as `/srv/node/{device_name}`. This recommended structure allows an administrator of OpenStack Object Storage to understand which disk is being used by Swift in a meaningful way.

In order to accommodate the metadata used by OpenStack Object Storage, we increase the inode size to 1024. This is set at the time of the format with the `-i size=1024` parameter.

Further performance considerations are set at mount time. We don't need to record file access times (`noatime`) and directory access times (`nodiratime`). Barrier support flushes the write-back cache to disk at an appropriate time. Disabling this yields a performance boost, as the highly available nature of OpenStack Object Storage allows for failure of a drive (and therefore, write of data), so this safety net in our filesystem can be disabled (with the `nobarrier` option) to increase speed.

Configuring Object Storage replication

For a highly redundant and scalable object storage system, replication is a key requirement. Rsync is responsible for performing the replication of the objects stored in our OpenStack Object Storage environment, and it is mandatory that this is configured correctly for Swift to operate. Rsync is configured so that the three services used by Swift (account server, container server, and object server) are set up as Rsync modules. The ccount server provides information about the user, the container server provides information about the containers owned by the user, and the object server is responsible for the data stored in the container.

Getting ready

Ensure that you are logged into the `swift` storage nodes. If you created these nodes with `vagrant`, you will carry out these actions on all five storage nodes. You can access each by issuing the following commands:

```
vagrant ssh swift-01
vagrant ssh swift-02
vagrant ssh swift-03
vagrant ssh swift-04
vagrant ssh swift-05
```

How to do it...

Configuring replication in OpenStack Object Storage means configuring the `rsync` service on each of the storage nodes. The following steps set up Rsync synchronization modules configured for each of our OpenStack Object Storage services—account server, container server, and object server:

1. We first create our `/etc/rsyncd.conf` file in its entirety, as follows:

```
uid = swift
gid = swift
log file = /var/log/rsyncd.log
pid file = /var/run/rsyncd.pid
address = 172.16.0.221 # Amend for each storage node's management
# IP address

[account]
max connections = 25
```

```
path = /srv/node/
read only = false
lock file = /var/lock/account.lock

[container]
max connections = 25
path = /srv/node/
read only = false
lock file = /var/lock/container.lock

[object]
max connections = 25
path = /srv/node/
read only = false
lock file = /var/lock/object.lock
```

2. Since the `rsync` process will be reading and writing files as the `swift` user and group, ensure that the path used (`/srv/node`) and any files and directories in here are owned by the `swift:swift` user/group, as shown here:

   `sudo chown -R swift:swift /srv/node`

3. Once complete, we enable `rsync` and start the service:

   ```
   sudo sed -i 's/=false/=true/' /etc/default/rsync
   sudo service rsync start
   ```

Repeat the step for each storage node in the environment.

How it works...

This recipe described how to configure `rsyncd.conf` appropriately for use with Swift. We configured various `rsync` modules that become targets on our Rsync server. Additionally, each section of the `rsyncd.conf` file has a number of configuration directives, such as max connections, read only, and the lock file. While most of these values should be self-explanatory, it is important to pay attention to the max connections value. In our test environment, this is set to not overwhelm the small servers that we are running Swift on. In the real world, you will want to tune the maximum connections value per guidance provided in the Rsync documentation. A full discussion of this, however, is beyond the scope of this book.

Configuring OpenStack Object Storage – storage services

The account server lists the available containers on our nodes. The container servers contain object servers seen in our OpenStack Object Storage environment. The object server contains the actual objects seen in our OpenStack Object Storage environment. The following steps must be conducted on all of the storage nodes in our environment.

Getting ready

Ensure that you are logged in to the `swift` storage nodes. If you created these nodes with `vagrant`, you will carry out these actions on all five storage nodes. You can access each by issuing the following commands:

```
vagrant ssh swift-01
vagrant ssh swift-02
vagrant ssh swift-03
vagrant ssh swift-04
vagrant ssh swift-05
```

How to do it...

For this recipe, we're creating four different account server configuration files that differ only in the port that the service will run on and the path on our single disk that corresponds to that service on that particular port. To create the configuration files, follow these steps:

1. We begin by creating the account server configuration file for our first node. Edit `/etc/swift/account-server.conf` with the following contents:

```
[DEFAULT]
devices = /srv/node
bind_port = 6002
user = swift
log_facility = LOG_LOCAL2

[pipeline:main]
pipeline = account-server
```

```
[app:account-server]
use = egg:swift#account

[account-replicator]
vm_test_mode = yes

[account-auditor]

[account-reaper]
```

2. Next, we edit the container server configuration file for the same node. Edit `/etc/swift/container-server.conf` with the following contents:

```
[DEFAULT]
devices = /srv/node
mount_check = false
bind_port = 6001
user = swift
log_facility = LOG_LOCAL2


[pipeline:main]
pipeline = container-server

[app:container-server]
use = egg:swift#container

[account-replicator]
vm_test_mode = yes

[account-updater]

[account-auditor]

[account-sync]

[container-auditor]

[container-replicator]

[container-updater]
```

3. We then configure the final service, the object server, by editing the `/etc/swift/object-server.conf` with the following contents:

```
[DEFAULT]
devices = /srv/node
mount_check = false
bind_port = 6000
user = swift
log_facility = LOG_LOCAL2

[pipeline:main]
pipeline = object-server

[app:object-server]
use = egg:swift#object

[object-replicator]
vm_test_mode = yes

[object-updater]

[object-auditor]
```

4. Create the Swift configuration file, `/etc/swift/swift.conf`, with the same contents as those detailed in step 2 of the *Configuring OpenStack Object Storage – proxy server* recipe in this chapter:

```
[swift-hash]
# Random unique string used on all nodes
swift_hash_path_prefix=a4rUmUIgJYXpKhbh
swift_hash_path_suffix=NESuuUEqc6OXwy6X
```

Repeat the steps for all of the storage nodes in the environment.

How it works...

What we have configured here are the three services that run on each of the storage nodes—the `account server`, the `container server`, and the `object server`. Each of these services run on three different ports on our storage node as defined by the `bind_port` flag:

```
account-server: bind_port = 6000
container-server: bind_port = 6001
object-server: bind_port = 6002
```

We then refer to these ports (at the storage node's addresses) when we make the rings associated with OpenStack Object Storage.

They all reference the parent directory of the path before the directory where the devices are mounted. In this case, the `devices` flag refers to `/srv/node` because our disk is mounted at `/srv/node/sdb1`.

Making the Object Storage rings

The final step is to create the object ring, account ring, and container ring that each of our virtual nodes exists in. The OpenStack Object Storage rings keeps track of where our data exists in our cluster. There are three rings that OpenStack Object Storage understands: the account, container, and object rings. To facilitate quick rebuilding of the rings in our cluster, we will create a script that performs the necessary steps.

Getting ready

Ensure that you are logged in to the `swift-proxy` node and have the packages installed and configured for running Swift and have the five storage nodes installed and configured, as described earlier in this chapter. If you created the `swift-proxy` node with `vagrant`, you can execute the following command:

```
vagrant ssh swift-proxy
```

How to do it...

To create the three rings used by the OpenStack Object Storage service, carry out the following steps:

1. The most convenient way to create the rings for our OpenStack Object Storage environment is to create a script. Create `/usr/local/bin/remakerings` with the following contents:

This file can be downloaded from `http://bit.ly/OpenStackCookbookSwift`.

```
#!/bin/bash

cd /etc/swift
rm -f *.builder *.ring.gz backups/*.builder
backups/*.ring.gz

# Object Ring
swift-ring-builder object.builder create 18 3 1
swift-ring-builder object.builder add r1z1-
172.16.0.221:6000/sdb1 1
swift-ring-builder object.builder add r1z1-
172.16.0.222:6000/sdb1 1
swift-ring-builder object.builder add r1z1-
172.16.0.223:6000/sdb1 1
swift-ring-builder object.builder add r1z1-
172.16.0.224:6000/sdb1 1
swift-ring-builder object.builder add r1z1-
172.16.0.225:6000/sdb1 1
swift-ring-builder object.builder rebalance

# Container Ring
swift-ring-builder container.builder create 18 3 1
swift-ring-builder container.builder add r1z1-
172.16.0.221:6001/sdb1 1
swift-ring-builder container.builder add r1z1-
172.16.0.222:6001/sdb1 1
```

```
swift-ring-builder container.builder add r1z1-
172.16.0.223:6001/sdb1 1
swift-ring-builder container.builder add r1z1-
172.16.0.224:6001/sdb1 1
swift-ring-builder container.builder add r1z1-
172.16.0.225:6001/sdb1 1
swift-ring-builder container.builder rebalance

# Account Ring
swift-ring-builder account.builder create 18 3 1
swift-ring-builder account.builder add r1z1-
172.16.0.221:6002/sdb1 1
swift-ring-builder account.builder add r1z1-
172.16.0.222:6002/sdb1 1
swift-ring-builder account.builder add r1z1-
172.16.0.223:6002/sdb1 1
swift-ring-builder account.builder add r1z1-
172.16.0.224:6002/sdb1 1
swift-ring-builder account.builder add r1z1-
172.16.0.225:6002/sdb1 1
swift-ring-builder account.builder rebalance
```

2. Now, we can run the script as follows:

   ```
   sudo chmod +x /usr/local/bin/remakerings
   sudo /usr/local/bin/remakerings
   ```

   You will see an output similar to this:

```
Device d0r1z1-172.16.0.221:6000R172.16.0.221:6000/sdb1_"" with 1.0 weight got id 0
Device d1r1z1-172.16.0.222:6000R172.16.0.222:6000/sdb1_"" with 1.0 weight got id 1
Device d2r1z1-172.16.0.223:6000R172.16.0.223:6000/sdb1_"" with 1.0 weight got id 2
Device d3r1z1-172.16.0.224:6000R172.16.0.224:6000/sdb1_"" with 1.0 weight got id 3
Device d4r1z1-172.16.0.225:6000R172.16.0.225:6000/sdb1_"" with 1.0 weight got id 4
Reassigned 262144 (100.00%) partitions. Balance is now 0.00.
Device d0r1z1-172.16.0.221:6001R172.16.0.221:6001/sdb1_"" with 1.0 weight got id 0
Device d1r1z1-172.16.0.222:6001R172.16.0.222:6001/sdb1_"" with 1.0 weight got id 1
Device d2r1z1-172.16.0.223:6001R172.16.0.223:6001/sdb1_"" with 1.0 weight got id 2
Device d3r1z1-172.16.0.224:6001R172.16.0.224:6001/sdb1_"" with 1.0 weight got id 3
Device d4r1z1-172.16.0.225:6001R172.16.0.225:6001/sdb1_"" with 1.0 weight got id 4
Reassigned 262144 (100.00%) partitions. Balance is now 0.00.
Device d0r1z1-172.16.0.221:6002R172.16.0.221:6002/sdb1_"" with 1.0 weight got id 0
Device d1r1z1-172.16.0.222:6002R172.16.0.222:6002/sdb1_"" with 1.0 weight got id 1
Device d2r1z1-172.16.0.223:6002R172.16.0.223:6002/sdb1_"" with 1.0 weight got id 2
Device d3r1z1-172.16.0.224:6002R172.16.0.224:6002/sdb1_"" with 1.0 weight got id 3
Device d4r1z1-172.16.0.225:6002R172.16.0.225:6002/sdb1_"" with 1.0 weight got id 4
Reassigned 262144 (100.00%) partitions. Balance is now 0.00.
```

3. Once this has been completed (and this step can take a while), it creates three gzipped files in the `/etc/swift` directory called `/etc/swift/account.ring.gz`, `/etc/swift/container.ring.gz`, and `/etc/swift/object.ring.gz`. These files now need to be placed into the `/etc/swift` directory of all of our storage nodes.

Copy the `*.gz` files from the proxy server's `/etc/swift` directory to each of the storage node's `/etc/swift` directories.

How it works...

In Swift, a ring functions like a cereal box decoder ring. It keeps track of where various bits of data reside in a given Swift cluster. In our example, we have provided details for creating the rings, as well as executed a rebuild of said rings.

Creation of the rings is done using the `swift-ring-builder` command and involves the following steps, repeated for each ring type (object, container, and account):

1. To create the ring, we use the following syntax:

   ```
   swift-ring-builder builder_file create \
       part_power replicas min_part_hours
   ```

   This syntax specifies the builder file to create three parameters—`part_power`, `replicas`, and `min_part_hours`. This means `2^part_power` (18 is used in this instance) is the number of partitions to create, `replicas` are the number of replicas (3 is used in this case) of the data within the ring, and `min_part_hours` (1 is specified in this case) is the time in hours before a specific partition can be moved in succession.

2. To assign a device to a ring, we use the following syntax:

   ```
   swift-ring-builder builder_file add \
       zzone-ip:port/device_name weight
   ```

   Adding a node to the ring specifies the same `builder_file` created in the first step. We then specify a zone (for example, `1`, prefixed with `z`) that the device will be in; `ip (172.16.0.222)` is the IP address of the server that the device is in, `port` (for example, `6000`) is the port number that the server is running on, and `device_name` is the name of the device on the server (for example, `sdb1`). The weight is a float weight that determines how many partitions are put on the device, relative to the rest of the devices in the cluster.

3. A balanced Swift ring is one where the number of data exchanges between nodes is minimized, while still providing the configured number of replicas. A number of cases for rebalancing a Swift ring are provided in *Chapter 6, Using OpenStack Object Storage*, and *Chapter 7, Administering OpenStack Object Storage*. To rebalance the ring, we use the following syntax within the `/etc/swift` directory:

   ```
   swift-ring-builder builder_file rebalance
   ```

   The preceding command will distribute the partitions across the drives in the ring.

   The previous process is run for each of the rings—object, container, and account.

After the `swift-ring-builder` steps have finished, remember to copy the resultant `account.ring.gz`, `container.ring.gz`, and `object.ring.gz` files to each of the nodes in our environment, including other proxy servers we might have.

Stopping and starting OpenStack Object Storage

After OpenStack Object Storage services has been installed across all our nodes, it's time to start our services for storing objects and images in our OpenStack environment.

Getting ready

Ensure that you are logged in to all of the nodes and have the relevant packages installed and configured for running Swift. If you created this environment with `vagrant`, you can execute the following commands to access all the nodes:

```
vagrant ssh swift-proxy
vagrant ssh swift-01
vagrant ssh swift-02
vagrant ssh swift-03
vagrant ssh swift-04
vagrant ssh swift-05
```

How to do it...

Controlling OpenStack Object Storage services is achieved using the tool called `swift-init`. We can start, stop, and restart the various services on that node using this tool.

On the Object Storage nodes, we can start, stop, and restart all the services with the following commands:

```
sudo swift-init all start
sudo swift-init all stop
sudo swift-init all restart
```

On the proxy server node, we can start, stop, and restart the proxy service with the following commands:

```
sudo swift-init proxy-server start
sudo swift-init proxy-server stop
sudo swift-init proxy-server restart
```

On all the nodes, ensure that the services have all started with the `start` command.

How it works...

The OpenStack Object Storage services are simply started, stopped, and restarted using the following syntax:

```
sudo swift-init all {start, stop, restart}
sudo swift-init swift-proxy {start, stop, restart}
```

Setting up SSL access

Setting up **Secure Sockets Layer** (**SSL**) access provides secure access between the client and our OpenStack Object Storage environment in exactly the same way SSL provides secure access to any other web service. To do this, we configure our proxy server with *SSL certificates*.

In production, you wouldn't set up SSL directly on the proxy server. You would use a hardware Load Balancer or another appropriate device to do the SSL offloading. Setting up SSL as described in the following recipe is for testing and development purposes only.

Getting ready

Ensure that you are logged in to the `swift-proxy` node and have the packages installed and configured for running Swift. If you created this node with `vagrant`, you can execute the following command:

```
vagrant ssh swift-proxy
```

How to do it...

Configuration of OpenStack Object Storage to secure communication between the client and the proxy server is done as follows:

1. In order to provide SSL access to our proxy server, we first create the certificates:

   ```
   cd /etc/swift
   sudo openssl req -new -x509 -nodes -out cert.crt \
       -keyout cert.key
   ```

2. We need to answer the following questions that the certificate process asks us:

   ```
   Generating a 2048 bit RSA private key
   ....................+++
   ............................................................+++
   writing new private key to 'cert.key'
   -----
   You are about to be asked to enter information that will be incorporated
   into your certificate request.
   What you are about to enter is what is called a Distinguished Name or a DN.
   There are quite a few fields but you can leave some blank
   For some fields there will be a default value,
   If you enter '.', the field will be left blank.
   -----
   Country Name (2 letter code) [AU]:GB
   State or Province Name (full name) [Some-State]:.
   Locality Name (eg, city) []:
   Organization Name (eg, company) [Internet Widgits Pty Ltd]:Cookbook
   Organizational Unit Name (eg, section) []:
   Common Name (e.g. server FQDN or YOUR name) []:192.168.100.210
   Email Address []:
   ```

3. Once created, we configure our proxy server to use the certificate and key by editing the `/etc/swift/proxy-server.conf` file, as shown here:

   ```
   bind_port = 443
   cert_file = /etc/swift/cert.crt
   key_file = /etc/swift/cert.key
   ```

4. With this in place, we can restart the proxy server using the `swift-init` command to pick up the change:

   sudo swift-init proxy-server restart

5. We now need to update our Keystone endpoint to reflect this change. We do this by first removing the current entry, and then adding the endpoint with the change of details. First, source your environment variables so that you have admin privileges, or set the following:

```
export ENDPOINT=192.168.100.200
export SERVICE_TOKEN=ADMIN
export SERVICE_ENDPOINT=https://${ENDPOINT}:35357/v2.0
export OS_KEY=/vagrant/cakey.pem
export OS_CACERT=/vagrant/ca.pem
```

6. List the endpoints to verify the entry to remove by issuing the following command:

   keystone endpoint-list

   This will bring back output such as the following. The Swift endpoint has been highlighted and output truncated to fit the page.

id	region	publicurl
05e3619f45a24f8ba92cf49a6c56f222	RegionOne	http://172.16.0.211:8776/v1/%(tenant_id)s
144c754040a14ce29024298d9170956b	RegionOne	http://192.168.100.200:9696
3482d9ccfe2241699be53cdf2de86f28	RegionOne	https://192.168.100.200:5000/v2.0
7807ae8bf89e4b429012b095399bf13c	RegionOne	http://192.168.100.200:8773/services/Cloud
bd46a06576a3489ba9f9a8a7eaa2b2bd	RegionOne	http://swift-proxy:8080/v1/AUTH_$(tenant_id)s
caacafe99f304cc5a0ab4f786f25c048	RegionOne	http://192.168.100.200:9292/v2
d14fafa3f74f4a1fa77b91eb2d482d2c	RegionOne	http://192.168.100.200:8774/v2/$(tenant_id)s

7. To remove the Swift endpoint, execute the following command:

   keystone endpoint-delete bd46a06576a3489ba9f9a8a7eaa2b2bd

8. We then add in the correct endpoint with the new values:

```
PUBLIC_URL="https://192.168.100.209:443/v1/AUTH_\
$(tenant_id)s"

ADMIN_URL="https://172.16.0.209:443/v1"

INTERNAL_URL=="https://172.16.0.209:443/v1/AUTH_\
$(tenant_id)s"
```

```
keystone endpoint-create --region RegionOne \
    --service_id $SWIFT_SERVICE_ID \
    --publicurl $PUBLIC_URL \
    --adminurl $ADMIN_URL \
    --internalurl $INTERNAL_URL
```

How it works...

Configuring OpenStack Object Storage to use SSL involves configuring the proxy server to use SSL. We first configure a self-signed certificate using the `openssl` command, which asks for various fields to be filled in. An important field is the **Common Name** field. Put in the **Fully Qualified Domain Name** (**FQDN**) hostname or IP address that you would use to connect to the Swift server.

Once that has been done, we specify the port that we want our proxy server to listen on. As we are configuring an SSL HTTPS connection, we will use the standard TCP port 443 that HTTPS defaults to. We also specify the certificate and key that we created in the first step so that when a request is made, this information is presented to the end user to allow secure data transfer. With this in place, we restart our proxy server to listen on port 443.

Finally, we modify the entry in Keystone to reflect this change. To do this, we identify the endpoint ID of the Swift service by first list the endpoints. After this, we delete this endpoint with the `keystone endpoint-delete $ENDPOINT_ID` command and add in the correct ones, we ensure that we specify `https` and port `443`.

With this in place, we can carry on using Swift as usual and the end user won't need to modify anything to take advantage of this change.

6

Using OpenStack Object Storage

In this chapter, we will cover the following recipes:

- Installing the swift client tool
- Creating containers
- Uploading objects
- Uploading large objects
- Listing containers and objects
- Downloading objects
- Deleting containers and objects
- Using OpenStack Object Storage ACLs
- Using Container Synchronization between two Swift Clusters

Introduction

Now that we have an OpenStack Object Storage environment running, we can use it to store our files. To do this, we can use the `swift` client tool. This allows us to operate our OpenStack Object Storage environment by allowing us to create containers, upload files, retrieve them, and set required permissions on them, as appropriate.

Installing the swift client tool

In order to operate our OpenStack Object Storage environment, we need to install an appropriate tool on our client. Swift ships with the `swift` tool, which allows us to upload, download, and modify files in our OpenStack Object Storage environment.

Getting ready

Ensure you are logged in to a Ubuntu host that has access to our OpenStack environment on the `192.168.100.0/24` public network. This host will be used to run client tools against the OpenStack environment created. If you are using the accompanying Vagrant environment, you can use the `controller` node. It has the `python-swiftclient` package that provides the `swift` command-line client.

If you created this node with Vagrant, you can execute the following command:

```
vagrant ssh controller
```

Ensure you have set the following credentials (adjust the path to your certificates and key file to match your environment if not using the Vagrant environment):

```
export OS_TENANT_NAME=cookbook
export OS_USERNAME=admin
export OS_PASSWORD=openstack
export OS_AUTH_URL=https://192.168.100.200:5000/v2.0/
export OS_NO_CACHE=1
export OS_KEY=/vagrant/cakey.pem
export OS_CACERT=/vagrant/ca.pem
```

How to do it...

We download and install the `swift` client conveniently from the Ubuntu repositories using the familiar `apt-get` utility as follows:

1. Installation of the `swift` client is done by installing the swift package as well as requiring the `Python` libraries for the OpenStack Identity Service: Keystone. We do this using the following commands:

   ```
   sudo apt-get update
   sudo apt-get install python-swiftclient python-keystone
   ```

2. No further configuration is required. To test that you have successfully installed `swift` and can connect to your OpenStack Object Storage server, issue the following command:

   ```
   swift stat -v
   ```

3. This will output the statistics of our OpenStack Object Storage environment to which the `admin` user, who is a member of the `cookbook` tenant, has access. An example is shown in the following screenshot:

```
     StorageURL: http://swift-proxy:8080/v1/AUTH_51e03fdce75e4b088ad1713d95a59e6e
     Auth Token: ce6e955daf1d44d9afc353a0ff7d7d86
        Account: AUTH_51e03fdce75e4b088ad1713d95a59e6e
     Containers: 0
        Objects: 0
          Bytes: 0
   Content-Type: text/plain; charset=utf-8
    X-Timestamp: 1435349039.35466
     X-Trans-Id: tx7b4dd493da5747bbb6c0c-00558db02f
X-Put-Timestamp: 1435349039.35466
```

How it works...

The `swift` client package is easily installed under Ubuntu and it requires no further configuration after downloading as all parameters needed to communicate with OpenStack Object Storage using the command line.

Creating containers

A **container** can be thought of as a root folder under our OpenStack Object Storage. It allows for objects to be stored within it. Creating objects and containers can be achieved in a number of ways. A simple way is by using the `swift` client tool.

Getting ready

Ensure you are logged in to a Ubuntu host that has access to our OpenStack environment on the 192.168.100.0/24 public network. This host will be used to run client tools against the OpenStack environment created. If you are using the accompanying Vagrant environment, you can use the `controller` node. This node has the `python-swiftclient` package that provides the `swift` command-line client.

If you created this node with Vagrant, you can execute the following command:

```
vagrant ssh controller
```

Ensure you have set the following credentials (adjust the path to your certificates and key file to match your environment if not using the Vagrant environment):

```
export OS_TENANT_NAME=cookbook
export OS_USERNAME=admin
export OS_PASSWORD=openstack
export OS_AUTH_URL=https://192.168.100.200:5000/v2.0/
export OS_NO_CACHE=1
export OS_KEY=/vagrant/cakey.pem
export OS_CACERT=/vagrant/ca.pem
```

How to do it...

Carry out the following steps to create a container under OpenStack Object Storage:

1. To create a container named `test` under our OpenStack Object Storage server using the `swift` tool, we use the following command:

   ```
   swift post test
   ```

2. We can verify the creation of our container by listing the containers in our OpenStack Object Storage environment. To list containers, execute the following command:

   ```
   swift list test
   ```

   This will simply list the containers in our OpenStack Object Storage environment, as shown in the following section:

How it works...

Creation of containers using the supplied `swift` tool is very simple. The syntax uses the `post` parameter for this purpose:

```
swift post container_name
```

Uploading objects

Objects are the files or directories that are stored within a container. You can upload objects in a number of ways. A simple way is by using the `swift` client tool. This allows you to create, delete, and modify containers and objects in the OpenStack Object Storage environment. Individual objects up to 5 GB in size can be uploaded to OpenStack Object Storage using the methods described in this recipe.

Getting ready

Ensure you are logged in to a Ubuntu host that has access to our OpenStack environment on the 192.168.100.0/24 public network. This host will be used to run client tools against the OpenStack environment created. If you are using the accompanying Vagrant environment, as described in the *Preface*, you can use the `controller` node. This node has the `python-swiftclient` package that provides the `swift` command-line client.

If you created this node with Vagrant, you can execute the following command:

```
vagrant ssh controller
```

Ensure you have set the following credentials (adjust the path to your certificates and key file to match your environment if not using the Vagrant environment):

```
export OS_TENANT_NAME=cookbook
export OS_USERNAME=admin
export OS_PASSWORD=openstack
export OS_AUTH_URL=https://192.168.100.200:5000/v2.0/
export OS_NO_CACHE=1
export OS_KEY=/vagrant/cakey.pem
export OS_CACERT=/vagrant/ca.pem
```

How to do it...

Carry out the following steps to upload objects in our OpenStack Object Storage environment.

Uploading files

Use the following steps to upload files:

1. Create a 500 MB file under `/tmp` as an example file that will be uploaded:

   ```
   dd if=/dev/zero of=/tmp/example-500Mb bs=1M count=500
   ```

2. Upload this file to your OpenStack Object Storage account using the following command:

   ```
   swift upload test /tmp/example-500Mb
   ```

Uploading directories and their contents

Use the following steps to upload directories:

1. Create a directory and two files to upload to our OpenStack Object Storage environment:

```
mkdir /tmp/test
dd if=/dev/zero of=/tmp/test/test1 bs=1M count=20
dd if=/dev/zero of=/tmp/test/test2 bs=1M count=20
```

2. To upload directories and their contents, we issue the same command but just specify the directory. The files within the directory are recursively uploaded. The command is as follows:

```
swift upload test /tmp/test
```

Uploading multiple objects

We can upload a number of objects using a single command. To do this, we simply specify each of them on our command line. To upload our `test1` and `test2` files, we issue the following command:

```
swift upload test /tmp/test/test1 /tmp/another/test2
```

How it works...

Uploading files to our OpenStack Object Storage environment is simple with the help of the `swift` client tool. We can upload individual files or complete directories. The syntax is as follows:

```
swift upload container_name file|directory {file|directory … }
```

Note that, when uploading files, the objects that are created are of the form that we specify to the `swift` client, including the full paths. For example, uploading `/tmp/example-500Mb` uploads that object as `tmp/example-500Mb`. This is because OpenStack Object Storage is not the traditional tree-based hierarchical file system that our computers and desktops usually employ, where paths are delimited by a single slash (/ or \). OpenStack Object Storage consists of a flat set of objects that exist in containers where that slash forms the object name itself.

Uploading large objects

Individual objects up to 5 GB in size can be uploaded to OpenStack Object Storage. However, by splitting the objects into segments, the download size of a single object is virtually unlimited. Segments of the larger object are uploaded and a special manifest file is created that, when downloaded, sends all the segments concatenated as a single object. By splitting objects into smaller chunks, you also gain efficiency by allowing parallel uploads.

Getting ready

Ensure you are logged in to a Ubuntu host that has access to our OpenStack environment on the 192.168.100.0/24 public network. This host will be used to run client tools against the OpenStack environment created. If you are using the accompanying Vagrant environment, as described in the *Preface*, you can use the `controller` node. It has the `python-swiftclient` package that provides the `swift` command line client.

If you created this node with Vagrant, you can execute the following command:

```
vagrant ssh controller
```

Ensure you have set the following credentials (adjust the path to your certificates and key file to match your environment if not using the Vagrant environment):

```
export OS_TENANT_NAME=cookbook
export OS_USERNAME=admin
export OS_PASSWORD=openstack
export OS_AUTH_URL=https://192.168.100.200:5000/v2.0/
export OS_NO_CACHE=1
export OS_KEY=/vagrant/cakey.pem
export OS_CACERT=/vagrant/ca.pem
```

How to do it...

Carry out the following steps to upload large objects split into smaller segments:

1. Create a 1 GB file under `/tmp` as an example file to upload:

   ```
   dd if=/dev/zero of=/tmp/example-1Gb bs=1M count=1024
   ```

2. Rather than uploading this file as a single object, we will utilize segmenting to split this into smaller chunks (in this case, 100-MB segments). To do this, we specify the size of the segments with the `-S` option, as follows:

   ```
   swift upload test -S 102400000 /tmp/example-1Gb
   ```

Note that the size specified by the `-S` flag is specified in bytes.

You will see output similar to the following screenshot that shows the status of each upload:

```
tmp/example-1Gb segment 7
tmp/example-1Gb segment 5
tmp/example-1Gb segment 2
tmp/example-1Gb segment 0
tmp/example-1Gb segment 3
tmp/example-1Gb segment 6
tmp/example-1Gb segment 4
tmp/example-1Gb segment 10
tmp/example-1Gb segment 1
tmp/example-1Gb segment 8
tmp/example-1Gb segment 9
tmp/example-1Gb
```

How it works...

OpenStack Object Storage is very good at storing and retrieving large objects. To efficiently do this in our OpenStack Object Storage environment, we have the ability to split large objects into smaller objects with OpenStack Object Storage, maintaining this relationship between the segments and the objects that appear as a single file. This allows us to upload large objects in parallel, rather than streaming a single large file. To achieve this, we use the following syntax:

```
swift upload container_name -S bytes_to_split large_file
```

Now, when we list our containers under our account, we have an extra container named `test_segments` that holds the actual segmented data fragments for our file. Our test container holds the view that our large object is a single object. Behind the scenes, the metadata within this single object will pull back the individual objects from the `test_segments` container to reconstruct the large object. The command as follows:

```
swift list
```

When the preceding command is executed, we get the following output:

```
test
test_segments
```

Now execute the following command:

```
swift list test
```

The following output is generated:

```
tmp/example-1Gb
```

You can also inspect the segments by listing the `test_segments` container with the following command:

```
swift list test_segments
```

You will get the following output:

```
tmp/example-1Gb/1435350204.204782/1073741824/102400000/00000000
tmp/example-1Gb/1435350204.204782/1073741824/102400000/00000001
tmp/example-1Gb/1435350204.204782/1073741824/102400000/00000002
tmp/example-1Gb/1435350204.204782/1073741824/102400000/00000003
tmp/example-1Gb/1435350204.204782/1073741824/102400000/00000004
tmp/example-1Gb/1435350204.204782/1073741824/102400000/00000005
tmp/example-1Gb/1435350204.204782/1073741824/102400000/00000006
tmp/example-1Gb/1435350204.204782/1073741824/102400000/00000007
tmp/example-1Gb/1435350204.204782/1073741824/102400000/00000008
tmp/example-1Gb/1435350204.204782/1073741824/102400000/00000009
tmp/example-1Gb/1435350204.204782/1073741824/102400000/00000010
```

Listing containers and objects

The `swift` client tool allows you to easily list containers and objects within your OpenStack Object Storage account.

Getting ready

Ensure you are logged in to a Ubuntu host that has access to our OpenStack environment on the 192.168.100.0/24 public network. This host will be used to run client tools against the OpenStack environment created. If you are using the accompanying Vagrant environment, as described in the *Preface*, you can use the `controller` node. It has the `python-swiftclient` package that provides the `swift` command-line client.

If you created this node with Vagrant, you can execute the following command:

```
vagrant ssh controller
```

Ensure you have set the following credentials (adjust the path to your certificates and key file to match your environment if not using the Vagrant environment):

```
export OS_TENANT_NAME=cookbook
export OS_USERNAME=admin
export OS_PASSWORD=openstack
export OS_AUTH_URL=https://192.168.100.200:5000/v2.0/
export OS_NO_CACHE=1
export OS_KEY=/vagrant/cakey.pem
export OS_CACERT=/vagrant/ca.pem
```

How to do it...

Carry out the following to list objects within our OpenStack Object Storage environment.

Listing all objects in a container

Let's list all the objects in a container:

1. In the preceding recipes, we uploaded a small number of files. To simply list the objects within our `test` container, we issue the following command:

   ```
   swift list test
   ```

   The preceding command will give you an output like this:

   ```
   tmp/example-500Mb
   tmp/test/test1
   tmp/test/test2
   ```

Listing specific object paths in a container

Let's list all the specific object paths in a container:

1. To list just the files within the `tmp/test` path, we specify this with the `-p` parameter:

   ```
   swift list -p tmp/test test
   ```

   The preceding command will list our two files:

   ```
   tmp/test/test1
   tmp/test/test2
   ```

2. We can put partial matches in the `-p` parameter too. For example, we issue the following command to list all files starting with `tmp/ex`:

   ```
   swift list -p tmp/ex test
   ```

   The preceding command will list files that match the string we specified:

   ```
   tmp/example-500Mb
   ```

How it works...

The `swift` tool is a basic but versatile utility that allows us to do many of the things we want to do with files. Listing them in a way that suits the user is also possible. To simply list the contents of our container, use the following syntax:

```
swift list {container_name}
```

To list a file in a particular path within the container, we add in the `-p` parameter to the syntax:

```
swift list -p path {container_name}
```

Downloading objects

Now that we have configured OpenStack Object Storage, we can also retrieve the stored objects using our `swift` client.

Getting ready

Ensure you are logged in to a Ubuntu host that has access to our OpenStack environment on the 192.168.100.0/24 public network. This host will be used to run client tools against the OpenStack environment created. If you are using the accompanying Vagrant environment, as described in the *Preface*, you can use the `controller` node. This has the `python-swiftclient` package installed that provides the `swift` command-line client.

If you created this node with Vagrant, you can execute the following command:

```
vagrant ssh controller
```

Ensure you have set the following credentials (adjust the path to your certificates and key file to match your environment if not using the Vagrant environment):

```
export OS_TENANT_NAME=cookbook
export OS_USERNAME=admin
export OS_PASSWORD=openstack
export OS_AUTH_URL=https://192.168.100.200:5000/v2.0/
export OS_NO_CACHE=1
export OS_KEY=/vagrant/cakey.pem
export OS_CACERT=/vagrant/ca.pem
```

How to do it...

We will download objects from our OpenStack Object Storage environment using different `swift` client options.

Downloading objects

To download the `tmp/test/test1` object, we issue the following command:

```
swift download test tmp/test/test1
```

The preceding command downloads the object to our filesystem. As we downloaded a file with the full path, this directory structure is preserved. So, we end up with a new directory structure of `tmp/test` with a file called `test1`.

Downloading objects with the -o parameter

To download the file without preserving the file structure, or to simply rename it to something else, we specify the `-o` parameter:

```
swift download test tmp/test/test1 -o test1
```

Downloading all objects from a container

We can also download complete containers to our local filesystem. To do this, we simply specify the container we want to download:

```
swift download test
```

The preceding command will download all objects found under the `test` container.

Downloading all objects from our OpenStack Object Storage account

We can download all objects that reside under our OpenStack Object Storage account. If we have multiple containers, all objects from all containers will be downloaded. We do this with the `--all` parameter:

```
swift download --all
```

The preceding command will download all objects with full paths preceded by the container name, as shown here:

```
test/tmp/test/test1
test/tmp/test/test2
test/tmp/example-500Mb
```

How it works...

The `swift` client is a basic but versatile tool that allows us to do many of the things we want to do with files. You can download `objects` and `containers` using the following syntax:

```
swift download container_name {object … }
```

To download an object and rename the file on the local filesystem, we use the `-o` parameter to specify a different local filename:

```
swift download container_name object -o renamed_object
```

To download all `objects` from our account (for example, from all containers), we specify the following syntax:

```
swift download --all
```

Deleting containers and objects

The `swift` client tool allows us to directly delete containers and objects within our OpenStack Object Storage environment.

Getting ready

Ensure you are logged in to a Ubuntu host that has access to our OpenStack environment on the 192.168.100.0/24 public network. This host will be used to run client tools against the OpenStack environment created. If you are using the accompanying Vagrant environment, as described in the *Preface*, you can use the `controller` node. It has the `python-swiftclient` package that provides the `swift` command-line client.

If you created this node with Vagrant, you can execute the following command:

```
vagrant ssh controller
```

Ensure you have set the following credentials (adjust the path to your certificates and key file to match your environment if not using the Vagrant environment):

```
export OS_TENANT_NAME=cookbook
export OS_USERNAME=admin
export OS_PASSWORD=openstack
export OS_AUTH_URL=https://192.168.100.200:5000/v2.0/
export OS_NO_CACHE=1
export OS_KEY=/vagrant/cakey.pem
export OS_CACERT=/vagrant/ca.pem
```

How to do it...

We will delete objects in our OpenStack Object Storage environment using different `swift` client options.

Deleting objects

To delete the object `tmp/test/test1`, we issue the following command:

```
swift delete test tmp/test/test1
```

This deletes the `tmp/test/test1` object from the `test` container.

Deleting multiple objects

To delete the `tmp/test/test2` and `tmp/example-500Mb` objects, we issue the following command:

```
swift delete test tmp/test/test2 tmp/example-500Mb
```

This deletes the `tmp/test/test2` and `tmp/example-500Mb` objects from the `test` container.

Deleting containers

To delete our `test` container, we issue the following command:

```
swift delete test
```

This will delete the *container*, any *objects* under this container, and any segment objects if the object was split when originally uploaded.

Deleting everything from our account

To delete all containers and objects in our account, we issue the following command:

```
swift delete --all
```

This will delete *all* containers and any objects under these containers.

How it works...

The `swift` client is a basic but versatile tool that allows us to do many of the things we want to do with files. You can delete objects and containers using the following syntax:

```
swift delete {container_name} {object … }
```

To download all objects from our account (for example, from all containers), we use the following syntax:

```
swift delete --all
```

Using OpenStack Object Storage ACLs

Access Control Lists (**ACLs**) allow us to have greater control over individual objects and containers without requiring full read/write access to a particular container. With ACLs, you can expose containers globally or restrict them to individual tenants and users.

Getting ready

Ensure you are logged in to a Ubuntu host that has access to our OpenStack environment on the 192.168.100.0/24 public network. This host will be used to run client tools against the OpenStack environment created. If you are using the accompanying Vagrant environment, as described in the *Preface*, you can use the `controller` node. It has the `python-swiftclient` package installed that provides the `swift` command-line client.

If you created this node with Vagrant, you can execute the following command:

```
vagrant ssh controller
```

Ensure you have set the following credentials (adjust the path to your certificates and key file to match your environment if not using the Vagrant environment):

```
export OS_TENANT_NAME=cookbook
export OS_USERNAME=admin
export OS_PASSWORD=openstack
export OS_AUTH_URL=https://192.168.100.200:5000/v2.0/
export OS_NO_CACHE=1
export OS_KEY=/vagrant/cakey.pem
export OS_CACERT=/vagrant/ca.pem
```

How to do it...

Carry out the following steps:

1. We will first create an account in our OpenStack Identity Server that is only a `Member` in the cookbook `tenant`. We will call this user `user`. The code is as follows:

   ```
   export ENDPOINT=192.168.100.200
   export SERVICE_TOKEN=ADMIN
   export SERVICE_ENDPOINT=https://${ENDPOINT}:35357/v2.0
   export OS_KEY=/vagrant/cakey.pem
   ```

```
export OS_CACERT=/vagrant/ca.pem

# First get TENANT_ID related to our 'cookbook' tenant
TENANT_ID=$(keystone tenant-list \
    | awk ' / cookbook / {print $2}')

# We then create the user specifying the TENANT_ID
keystone user-create \
    --name test_user \
    --tenant_id $TENANT_ID \
    --pass openstack \
    --email user@localhost \
    --enabled true

# We get this new user's ID
USER_ID=$(keystone user-list | awk ' / user / {print $2}')

# We get the ID of the 'Member' role
ROLE_ID=$(keystone role-list \
    | awk ' / Member / {print $2}')

# Finally add the user to the 'Member' role in cookbook
keystone user-role-add \
    --user $USER_ID \
    --role $ROLE_ID \
    --tenant_id $TENANT_ID
```

2. After creating our new user, we will now create a container using a user that has admin privileges (and therefore a container that our new user initially doesn't have access to), as follows:

   swift post testACL

3. We will then set this container to be read-only for our user named `test_user`:

   swift post -r test_user testACL

4. We will upload a file to this container using our new user:

   swift upload testACL /tmp/test/test1

This brings back an "HTTP 403 Forbidden" message similar like this:

```
Object HEAD failed: https://proxy-server:8080/v1/AUTH_53d87d9b6679
4904aa2c84c17274392b/testACL/tmp/test/test1 403 Forbidden
```

5. We will now give write access to the `testACL` container for our user by allowing write access to the container:

```
swift post -w test_user -r test_user testACL
```

6. When we try to upload the file again, it is successful:

```
swift upload testACL /tmp/test/test1
```

How it works

Granting access control is done on a *container* basis and is achieved at the *user* level. When a user creates a container, other users can be granted that access by adding them to the container. The users will then be granted read and write access to containers, for example:

```
swift post -w user -r user container
```

Using Container Synchronization between two Swift Clusters

Replicating container content from one Swift Cluster to another in a remote location is a useful feature for disaster recovery and running active/active datacenters. This feature allows a user to upload objects as normal to a particular container, and have those contents upload to a nominated container in a remote cluster automatically.

Getting ready

Ensure you are logged in to both swift proxy servers that will be used for the replication. An example of this feature can be found with the Swift Vagrant environment at `https://github.com/OpenStackCookbook/VagrantSwift`. If you created these nodes with this environment, ensure that you have both `swift` and `swift2` running and you have a shell on both by executing the following command:

```
vagrant ssh swift
vagrant ssh swift2
```

How to do it...

To set up Container Sync replication, carry out the following steps:

1. On both Proxy Servers, edit `/etc/swift/proxy-server.conf` to add in the `container_sync` to the pipeline:

   ```
   [pipeline:main]
   # Order of execution of modules defined below
   pipeline = catch_errors healthcheck cache container_sync authtoken
   keystone proxy-server
   [filter:container_sync]
   use = egg:swift#container_sync
   ```

2. On each Proxy Server, create `/etc/swift/container-sync-realms.conf` with the following contents:

   ```
   [realm1]
   key = realm1key
   cluster_swift = http://swift:8080/v1/
   cluster_swift2 = http://swift2:8080/v1/
   ```

3. On each Proxy Server, issue the following command to pick up the changes:

   ```
   swift-init proxy-server restart
   ```

4. On the first Swift cluster (`swift`), identify the account on the second cluster (`swift2`), where the first cluster will sync:

   ```
   swift --insecure -V2.0 -A https://swift2:5000/v2.0
       -U cookbook:admin
       -K openstack
   ```

   The preceding command shows an output similar to the following (note the `Account:` line):

   ```
           Account: AUTH_d81683a9a2dd46cf9cac88c5b8eaca1a
        Containers: 0
           Objects: 0
             Bytes: 0
      Content-Type: text/plain; charset=utf-8
       X-Timestamp: 1421140955.13054
        X-Trans-Id: tx32e023c22538426096070-0054b4e3db
   X-Put-Timestamp: 1421140955.13054
   ```

Note that we're using the `--insecure` flag on this command as `Swift2` is running a self-signed certificate and we don't have access to the generated CA file from our Swift node. If you copy this file across so it is accessible, you can omit this flag.

5. Set up a container called `container1` on the first `swift` cluster that synchronizes content to a container called `container2` on the second cluster, `swift2`:

```
swift -V2.0 -A https://controller:5000/v2.0
    -U cookbook:admin -K openstack post
    -t '//realm1/swift2/AUTH_d81683a9a2dd46cf9cac88c5b8eaca1a/
container2'
    -k 'myKey' container1
```

6. Set up the `container2` container referenced in the previous step on the second cluster that can also synchronize content back to `container1` on the first cluster (two-way sync) as follows. Note that we're running this command from the node called `swift` and remotely creating the container on `swift2`:

```
swift --insecure -V2.0 -A https://swift2:5000/v2.0
    -U cookbook:admin
    -K openstack
    post container2
```

7. Upload a file to `container1` on `swift1`:

```
swift -V2.0 -A https://controller:5000/v2.0
    -U cookbook:admin -K openstack
    upload container1 my_example_file
```

8. You can now view the contents on `container2` on `swift2` that will show the same files listed in `container1` on `swift`.

If the file hasn't appeared yet on `container2` on the second `swift` cluster, run the following:

`swift-init` container-sync once

How it works...

Container Synchronization is an excellent feature when multiple datacenters are running and our disaster recovery plan requires data to be kept consistent in each datacenter. Container sync operates at the container level, so we can control where our data is synced to.

To enable this feature, we modify the pipeline in the `/etc/swift/proxy-server.conf` file to notify Swift to run Container Sync jobs.

Once configured, we create a file called `/etc/swift/container-sync-realms.conf` that has the following structure:

```
[realm_name]
key = realm_name_key
cluster_name_of_cluster = http://swift1_proxy_server:8080/v1/
cluster_name_of_cluster2 = http://swift2_proxy_server:8080/v1/
```

This structure is important and is referenced when we create the synchronization on the containers shown in the following syntax:

```
swift post
    -t '//realm_name/name_of_cluster2/AUTH_UUID/container_name'
    -k 'mykey' container_name_to_be_syncd
```

The `AUTH_UUID` comes from the following command shown that gives us the Swift account associated with the user on the remote (receiving) Swift:

```
swift -V2.0 -A https://cluster2:5000/v2.0
    -U tenant:user -K password
    stat
```

The key is then used—along with the key references in the `/etc/swift/container-sync-realms.conf` file—to create our shared secret that is used for authentication between the containers.

As a result of this configuration, when we upload a file to the container created on our first cluster that has been instructed to sync with the second, the file will automatically sync in the background.

There's more...

Container Synchronization is one approach that allows different Swift clusters to replicate data between them. Another approach is using Global Clusters. For more information, visit `https://swiftstack.com/blog/2013/07/02/swift-1-9-0-release/`.

7
Administering OpenStack Object Storage

In this chapter, we will cover the following recipes:

- Managing the OpenStack Object Storage clusters with swift-init
- Checking cluster health
- Managing the Swift cluster capacity
- Removing nodes from a cluster
- Detecting and replacing failed hard drives
- Collecting usage statistics

Introduction

Day-to-day administration of our OpenStack Object Storage cluster involves ensuring that the files within the cluster are replicated to the right number of nodes, reporting on usage within the cluster, and dealing with any failures with the cluster. This chapter builds upon the work done in *Chapters 6, Using OpenStack Object Storage*, to show you the tools and processes required to administer OpenStack Object Storage.

Managing the OpenStack Object Storage cluster with swift-init

Services in our OpenStack Object Storage environment can be managed using the `swift-init` tool. This tool allows us to control all the daemons in OpenStack Object Storage in a convenient way. For information on installing and configuring the Swift services or daemons, see *Chapter 5, Swift – OpenStack Object Storage*.

Getting ready

Login to any OpenStack Object Storage node. If using the `vagrant` environment, these can be accessed by using the following commands:

```
vagrant ssh swift-proxy

vagrant ssh swift-01

vagrant ssh swift-02

vagrant ssh swift-03

vagrant ssh swift-04

vagrant ssh swift-05
```

How to do it...

The `swift-init` tool can be used to control any of the running daemons in our OpenStack Object Storage cluster rather than calling individual `init` scripts, which makes it a convenient tool.

To control OpenStack Object Storage proxy, use the following command:

```
swift-init proxy-server { command }
```

To control OpenStack Object Storage object daemons, use the following commands:

```
swift-init object { command }
swift-init object-replicator {command }
swift-init object-auditor { command }
swift-init object-updater { command }
```

To control OpenStack Object Storage container daemons, use the following commands:

```
swift-init container { command }
swift-init container-update { command }
swift-init container-replicator { command }
swift-init container-auditor { command }
```

To control OpenStack Object Storage account daemons, use the following commands:

```
swift-init account { command }
swift-init account-auditor { command }
swift-init account-reaper { command }
swift-init account-replicator { command }
```

To control all daemons, use the following command:

```
swift-init all { command }
```

The { `command` } term can be one of the following:

Command	Description
`stop`, `start`, and `restart`	As stated, the `start` and `stop` commands are used to `start` and `stop` the daemon objects. The `restart` command will include both functions of the `stop` and `start` commands successively.
`force-reload` and `reload`	A graceful shutdown and restart.
`shutdown`	Shutdown after waiting for current processes to finish.
`no-daemon`	Start a server within the current shell.
`no-wait`	Spawn server and return immediately.
`once`	Start server and run one pass.
`status`	Display the status of the processes for the server.

How it works...

The `swift-init` tool is a single tool that can be used to manage any of the running OpenStack Object Storage daemons. This allows for consistency in managing our cluster.

There's more...

Explanation of the various features and services of Swift can be found at `http://docs.openstack.org/developer/swift/admin_guide.html`.

Checking cluster health

We can measure the health of our cluster by using the `swift-dispersion-report` tool. This is done by checking the set of our distributed containers to ensure that the objects are in their proper places within the cluster.

Getting ready

Ensure you are logged in to the `swift-proxy` nodes. If you created this node with Vagrant, you can access it by using the following command:

```
vagrant ssh swift-proxy
```

How to do it...

Carry out the following steps to set up the `swift-dispersion` tool to report on cluster health:

1. We create the configuration file (`/etc/swift/dispersion.conf`) required by the `swift-dispersion` tool, as follows:

```
[dispersion]
auth_url = https://192.168.100.200:5000/v2.0
auth_user = cookbook:admin
auth_key = openstack
auth_version = 2.0
keystone_api_insecure = yes
```

We're using `keystone_api_insecure` in this environment because we are using a self-signed certificate for our keystone endpoint. This skips the validation of the certificate.

2. Now, we need to create containers and objects throughout our cluster so that they are in distinct places. We use the `swift-dispersion-populate` tool, as follows:

```
sudo swift-dispersion-populate
```

This produces an output similar to the following:

```
Created 2621 containers for dispersion reporting, 1m, 0 retries
Created 2621 objects for dispersion reporting, 2m, 0 retries
```

3. Once these containers and objects have been set up, we can run `swift-dispersion-report`:

   `sudo swift-dispersion-report`

   This produces the following report output:

```
Querying containers: 1101 of 2622, 37s left, 0 retries

Queried 2622 containers for dispersion reporting, 1m, 0 retries
100.00% of container copies found (7866 of 7866)
Sample represents 1.00% of the container partition space
Queried 2621 objects for dispersion reporting, 30s, 0 retries
There were 2621 partitions missing 0 copy.
100.00% of object copies found (7863 of 7863)
Sample represents 1.00% of the object partition space
```

4. We then set up a `cron` job that repeatedly checks the health of these containers and objects:

```
echo "/usr/bin/swift-dispersion-report" \
    | sudo tee -a /etc/cron.hourly/swift-dispersion-report
```

How it works...

The health of objects can be measured by checking whether the replicas are correct. If our OpenStack Object Storage cluster replicates an object three times and two of these three objects are in the correct place, the object would be 66.66 percent healthy.

To ensure we have enough replicated objects in our cluster, we populate it with the `swift-dispersion-populate` tool, which creates 2,621 containers and objects, thereby increasing our cluster size. Once in place, we can then set up a `cron` job that will run hourly to ensure our cluster is consistent which therefore gives a good indication whether our cluster is healthy.

By setting up a `cron` job on our proxy node (which has access to all our nodes), we can constantly measure the health of our entire cluster. In our example, the `cron` job runs hourly, executing the `swift-dispersion-report` tool.

Managing the Swift cluster capacity

A **zone** is a group of nodes that is as isolated as possible from other nodes (separate servers, network, power, and geography). A Swift **ring** function similar to a cereal box decoder ring, allowing the Swift services to locate each object. The ring guarantees that every replica is stored in a separate zone. To increase the capacity of our environment, we can add an extra zone to which data will then be replicated. In this example, we will add an extra storage node with `172.16.0.212` as its IP address and `/dev/sdb` as its second disk. This node will be used for our OpenStack Object Storage. This node makes up the only node in this zone.

To add additional capacity to existing zones, we repeat the instructions for each existing zone in our cluster. For example, the following steps assume that zone 5 (`z5`) does not exist, so this gets created when we build the rings. To simply add additional capacity to existing zones, we specify the new servers in the existing zones (zones 1-4). The instructions remain the same throughout.

Getting ready

Ensure you are logged in to the `swift-proxy` nodes. If you created this node with Vagrant, you can access it by issuing the following command:

```
vagrant ssh swift-proxy
```

How to do it...

To add an extra zone to our OpenStack Object Storage cluster, carry out the following steps:

1. Create a proxy server.
2. Create a storage node.

Proxy server creation

To create a proxy server, follow these steps:

1. Add the following entries to the ring, where `STORAGE_LOCAL_NET_IP` is the IP address of our new node and `ZONE` is our new zone:

> Ensure that you run these commands while in the `/etc/swift` directory.

```
cd /etc/swift

ZONE=5
STORAGE_LOCAL_NET_IP=172.16.0.212
WEIGHT=100
DEVICE=sdb1

swift-ring-builder account.builder add z$ZONE-
$STORAGE_LOCAL_NET_IP:6002/$DEVICE $WEIGHT
swift-ring-builder container.builder add z$ZONE-
$STORAGE_LOCAL_NET_IP:6001/$DEVICE $WEIGHT
swift-ring-builder object.builder add z$ZONE-
$STORAGE_LOCAL_NET_IP:6000/$DEVICE $WEIGHT
```

2. We need to verify the contents of the rings by issuing the following commands:

```
swift-ring-builder account.builder
swift-ring-builder container.builder
swift-ring-builder object.builder
```

3. Finally, we rebalance the rings, which could take some time to run:

```
swift-ring-builder account.builder rebalance
swift-ring-builder container.builder rebalance
swift-ring-builder object.builder rebalance
```

4. Then, we need to copy `account.ring.gz`, `container.ring.gz` and `object.ring.gz` in our new storage node and all other storage nodes:

```
scp *.ring.gz $STORAGE_LOCAL_NET_IP:/tmp
# And other scp to other storage nodes
```

Storage node creation

To create a storage node, follow these steps:

1. We first move the copied `account.ring.gz`, `container.ring.gz`, and `object.ring.gz` files to the `/etc/swift` directory and ensure they're owned by `swift`:

```
mv /tmp/*.ring.gz /etc/swift
chown swift:swift /etc/swift/*.ring.gz
```

   Prepare the storage on this node, as described in the *Configuring physical storage for use with Swift* recipe in *Chapter 5, Swift – OpenStack Object Storage*.

2. Edit the /etc/swift/swift.conf file so that the [swift-hash] section is similar on all nodes, as shown here:

```
[swift-hash]
# Random unique string used on all nodes
swift_hash_path_prefix=a4rUmUIgJYXpKhbh
swift_hash_path_suffix=NESuuUEqc6OXwy6X
```

3. We now need to create the appropriate /etc/rsyncd.conf file with the following content:

```
uid = swift
gid = swift
log file = /var/log/rsyncd.log
pid file = /var/run/rsyncd.pid
address = 172.16.0.212

[account]
max connections = 2
path = /srv/node/
read only = false
lock file = /var/lock/account.lock

[container]
max connections = 2
path = /srv/node/
read only = false
lock file = /var/lock/container.lock

[object]
max connections = 2
path = /srv/node/
read only = false
lock file = /var/lock/object.lock
```

4. Enable and start rsync with the following commands:

```
sed -i 's/=false/=true/' /etc/default/rsync
service rsync start
```

5. We need to create the /etc/swift/account-server.conf file with the following content:

```
[DEFAULT]
bind_ip = 172.16.0.212
workers = 2

[pipeline:main]
```

```
pipeline = account-server

[app:account-server]
use = egg:swift#account

[account-replicator]

[account-auditor]

[account-reaper]
```

6. Create the `/etc/swift/container-server.conf` file with the following content:

```
[DEFAULT]
bind_ip = 172.16.0.212
workers = 2

[pipeline:main]
pipeline = container-server

[app:container-server]
use = egg:swift#container

[container-replicator]

[container-updater]

[container-auditor]
```

7. Finally, create the `/etc/swift/object-server.conf` file with the following content:

```
[DEFAULT]
bind_ip = 172.16.0.212
workers = 2

[pipeline:main]
pipeline = object-server

[app:object-server]
use = egg:swift#object

[object-replicator]

[object-updater]

[object-auditor]
```

8. We can now start this storage node, which we have configured to be in our fifth zone, as follows:

   ```
   swift-init all start
   ```

How it works...

Adding extra capacity by adding additional nodes or zones is done in the following two steps:

1. Configure the zones and nodes on the proxy server.
2. Configure the storage node(s).

For each storage node and the devices on those storage nodes, we run the following command to add the storage node and device to our new zone:

```
swift-ring-builder account.builder add zzone-storage_ip:6002/device
weight
swift-ring-builder container.builder add zzone-storage_ip:6001/device
weight
swift-ring-builder object.builder add zzone-storage_ip:6000/device
weight
```

Once this has been configured on our proxy node, we rebalance the rings. This updates the object, account, and container rings. We copy the updated gzipped files, as well as the Swift hash key used within our environment for all our storage node(s).

On the storage node, we simply run through the following steps:

1. Configure the disk (partition and format with `XFS`).
2. Configure and start `rsyncd`.
3. Configure the account, container, and object services.
4. Start the OpenStack Object Storage services on the storage node(s).

Data is then redistributed within our OpenStack Object Storage environment onto this new zone's node.

Removing nodes from a cluster

There may be times when we need to scale back or remove a failed node from for service. We can do this by removing nodes from the zones in our cluster. In the following example, we will remove the node `172.16.0.212` in `z5`, which only has one storage device attached, which is `/dev/sdb1`.

Getting ready

Ensure you are logged in to the `swift-proxy` nodes. If you created this node with Vagrant, you can access it by issuing the following command:

```
vagrant ssh swift-proxy
```

How to do it...

To remove a storage node from a zone, you need to make changes in the proxy server configuration, which is highlighted in the next section.

Proxy Server

We need to make changes in our proxy server configuration by following these steps:

1. To remove a node from OpenStack Object Storage, we first set its `weight` parameter to `0` so that data is drained away from this node when the rings get rebalanced:

   ```
   cd /etc/swift


   swift-ring-builder account.builder set_weight z5-
   172.16.0.212:6002/sdb1 0
   swift-ring-builder container.builder set_weight z5-
   172.16.0.212:6001/sdb1 0
   swift-ring-builder object.builder set_weight z5-
   172.16.0.212:6000/sdb1 0
   ```

2. We then rebalance the rings as follows:

   ```
   swift-ring-builder account.builder rebalance
   swift-ring-builder container.builder rebalance
   swift-ring-builder object.builder rebalance
   ```

3. Once this is done, we can remove the node in this zone from the ring using the following commands:

   ```
   swift-ring-builder account.builder remove z5-
   172.16.0.212:6002/sdb1
   swift-ring-builder container.builder remove z5-
   172.16.0.212:6001/sdb1
   swift-ring-builder object.builder remove z5-
   172.16.0.212:6000/sdb1
   ```

4. We then copy the resulting `account.ring.gz`, `container.ring.gz`, and `object.ring.gz` files over to the rest of nodes in our cluster. We are now free to decommission this storage node by physically removing this device.

How it works...

Manually removing a node from our OpenStack Object Storage cluster is done in three steps:

1. Set the node's `weight` parameter to `0`, so data isn't being replicated to it, by using the `swift-ring-builder <ring> set_weight` command.
2. Rebalance the rings to update the data replication.
3. Remove the node from the OpenStack Object Storage cluster using the `swift-ring-builder <ring> remove` command. Once done, we are then free to decommission that node. We repeat this for each node (or device) in the zone.

Detecting and replacing failed hard drives

OpenStack Object Storage won't be of much use if it cannot access the hard drives where our data is stored; therefore, being able to detect and replace failed hard drives is essential. OpenStack Object Storage can be configured to detect hard drive failures with the `swift-drive-audit` command. This will allow us to detect failures so that we can replace the failed hard drive, which is essential to the system health and performance.

Getting ready

Ensure that you are logged in to the `swift-proxy` nodes. If you created this node with Vagrant, you can access it by issuing the following commands:

```
vagrant ssh swift-proxy
vagrant ssh swift-01
```

How to do it...

To detect a failing hard drive, carry out the following steps:

Storage node

We need to follow these steps to make changes in our storage node:

1. We first need to configure a `cron` job that monitors `/var/log/kern.log` for failed disk errors on our storage nodes. To do this, we create a configuration file named `/etc/swift/swift-drive-audit.conf` as follows:

   ```
   [drive-audit]
   log_facility=LOG_LOCAL0
   log_level=INFO
   ```

```
device_dir=/srv/node
minutes=60
error_limit=1
```

2. We then add a `cron` job that executes `swift-drive-audit` hourly, or as often as needed for your environment:

   ```
   echo '/usr/bin/swift-drive-audit /etc/swift/swift-drive-audit.conf' | sudo tee -a /etc/cron.hourly/swift-drive-audit
   ```

3. With this in place, when a drive has been detected as faulty, the script will unmount it so that OpenStack Object Storage can work around the issue. Therefore, when a disk has been marked as faulty and taken offline, you can now replace it.

> Without `swift-drive-audit` taking care of this automatically, you would have to manually to ensure that the disk has been dismounted and removed from the ring.

4. Once the disk has been physically replaced, we can follow the instructions described in the *Managing the Swift cluster capacity* recipe in this chapter to add our node or device back into our cluster.

How it works...

Detection of failed hard drives can be picked up automatically by the `swift-drive-audit` tool, which we set up as a `cron` job to run hourly. This looks in `/var/log/kern.log` for any drive failures. By default, Ubuntu 14.04 logs hardware system information to this file. With this in place, it detects failures, unmounts the drive so that it cannot be used, and updates the ring so that data isn't being stored or replicated to it.

Once the drive has been removed from the rings, we can run maintenance on that device and replace the drive.

With a new drive in place, we can then put the device back in service on the storage node by adding it back into the rings. We can then rebalance the rings by running the `swift-ring-builder` commands.

Collecting usage statistics

OpenStack Object Storage can report on usage metrics by using the `swift-recon` middleware added to our `object-server` configuration. By using a tool named `swift-recon`, we can then query these collected metrics.

Getting ready

Ensure that you are logged in to all of the nodes and have the relevant packages installed and configured for running Swift. If you created this environment with Vagrant, you can execute the following commands to access all the nodes:

```
vagrant ssh swift-proxy

vagrant ssh swift-01

vagrant ssh swift-02

vagrant ssh swift-03

vagrant ssh swift-04

vagrant ssh swift-05
```

How to do it...

To collect usage statistics from our OpenStack Object Storage cluster, carry out the following steps:

1. We first need to modify our `/etc/swift/object-server.conf` configuration file on storage nodes to include the `swift-recon` middleware, so that it looks similar to the following:

   ```
   [DEFAULT]
   bind_ip = 0.0.0.0
   workers = 2

   [pipeline:main]
   pipeline = recon object-server

   [app:object-server]
   use = egg:swift#object

   [object-replicator]

   [object-updater]

   [object-auditor]

   [filter:recon]
   use = egg:swift#recon
   recon_cache_path = /var/cache/swift
   ```

In the example vagrant environment, we are running a number of Swift nodes collapsed into a single host. As such, we need to edit each of the simulated node object-server configuration files in `/etc/swift/object-server/` directory.

2. Once this is in place, we simply restart our `object-server` service using `swift-init`:

   ```
   swift-init object-server restart
   ```

Now that the command is running, we can use the `swift-recon` tool on the proxy server to get usage statistics:

- Disk usage:

  ```
  swift-recon -d
  ```

  The preceding command will report on disk usage in our cluster.

  ```
  swift-recon -d -z5
  ```

  The preceding command will report on disk usage in zone 5.

- Load average:

  ```
  swift-recon -l
  ```

  The preceding command will report on the load average in our cluster.

  ```
  swift-recon -l -z5
  ```

  The preceding command will report on load average of the nodes in zone 5.

- Quarantined statistics:

  ```
  swift-recon -q
  ```

  The preceding command will report on any quarantined containers, objects, and accounts in the cluster.

  ```
  swift-recon -q -z5
  ```

  The preceding command will report on this information for zone 5 only.

- Check for unmounted devices:

  ```
  swift-recon -u
  ```

  The preceding command will check for any unmounted drives in our cluster.

  ```
  swift-recon -z5 -u
  ```

  The preceding command will work the same way for zone 5 only.

- Check replication metrics:

  ```
  swift-recon -r
  ```

  The preceding command will report on replication status within our cluster.

  ```
  swift-recon -r -z5
  ```

  The preceding command will just perform this for nodes in zone 5.

  We can perform all these actions with a single command to get all telemetry data back about our cluster:

  ```
  swift-recon --all
  ```

  We can just get this information for nodes within zone 5 by adding `-z5` at the end, as follows:

  ```
  swift-recon --all -z5
  ```

  Finally, you can also check for any asynchronous pending objects in our environment by running a `cron` job periodically. This `cron` job can be set up as follows:

  ```
  */5 * * * * swift /usr/bin/swift-recon-cron /etc/swift/object-server.conf
  ```

How it works...

To enable usage statistics within OpenStack Object Storage, we add in the `swift-recon` middleware so that metrics are collected. We add this to the object server by adding the following lines to `/etc/swift/object-server.conf` on each of our storage nodes:

```
[pipeline:main]
pipeline = recon object-server

[filter:recon]
use = egg:swift#recon
recon_cache_path = /var/cache/swift
```

With this in place and our object servers restarted, we can query this telemetry data by using the `swift-recon` tool. We can collect the statistics from the cluster as a whole, or from specific zones with the `-z` parameter.

Note that we can also collect all or multiple statistics by specifying the `--all` flag or appending multiple flags to the command line. For example, to collect load average and replication statistics from our nodes in zone 5, we would execute the following command:

```
swift-recon -r -l -z5
```

8
Cinder – OpenStack Block Storage

In this chapter, we will cover the following recipes:

- Configuring Cinder-volume services
- Configuring OpenStack Compute for Cinder-volume
- Creating volumes
- Attaching volumes to an instance
- Detaching volumes from an instance
- Deleting volumes
- Configuring third-party volume services
- Working with Cinder snapshots
- Booting from volumes

Introduction

Data written to currently running instances on disks is not persistent—when you terminate such instances, any disk writes will be lost. Volumes are persistent storage that you can attach to your running OpenStack `compute` instances; the best analogy is that of a USB drive that you can attach to an instance. Similar to USB drives, you can only attach instances to one computer at a time.

In prior OpenStack releases, volume services were provided by `nova-volume`, which has evolved over time into OpenStack Block Storage; that is, **Cinder**. OpenStack Block Storage is very similar to *Amazon EC2's Elastic Block Storage*—the difference is in how volumes are presented to the running instances. In OpenStack `compute`, volumes can easily be managed using an iSCSI-exposed LVM volume group named `cinder-volumes`. So, this iSCSI volume group must be present on any host running the Cinder volume service.

At times, managing OpenStack Block Storage can be confusing as Cinder volume is the running service name, and `cinder-volumes` is the name of the LVM volume group that is exposed by the `cinder-volumes` service.

In this chapter, we will be adding an additional node to run our OpenStack Block Storage services. The following diagram describes this environment and where Cinder fits:

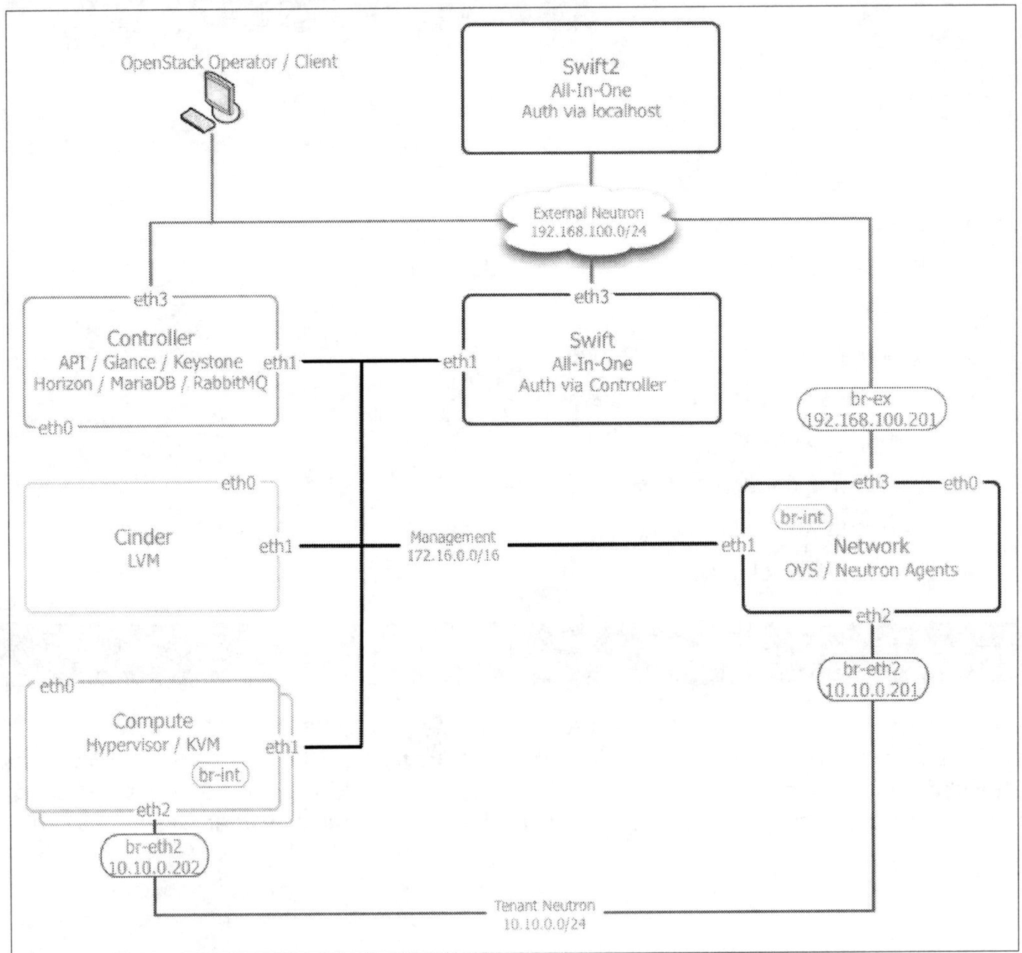

Configuring Cinder-volume services

In this recipe, we will configure an additional server running Ubuntu 14.04 LTS to host the volumes, and we'll explore the prerequisites of Cinder-volume when it comes to attaching volumes to our instances.

Getting ready

To use Cinder volumes, you will need to have an additional host running Ubuntu 14.04 LTS. This host will be configured to provide a loopback filesystem on which we will build the LVM volumes and install the required services for Cinder.

If you are using the Vagrant environment that accompanies this book, be sure to login to the `cinder` node with the following commands:

```
vagrant up cinder
vagrant ssh cinder
```

The terms OpenStack Block Storage and Cinder will be used interchangeably in this chapter.

How to do it...

First, we will set up a loopback filesystem and set up LVM appropriately. After that, we will install and configure prerequisites such as `open-iscsi`. Finally, we will configure Cinder.

To configure your new host for `cinder-volume`, perform the following steps:

1. First login to the new host.
2. Install the prerequisites using the following commands:

   ```
   # Install some dependencies
   sudo apt-get update
   sudo apt-get install linux-headers-`uname -r` \
       build-essential python-mysqldb xfsprogs

   sudo apt-get install cinder-api cinder-scheduler \
       cinder-volume open-iscsi python-cinderclient tgt \
       iscsitarget iscsitarget-dkms
   ```

3. Now we need to restart `open-iscsi` using the following command:

```
sudo service open-iscsi restart
```

To create a loopback filesystem and set up LVM for `cinder-volume`, perform the following steps.

4. Next, we create a 5-GB file that will be used for the loopback filesystem:

```
dd if=/dev/zero of=cinder-volumes bs=1 count=0 seek=5G
```

Once that file is created, we create the loopback filesystem:

```
sudo losetup /dev/loop2 cinder-volumes
```

5. Finally, we create the LVM setup required for `cinder-volume` using the following command:

```
sudo pvcreate /dev/loop2
sudo vgcreate cinder-volumes /dev/loop2
```

It is important to note that this is not a persistent filesystem. Rather, it is shown here for demonstration. In a production setup, you would use an actual volume, rather than a loopback file, and set it up to mount persistently.

How it works...

In order for us to use `cinder-volume`, also change the formatting, we need to prepare a suitable disk or partition that has been configured as an LVM volume and that is specifically named `cinder-volumes`. For our book, we simply create a loopback filesystem that we can then set up to be part of this LVM volume group. In a physical installation, the steps are no different. We simply configure a partition to be of type `8e` (Linux LVM) in `fdisk` and then add this partition to a volume group named `cinder-volumes`.

Once done, we then install the required Cinder-volume packages and supporting services. As Cinder-volume uses iSCSI as the mechanism for attaching a volume to an instance, we install the appropriate packages that are required to run iSCSI targets.

Configuring OpenStack Compute for Cinder-volume

We now need to tell our OpenStack `compute` service about our new Cinder-volume service.

Getting ready

As we are performing this setup in a multi-node environment, you will need to be logged into your `controller`, `compute`, and `cinder` nodes.

If you are using the Vagrant environment that accompanies this book, you can log in to these nodes as follows:

```
vagrant ssh controller
vagrant ssh cinder
```

This recipe assumes you have created an `openrc` file. To create an `openrc` file on each node where you need it, open a text file named `openrc` and add the following contents:

```
export OS_TENANT_NAME=cookbook
export OS_USERNAME=admin
export OS_PASSWORD=openstack
export OS_AUTH_URL=https://192.168.100.200:5000/v2.0/
export OS_KEY=/path/to/cakey.pem
export OS_CACERT=/path/to/ca.pem
```

How to do it...

In our multi-node installation, we will need to configure the `controller`, `compute`, and `cinder` nodes. Thus, we have broken down the instructions in that order.

To configure your OpenStack `controller` node for `cinder-volume`, perform the following steps:

1. In our multi-node configuration, the OpenStack `controller` node is responsible for authentication (Keystone) as well as hosting the Cinder database. First, log in to the `controller` to configure authentication by running the following code:

```
source openrc
keystone service-create \
    --name volume \
    --type volume \
```

```
    --description 'Volume Service'

CINDER_SERVICE_ID=$(keystone service-list | awk '/\ volume\
/ {print $2}')

PUB_CINDER_ENDPOINT="192.168.0.211"
INT_CINDER_ENDPOINT="172.16.0.211"

PUBLIC="http://$PUB_CINDER_ENDPOINT:8776/v1/%(tenant_id)s"

ADMIN="http://$INT_CINDER_ENDPOINT:8776/v1/%(tenant_id)s"

INTERNAL=$PUBLIC

keystone endpoint-create \
    --region RegionOne \
    --service_id $CINDER_SERVICE_ID \
    --publicurl $PUBLIC \
    --adminurl $ADMIN \
    --internalurl $INTERNAL

keystone user-create \
    --name cinder \
    --pass cinder \
    --tenant_id $SERVICE_TENANT_ID \
    --email cinder@localhost --enabled true

CINDER_USER_ID=$(keystone user-list \
    | awk '/\ cinder \ / {print $2}')

keystone user-role-add \
    --user $CINDER_USER_ID \
    --role $ADMIN_ROLE_ID \
    --tenant_id $SERVICE_TENANT_ID
```

2. Next we create the MariaDB/MySQL database for use with Cinder:

```
MYSQL_ROOT_PASS=openstack

MYSQL_CINDER_PASS=openstack

mysql -uroot -p$MYSQL_ROOT_PASS \
    -e 'CREATE DATABASE cinder;'
```

```
mysql -uroot -p$MYSQL_ROOT_PASS \
    -e "GRANT ALL PRIVILEGES ON cinder.* TO 'cinder'@'%';"

mysql -uroot -p$MYSQL_ROOT_PASS \
    -e "SET PASSWORD FOR 'cinder'@'%' =
PASSWORD('$MYSQL_CINDER_PASS');"
```

3. Add the following lines to the `/etc/nova/nova.conf` file under the `[Default]` section:

```
volume_driver=nova.volume.driver.ISCSIDriver

enabled_apis=ec2,osapi_compute,metadata
volume_api_class=nova.volume.cinder.API
iscsi_helper=tgtadm
```

4. Now restart the `nova` services:

```
for P in $(ls /etc/init/nova* | cut -d'/' -f4 | cut -d'.' -f1)
do
  sudo stop ${P}
  sudo start ${P}
done
```

To configure the OpenStack `compute` nodes for Cinder, perform the following steps:

1. Next on our list for configuration are the OpenStack `compute` nodes. We will show you how to configure the first node. You will need to replicate this configuration against all of your `compute` nodes. Start by logging in to a `compute` node:

```
vagrant ssh compute-01
```

2. Add the following lines to the `/etc/nova/nova.conf` file under the `[Default]` section:

```
volume_driver=nova.volume.driver.ISCSIDriver
enabled_apis=ec2,osapi_compute,metadata
volume_api_class=nova.volume.cinder.API
iscsi_helper=tgtadm
```

3. Now restart the `nova` services:

```
for P in $(ls /etc/init/nova* | cut -d'/' -f4 | cut -d'.' -f1)
do
  sudo stop ${P}
  sudo start ${P}
done
```

To configure the Cinder node with the `cinder-volume` service, log into the Cinder node and perform the following steps:

1. Add the following lines to `/etc/cinder/cinder.conf` to enable communication with Keystone on its internal address as follows:

```
[keystone_authtoken]
auth_uri = https:// 192.168.100.200:35357/v2.0/
identity_uri = https://192.168.100.200:5000
admin_tenant_name = service
admin_user = cinder
admin_password = cinder
insecure = True
```

2. Next we modify `/etc/cinder/cinder.conf` to configure the database, iSCSI, and RabbitMQ. Ensure `cinder.conf` has the following lines:

```
[DEFAULT]
rootwrap_config=/etc/cinder/rootwrap.conf

[database]
backend=sqlalchemy
connection = mysql://cinder:openstack@172.16.0.200/cinder


iscsi_helper=tgtadm
volume_name_template = volume-%s
volume_group = cinder-volumes
verbose = True
auth_strategy = keystone


# Add these when not using the defaults.
rabbit_host = 172.16.0.200
rabbit_port = 5672

state_path = /var/lib/cinder/
```

3. To wrap up, we populate the Cinder database and restart the Cinder services:

```
cinder-manage db sync
cd /etc/init.d/; for i in $( ls cinder-* ); do sudo service $i
restart; done
```

How it works...

In our multi-node OpenStack configuration, we have to perform configuration across our environment to enable the `cinder-volume` service. On the OpenStack `controller` node, we created a Keystone service, endpoint, and user. We additionally assigned the `cinder` user and the `admin` role within the `service` tenant. On the `controller`, we created a `cinder` MySQL database and modified `nova.conf` to allow the use of Cinder.

On our `compute` nodes, the modifications were much simpler as we only needed to modify `nova.conf` to enable Cinder.

Finally, we configured the Cinder node itself. We did this by enabling Keystone, initializing the Cinder database, and connecting the Cinder service to its MySQL database. After this, we wrapped up by restarting the Cinder services.

Creating volumes

Now that we have created a Cinder volume service, we can create volumes for use by our instances. We do this under our Ubuntu client using one of the Cinder client tools, `python-cinderclient`, so we are creating volumes specific to our tenancy (project).

Getting ready

To begin with, ensure you are logged in to your Ubuntu client that has access to the Cinder client tools. If using the Vagrant environment that accompanies the book, you can access these tools from the `cinder` node:

```
vagrant ssh cinder
```

This recipe assumes you have created an `openrc` file. To create an `openrc` file on each node where you need it, open a text file named `openrc` and add the following contents:

```
export OS_TENANT_NAME=cookbook
export OS_USERNAME=admin
export OS_PASSWORD=openstack
export OS_AUTH_URL=https://192.168.100.200:5000/v2.0/
export OS_KEY=/path/to/cakey.pem
export OS_CACERT=/path/to/ca.pem
```

These packages can be installed using the following command:

```
sudo apt-get update
sudo apt-get install python-cinderclient
```

How to do it...

Carry out the following steps to create a volume using Cinder client:

1. First create the volume that we will attach to our instance by running the following command:

   ```
   source openrc
   cinder create --display-name cookbook 1
   ```

2. On completion, the command returns the following output:

```
+---------------------+--------------------------------------+
|       Property      |                Value                 |
+---------------------+--------------------------------------+
|     attachments     |                  []                  |
|  availability_zone  |                 nova                 |
|       bootable      |                false                 |
|      created_at     |      2015-07-03T20:55:40.704025      |
| display_description |                 None                 |
|     display_name    |               cookbook               |
|      encrypted      |                False                 |
|          id         | 06ab21fb-bc76-4216-9491-6c1918c1dab2 |
|       metadata      |                  {}                  |
|         size        |                  1                   |
|     snapshot_id     |                 None                 |
|     source_volid    |                 None                 |
|        status       |               creating               |
|     volume_type     |                 None                 |
+---------------------+--------------------------------------+
```

How it works...

Creating Cinder *volumes* for use within our project, `cookbook`, is very straightforward.

With the Cinder client, we use the `create` option with the following syntax:

```
cinder create --display_name volume_name size_Gb
```

Here, `volume_name` can be any arbitrary name with no spaces. We can see the actual LVM volumes on `cinder-volumes`, using the usual LVM tools, as follows:

```
sudo lvdisplay cinder-volumes
```

You will get the following output:

```
--- Logical volume ---
LV Path                /dev/cinder-volumes/volume-06ab21fb-bc76-4216-9491-6c1918c1dab2
LV Name                volume-06ab21fb-bc76-4216-9491-6c1918c1dab2
VG Name                cinder-volumes
LV UUID                gg1gKl-X34n-q9xU-xGbc-7C8x-tIxF-yaPU6B
LV Write Access        read/write
LV Creation host, time cinder, 2015-07-03 15:55:40 -0500
LV Status              available
# open                 0
LV Size                1.00 GiB
Current LE             256
Segments               1
Allocation             inherit
Read ahead sectors     auto
- currently set to     256
Block device           252:2
```

Notice the `LV` name matches the ID of the volume created with Cinder.

Attaching volumes to an instance

Now that we have a usable volume, we can attach this to any instance. We do this by using the `nova volume-attach` command in the Nova client.

Getting ready

To begin with, ensure you are logged in to the Ubuntu client that has access to the Nova client tools. If using the Vagrant environment that accompanies the book, you can access these tools from the `controller` node by running this command:

```
vagrant ssh controller
```

This recipe assumes you have created an `openrc` file. To create an `openrc` file on each node where you need it, open a text file named `openrc` and add the following contents:

```
export OS_TENANT_NAME=cookbook
export OS_USERNAME=admin
export OS_PASSWORD=openstack
export OS_AUTH_URL=https://192.168.100.200:5000/v2.0/
export OS_KEY=/path/to/cakey.pem
export OS_CACERT=/path/to/ca.pem
```

These packages can be installed using the following commands:

```
sudo apt-get update
sudo apt-get install python-novaclient
```

How to do it...

Carry out the following steps to attach a volume to an instance using the Nova client:

1. If you have no instance running, spin one up. Once it is running, run the `nova list` command and note the instance ID:

```
source openrc
nova list --fields name
```

   The following output is generated:

```
+--------------------------------------+-------+
| ID                                   | Name  |
+--------------------------------------+-------+
| f9659289-82f1-435f-98fc-add99c7a611b | test1 |
+--------------------------------------+-------+
```

2. Using the instance ID, we can attach the volume to our running instance, as follows:

```
nova volume-attach <instance_id> <volume_id> /dev/vdc
```

3. The preceding command will output the name of the volume when successful. To view this, log into your running instance and view the volume that is now attached by running the following:

```
sudo fdisk -l /dev/vdc
```

4. We should see 1 GB of space available for the running instance. As this is like adding a fresh disk to a system, you need to format it for use and then mount it as part of your filesystem, as shown here:

```
sudo mkfs.ext4 /dev/vdc
sudo mkdir /mnt1
sudo mount /dev/vdc /mnt1
```

5. We should now see the newly-attached disk available at `/mnt1`, as shown here:

```
df -h
Filesystem   Size Used Avail Use% Mounted on
/dev/vda     1.4G 602M 733M 46% /
devtmpfs     248M  12K 248M  1% /dev
none          50M 216K  50M  1% /run
none        5.0M    0 5.0M  0% /run/lock
none        248M    0 248M  0% /run/shm
/dev/vdb     5.0G 204M 4.6G  5% /mnt
/dev/vdc         1.0G  204M  784M   5% /mnt1
```

How it works...

Attaching a Cinder *volume* is no different from plugging in a USB stick on your own computer; similar to a USB stick, a Cinder volume can only be attached to a single host and must be formatted and mounted.

Under Nova client, the option `volume-attach` takes the following syntax:

```
nova volume-attach instance_id volume_id device
```

The `instance_id` parameter is the ID returned from the Nova list for the instance that we want to attach the volume to. The `volume_id` is the name of the device within the instance that we will use to mount the volume that can be retrieved using the `nova volume-list`. This device is the device that will be created on our instance that we use to mount the volume.

Detaching volumes from an instance

As Cinder volumes can only be attached to one host at a time, you need to detach it from one instance before attaching it to another. To detach a volume, we use another Nova client option called `volume-detach`.

Getting ready

To begin with, ensure you are logged in to the Ubuntu host that has access to Nova client tools. If using the Vagrant environment that accompanies the book, you can access these tools from the `controller` node:

```
vagrant ssh controller
```

This recipe assumes you have created an `openrc` file. To create an `openrc` file on each node where you need it, open a text file named `openrc`, and add the following contents:

```
export OS_TENANT_NAME=cookbook
export OS_USERNAME=admin
export OS_PASSWORD=openstack
export OS_AUTH_URL=https://192.168.100.200:5000/v2.0/
export OS_KEY=/path/to/cakey.pem
export OS_CACERT=/path/to/ca.pem
```

These packages can be installed using the following commands:

```
sudo apt-get update
sudo apt-get install python-novaclient
```

How to do it...

To detach a volume using Nova client, carry out the following steps:

1. First, we identify the volumes attached to running instances by running the following command:

   nova volume-list

   This returns the following output:

```
+--------------------------------------+-----------+--------------+------+-------------+-------------+
| ID                                   | Status    | Display Name | Size | Volume Type | Attached to |
+--------------------------------------+-----------+--------------+------+-------------+-------------+
| 06ab21fb-bc76-4216-9491-6c1918c1dab2 | available | cookbook     | 1    | None        |             |
+--------------------------------------+-----------+--------------+------+-------------+-------------+
```

2. On the instance that has the volume mounted, we must first `unmount` it with the following command (if using the earlier example, this is on `/mnt1`):

   sudo unmount /mnt1

3. Back on the Ubuntu client, where Nova client is installed, we can now detach this volume with the following command:

   nova volume-detach <instance_id> <volume_id>

Now we can attach this to another running instance and the data will be preserved.

How it works...

Detaching Cinder volumes is no different from removing a USB stick from a computer. We first unmount the volume from our running instance. Then we detach the volume from the running instance using `nova volume-detach` from the Nova Client.

The `nova volume-detach` command has the following syntax:

nova volume-detach instance_id volume_id

The `instance_id` parameter is the ID from the `attached to` column returned from the `nova volume-list` command, and this notifies which ID we want to detach the volume from.

The `volume_id` parameter is the ID listed in the ID column from the `nova volume-list` command.

Deleting volumes

At some point, you will no longer need the volumes you have created. To remove the volumes from the system permanently so they are no longer available, we simply pull out another tool from the Nova client—the `volume-delete` option.

Getting ready

Ensure that you are logged in to the Ubuntu host where Nova client is installed and have sourced in your OpenStack environment credentials. If you are using the Vagrant environment that accompanies this book, be sure to log in to the `controller` node with the following command:

```
vagrant ssh controller
```

This is a one-way deletion of data. It's gone unless you've got a backup—you should be sure that you *really* want it gone.

How to do it...

To delete a volume using Nova client, carry out the following steps:

1. First we list the volumes available to identify the volume we want to delete with the following command:

   ```
   cinder list
   ```

2. We now simply use the volume ID to delete this from the system with the following command:

   ```
   cinder delete <volume_id>
   ```

On deletion, the volume you have deleted will be printed on the screen.

How it works...

Deleting images removes the LVM volume from use within our system. To do this, we simply specify the volume ID as a parameter to `nova volume-delete` (when using the Nova client), ensuring that the volume is not in use.

Configuring third-party volume services

The OpenStack Block storage project, Cinder, relies on Linux iSCSI by default. While that is fairly robust, you may need to integrate OpenStack into your existing environment or wish to use more advanced features provided by third-party storage devices. In this section, we will show you how to configure Cinder to use a different storage provider plugin.

Getting ready

Ensure that you are logged in to the Ubuntu host where the `cinder-api` service is installed, and have sourced in your OpenStack environment credentials.

> This example highlights the use of the NFS backend for Cinder. It is important to note that, while this setup is straightforward, you should consult vendor documentation for other third-party drivers.

How to do it...

To change the Cinder volume driver to NFS, carry out the following steps:

1. You will need a properly configured NFS server and to create a file called `/etc/cinder/nfsshares` on the node where `cinder-api` is running that contains one line per NFS volume in the following format:

   ```
   cinder.book:/exports
   ```

2. Next, you will need to edit your `/etc/cinder/cinder.conf` file so that it contains the following line:

   ```
   volume_driver = cinder.volume.drivers.nfs.NfsDriver
   ```

   The file should also contain the following line:

   ```
   nfs_shares_config = /etc/cinder/nfsshares
   ```

   The final file will look like the following:

   ```
   [DEFAULT]
   rootwrap_config=/etc/cinder/rootwrap.conf
   api_paste_config = /etc/cinder/api-paste.ini
   volume_driver = cinder.volume.drivers.nfs.NfsDriver
   nfs_shares_config = /etc/cinder/nfsshares
   ```

```
verbose = True
use_syslog = True
syslog_log_facility = LOG_LOCAL0

auth_strategy = keystone

rabbit_host = 172.16.0.200
rabbit_port = 5672
state_path = /var/lib/cinder/

[database]
backend=sqlalchemy
connection = mysql://cinder:openstack@172.16.0.200/cinder

[keystone_authtoken]
auth_uri = https://192.168.100.200:35357/v2.0/
identity_uri = https://192.168.100.200:5000
admin_tenant_name = service
admin_user = cinder
admin_password = cinder
signing_dir = \$state_path/keystone-signing
insecure = True
```

3. Finally, restart the Cinder services:

```
cd /etc/init/; for c in $( ls cinder-* | cut -d '.' -f1) ; \
do sudo stop $c; start $c; done
```

How it works...

The `/etc/cinder/nfsshares` file lets Cinder know which NFS servers and shares to connect to for volume placement, while the `volume_driver` tells Cinder to use a different storage back end. The `nfs_shares_config` variable tells the Cinder services where to look for additional configuration details. Once the services are restarted, Cinder is able to use the specified NFS servers for volume storage.

Working with Cinder snapshots

Within Cinder, volume snapshots provide a way to non-disruptively copy a volume. This allows for volume backups. It also enables more advanced backup features and provides the ability to boot an instance from a given snapshot or point in time.

In this section, we will show you how to create a snapshot, refresh a snapshot, and delete a given snapshot.

Getting ready

Ensure that you are logged in to the Ubuntu host where the Cinder command-line utilities are installed and source your OpenStack environment admin credentials.

How to do it...

1. To create a snapshot, the volume must not be attached to an instance. To list your current volumes, you can use the `cinder list` command:

   `$ cinder list`

   Here's the output:

```
+--------------------------------------+-----------+--------------+------+-------------+----------+-------------+
|                  ID                  |   Status  | Display Name | Size | Volume Type | Bootable | Attached to |
+--------------------------------------+-----------+--------------+------+-------------+----------+-------------+
| b3e0f6b2-19cb-436f-a190-4b5c66ba2daf | available |     demo     |  1   |     None    |  false   |             |
+--------------------------------------+-----------+--------------+------+-------------+----------+-------------+
```

If the volume you wish to take a snapshot of has an `in-use` status, you will need to detach it using the instructions in the *Detaching volumes from an instance* recipe in this chapter.

2. As our volume is available, we will create a snapshot of the volume using the `cinder snapshot-create` command:

   `cinder snapshot-create b3e0f6b2-19cb-436f-a190-4b5c66ba2daf`

   Here's the output:

```
+---------------------+--------------------------------------+
|       Property      |                Value                 |
+---------------------+--------------------------------------+
|      created_at     |      2015-03-03T03:34:28.863739      |
| display_description |                 None                 |
|     display_name    |                 None                 |
|          id         | 855de1d1-1e43-4b19-93eb-5c60059890a7 |
|       metadata      |                  {}                  |
|         size        |                  1                   |
|        status       |               creating               |
|      volume_id      | b3e0f6b2-19cb-436f-a190-4b5c66ba2daf |
+---------------------+--------------------------------------+
```

3. Once the snapshot is complete, you can reattach it to an instance and continue operations. If using snapshots as part of an ongoing test/validation process or part of a backup scheme, you may want to update the snapshot with fresh data. To do this, we use the cinder `snapshot-reset-state` command, which produces no output if successful.

4. Finally, you will need to delete snapshots. To do this, use the `cinder snapshot-delete` command as follows:

   ```
   cinder snapshot-delete 63c3173b-4f30-4240-99f2-fd2e82cb757e
   ```

   Confirm whether the volume is deleted with the `cinder snapshot-list` command:

   ```
   cinder snapshot-list
   ```

   Here's the output:

   ```
   +----+-----------+--------+--------------+------+
   | ID | Volume ID | Status | Display Name | Size |
   +----+-----------+--------+--------------+------+
   +----+-----------+--------+--------------+------+
   ```

How it works...

Cinder volume snapshots provide a flexible way to clone volumes for backup, attaching to other instances and more. The `cinder snapshot-` commands we used here—specifically `cinder snapshot-create`, `cinder snapshot-list`, `cinder snapshot-reset-state`, and `cinder-snapshot-delete`—instruct Cinder to work with the storage driver to perform snapshot-specific actions: `create`, `list`, `update`, and `delete`, respectively. The specific implementation of a particular *snapshot* depends on the underlying driver.

Booting from volumes

Booting from a Cinder volume gives a number of benefits as an OpenStack Operator. You can provide a level of resiliency to your instances, or you can enable Live-Migration of an instance where you are not counting on Libvirt to migrate the disk for you.

Getting ready

Ensure you are logged in to the Ubuntu host where the cinder command-line utilities are installed and source your OpenStack environment admin credentials.

How to do it...

To boot an instance from a volume, we first need to select an image to boot from as well as a flavor of our choice. The steps are follows:

1. Get the UUID of the image to boot:

   `nova image-list`

   The command generates the following output:

```
+--------------------------------------+--------------+--------+--------+
| ID                                   | Name         | Status | Server |
+--------------------------------------+--------------+--------+--------+
| bbcf92a3-658b-4185-8686-7fb2f77b66a0 | cirros-image | ACTIVE |        |
| f5eba890-4660-4ee8-92d0-d7972510b7d6 | trusty-image | ACTIVE |        |
+--------------------------------------+--------------+--------+--------+
```

2. Get the flavor ID for `m1.tiny`:

   `nova flavor-list`

   The command generates the following output:

```
+----+-----------+-----------+------+-----------+------+-------+-------------+-----------+
| ID | Name      | Memory_MB | Disk | Ephemeral | Swap | VCPUs | RXTX_Factor | Is_Public |
+----+-----------+-----------+------+-----------+------+-------+-------------+-----------+
| 1  | m1.tiny   | 512       | 1    | 0         |      | 1     | 1.0         | True      |
| 2  | m1.small  | 2048      | 20   | 0         |      | 1     | 1.0         | True      |
| 3  | m1.medium | 4096      | 40   | 0         |      | 2     | 1.0         | True      |
| 4  | m1.large  | 8192      | 80   | 0         |      | 4     | 1.0         | True      |
| 5  | m1.xlarge | 16384     | 160  | 0         |      | 8     | 1.0         | True      |
+----+-----------+-----------+------+-----------+------+-------+-------------+-----------+
```

3. Since our lab environment is configured with two networks, we will need to choose the network to attach our instance to. First, list available networks:

   `neutron net-list`

   The available networks will be displayed:

```
+--------------------------------------+--------------------+-------------------------------------------------------+
| id                                   | name               | subnets                                               |
+--------------------------------------+--------------------+-------------------------------------------------------+
| 0375e772-b021-425c-bc17-5a3263247fb8 | cookbook_network_1 | 37ca3149-ee6b-4288-b074-03a4e1635b7c 10.200.0.0/24    |
| 706c9118-68d9-4751-932c-3dc94ec6f4ed | ext_net            | 889c1ef7-09af-48d2-85bf-6971446e2eb7 192.168.100.0/24 |
+--------------------------------------+--------------------+-------------------------------------------------------+
```

4. Finally, we issue the `nova boot` command:

```
nova boot \
     --flavor m1.tiny \
     --block-device source=image,id=trusty-
image,shutdown=preserve,dest=volume,size=15,bootindex=0 \
    --key_name demokey \
     --nic net-id=03575e772-b021-425c-bc17-5a3263247fb8 \
     --config-drive=true \
     CookBook_Instance
```

How it works...

As you can see, in the final step we passed a lot of new parameters to `nova boot` to tell Nova to use Cinder while booting the image. Specifically, `--block-device`, along with its sub-parameters `source`, `id`, `shutdown`, `destination`, `size`, and `boot index`, tell Nova to boot from a specific image (`source` and `id`), to preserve the Cinder volume when you shutdown the instance (`shutdown`), and that the destination is to be a cinder-volume of a specific size (`dest` and `size`).

9
More OpenStack

In this chapter, we will cover the following recipes:

- Using cloud-init to run post-installation commands
- Using cloud-config to run the post-installation configuration
- Installing OpenStack Telemetry
- Using OpenStack Telemetry to interrogate usage statistics
- Installing Neutron LBaaS
- Using Neutron LBaaS
- Configuring Neutron FWaaS
- Using Neutron FWaaS
- Installing the Heat OpenStack Orchestration service
- Using Heat to spin up instances

Introduction

So far in this book, we have discussed how to build and operate an OpenStack Cloud. By necessity, we were exceedingly pragmatic in doing so and erred on the side of showing you the most useful bits to get you up-and-running. In this chapter, we will cover a number of OpenStack-related projects, functions, and features that will enhance your understanding and ability to effectively design, implement, and operate your OpenStack Cloud. So, grab your super-hero cape and let's get started.

Using cloud-init to run post-installation commands

Cloud-init was originally developed by Canonical and is the *de facto* standard for running post-installation commands and configuration on a cloud instance. When an instance is launched, if cloud-init is part of the image being used, it will look for metadata information passed to it at launch time to do post-installation execution of commands. When a shell script is used (as demonstrated in the following *How to do it...* section of this recipe), it can be analogous to running commands in the `/etc/rc.local` working directory of a Linux machine. Cloud-init relies on data being sent from the `nova-metadata` API service. An instance looks for data associated with the particular instance and executes it accordingly. This section will cover the basics of using cloud-init.

Getting ready

Ensure that you are logged into a Ubuntu host that has access to our OpenStack environment on the `192.168.100.0/24` public network. This host will be used to run client tools against the OpenStack environment created. If you are using the accompanying Vagrant environment, as described in the *Preface*, you can use the `controller` node. This has the `python-novaclient` package that provides the `nova` command-line client.

If you created this node with Vagrant, you can execute the following command:

```
vagrant ssh controller
```

Ensure that you have set the following credentials (adjust the path to your certificates and key file to match your environment if you're not using the Vagrant environment):

```
export OS_TENANT_NAME=cookbook
export OS_USERNAME=admin
export OS_PASSWORD=openstack
export OS_AUTH_URL=https://192.168.100.200:5000/v2.0/
export OS_NO_CACHE=1
export OS_KEY=/vagrant/cakey.pem
export OS_CACERT=/vagrant/ca.pem
```

How to do it...

For this section, we will demonstrate how to run a script that brings up all interfaces on a standard Ubuntu image. Without this approach, if you run a Ubuntu image with more than one network interface, only the first interface `eth0` is brought up.

In this example, we will launch a Ubuntu instance with two Neutron networks and pass a shell script on the command line to bring up all interfaces. The steps are as follows:

1. We first create a small shell script to demonstrate the ability to pass shell scripts to an instance. Create a file called `multi-nic.sh` in the current directory with the following content:

```
#!/bin/bash
ifconfig -a | awk '/^eth/ {print $1}' | while read I

do

    dhclient $I

done
```

2. We can then simply pass this file as an argument to the `nova boot` line with the `--user-data` flag as follows:

```
nova boot
    --flavor m1.tiny
    --image trusty-image
    --nic net-id=e8e4ed14-97a6-4715-a065-3ff0347f40dd
    --nic net-id=8cb0f8f3-c529-45fe-ac5f-bd00c9814005
    --user-data ./multi-nic.sh
    myInstance
```

The second `nic`, and `eth1`, lines will now have an IP associated with it.

The `net-id` value can be found by running the `neutron net-list` command and looking up the ID associated with the network you want to use. You can specify any number of `--nic` flags (limited by the amount the image supports).

How it works...

Cloud-init is a very powerful system that is the cornerstone of hands-free orchestration of your instances. By providing the ability to run post-installation scripts, cloud-init paves the way for full-stack system automation and integration with third-party configuration management utilities.

To be able to execute a cloud-init script that is similar to an `rc.local` script, start the file with `#!`, followed by the interpreter such as `/bin/bash` or `/bin/python`. This tells cloud-init to run this script very late into the boot sequence after the initial services have started.

Cloud-init also supports a wide range of other features ranging from running upstart jobs (if the file begins with `#upstart-job`), which will place the file in `/etc/init` and execute this as any other type of upstart job, to the ability to consume the `gzip` files. These files get unzipped and executed for that file type as normal. Using the `gzip` files is very common as the input size is limited to 16,384 bytes.

There's more...

More information on cloud-init can be found at `http://cloud-init.readthedocs.org/`.

Using cloud-config to run the post-installation configuration

Cloud-config is a feature of cloud-init and is the simplest way to install packages via `apt` and configure our instances. With cloud-config, we can use a **Yet Another Markup Language** (**YAML**) file to describe how an instance is configured, which would require more effort if performed with shell scripts.

Getting ready

Ensure you are logged into a Ubuntu host that has access to our OpenStack environment on the `192.168.100.0/24` public network. This host will be used to run client tools against the OpenStack environment created. If you are using the accompanying Vagrant environment, as described in the *Preface*, you can use the `controller` node. This has the `python-novaclient` package that provides the `nova` command-line client.

If you created this node with Vagrant, you can execute the following command:

```
vagrant ssh controller
```

Ensure you have set the following credentials (adjust the path to your certificates and key file to match your environment if not using the Vagrant environment):

```
export OS_TENANT_NAME=cookbook
export OS_USERNAME=admin
export OS_PASSWORD=openstack
```

```
export OS_AUTH_URL=https://192.168.100.200:5000/v2.0/
export OS_NO_CACHE=1
export OS_KEY=/vagrant/cakey.pem
export OS_CACERT=/vagrant/ca.pem
```

How to do it...

In this section, we will demonstrate the configuration of the instance's hostname and installation of the Apache web server, as well as creation of groups and users. The steps are as follows:

1. We first create the `.yaml` file describing this behavior. Create a file called `webserver.yaml` in the current directory with the following content:

```
#cloud-config
hostname: myWebserver
fqdn: mywebserver.cook.book
manage_etc_hosts: true
groups:
 - developers
users:
 - auser
   gecos: A User
   primary-group: users
   groups: users, developers
   passwd: $6r$j632wezy/grasdfds7/efew7fwq/fdfws.8ewfwefwe
packages
 - apache2
```

2. We can simply pass this file as an argument to the `nova boot` line with the `--user-data` flag, as follows:

```
nova boot
    --flavor m1.tiny
    --image trusty-image
    --nic net-id=e8e4ed14-97a6-4715-a065-3ff0347f40dd
    --user-data ./webserver.yaml
    myWebserver
```

The `net-id` value can be found by running the `neutron net-list` command and looking up the `id` associated with the network you want to use.

3. The output can be seen with the `nova console-log` command. Cloud-init will interpret this cloud-config data and as a result will output commands such as `apt-get update` and `apt-get install`. At the end of the cloud-config run, your web server will be accessible.

> Note that the output of `nova list`, which shows the status of the instance, will show as `Active` despite the fact that cloud-init might not have completed yet. Be aware of this if you are relying on this status to check whether a service running on the instance is ready or not.
>
> Remember to open up the relevant security group ports for the services running on the instances too.

How it works...

Cloud-config is a feature of cloud-init and is a very simple method for the post-configuration tasks of our instances. A number of configuration options are available.

In the preceding example, we set the following line:

```
#cloud-config
```

Any file starting with this on the first line will be interpreted by cloud-init as cloud-config data.

The `hostname` parameter sets the short hostname of the instance.

The `fqdn` parameter sets the fully qualified domain name of the instance.

The `manage_etc_hosts: true` line allows us to modify the entries of `/etc/hosts` with the preceding information.

Adding users to the instance is simple when used with the groups and users statements. We simply list the groups to be added to the system and the users. Each user section begins with:

```
  - name: username
```

This line is followed by the system information you'd expect to see. The next user will start with the next section as follows:

```
  - name: anotheruser
```

Package installation starts with the packages and we simply list each package we want to install, as shown in the following code. Ensure there is an Internet connection available to your instances if you are accessing them outside your network:

```
packages
- apache2
- openssl
```

If the outside world isn't available, you can configure `apt` to point to a repository internally:

```
apt_mirror: http://internal-apt.cook.book/ubuntu/
apt_mirror_search_dns: false
```

This method is great for installation of packages for instances that cannot reach the Internet.

There's more...

Cloud-config can do a lot more than just install packages. Cloud-config can be used to install and run Chef recipes and puppet manifests, allowing you to integrate your OpenStack instances into your favorite orchestration and configuration management system. More information on cloud-config can be found at `http://cloud-init.readthedocs.org/`.

Cloud-init is not just limited to Linux-based instances. Cloudbase-init from Cloudbase brings the same ability to Windows instances also. Visit `http://www.cloudbase.it/cloud-init-for-windows-instances/` for more information on how to set up a cloud-init instance in Windows with Powershell.

Installing OpenStack Telemetry

The OpenStack Telemetry project, also called Ceilometer, provides you with the ability to collect metering data of the physical and virtual resources comprising deployed OpenStack components and persist this data for subsequent retrieval and analysis. It can also trigger actions when the defined criteria are met.

Getting ready

Ensure you have suitable servers running the OpenStack components. If you are using the accompanying Vagrant environment, as described in the *Preface*, we will use the same `controller` and `compute-01` nodes for this recipe.

We will be installing Ceilometer packages on a `controller` node and a `compute` node. Ensure you are logged into the `controller` and `compute-01` nodes in our environment. If you created these nodes with Vagrant, you can execute the following command:

```
vagrant ssh controller
vagrant ssh compute-01
```

How to do it...

To enable the Telemetry (`ceilometer`) service, first carry out the following steps on the controller node:

1. Ceilometer requires its own database to store all the data it collects. We will install MongoDB and the required dependencies to use with OpenStack's Telemetry service. On a `controller` node, execute the following command:

   ```
   sudo apt-get install mongodb python-pymongo python-bson
   ```

2. After installing MongoDB, edit the MongoDB configuration file `/etc/mongodb.conf` on the `controller` node and set the `bind_ip` parameter:

   ```
   bind_ip = 172.16.0.200
   ```

3. Restart MongoDB as follows:

   ```
   sudo service mongodb restart
   ```

4. MongoDB uses JavaScript syntax for its commands. To configure MongoDB for use with Ceilometer, add the `ceilometer user` by issuing the following command:

   ```
   db.addUser( { user: "ceilometer",
                 pwd: "openstack",
                 roles: [ "readWrite", "dbAdmin" ]
               } );
   ```

5. Keystone needs to be aware of Ceilometer, so ensure that there are Keystone credentials for the `ceilometer` service by executing the following commands:

   ```
   keystone user-create --name=ceilometer --pass=ceilometer \
   --email=ceilomoter@localhost
   keystone user-role-add --user=ceilometer \
   --tenant=service --role=admin
   ```

6. We then add the following service and `endpoint` for Ceilometer in Keystone by executing the following commands:

   ```
   keystone service-create --name=ceilometer \
   --type=telemetry \
   --description="Ceilometer Metering Service"
   METERING_SERVICE_ID=$(keystone service-list \
   | awk '/\ ceilometer\ / {print $2}')
   keystone endpoint-create \
     --region RegionOne \
   ```

```
--service-id=${METERING_SERVICE_ID} \
--publicurl=http://192.168.100.200:8777 \
--internalurl=http://192.168.100.200:8777 \
--adminurl=http://192.168.100.200:8777
```

7. We are now ready to install the required `ceilometer` packages using `apt`:

```
sudo apt-get update
sudo apt-install ceilometer-api \
ceilometer-collector \
ceilometer-agent-central \
python-ceilometerclient
```

8. Configure `ceilometer` by editing the `/etc/ceilometer/ceilometer.conf` file. It should contain the following configuration to work with our environment:

```
[DEFAULT]
policy_file = /etc/ceilometer/policy.json
verbose = true
debug = true
insecure = true

##### AMQP #####
notification_topics = notifications,glance_notifications

rabbit_host=172.16.0.200
rabbit_port=5672
rabbit_userid=guest
rabbit_password=guest
rabbit_virtual_host=/
rabbit_ha_queues=false

[database]
connection=mongodb://ceilometer:openstack@172.16.0.200:
27017/ceilometer

[api]
host = 172.16.0.200
port = 8777

[keystone_authtoken]
auth_uri = https://192.168.100.200:35357/v2.0/
```

```
identity_uri = https://192.168.100.200:5000
admin_tenant_name = service
admin_user = ceilometer
admin_password = ceilometer
revocation_cache_time = 10
insecure = True

[service_credentials]
os_auth_url = https://192.168.100.200:5000/v2.0
os_username = ceilometer
os_tenant_name = service
os_password = ceilometer
insecure = True
```

9. We restart all `ceilometer` services:

```
sudo service ceilometer-agent-central restart
sudo service ceilometer-agent-notification restart
sudo service ceilometer-alarm-evaluator restart
sudo service ceilometer-alarm-notifier restart
sudo service ceilometer-api restart
sudo service ceilometer-collector restart
```

   Now that `controller` node is set up, we proceed to install the Ceilometer agent on a `compute-01` node.

10. On a `compute-01` node, install the `ceilometer` agent:

```
sudo apt-get install ceilometer-agent-compute
```

11. Edit the `/etc/ceilometer/ceilometer.conf` file and insert the following lines:

```
[DEFAULT]
policy_file = /etc/ceilometer/policy.json
verbose = true
debug = true
insecure = true

##### AMQP #####
notification_topics = notifications,glance_notifications

rabbit_host=172.16.0.200
rabbit_port=5672
rabbit_userid=guest
```

```
rabbit_password=guest
rabbit_virtual_host=/
rabbit_ha_queues=false

[database]
connection=mongodb://ceilometer:openstack@172.16.0.200:
27017/ceilometer

[api]
host = 172.16.0.200
port = 8777

[keystone_authtoken]
auth_uri = https://192.168.100.200:35357/v2.0/
identity_uri = https://192.168.100.200:5000
admin_tenant_name = service
admin_user = ceilometer
admin_password = ceilometer
revocation_cache_time = 10
insecure = True
[service_credentials]
os_auth_url = https://192.168.100.200:5000/v2.0
os_username = ceilometer
os_tenant_name = service
os_password = ceilometer
insecure = True
```

12. Add the `Ceilometer` section to the `/etc/nova/nova.conf` configuration file:

```
# Ceilometer
instance_usage_audit=True
instance_usage_audit_period=hour
notify_on_state_change=vm_and_task_state
notification_driver=nova.openstack.common.notifier.
rpc_notifier
```

13. Restart the `nova` services:

```
sudo service nova-compute restart
```

14. Restart the Ceilometer agent:

```
sudo service ceilometer-agent-compute restart
```

Your `compute` node is now reporting all its usage statistics to the `controller` node.

How it works...

We installed and configured MongoDB on our `controller` node. We set up MongoDB to listen on the internal controller IP, which is similar to the RabbitMQ service. Ceilometer uses Keystone for communication, so we also created a `ceilometer user` and services using `keystone` commands. After creating the `ceilometer user`, we installed and configured `ceilometer` packages. The configuration file for Ceilometer is `/etc/ceilometer/ceilometer.conf`. Apart from the `[api]`, `[keystone_authtoken]`, and `[service_credentials]` sections, we also specified the database connection section:

```
[database]
connection=mongodb://ceilometer:openstack@172.16.0.200:27017/
ceilometer
```

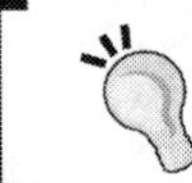

To properly configure the MongoDB database for production use, refer to the MongoDB documentation at `http://docs.mongodb.org/manual/`.

We could have used any supported database, such as MongoDB, MySQL, PostgreSQL, HBase, and DB2.

After configuring the `controller` node, we set up the `compute-01` node by installing the Ceilometer agent. We then updated the `/etc/ceilometer.conf` and `/etc/nova/nova.conf` files. Now, the Ceilometer service is ready to be used.

Using OpenStack Telemetry to interrogate usage statistics

With the telemetry modules installed and configured, we can now use the Ceilometer command line to interrogate resource usage statistics. We do this by retrieving meters that were set up for our environment and in listing the data.

Getting ready

Ensure that you are logged into a Ubuntu host that has access to our OpenStack environment on the `192.168.100.0/24` public network. This host will be used to run client tools against the OpenStack environment created. If you are using the accompanying Vagrant environment, as described in the *Preface*, you can use the `controller` node. This has the `python-ceilometer` package that provides the `ceilometer` command-line client.

If you created this node with Vagrant, you can execute the following command:

```
vagrant ssh controller
```

Ensure that you have set the following credentials (adjust the path to your certificates and key file to match your environment if not using the Vagrant environment):

```
export OS_TENANT_NAME=cookbook
export OS_USERNAME=admin
export OS_PASSWORD=openstack
export OS_AUTH_URL=https://192.168.100.200:5000/v2.0/
export OS_NO_CACHE=1
export OS_KEY=/vagrant/cakey.pem
export OS_CACERT=/vagrant/ca.pem
vagrant ssh controller
```

How to do it...

We will first list the meters available in our environment:

1. We will list the meters available in our environment:

   ```
   ceilometer meter-list
   ```

   The preceding command will display the following information:

Name	Type	Unit	Resource ID	User ID	Project ID
cpu	cumulative	ns	4be430e2-9b12	37e4ba2f	d27f89204b8
cpu_util	gauge	%	4be430e2-9b12	37e4ba2f	d27f89204b8
disk.device.read.bytes	cumulative	B	4be430e2-9b12	37e4ba2f	d27f89204b8
disk.device.read.requests	cumulative	request	4be430e2-9b12	37e4ba2f	d27f89204b8
disk.device.write.bytes	cumulative	B	4be430e2-9b12	37e4ba2f	d27f89204b8
disk.device.write.requests	cumulative	request	4be430e2-9b12	37e4ba2f	d27f89204b8
disk.read.bytes	cumulative	B	4be430e2-9b12	37e4ba2f	d27f89204b8
disk.read.bytes.rate	gauge	B/s	4be430e2-9b12	37e4ba2f	d27f89204b8
disk.read.requests	cumulative	request	4be430e2-9b12	37e4ba2f	d27f89204b8
disk.read.requests.rate	gauge	request/s	4be430e2-9b12	37e4ba2f	d27f89204b8
disk.write.bytes	cumulative	B	4be430e2-9b12	37e4ba2f	d27f89204b8
disk.write.bytes.rate	gauge	B/s	4be430e2-9b12	37e4ba2f	d27f89204b8
disk.write.requests	cumulative	request	4be430e2-9b12	37e4ba2f	d27f89204b8
disk.write.requests.rate	gauge	request/s	4be430e2-9b12	37e4ba2f	d27f89204b8
image	gauge	image	b8ab5287-081a	None	d27f89204b8
image	gauge	image	e5f33281-c497	None	d27f89204b8
image.size	gauge	B	b8ab5287-081a	None	d27f89204b8
image.size	gauge	B	e5f33281-c497	None	d27f89204b8
instance	gauge	instance	4be430e2-9b12	37e4ba2f	d27f89204b8
instance:m1.tiny	gauge	instance	4be430e2-9b12	37e4ba2f	d27f89204b8
network.incoming.bytes	cumulative	B	instance-0000	37e4ba2f	d27f89204b8
network.incoming.bytes.rate	gauge	B/s	instance-0000	37e4ba2f	d27f89204b8
network.incoming.packets	cumulative	packet	instance-0000	37e4ba2f	d27f89204b8
network.incoming.packets.rate	gauge	packet/s	instance-0000	37e4ba2f	d27f89204b8
network.outgoing.bytes	cumulative	B	instance-0000	37e4ba2f	d27f89204b8
network.outgoing.bytes.rate	gauge	B/s	instance-0000	37e4ba2f	d27f89204b8
network.outgoing.packets	cumulative	packet	instance-0000	37e4ba2f	d27f89204b8
network.outgoing.packets.rate	gauge	packet/s	instance-0000	37e4ba2f	d27f89204b8

2. Narrow down the meter list by a particular VM:

   ceilometer meter-list --query resource=4be430e2-9b12

   We get the following output:

Name	Type	Unit	Resource ID	User ID	Project ID
cpu	cumulative	ns	4be430e2-9b12	37e4ba2f	d27f89204b
cpu_util	gauge	%	4be430e2-9b12	37e4ba2f	d27f89204b
disk.read.bytes	cumulative	B	4be430e2-9b12	37e4ba2f	d27f89204b
disk.read.bytes.rate	gauge	B/s	4be430e2-9b12	37e4ba2f	d27f89204b
disk.read.requests	cumulative	request	4be430e2-9b12	37e4ba2f	d27f89204b
disk.read.requests.rate	gauge	request/s	4be430e2-9b12	37e4ba2f	d27f89204b
disk.write.bytes	cumulative	B	4be430e2-9b12	37e4ba2f	d27f89204b
disk.write.bytes.rate	gauge	B/s	4be430e2-9b12	37e4ba2f	d27f89204b
disk.write.requests	cumulative	request	4be430e2-9b12	37e4ba2f	d27f89204b
disk.write.requests.rate	gauge	request/s	4be430e2-9b12	37e4ba2f	d27f89204b
instance	gauge	instance	4be430e2-9b12	37e4ba2f	d27f89204b
instance:m1.tiny	gauge	instance	4be430e2-9b12	37e4ba2f	d27f89204b

3. We can view sample data for different meters related to our VM. To view the sample data, use the following command:

   ceilometer sample-list -m disk.write.bytes

   This will provide a lot of raw data:

Resource ID	Name	Type	Volume	Unit	Timestamp
4be430e2-9b12-4e1b-941c-58b5d0f0918b	disk.write.bytes	cumulative	707003392.0	B	2015-04-20T08:48:16
4be430e2-9b12-4e1b-941c-58b5d0f0918b	disk.write.bytes	cumulative	707003392.0	B	2015-04-20T08:38:16
4be430e2-9b12-4e1b-941c-58b5d0f0918b	disk.write.bytes	cumulative	707003392.0	B	2015-04-20T08:28:16
4be430e2-9b12-4e1b-941c-58b5d0f0918b	disk.write.bytes	cumulative	707003392.0	B	2015-04-20T08:18:16
4be430e2-9b12-4e1b-941c-58b5d0f0918b	disk.write.bytes	cumulative	706917376.0	B	2015-04-20T08:08:16
4be430e2-9b12-4e1b-941c-58b5d0f0918b	disk.write.bytes	cumulative	706917376.0	B	2015-04-20T07:58:16
4be430e2-9b12-4e1b-941c-58b5d0f0918b	disk.write.bytes	cumulative	706917376.0	B	2015-04-20T07:48:16
4be430e2-9b12-4e1b-941c-58b5d0f0918b	disk.write.bytes	cumulative	706917376.0	B	2015-04-20T07:38:16
4be430e2-9b12-4e1b-941c-58b5d0f0918b	disk.write.bytes	cumulative	706917376.0	B	2015-04-20T07:28:16
4be430e2-9b12-4e1b-941c-58b5d0f0918b	disk.write.bytes	cumulative	706917376.0	B	2015-04-20T07:18:16
4be430e2-9b12-4e1b-941c-58b5d0f0918b	disk.write.bytes	cumulative	706810880.0	B	2015-04-20T07:08:16

   We trimmed the preceding output for readability; usually there will be a lot more data.

4. Ceilometer comes with some helpful tools to perform calculations and provide statistics. We can now get the statistics for individual meters and investigate the `disk write` rate:

   ceilometer statistics --meter disk.write.bytes.rate

   The preceding command will provide the following output:

Period	Period Start	Period End	Max	Min	Avg	Sum	Count	Duration	Duration Start	Duration End
0	2015-04-14T03:58:15	2015-04-14T03:58:15	134778.88	0.0	1329.6	1163356.4	875	529201.0	2015-04-14T03:58:15	2015-04-20T06:58:16

5. Ceilometer allows custom queries. To view the data for a particular date range, we will enter start and end times:

   ```
   ceilometer  statistics -m disk.write.bytes.rate \
   -q 'timestamp>2015-04-14T22:38:15; \
   timestamp<=2015-04-19T04:28:15' --period 60
   ```

   The preceding command will give us a lot of data for a given range. Here is the truncated output:

Period	Period Start	Period End	Max	Min	Avg	Sum	Count	Duration	Duration Start	Duration End
60	2015-04-14T22:48:15	2015-04-14T22:49:15	0.0	0.0	0.0	0.0	1	0.0	2015-04-14T22:48:15	2015-04-14T22:48:15
60	2015-04-14T22:58:15	2015-04-14T22:59:15	0.0	0.0	0.0	0.0	1	0.0	2015-04-14T22:58:15	2015-04-14T22:58:15
60	2015-04-14T23:08:15	2015-04-14T23:09:15	0.0	0.0	0.0	0.0	1	0.0	2015-04-14T23:08:15	2015-04-14T23:08:15
60	2015-04-14T23:18:15	2015-04-14T23:19:15	177.4	177.4	177.4	177.4	1	0.0	2015-04-14T23:18:15	2015-04-14T23:18:15
60	2015-04-14T23:28:15	2015-04-14T23:29:15	0.0	0.0	0.0	0.0	1	0.0	2015-04-14T23:28:15	2015-04-14T23:28:15
60	2015-04-14T23:38:15	2015-04-14T23:39:15	0.0	0.0	0.0	0.0	1	0.0	2015-04-14T23:38:15	2015-04-14T23:38:15
60	2015-04-14T23:48:15	2015-04-14T23:49:15	0.0	0.0	0.0	0.0	1	0.0	2015-04-14T23:48:15	2015-04-14T23:48:15
60	2015-04-14T23:58:15	2015-04-14T23:59:15	0.0	0.0	0.0	0.0	1	0.0	2015-04-14T23:58:15	2015-04-14T23:58:15
60	2015-04-15T00:08:15	2015-04-15T00:09:15	0.0	0.0	0.0	0.0	1	0.0	2015-04-15T00:08:15	2015-04-15T00:08:15
60	2015-04-15T00:18:15	2015-04-15T00:19:15	129.7	129.7	129.7	129.7	1	0.0	2015-04-15T00:18:15	2015-04-15T00:18:15
60	2015-04-15T00:28:15	2015-04-15T00:29:15	0.0	0.0	0.0	0.0	1	0.0	2015-04-15T00:28:15	2015-04-15T00:28:15
60	2015-04-15T00:38:15	2015-04-15T00:39:15	61.44	61.44	61.44	61.44	1	0.0	2015-04-15T00:38:15	2015-04-15T00:38:15
60	2015-04-15T00:48:15	2015-04-15T00:49:15	0.0	0.0	0.0	0.0	1	0.0	2015-04-15T00:48:15	2015-04-15T00:48:15
60	2015-04-15T00:58:15	2015-04-15T00:59:15	0.0	0.0	0.0	0.0	1	0.0	2015-04-15T00:58:15	2015-04-15T00:58:15
60	2015-04-15T01:08:15	2015-04-15T01:09:15	0.0	0.0	0.0	0.0	1	0.0	2015-04-15T01:08:15	2015-04-15T01:08:15
60	2015-04-15T01:18:15	2015-04-15T01:19:15	129.7	129.7	129.7	129.7	1	0.0	2015-04-15T01:18:15	2015-04-15T01:18:15
60	2015-04-15T01:28:15	2015-04-15T01:29:15	0.0	0.0	0.0	0.0	1	0.0	2015-04-15T01:28:15	2015-04-15T01:28:15
60	2015-04-15T01:38:15	2015-04-15T01:39:15	0.0	0.0	0.0	0.0	1	0.0	2015-04-15T01:38:15	2015-04-15T01:38:15
60	2015-04-15T01:48:15	2015-04-15T01:49:15	0.0	0.0	0.0	0.0	1	0.0	2015-04-15T01:48:15	2015-04-15T01:48:15
60	2015-04-15T01:58:15	2015-04-15T01:59:15	0.0	0.0	0.0	0.0	1	0.0	2015-04-15T01:58:15	2015-04-15T01:58:15
60	2015-04-15T02:08:15	2015-04-15T02:09:15	0.0	0.0	0.0	0.0	1	0.0	2015-04-15T02:08:15	2015-04-15T02:08:15
60	2015-04-15T02:18:15	2015-04-15T02:19:15	129.7	129.7	129.7	129.7	1	0.0	2015-04-15T02:18:15	2015-04-15T02:18:15
60	2015-04-15T02:28:15	2015-04-15T02:29:15	0.0	0.0	0.0	0.0	1	0.0	2015-04-15T02:28:15	2015-04-15T02:28:15
60	2015-04-15T02:38:15	2015-04-15T02:39:15	0.0	0.0	0.0	0.0	1	0.0	2015-04-15T02:38:15	2015-04-15T02:38:15
60	2015-04-15T02:48:15	2015-04-15T02:49:15	0.0	0.0	0.0	0.0	1	0.0	2015-04-15T02:48:15	2015-04-15T02:48:15
60	2015-04-15T02:58:15	2015-04-15T02:59:15	0.0	0.0	0.0	0.0	1	0.0	2015-04-15T02:58:15	2015-04-15T02:58:15
60	2015-04-15T03:08:15	2015-04-15T03:09:15	0.0	0.0	0.0	0.0	1	0.0	2015-04-15T03:08:15	2015-04-15T03:08:15
60	2015-04-15T03:18:15	2015-04-15T03:19:15	129.7	129.7	129.7	129.7	1	0.0	2015-04-15T03:18:15	2015-04-15T03:18:15
60	2015-04-15T03:28:15	2015-04-15T03:29:15	0.0	0.0	0.0	0.0	1	0.0	2015-04-15T03:28:15	2015-04-15T03:28:15
60	2015-04-15T03:38:15	2015-04-15T03:39:15	0.0	0.0	0.0	0.0	1	0.0	2015-04-15T03:38:15	2015-04-15T03:38:15
60	2015-04-15T03:48:15	2015-04-15T03:49:15	0.0	0.0	0.0	0.0	1	0.0	2015-04-15T03:48:15	2015-04-15T03:48:15
60	2015-04-15T03:58:15	2015-04-15T03:59:15	0.0	0.0	0.0	0.0	1	0.0	2015-04-15T03:58:15	2015-04-15T03:58:15
60	2015-04-15T04:08:15	2015-04-15T04:09:15	0.0	0.0	0.0	0.0	1	0.0	2015-04-15T04:08:15	2015-04-15T04:08:15
60	2015-04-15T04:18:15	2015-04-15T04:19:15	402.7	402.7	402.7	402.7	1	0.0	2015-04-15T04:18:15	2015-04-15T04:18:15
60	2015-04-15T04:28:15	2015-04-15T04:29:15	0.0	0.0	0.0	0.0	1	0.0	2015-04-15T04:28:15	2015-04-15T04:28:15

6. To investigate statistics for cumulative data, we will check network outgoing bytes with the following command:

   ```
   ceilometer statistics -m network.outgoing.bytes
   ```

   The preceding command will give us the following output:

Period	Period Start	Period End	Max	Min	Avg
0	2015-04-14T03:48:15	2015-04-14T03:48:15	56915.0	25157.0	41814.138009

Sum	Count	Duration	Duration Start	Duration End
36963698.0	884	534601.0	2015-04-14T03:48:15	2015-04-20T08:18:16

Here, we wrapped the table output for easier readability. Normally, all columns would be presented together.

The main difference is that, in addition to all the other columns as before, we now have a `Sum` column that has the total sum of all outgoing bytes.

7. To list a running sum of bytes for outgoing networks, we will use a query for a specific time range:

```
ceilometer statistics -m network.outgoing.bytes \
-q 'timestamp>2015-04-14T22:38:15;\
timestamp<=2015-04-19T04:28:15' --period 60
```

We will get the following output:

Period Start	Period End	Max	Min	Avg	Sum	Duration Start	Duration End
2015-04-14T22:48:15	2015-04-14T22:49:15	31323.0	31323.0	31323.0	31323.0	2015-04-14T22:48:15	2015-04-14T22:48:15
2015-04-14T22:58:15	2015-04-14T22:59:15	31323.0	31323.0	31323.0	31323.0	2015-04-14T22:58:15	2015-04-14T22:58:15
2015-04-14T23:08:15	2015-04-14T23:09:15	31323.0	31323.0	31323.0	31323.0	2015-04-14T23:08:15	2015-04-14T23:08:15
2015-04-14T23:18:15	2015-04-14T23:19:15	31323.0	31323.0	31323.0	31323.0	2015-04-14T23:18:15	2015-04-14T23:18:15
2015-04-14T23:28:15	2015-04-14T23:29:15	31323.0	31323.0	31323.0	31323.0	2015-04-14T23:28:15	2015-04-14T23:28:15
2015-04-14T23:38:15	2015-04-14T23:39:15	31323.0	31323.0	31323.0	31323.0	2015-04-14T23:38:15	2015-04-14T23:38:15
2015-04-14T23:48:15	2015-04-14T23:49:15	31323.0	31323.0	31323.0	31323.0	2015-04-14T23:48:15	2015-04-14T23:48:15
2015-04-14T23:58:15	2015-04-14T23:59:15	31323.0	31323.0	31323.0	31323.0	2015-04-14T23:58:15	2015-04-14T23:58:15
2015-04-15T00:08:15	2015-04-15T00:09:15	31323.0	31323.0	31323.0	31323.0	2015-04-15T00:08:15	2015-04-15T00:08:15
2015-04-15T00:18:15	2015-04-15T00:19:15	31323.0	31323.0	31323.0	31323.0	2015-04-15T00:18:15	2015-04-15T00:18:15
2015-04-15T00:28:15	2015-04-15T00:29:15	31323.0	31323.0	31323.0	31323.0	2015-04-15T00:28:15	2015-04-15T00:28:15
2015-04-15T00:38:15	2015-04-15T00:39:15	31707.0	31707.0	31707.0	31707.0	2015-04-15T00:38:15	2015-04-15T00:38:15
...							
2015-04-19T03:58:15	2015-04-19T03:59:15	48345.0	48345.0	48345.0	48345.0	2015-04-19T03:58:16	2015-04-19T03:58:16
2015-04-19T04:08:15	2015-04-19T04:09:15	48345.0	48345.0	48345.0	48345.0	2015-04-19T04:08:16	2015-04-19T04:08:16
2015-04-19T04:18:15	2015-04-19T04:19:15	48345.0	48345.0	48345.0	48345.0	2015-04-19T04:18:16	2015-04-19T04:18:16

We can see the cumulative running total during the specified time interval. For the sake of readability, we removed the `Period`, `Count`, and `Duration` columns and some data in the middle of the time range.

How it works...

Ceilometer collects data from various OpenStack components. We have viewed meters that were set up for our environment and queried data based on the date range. Ceilometer provides three types of data—cumulative, gauge, and delta. We have looked at gauge data, which provided information about the disk write rate. We also looked at cumulative data for a date interval. To list the Ceilometer meters, use the following command:

```
ceilometer meter-list
```

To view sample data for individual meters, we used the `-m` or `--meter` flags with the following command:

```
ceilometer sample-list -m disk.write.bytes
```

Ceilometer also provides statistics for the various data it collects. To view statistics, we issue the following command:

```
ceilometer statistics --meter disk.write.bytes.rate
```

The preceding command also accepts queries in the following format:

```
ceilometer statistics -m disk.write.bytes.rate -q \
'timestamp>2015-04-14T22:38:15;\
timestamp<=2015-04-19T04:28:15' --period 60
```

Ceilometer collects, stores, and queries what can be middling-to-large amounts of data or *big* data—depending on the number of hosts and meters configured. While it is beyond the scope of this book to teach you how to handle middling-to-large data problems, it is recommended that, if you deploy Ceilometer in production, you should host its operations where it will not otherwise impact your workloads.

Installing Neutron LBaaS

Unlike its cartoon namesake Jimmy Neutron, OpenStack Neutron has an extensible plugin mechanism that enables more network features through the Neutron API. By enabling the **Load-Balancer-as-a-Service** (**LBaaS**) agent plugin on our Network node, we are able to create and manage Load Balancers through Neutron API calls. There are drivers for many hardware vendors; the following example uses the HA Proxy reference driver for Open vSwitch.

To install Neutron LBaaS, we install the LBaaS agent on the `network` node and configure Neutron on both the `network` and `controller` nodes to pick up the service.

Getting ready

Ensure that you have a suitable server running the OpenStack network components. If you are using the accompanying Vagrant environment, as described in the *Preface*, we will use the same `network` node for this recipe.

Ensure that you are logged into the `network` node as well as the `controller` node in our environment. If you created these nodes with Vagrant, you can execute the following command:

```
vagrant ssh network
vagrant ssh controller
```

How to do it...

To enable the Neutron LBaaS feature, first carry out the following steps on the `network` node:

1. We install the LBaaS agent using `apt`:

   ```
   sudo apt-get update
   sudo add-apt-repository ppa:openstack-ubuntu-testing/kilo
   neutron-lbaas-agent haproxy
   ```

2. We enable the Load Balance service in the `[Default]` section of the `/etc/neutron/neutron.conf` file by adding `lbaas` to the `service_plugins` line as follows:

   ```
   service_plugins = lbaas
   ```

The `service_plugins` line is a comma-delimited list, for example:

```
service_plugins = lbaas,router
```

3. We enable the HA Proxy Load Balancer service by adding the following lines to `/etc/neutron/neutron.conf`:

   ```
   [service_providers]
   service_provider =
   LOADBALANCER:Haproxy:neutron.services.loadbalancer.drivers.
   haproxy.plugin_driver.HaproxyOnHostPluginDriver:default
   ```

4. We then edit the `/etc/neutron/lbaas_agent.ini` file to have the following lines:

   ```
   [DEFAULT]
   debug = False
   interface_driver =
   neutron.agent.linux.interface.OVSInterfaceDriver
   device_driver =
   neutron.services.loadbalancer.drivers.haproxy.
   namespace_driver.HaproxyNSDriver
   ```

```
[haproxy]
loadbalancer_state_path = $state_path/lbaas
user_group = nogroup
```

5. On the `network` node, we start the Neutron LBaaS agent:

   sudo start neutron-lbaas-agent

6. On the `controller` node, where our Neutron API is running, we edit the `/etc/neutron/neutron.conf` file to match the same configuration presented previously. Under the `[Default]` section, we enable the Load Balance service by adding `lbaas` to the `service_plugins` line:

   ```
   service_plugins = lbaas
   ```

The `service_plugins` line is a comma-delimited list, for example:

```
service_plugins = lbaas,router
```

7. We then enable the HA Proxy Load Balance service by adding the following lines to the `/etc/neutron/neutron.conf` configuration file:

   ```
   [service_providers]
   service_provider =
   LOADBALANCER:Haproxy:neutron.services.loadbalancer.drivers.
   haproxy.plugin_driver.HaproxyOnHostPluginDriver:default
   ```

8. On the `controller` node, we restart the Neutron API service:

   sudo restart neutron-server

9. Horizon, the OpenStack Dashboard, can also be configured for use with Neutron's LBaaS. To enable this feature, edit the `/etc/openstack-dashboard/local_settings.py` file to insert the following lines:

   ```
   OPENSTACK_NEUTRON_NETWORK = {
       'enable_lb': True,
       ...
   }
   ```

10. Restart Apache to pick up the changes:

    service apache2 restart

How it works...

We have enabled the Neutron LBaaS plugin in our environment by first installing the Neutron LBaaS agent package on our `network` node, and then configuring this for use with HA Proxy. The `/etc/neutron/neutron.conf` file notifies our `neutron` services of this feature with the following lines:

```
[Default]
service_plugins = lbaas
[Service_Providers]
service_provider =
LOADBALANCER:Haproxy:neutron.services.loadbalancer.drivers.haproxy
.plugin_driver.HaproxyOnHostPluginDriver:default
```

The specific configuration of the LBaaS Agent is achieved in the `/etc/neutron/lbaas-agent.ini` file on the node running the agent, which is our `network` node.

We then notify the Neutron API service running on the `controller` about the Neutron LBaaS plugin. We copy the same `neutron.conf` settings file created here onto the `controller` node and restart the Neutron Server API service.

Using Neutron LBaaS

With Neutron LBaaS now installed, we can use this through the Neutron API and command line. This allows us to create simple HA Proxy Load Balance services for our instances. We do this by creating Load Balance pools and adding the running instances to those pools. Optionally, we can add in monitoring to help the Load Balancer decide whether to send traffic to an instance or not.

In this section, we will configure a basic HTTP Load Balancer pool with two instances running Apache. The result will be the ability to use the HTTP Load Balancer pool address to send traffic to two instances running Apache.

Getting ready

Ensure you are logged into a Ubuntu host that has access to our OpenStack environment on the `192.168.100.0/24` public network. This host will be used to run client tools against the OpenStack environment created. If you are using the accompanying Vagrant environment, as described in the *Preface*, you can use the `controller` node. This node has the `python-neutronclient` package that provides the `neutron` command-line client.

If you created this node with Vagrant, you can execute the following command:

```
vagrant ssh controller
```

Ensure you have set the following credentials (adjust the path to your certificates and key file to match your environment if not using the Vagrant environment):

```
export OS_TENANT_NAME=cookbook
export OS_USERNAME=admin
export OS_PASSWORD=openstack
export OS_AUTH_URL=https://192.168.100.200:5000/v2.0/
export OS_NO_CACHE=1
export OS_KEY=/vagrant/cakey.pem
export OS_CACERT=/vagrant/ca.pem
```

How to do it...

We will first create the Load Balancer pool then add in members (instances) running Apache to this pool. The steps are as follows:

1. We first list the subnets available in our environment and choose the subnet on which the Load Balancer will be created:

   ```
   neutron subnet-list
   ```

   The preceding command will give an output similar to this:

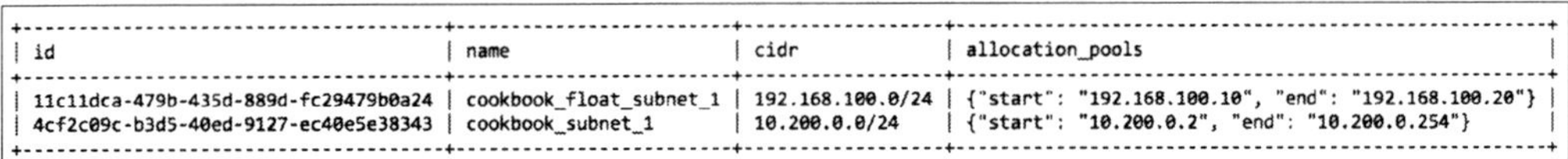

id	name	cidr	allocation_pools
11c11dca-479b-435d-889d-fc29479b0a24	cookbook_float_subnet_1	192.168.100.0/24	{"start": "192.168.100.10", "end": "192.168.100.20"}
4cf2c09c-b3d5-40ed-9127-ec40e5e38343	cookbook_subnet_1	10.200.0.0/24	{"start": "10.200.0.2", "end": "10.200.0.254"}

2. We take the `subnet-id` value of the subnet we want and use this to create the Load Balance pool as follows. Here we're using one of the private subnets, `cookbook_subnet_1`:

   ```
   neutron lb-pool-create \
       --description "Web Load Balancer" \
       --lb-method ROUND_ROBIN \
       --name Web-Load-Balancer \
       --protocol HTTP \
       --subnet-id 11c11dca-479b-435d-889d-fc29479b0a24
   ```

This creates output similar to this:

```
Created a new pool:
+------------------------+--------------------------------------+
| Field                  | Value                                |
+------------------------+--------------------------------------+
| admin_state_up         | True                                 |
| description            | Web Load Balancer                    |
| health_monitors        |                                      |
| health_monitors_status |                                      |
| id                     | 546e1f04-b059-453e-a619-c0e4efff8a52 |
| lb_method              | ROUND_ROBIN                          |
| members                |                                      |
| name                   | Web-Load-Balancer                    |
| protocol               | HTTP                                 |
| provider               | haproxy                              |
| status                 | PENDING_CREATE                       |
| status_description     |                                      |
| subnet_id              | 624ff352-2bca-40a2-bb45-efe0b824a6a1 |
| tenant_id              | 61fbdb985a834dce8f68f8dfabd73bd0     |
| vip_id                 |                                      |
+------------------------+--------------------------------------+
```

3. We now add the members to this Load Balancer pool. To do this, ensure two instances are running Apache. We can follow the *Using cloud-config to run the post-installation configuration* recipe in this chapter to create appropriate servers on the same network as the subnet used:

   ```
   nova boot \
       --flavor m1.tiny \
       --image trusty-image \
       --nic net-id=25153759-994f-4835-9b13-bf0ec77fb336 \
       --user-data ./webserver.yaml \
       --max-count 2 \
       webServer
   ```

4. With two web servers running, we can take assigned IPs and assign them to the created Load Balancer pool, `Web-Load-Balancer`:

   ```
   nova list
   ```

   You will get an output similar to this:

ID	Name	Status	Task State	Power State	Networks
2b672837-cc50-45b1-898e-5ce6bb68652c	test1	ACTIVE	-	Running	cookbook_network_1=11.200.0.2, 192.168.100.11
0ab5d1ed-7c17-45ca-9d41-daf48e27af20	webserver-0ab5d1ed-7c17-45ca-9d41-daf48e27af20	ACTIVE	-	Running	cookbook_network_1=11.200.0.5
3d1eba44-25a1-4aa9-8ce9-085531dbd5e1	webserver-3d1eba44-25a1-4aa9-8ce9-085531dbd5e1	ACTIVE	-	Running	cookbook_network_1=11.200.0.6

5. We take the first IP, `10.200.0.4`, and add it to the pool:

   ```
   neutron lb-member-create \
       --address 10.200.0.4 \
       --protocol-port 80 \
       Web-Load-Balancer
   ```

   You will get the following output:

   ```
   Created a new member:
   +--------------------+--------------------------------------+
   | Field              | Value                                |
   +--------------------+--------------------------------------+
   | address            | 10.200.0.4                           |
   | admin_state_up     | True                                 |
   | id                 | 5cade31f-7208-4623-88d2-f0d60818cce5 |
   | pool_id            | 7d1aef98-90ee-4b6f-82a2-1b4b39c3c444 |
   | protocol_port      | 80                                   |
   | status             | PENDING_CREATE                       |
   | status_description |                                      |
   | tenant_id          | 001504d6f08d4698824636fa00f4a0f2     |
   | weight             | 1                                    |
   +--------------------+--------------------------------------+
   ```

6. We repeat this for the IP of the second web server:

   ```
   neutron lb-member-create
       --address 10.200.0.5 \
       --protocol-port 80 \
       Web-Load-Balancer
   ```

7. We can view the status of pool members by issuing the following command:

   ```
   neutron lb-member-list
   ```

   The preceding command will give an output similar to this:

```
+--------------------------------------+-------------+---------------+--------+----------------+--------+
| id                                   | address     | protocol_port | weight | admin_state_up | status |
+--------------------------------------+-------------+---------------+--------+----------------+--------+
| af96b7f1-e2b0-4f5c-ae70-7e99a75079bf | 11.200.0.5 |            80 |      1 | True           | ACTIVE |
| ee1aa038-53d5-44df-ae29-89af7548d9fc | 11.200.0.6 |            80 |      1 | True           | ACTIVE |
+--------------------------------------+-------------+---------------+--------+----------------+--------+
```

8. We now need to create the **Virtual IP** (**VIP**) to access the Load Balance pool and the instances sitting behind it. We will create this VIP on the public network:

   ```
   neutron subnet-list
   ```

The preceding command will give an output similar to this:

```
+--------------------------------------+--------------------------+------------------+------------------------------------------------------+
| id                                   | name                     | cidr             | allocation_pools                                     |
+--------------------------------------+--------------------------+------------------+------------------------------------------------------+
| 11c11dca-479b-435d-889d-fc29479b0a24 | cookbook_float_subnet_1  | 192.168.100.0/24 | {"start": "192.168.100.10", "end": "192.168.100.20"} |
| 4cf2c09c-b3d5-40ed-9127-ec40e5e38343 | cookbook_subnet_1        | 10.200.0.0/24    | {"start": "10.200.0.2", "end": "10.200.0.254"}       |
+--------------------------------------+--------------------------+------------------+------------------------------------------------------+
```

9. We take the floating/external subnet ID to create our publically accessible VIP:

```
neutron lb-vip-create \
    --name WebserverVIF \
    --protocol-port 80 \
    --protocol HTTP \
    --subnet-id 11c11dca-479b-435d-889d-fc29479b0a24 \
    Web-Load-Balancer
```

You will get output similar to this:

```
Created a new vip:
+---------------------+--------------------------------------+
| Field               | Value                                |
+---------------------+--------------------------------------+
| address             | 192.168.100.12                       |
| admin_state_up      | True                                 |
| connection_limit    | -1                                   |
| description         |                                      |
| id                  | c66c59a8-b34a-47e2-8239-63aa685c96c5 |
| name                | WebserverVIF                         |
| pool_id             | 7d1aef98-90ee-4b6f-82a2-1b4b39c3c444 |
| port_id             | 1b1f227c-9439-47fc-b6f9-e0c24e03b5b9 |
| protocol            | HTTP                                 |
| protocol_port       | 80                                   |
| session_persistence |                                      |
| status              | PENDING_CREATE                       |
| status_description  |                                      |
| subnet_id           | 11c11dca-479b-435d-889d-fc29479b0a24 |
| tenant_id           | 001504d6f08d4698824636fa00f4a0f2     |
+---------------------+--------------------------------------+
```

We can see it has an IP of `192.168.100.12`. We can use a web browser and point it to that address; it will be balancing the traffic between our two web servers.

How it works...

We create a Load Balancer pool with two instances as members, and then assign a VIP to the pool to be used to access the instances. To do this, we perform the following steps:

1. Create the Load Balance pool with `neutron lb-pool-create`.
2. Add the member instances to the pool with `neutron lb-member-create` by adding the IPs of the subnet used.
3. Create a VIP on the external floating IP range so the pool is accessible from the network using `neutron lb-vip-create`.
4. When creating the Load Balance pool, we use the following syntax:

```
neutron lb-pool-create \
    --description $DESCRIPTION \
    --lb-method $LB_METHOD \
    --name $LB_NAME \
    --protocol $PROTOCOL \
    --subnet-id $SUBNET_ID
```

Configuring Neutron FWaaS

After our work with the OpenStack Neutron LBaaS plugin, let's look at another useful plugin, **FireWall as a Service** (**FWaaS**). By enabling the FWaaS agent plugin on our `network` node, we are able to create and manage firewalls through Neutron API calls. There are drivers for many hardware vendors; the following example uses IPTables to provide the firewalling service.

We configure Neutron FWaaS on the nodes running the Neutron L3 agent (this will be the `network` node if not using **Distributed Virtual Routers** (**DVR**), or the `compute` node if using DVR) and configure Neutron Server API on the `controller` nodes to pick up the service. We can also expose the FWaaS feature in Horizon on the `controller` nodes.

Getting ready

Ensure that you have a suitable server running the OpenStack network components. If you are using the accompanying Vagrant environment, as described in the *Preface*, we will use the same `network` and `controller` nodes for this recipe.

Ensure that you are logged into the `network` node as well as the `controller` node in our environment. If you created these nodes with Vagrant, you can execute the following command:

```
vagrant ssh network
vagrant ssh controller
```

How to do it...

To enable the Neutron FWaaS feature, first carry out the following steps on the nodes running the L3 agent. In normal circumstances this will be the `network` node. If you are running DVR, this will be on the `compute` nodes. Follow these steps:

1. We enable the firewall service in the `[DEFAULT]` section of the `/etc/neutron/neutron.conf` file by adding `firewall` to the `service_plugins` line:

    ```
    service_plugins = firewall
    ```

The `service_plugins` line is a comma-delimited list, for example:

```
service_plugins = router, firewall
```

2. In the same file, we add the following lines to the `[SERVICE_PROVIDERS]` section:

    ```
    [SERVICE_PROVIDERS]
    service_provider =
    FIREWALL:Iptables:neutron.agent.linux.iptables_firewall.
    OVSHybridIptablesFirewallDriver:default
    ```

3. We then edit the `/etc/neutron/fwaas_driver.ini` file so it has the following content:

    ```
    [fwaas]
    driver = neutron.services.firewall.drivers.linux.iptables_fwaas.
    IptablesFwaasDriver
    enabled = True
    ```

4. Restart the `neutron-l3-agent` service to pick up these changes as follows:

    ```
    sudo restart neutron-l3-agent
    ```

5. On the `controller` node running the Neutron Server API and Horizon, make the same change to the `/etc/neutron/neutron.conf` file:

    ```
    [DEFAULT]
    service_plugins = firewall

    [SERVICE_PROVIDERS]
    ```

```
service_provider =
FIREWALL:Iptables:neutron.agent.linux.iptables_firewall.
OVSHybridIptablesFirewallDriver:default
```

Add `firewall` to the `service_plugins` list if something already exists here, such as `router`:

```
service_plugins = router, firewall
```

6. Restart the Neutron Server service to pick up this change:

   ```
   sudo restart neutron-server
   ```

7. Edit the `/etc/openstack-dashboard/local_settings.py` file to enable the FWaaS feature in Horizon:

   ```
   OPENSTACK_NEUTRON_NETWORK = {
       'enable_firewall': True,
       ...
   }
   ```

8. Restart Apache to pick up this change:

   ```
   sudo service apache2 restart
   ```

How it works...

We have enabled the Neutron FWaaS plugin in our environment by configuring the relevant Neutron configuration files on our nodes that are running the L3 agent (`network` nodes in the non-DVR mode or `compute` nodes in the DVR mode).

The `/etc/neutron/neutron.conf` file notifies our Neutron services of this feature with the following lines:

```
[DEFAULT]
service_plugins = firewall

[SERVICE_PROVIDERS]
service_provider =
FIREWALL:Iptables:neutron.agent.linux.iptables_firewall.
OVSHybridIptablesFirewallDriver:default
```

The specific configuration of the LBaaS agent is achieved in the `/etc/neutron/fwaas-driver.ini` file on the node running the L3 agent.

We then notify the Neutron API service running on the `controller` node about the Neutron FWaaS Plugin. We copy the same `neutron.conf` settings found earlier onto the `controller` node and restart the Neutron Server API service.

We can then enable this feature in Horizon by setting the configuration `enable_firewall` to `True` and restarting Apache to pick up this change.

Using Neutron FWaaS

With Neutron FWaaS now installed, we can use this service through the Neutron API and command line. This allows us to create perimeter firewall policies between our routed Neutron networks.

With a Neutron firewall in place on the L3 router, any traffic traversing that router will be inspected there before it is allowed to continue. This allows us to have a firewall between layers of an application. For example, you may have a standard multi-tiered web application where a web server communicates with a database server. With Neutron firewalls in place, we can allow only database traffic to traverse between the database and the web server. Policies at the router level can be seen as traditional edge perimeter firewall policies, whereas *security groups* can be seen as similar to host-based security. Policy driven security also fits well with traditional network security teams moving to an OpenStack environment and allows standards to be controlled at the network level, rather than the `compute` level.

The following diagram explains this logical view with a clear separation of services provided by **Neutron FWaaS**. In this example, the **Web App Tier** is on a different subnet to the **Database Tier** and the Neutron L3 router and **FWaaS** is routing traffic between the two. The policy applied here will allow the traffic to communicate between the database and web servers—for example, only allowing TCP port 3306 from the **Web App Tier** subnet to the **Database Tier** subnet:

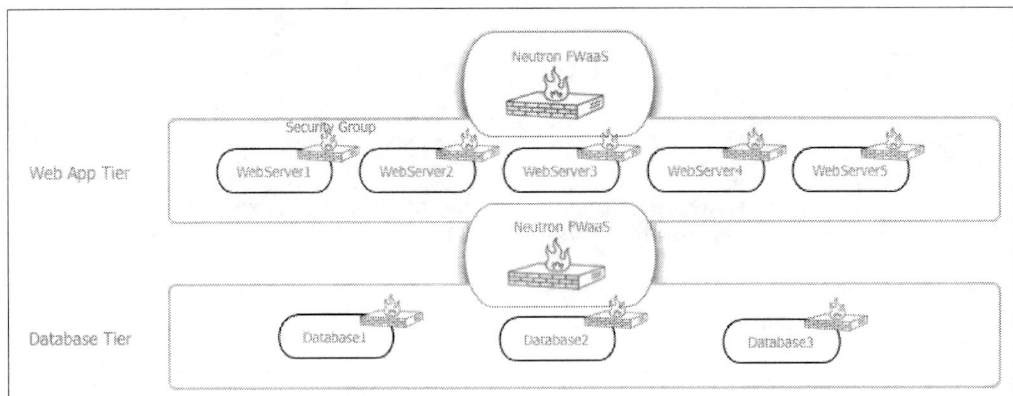

Getting ready

Ensure that you are logged into a Ubuntu host that has access to our OpenStack environment on the `192.168.100.0/24` public network. This host will be used to run client tools against the OpenStack environment created. If you are using the accompanying Vagrant environment, as described in the *Preface*, you can use the `controller` node. This has the `python-neutronclient` package that provides the `neutron` command-line client.

If you created this node with Vagrant, you can execute the following command:

```
vagrant ssh controller
```

Ensure that you have set the following credentials (adjust the path to your certificates and key file to match your environment if not using the Vagrant environment):

```
export OS_TENANT_NAME=cookbook
export OS_USERNAME=admin
export OS_PASSWORD=openstack
export OS_AUTH_URL=https://192.168.100.200:5000/v2.0/
export OS_NO_CACHE=1
export OS_KEY=/vagrant/cakey.pem
export OS_CACERT=/vagrant/ca.pem
vagrant ssh controller
```

How to do it...

In this section, we will create a firewall with a policy that has a rule to allow TCP port 80 connections and demonstrate its effect on the environment. The steps are as follows:

1. We first create the rule:

   ```
   neutron firewall-rule-create \
       --protocol tcp \
       --destination-port 80 \
       --action allow
   ```

You will get the following output:

```
Created a new firewall_rule:
+------------------------+--------------------------------------+
| Field                  | Value                                |
+------------------------+--------------------------------------+
| action                 | allow                                |
| description            |                                      |
| destination_ip_address |                                      |
| destination_port       | 80                                   |
| enabled                | True                                 |
| firewall_policy_id     |                                      |
| id                     | e43bade8-f50d-4655-bbf3-0030b7aa3dc8 |
| ip_version             | 4                                    |
| name                   |                                      |
| position               |                                      |
| protocol               | tcp                                  |
| shared                 | False                                |
| source_ip_address      |                                      |
| source_port            |                                      |
| tenant_id              | 68aa8242ee3c47279fcafa8fa6620311     |
+------------------------+--------------------------------------+
```

2. We then create a policy with the rules created:

```
neutron firewall-policy-create \
    --firewall-rules "e43bade8-f50d-4655-bbf3-0030b7aa3dc8" \
    allow-http-policy
```

This gives the following output:

```
Created a new firewall_policy:
+----------------+--------------------------------------+
| Field          | Value                                |
+----------------+--------------------------------------+
| audited        | False                                |
| description    |                                      |
| firewall_rules | e43bade8-f50d-4655-bbf3-0030b7aa3dc8 |
| id             | b12d0be0-9645-448a-b010-a8a8f47580d8 |
| name           | allow-http-policy                    |
| shared         | False                                |
| tenant_id      | 68aa8242ee3c47279fcafa8fa6620311     |
+----------------+--------------------------------------+
```

3. With the policy in place, we can now create the firewall by specifying the policy ID we just created:

```
neutron firewall-create
    --name cookbook-firewall
    b12d0be0-9645-448a-b010-a8a8f47580d8
```

You will get the following output:

```
Created a new firewall:
+--------------------+--------------------------------------+
| Field              | Value                                |
+--------------------+--------------------------------------+
| admin_state_up     | True                                 |
| description        |                                      |
| firewall_policy_id | b12d0be0-9645-448a-b010-a8a8f47580d8 |
| id                 | 1e0c0c8f-f8cf-46e2-bfd2-2b97f39d6ada |
| name               | cookbook-firewall                    |
| status             | CREATED                              |
| tenant_id          | 68aa8242ee3c47279fcafa8fa6620311     |
+--------------------+--------------------------------------+
```

4. We can list the available firewalls with the following command:

   neutron firewall-list

   The preceding command produces output similar to this:

```
+--------------------------------------+-------------------+--------------------------------------+
| id                                   | name              | firewall_policy_id                   |
+--------------------------------------+-------------------+--------------------------------------+
| 1e0c0c8f-f8cf-46e2-bfd2-2b97f39d6ada | cookbook-firewall | b12d0be0-9645-448a-b010-a8a8f47580d8 |
+--------------------------------------+-------------------+--------------------------------------+
```

5. We can show the details of the firewall, policy, and rules with the following set of commands. We begin with this command:

   neutron firewall-show 1e0c0c8f-f8cf-46e2-bfd2-2b97f39d6ada

   You will get the following output:

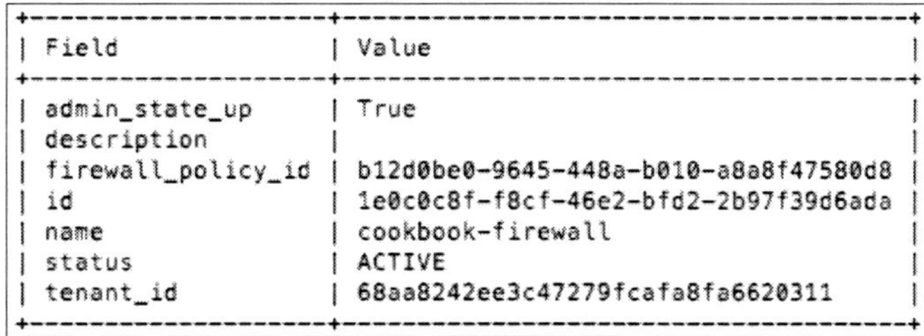

```
+--------------------+--------------------------------------+
| Field              | Value                                |
+--------------------+--------------------------------------+
| admin_state_up     | True                                 |
| description        |                                      |
| firewall_policy_id | b12d0be0-9645-448a-b010-a8a8f47580d8 |
| id                 | 1e0c0c8f-f8cf-46e2-bfd2-2b97f39d6ada |
| name               | cookbook-firewall                    |
| status             | ACTIVE                               |
| tenant_id          | 68aa8242ee3c47279fcafa8fa6620311     |
+--------------------+--------------------------------------+
```

The firewall will only show as **ACTIVE** if you have created a floating IP network, as this uses the L3 agent.

We execute this command:

```
neutron firewall-policy-show b12d0be0-9645-448a-b010-a8a8f47580d8
```

This gives the following output:

```
+----------------+--------------------------------------+
| Field          | Value                                |
+----------------+--------------------------------------+
| audited        | False                                |
| description    |                                      |
| firewall_rules | e43bade8-f50d-4655-bbf3-0030b7aa3dc8 |
| id             | b12d0be0-9645-448a-b010-a8a8f47580d8 |
| name           | allow-http-policy                    |
| shared         | False                                |
| tenant_id      | 68aa8242ee3c47279fcafa8fa6620311     |
+----------------+--------------------------------------+
```

We execute this command:

```
neutron firewall-rule-show e43bade8-f50d-4655-bbf3-0030b7aa3dc8
```

This gives the following output:

```
+------------------------+--------------------------------------+
| Field                  | Value                                |
+------------------------+--------------------------------------+
| action                 | allow                                |
| description            |                                      |
| destination_ip_address |                                      |
| destination_port       | 80                                   |
| enabled                | True                                 |
| firewall_policy_id     | b12d0be0-9645-448a-b010-a8a8f47580d8 |
| id                     | e43bade8-f50d-4655-bbf3-0030b7aa3dc8 |
| ip_version             | 4                                    |
| name                   |                                      |
| position               | 1                                    |
| protocol               | tcp                                  |
| shared                 | False                                |
| source_ip_address      |                                      |
| source_port            |                                      |
| tenant_id              | 68aa8242ee3c47279fcafa8fa6620311     |
+------------------------+--------------------------------------+
```

6. We will now spin up two instances on two different networks that are routed via our L3 routers:

```
# Create another network
neutron net-create anotherNet
SUBNET_ID=$(neutron subnet-create anotherNet \
    --name anotherSubnet 10.201.0.0/24
    | awk '/\ id\ / {print $4}')
```

```
# Connect to cookbook_router_1
neutron router-interface-add cookbook_router_1 ${SUBNET_ID}

# Get Network IDs
NET1=$(neutron net-list | awk '/network_1/ {print $2}')
NET2=$(neutron net-list | awk '/anotherNet/ {print $2}')

# Boot 2 instances
nova boot --flavor 1 --image cirros-image \
    --nic net-id=${NET1} net1-instance
nova boot --flavor 1 --image cirros-image \
    --nic net-id=${NET2} net2-instance
```

7. With a Neutron firewall policy in place on the L3 router between these two instances and networks, all other traffic is denied by default. This means we are unable to ping or SSH despite our default security group having this enabled. The policy rule we created allowed TCP port 80 traffic between our instances (source and destination were blank, meaning that the TCP port 80 would work in both directions). With a web server, say Apache, running on port 80 on either of the instances, we can execute the following command to test our firewall policy rule:

   `wget http://10.200.0.2/`

   This will return the following output if the test was successful:

```
--2015-02-09 04:22:37--  http://10.200.0.2/
Connecting to 10.200.0.2:80... connected.
HTTP request sent, awaiting response... 200 OK
```

Ensure that your local security group has a rule to allow TCP port 80 for this to work. Neutron firewall policy rules do not automatically override security group rules.

8. Now we will try to use **Secure Shell** (**SSH**) to connect the same instance:

   `ssh cirros@10.200.0.2`

   This `ssh` command will timeout because our firewall policy only allows TCP port 80 at present.

9. To add a rule to our Neutron firewall, we carry out the following steps. We first create a new firewall rule, specifying TCP port 22:

```
neutron firewall-rule-create \
    --protocol tcp \
    --destination-port 22 \
    --action allow
```

10. We can either update an existing policy, or create a new one specifically for this rule. We will create a new policy in this example:

```
neutron firewall-policy-create \
    --firewall-rules "451e65e0-a1c2-4cc1-8a5d-1ef0608ec1f6" \
    allow-ssh-policy
```

You will get an output similar to this:

```
Created a new firewall_policy:
+----------------+--------------------------------------+
| Field          | Value                                |
+----------------+--------------------------------------+
| audited        | False                                |
| description    |                                      |
| firewall_rules | 451e65e0-a1c2-4cc1-8a5d-1ef0608ec1f6 |
| id             | e78ba041-d1f3-4f9f-93c2-c6f0fc680e86 |
| name           | allow-ssh-policy                     |
| shared         | False                                |
| tenant_id      | 35735709193949ffa8fbfed613ac2d46     |
+----------------+--------------------------------------+
```

11. We then update the firewall with this new policy:

```
neutron firewall-update \
    --policy e78ba041-d1f3-4f9f-93c2-c6f0fc680e86 \
    cookbook-firewall
```

You will get a message saying that the firewall has been updated.

12. We can now test whether we can use SSH between our instances again:

```
ssh cirros@10.200.0.2
```

This will now connect to our instance (although a failure might occur because of incorrect credentials, the fact we got a message about the authentication failure proves TCP port 22 is open).

How it works...

Neutron firewalls are policy-driven firewall rules that exist on the router between different subnets. This allows a network administrator of our OpenStack cloud to create policies at a network level, instead of relying on users to maintain security group rules.

To create a Neutron firewall, carry out the following steps:

1. Create the firewall rule with `neutron firewall-rule-create`.
2. Create the policy with `neutron firewall-policy-create $RULE_ID`.
3. Create the firewall with the policy using `neutron firewall-create $POLICY_ID`.

The order of priority of rules when using Neutron firewalls is as follows:

1. Neutron firewall policy.
2. Security group rules.
3. Any host-based rules inside the running instance (for example, `iptables`).

It is important to ensure that we allow correct access to services running on the instances; security group rules exist to allow access for these running service. In other words, a network administrator might have a policy to allow TCP port 80 through the L3 router between subnets, but there needs to be a security group rule applied to the instance to allow TCP port 80 too.

Installing the Heat OpenStack Orchestration service

Heat is the OpenStack Orchestration service and provides a template-based system to define environments and resources in OpenStack. It is said that the Dragon Operator only ever needed OpenStack Heat and the nascent energies of the Universe to deploy on OpenStack. With Heat, you can describe Compute resources, the installation of software, and the relationship with Load Balancers and databases.

Getting ready

Ensure that you have a suitable server running the OpenStack components. If you are using the accompanying Vagrant environment, as described in the *Preface*, we will use the same `controller` node.

Ensure that you are logged into the `controller` node in our environment. If you created this node with Vagrant, you can execute the following command:

```
vagrant ssh controller
```

How to do it...

To install Heat, carry out the following steps on the `controller` node:

1. We create a `heat` database using the following commands:

   ```
   MYSQL_ROOT_PASS=openstack

   mysql -uroot
       -p$MYSQL_ROOT_PASS
       -e 'CREATE DATABASE heat;'
   ```

2. We create a `heat` user with the password `openstack` and with privileges to use this database:

   ```
   MYSQL_HEAT_PASS=openstack

   mysql -uroot -p${MYSQL_ROOT_PASS}
       -e "GRANT ALL PRIVILEGES ON heat.* TO 'heat'@'%'
   IDENTIFIED BY '${MYSQL_HEAT_PASS}';"

   mysql -uroot -p${MYSQL_ROOT_PASS}
       -e "GRANT ALL PRIVILEGES ON heat.* TO 'heat'@'localhost'
   IDENTIFIED BY '${MYSQL_HEAT_PASS}';"
   ```

3. Keystone needs to be aware of Heat, so first ensure that there are Keystone credentials for the Heat service by executing the following commands:

   ```
   keystone user-create \
       --name=heat \
       --pass=heat \
       --email=heat@localhost

   keystone user-role-add \
       --user=heat \
       --tenant=service \
       --role=admin
   ```

4. We then add the following two services and endpoints for Heat in Keystone by executing the following commands:

```
keystone service-create \
    --name=heat \
    --type=orchestration \
    --description="Heat Orchestration API"

ORCHESTRATION_SERVICE_ID=$(keystone service-list \
    | awk '/\ orchestration\ / {print $2}')

keystone endpoint-create
  --region RegionOne \
  --service-id=${ORCHESTRATION_SERVICE_ID} \
  --publicurl=http://172.16.0.200:8004/v1/$\(tenant_id\)s \
  --internalurl=http://172.16.0.200:8004/v1/$\(tenant_id\)s \
  --adminurl=http://172.16.0.200:8004/v1/$\(tenant_id\)s

keystone service-create \
    --name=heat-cfn \
    --type=cloudformation \
    --description="Heat CloudFormation API"

CLOUDFORMATION_SERVICE_ID=$(keystone service-list \
    | awk '/\ cloudformation\ / {print $2}')

keystone --insecure endpoint-create \
  --region RegionOne \
  --service-id=${CLOUDFORMATION_SERVICE_ID} \
  --publicurl=http://172.16.0.200:8000/v1/ \
  --internalurl=http://172.16.0.200:8000/v1 \
  --adminurl=http://172.16.0.200:8000/v1
```

5. We can now install the packages required for Heat using `apt`:

```
sudo apt-get install heat-api heat-api-cfn heat-engine
```

6. The Heat configuration file is `/etc/heat/heat.conf`. Edit this file to include the following lines:

```
[DEFAULT]
rabbit_host=172.16.0.200
rabbit_port=5672
rabbit_userid=guest
rabbit_password=guest
rabbit_virtual_host=/
rabbit_ha_queues=false
log_dir=/var/log/heat

[database]
backend=sqlalchemy
connection = mysql://heat:openstack@172.16.0.200/heat

[keystone_authtoken]
auth_uri = https://192.168.100.200:35357/v2.0
identity_uri = https://192.168.100.200:5000
admin_tenant_name = service
admin_user = heat
admin_password = heat
insecure = True
heat_watch_server_url = http://192.168.100.200:8003
heat_waitcondition_server_url =
http://192.168.100.200:8000/v1/waitcondition
heat_metadata_server_url = http://192.168.100.200:8000

[clients]
endpoint_type = internalURL

[clients_ceilometer]
endpoint_type = internalURL

[clients_cinder]
endpoint_type = internalURL

[clients_heat]
endpoint_type = internalURL

[clients_keystone]
endpoint_type = internalURL
```

```
[clients_neutron]
endpoint_type = internalURL

[clients_nova]
endpoint_type = internalURL

[clients_swift]
endpoint_type = internalURL

[clients_trove]
endpoint_type = internalURL

[ec2authtoken]
auth_uri = https://192.168.100.200:5000/v2.0

[heat_api]
bind_port = 8004

[heat_api_cfn]
bind_port = 8000

[heat_api_cloudwatch]
bind_port = 8003
```

7. Before we can start the services, we must create the Heat database tables and initial entries with the following command:

   ```
   heat-manage db_sync
   ```

8. We finally restart the services with the following commands:

   ```
   service heat-api restart
   service heat-api-cfn restart
   service heat-engine restart
   ```

How it works...

Heat, just as with any other OpenStack Service, requires credentials to be present in our database backend, with credentials and service endpoints defined in Keystone. We then use these credentials in the `/etc/heat/heat.conf` file that describes the service.

It is important to note that the initialization of the database with the `heat-manage db_sync` command is done before starting the services. This process prepares the table structure in our database for Heat to use.

Using Heat to spin up instances

With Heat, we can create a wide variety of templates—from spinning up basic instances to creating complete environments for an application. In this section, we will show the basics of Heat by spinning up an instance, attaching it to an existing Neutron network, and assigning a floating IP to it. Heat templates, known as **Heat Orchestration Templates** (**HOT**) are **Yet Another Markup Language** (**YAML**) based files. The files describe the resources being used, the type and size of the instances, and the network an instance will be attached to, among other pieces of information required to run that environment.

In this section, we will show how to use a HOT file to spin up two web servers running Apache that are connected to a third instance running HA Proxy.

Getting ready

Ensure you are logged into a Ubuntu host that has access to our OpenStack environment on the `192.168.100.0/24` public network. This host will be used to run client tools against the OpenStack environment created. If you are using the accompanying Vagrant environment, as described in the *Preface*, you can use `controller` node. This has the `python-heatclient` package that provides the `heat` command-line client.

> If you are using the provided Vagrant environment, this public network isn't routed to the Internet as a physical environment will be. The result is that our instances have no way to access remote packages for installation as described in the Heat templates. To overcome this, we can run a proxy server, such as Squid, on our host running this virtual environment. This should be configured to allow access on the `192.168.100.0/24` network. The example HOT file assumes Squid to be running at the address `http://192.168.100.1:3128/`, which has been assigned on a physical host.

If you created this node with Vagrant, you can execute the following command:

```
vagrant ssh controller
```

Ensure that you have set the following credentials (adjust the path to your certificates and key file to match your environment if not using the Vagrant environment):

```
export OS_TENANT_NAME=cookbook
export OS_USERNAME=admin
export OS_PASSWORD=openstack
```

```
export OS_AUTH_URL=https://192.168.100.200:5000/v2.0/
export OS_NO_CACHE=1
export OS_KEY=/vagrant/cakey.pem
export OS_CACERT=/vagrant/ca.pem
```

How to do it...

In this section, we will download a HOT file called `cookbook.yaml`, which will describe our instance and the network to attach it to. The steps are as follows:

1. First, we download the HOT file from the Cookbook GitHub repository using the following command:

   ```
   wget -O cookbook.yaml \
   https://raw.githubusercontent.com/OpenStackCookbook/
   OpenStackCookbook/master/cookbook.yaml
   ```

2. Heat takes input parameters from the command line or from an environment file that gets passed to the template. These parameters are seen at the top of the HOT file as shown in the following code:

   ```
   parameters:
     key_name:
       type: string
       description: Name of keypair to assign to servers
     image:
       type: string
       description: Name of image to use for servers
     flavor:
       type: string
       description: Flavor to use for servers
     public_net_id:
       type: string
       description: >
         ID of public network for which floating IP addresses
   will be allocated
     private_net_id:
       type: string
       description: ID of private network into which servers
   get deployed
     private_subnet_id:
       type: string
       description: ID of private sub network into which
   servers get deployed
   ```

3. As you can see, we have to pass in various parameters when we launch this template. Ensure that you have these details by running the following commands:

   ```
   nova keypair-list
   nova image-list
   nova flavor-list
   neutron net-list
   ```

   The neutron net-list output may look similar to this:

```
+--------------------------------------+---------------------+------------------------------------------------------+
| id                                   | name                | subnets                                              |
+--------------------------------------+---------------------+------------------------------------------------------+
| 5e5d24bd-9d1f-4ed1-84b5-0b7e2a9a233b | ext_net             | 11c11dca-479b-435d-889d-fc29479b0a24 192.168.100.0/24 |
| 25153759-994f-4835-9b13-bf0ec77fb336 | cookbook_network_1  | 4cf2c09c-b3d5-40ed-9127-ec40e5e38343 10.200.0.0/24   |
+--------------------------------------+---------------------+------------------------------------------------------+
```

4. With the information at hand, we create an environment file that will be used to store our parameters. These parameters will be passed to the HOT file when we launch the stack. Create `cookbook-env.yaml` in the same directory as `cookbook.yaml` with the following lines, based on the output of the previous commands:

   ```
   parameters:
     key_name: demokey
     image: trusty-image
     flavor: m1.tiny
     public_net_id: 5e5d24bd-9d1f-4ed1-84b5-0b7e2a9a233b
     private_net_id: 25153759-994f-4835-9b13-bf0ec77fb336
     private_subnet_id: 4cf2c09c-b3d5-40ed-9127-ec40e5e38343
   ```

5. We're now ready to launch this stack with the following commands:

   ```
   heat stack-create haproxy101 \
       --template-file=cookbook.yaml \
       --environment-file=cookbook-env.yaml
   ```

   This will produce the following output:

```
+--------------------------------------+------------+--------------------+----------------------+
| id                                   | stack_name | stack_status       | creation_time        |
+--------------------------------------+------------+--------------------+----------------------+
| 5484d8ec-62ae-4c59-80f2-ce9a8ada9098 | haproxy101 | CREATE_IN_PROGRESS | 2015-02-23T16:38:54Z |
+--------------------------------------+------------+--------------------+----------------------+
```

6. To view a list of stacks, execute the following command:

   heat stack-list

   You will get a list of stacks that are currently running:

```
+--------------------------------------+------------+-----------------+----------------------+
| id                                   | stack_name | stack_status    | creation_time        |
+--------------------------------------+------------+-----------------+----------------------+
| 5484d8ec-62ae-4c59-80f2-ce9a8ada9098 | haproxy101 | CREATE_COMPLETE | 2015-02-23T16:38:54Z |
+--------------------------------------+------------+-----------------+----------------------+
```

7. A section in the template references outputs. Outputs allow a user to interrogate these values so they can access the running stack; without this, the user would have to do more digging into the running systems to find out which IP addresses were assigned to the instances that make up the stack. To see a list of outputs associated with our running stack, execute the following command:

   heat output-list

   You will get the following output:

```
+-------------------------+------------------------------------------------+
| output_key              | description                                    |
+-------------------------+------------------------------------------------+
| haproxy_public_ip       | Floating IP address of haproxy in public network |
| webserver1_private_ip   | IP address of webserver1 in private network    |
| webserver2_private_ip   | IP address of webserver2 in private network    |
+-------------------------+------------------------------------------------+
```

8. To view a particular value, we will access the public IP (floating IP) assigned to our HA Proxy so that we can access the websites that are running on private addresses behind the Load Balancer:

   heat output-show haproxy101 haproxy_public_ip

   This gives you the IP address:

   192.168.100.12

9. We can then use the address `http://192.168.100.12/` to send the request to either of the web servers running configured as part of this HA Proxy Load Balancer demonstration.

How it works...

HOT are *YAML* files (also known as *stacks*) that describe our environment. The basic templates generally have the following structure:

```
description:
parameters:
resources:
outputs:
```

- The `description:` section: This section helps a user understand what is expected to occur when the template is used.
- The `parameters:` section: This section defines the input variables—for example, the type of image(s) to be used, the network(s) to attach the instances on, and key pair names to be associated with the instances. Parameters are arbitrary and can contain any information you may need to execute the template properly. The `parameters:` section works with the information found in the accompanying environment file (as specified by `--environment-file= parameter`). Each parameter must either have a default value or be specified in the environment file for the stack to launch successfully.
- The `resources:` section: This section is the biggest as it describes the environment. It can describe the instances that will be used, the naming of them, what networks to attach, how all of the elements relate to each other, and how the environment is orchestrated. Explanations of how best to write these resources are beyond the scope of this book.
- The `outputs:` section: This section refers to the *return* values from the stack execution. For example, a user will need to know how to access a particular stack that has just been created. Random IPs and hostnames can all be assigned as part of the normal operation of running stacks, so you should be able to ask for the right information in order to access the environment.

10

Using the OpenStack Dashboard

In this chapter, we will cover the following recipes:

- Installing OpenStack Dashboard
- Using OpenStack Dashboard for key management
- Using OpenStack Dashboard to manage Neutron networks
- Using OpenStack Dashboard for security group management
- Using OpenStack Dashboard to launch instances
- Using OpenStack Dashboard to terminate instances
- Using OpenStack Dashboard to connect to instances using a VNC
- Using OpenStack Dashboard to add new tenants - projects
- Using OpenStack Dashboard for user management
- Using OpenStack Dashboard with LBaaS
- Using OpenStack Dashboard with OpenStack Orchestration

Introduction

Managing our OpenStack environment through a command-line interface allows us to have complete control of our cloud environment, but having a web-based interface that operators and administrators can use to manage their environments and instances makes this process easier. OpenStack Dashboard, known as Horizon, provides this graphical, web-based, user interface. Horizon is a web service that runs from an Apache installation, using Python's **Web Service Gateway Interface** (**WSGI**) and Django, a rapid development web framework.

With OpenStack Dashboard installed, we can manage all the core components of our OpenStack environment.

Installing OpenStack Dashboard

Installing OpenStack Dashboard is a straightforward process using Ubuntu's package repository.

Getting ready

Ensure that you are logged in to the OpenStack `controller` node. If you use Vagrant to create this as described in the *Installing the OpenStack Identity service* recipe of *Chapter 1, Keystone – OpenStack Identity Service*, we can access this with the following command:

```
vagrant ssh controller
```

How to do it...

To install OpenStack Dashboard, we simply install the required packages and dependencies by following these steps:

1. Install the required packages as follows:

   ```
   sudo apt-get update
   sudo apt-get install openstack-dashboard
   ```

2. We can configure the OpenStack Dashboard by editing the `/etc/openstack-dashboard/local_settings.py` file, thus:

   ```
   OPENSTACK_HOST = "192.168.100.200"
   OPENSTACK_KEYSTONE_URL = "http://%s:5000/v2.0" %
   OPENSTACK_HOST
   OPENSTACK_KEYSTONE_DEFAULT_ROLE = "_member_"
   CACHES = {
       'default': {
           'BACKEND':
   'django.core.cache.backends.memcached.MemcachedCache',
           'LOCATION': '127.0.0.1:11211',
       }
   }
   ALLOWED_HOSTS = '*'
   ```

3. Now we need to configure OpenStack Compute to use our **Virtual Network Console** (**VNC**) proxy service that can be used through our OpenStack Dashboard interface. To do so, add the following lines to `/etc/nova/nova.conf`:

```
# NoVNC
novnc_enabled=true
novncproxy_host=192.168.100.200
novncproxy_base_url=http://192.168.100.200:6080/vnc_auto.
html
novncproxy_port=6080

xvpvncproxy_port=6081
xvpvncproxy_host=192.168.100.200
xvpvncproxy_base_url=http://192.168.100.200:6081/console

vncserver_proxyclient_address=192.168.100.200
vncserver_listen=0.0.0.0
```

4. Restart `nova-api` to pick up the changes:

```
sudo restart nova-api
sudo restart nova-compute
sudo service apache2 restart
```

Installing OpenStack Dashboard under Ubuntu gives a slightly different look and feel from a stock installation of Dashboard. The functions remain the same, although Ubuntu adds an additional feature to allow the user to download environment settings for the Canonicals' orchestration tool, Juju. To remove the Ubuntu theme, execute the following command:

```
sudo dpkg --purge openstack-dashboard-ubuntu-theme
```

How it works...

Installing the OpenStack Dashboard, Horizon, is done using the Ubuntu package repository. Given that the OpenStack Dashboard runs over an Apache web server, we have to restart the web server to pick up the changes.

We also include the VNC Proxy service. It provides us with a great feature to access our instances over the network, through the web interface.

For the remainder of this chapter, the screenshots show the standard OpenStack interface after the removal of the Ubuntu theme.

Using OpenStack Dashboard for key management

The **Secure Shell** (**SSH**) key pairs allow users to connect to Linux instances without requiring to input passwords and is the default access mechanism for almost all Linux images that you will use for OpenStack. Users can manage their own key pairs through the OpenStack Dashboard. Usually, this is the first task a new user has to do when given access to our OpenStack environment.

Getting ready

Load a web browser, point it to our OpenStack Dashboard address at `http://192.168.100.200/`, and log in as a user, such as the `demo` user created in the *Adding users to Keystone* recipe of *Chapter 1, Keystone – OpenStack Identity Service*, with the password `openstack`.

How to do it...

Management of the logged-in user's key pairs is achieved with the steps discussed in the following sections.

Adding key pairs

Key pairs can be added by performing the following steps:

1. A new key pair can be added to our system by clicking on the **Access & Security** tab under the **Project** | **Compute** section:

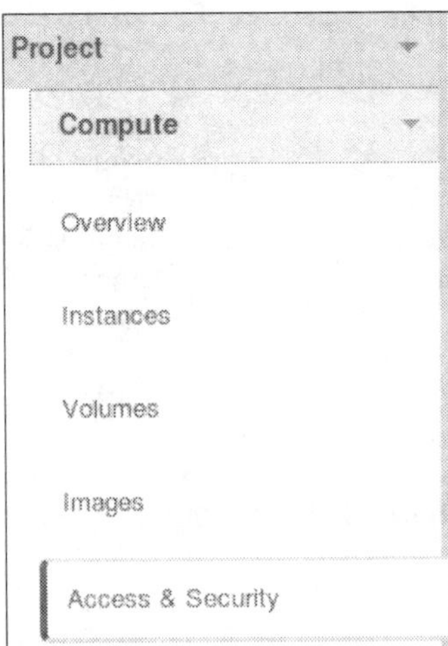

2. We will now see a screen allowing access to security settings and key pair management. Under the **Key Pairs** tab, there will be a list of valid key pairs that we can use when launching and accessing our instances. To create a new key pair, click on the **Create Key Pair** button:

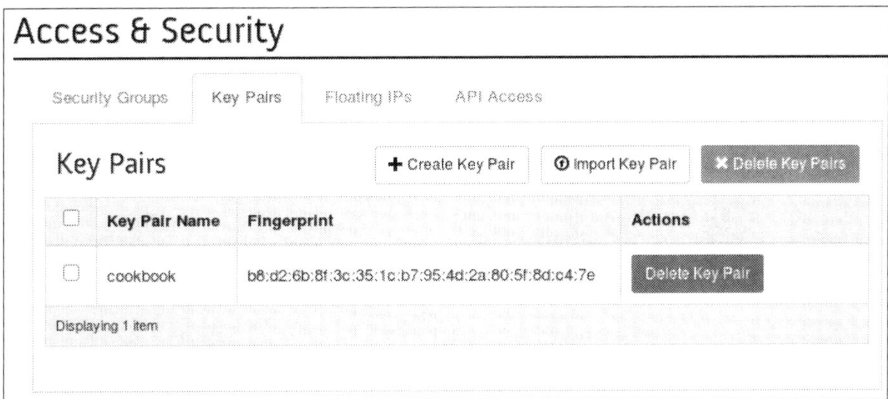

3. On the **Create Key Pair** screen, type in a meaningful name (for example, `demo`) ensuring there are no spaces in the name, and then click on the **Create Key Pair** button:

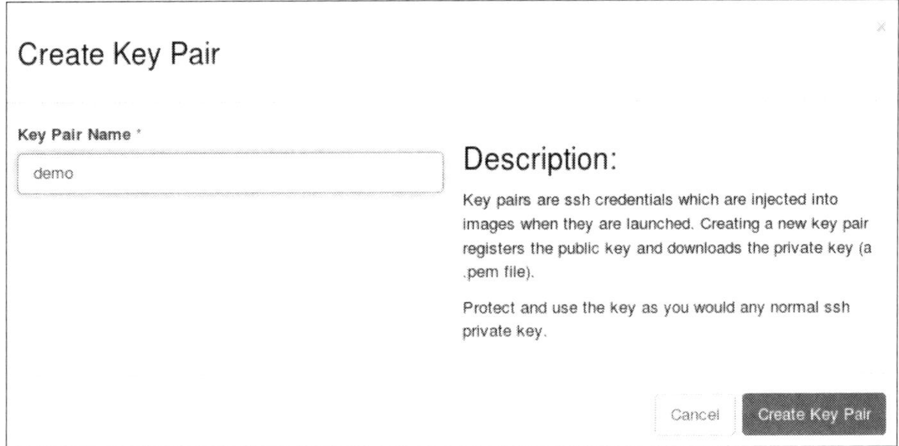

4. Once the key pair is created, we will be asked to save the private key portion of our key pair on the disk:

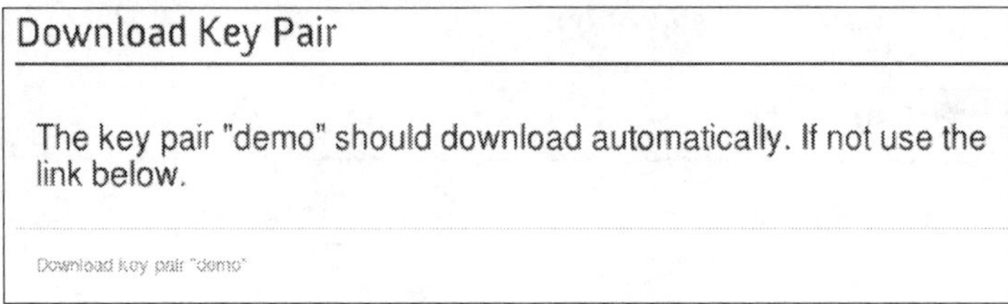

A private SSH key cannot be recreated, so keep this safe and store it safely and appropriately on the file system.

5. Click on the **Access & Security** tab to return to our list of key pairs. We will now see the newly created key pair listed. When launching instances, we can select this new key pair and gain access to it only by using the private key that we have stored locally:

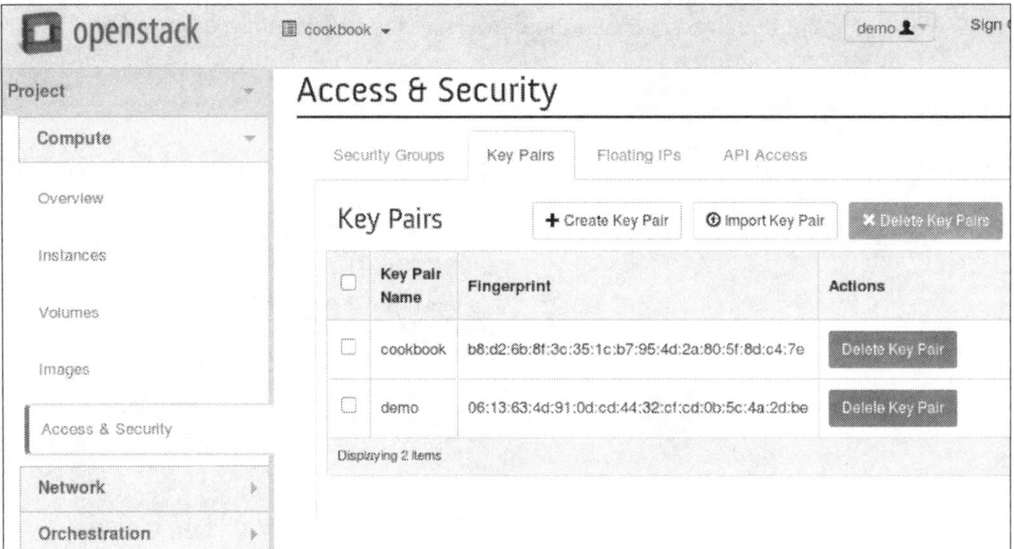

Deleting key pairs

Key pairs can be deleted by performing the following steps:

1. When key pairs are no longer required, we can delete them from our OpenStack environment. To do so, click on the **Access & Security** tab on the left of the screen.

2. We will then be presented with a screen allowing access to security settings and key pair management, as shown in the following screenshot. Under **Key Pairs**, there will be a list of key pairs that we can use to access our instances. To delete a key pair from our system, click on the **Delete Key Pair** button for the key pair that we want to delete:

3. We will be presented with a confirmation dialog box:

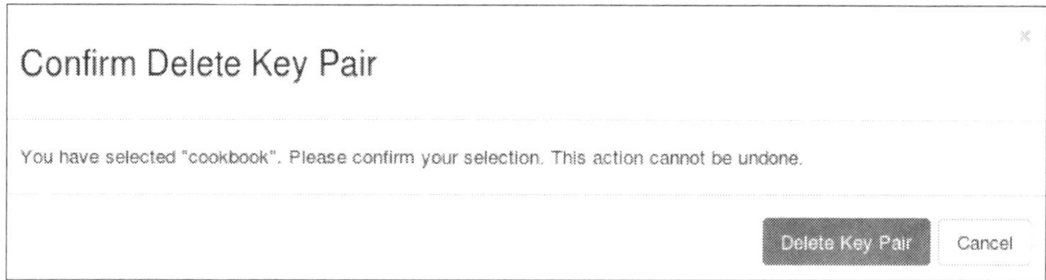

Once we click on the **Delete Key Pair** button, the key pair will be deleted.

Importing key pairs

If you have your own key pairs that you use to access other systems, these can be imported into your OpenStack environment so that you can continue to use them for accessing instances within your OpenStack Compute environment. To import key pairs, perform the following steps:

1. We can import key pairs that have been created in our traditional Linux-based environments into our OpenStack setup. If you don't have one already, run the following command from your Linux-based or other Unix-based host:

   ```
   ssh-keygen -t rsa -N "" -f id_rsa
   ```

2. This will produce the following two files on our client:
   - `.ssh/id_rsa`
   - `.ssh/id_rsa.pub`

3. The `.ssh/id_rsa` file is our private key and has to be protected, as it is the only key that matches the public portion of the key pair: `.ssh/id_rsa.pub`.

4. We can import this public key to use in our OpenStack environment so that, when an instance is launched, the public key is inserted into our running instance. To import the public key, ensure that you're at the **Access & Security** screen, and, then, under **Key pairs**, click on the **Import Key Pair** button:

5. We are presented with a screen that asks us to name our key pair and paste in the contents of our public key, as shown in the following screenshot. So, name the key pair and then copy-and-paste the contents of the public key into the space—for example, the contents of `.ssh/id_rsa.pub`. Once entered, click on the **Import Key Pair** button:

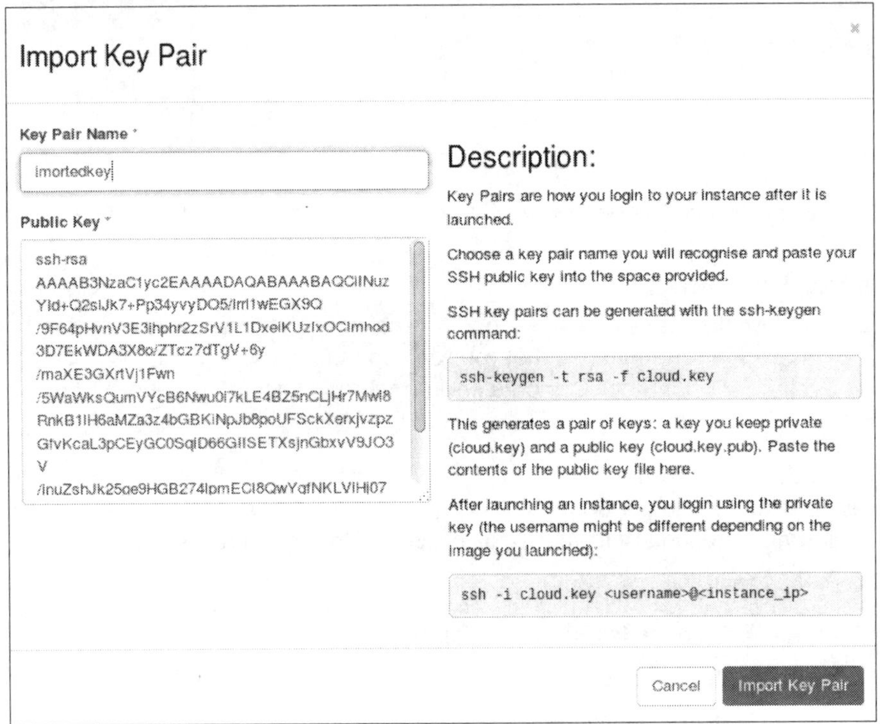

Once completed, we see the list of key pairs available for that user, including our imported key pair:

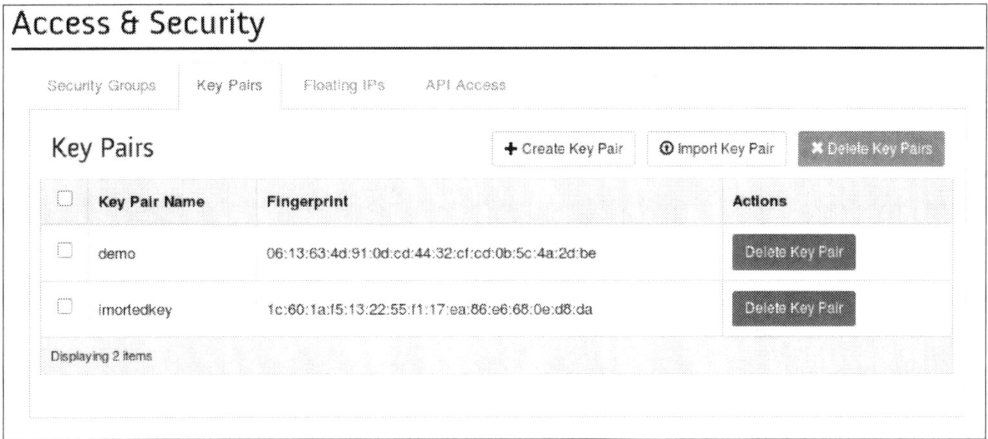

How it works...

Key pair management is important, as it provides a consistent and secure approach for accessing our running instances. Allowing the user to create, delete, and import key pairs to use within their tenants enables them to create more secure systems.

The OpenStack Dashboard allows a user to create key pairs easily. The user must ensure, though, that the private key that he/she downloads is kept secure.

While deleting a key pair is simple, the user must remember that deleted key pairs that are associated with running instances will remove access to the running system. Every key pair created is unique, regardless of the name. The name is simply a label, but the unique fingerprint of the key is required and cannot be recreated.

Importing key pairs has the advantage that we can use our existing secure key pairs that we have been using outside OpenStack within our new private cloud environment. This provides a consistent user experience when moving from one environment to another.

Using OpenStack Dashboard to manage Neutron networks

The OpenStack Dashboard has the ability to view, create, and edit Neutron networks, which makes managing complex software-defined networks much easier. Certain functions, such as creating shared networks and provider routers, require a user to be logged into the OpenStack Dashboard as a user with admin privileges, but any user can create private networks. To help with managing complex software-defined networks, the OpenStack Dashboard provides an automatically updating network topography.

Getting ready

Load a web browser, point it to our OpenStack Dashboard address at `http://192.168.100.200/`, and log in as a user, such as the `demo` user created in the *Adding users to Keystone* recipe of *Chapter 1, Keystone – OpenStack Identity Service*, with the password `openstack`.

How to do it...

In this section, we will learn the following topics:

- Creating networks
- Deleting networks
- Viewing networks

Creating networks

To create a private network for a logged in user, carry out the following steps:

1. To manage networks within our OpenStack Dashboard, select the **Networks** tab:

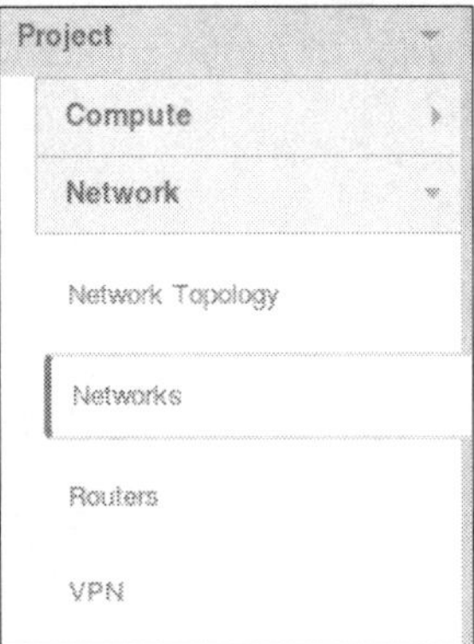

2. When this has been selected, we will be presented with a list of networks that we can assign to our instances:

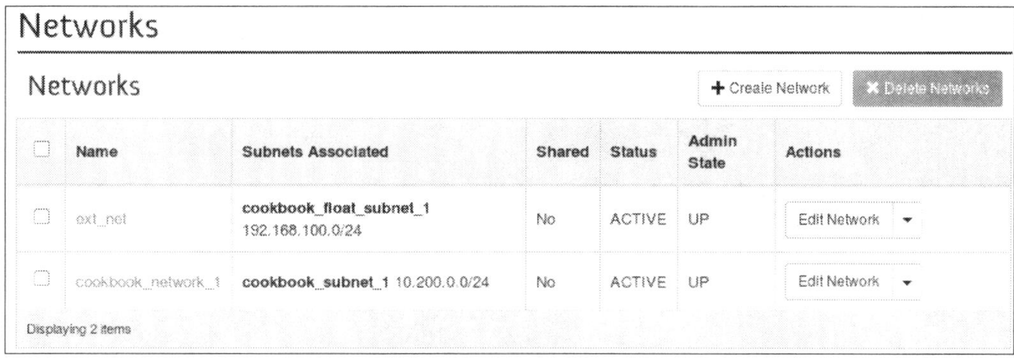

3. To create a new network, click on the **Create Network** button.
4. We are presented with a dialog box that first asks us to name our network:

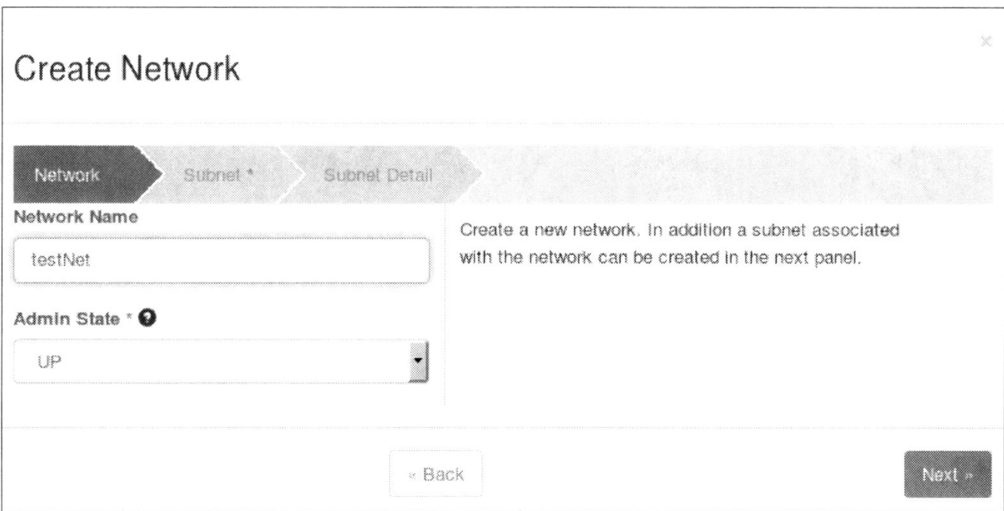

5. After choosing a name and keeping the **Admin State** set to `UP` (which means our network will be on and available for instances to connect to), we then assign a subnet to it by selecting the **Subnet** tab:

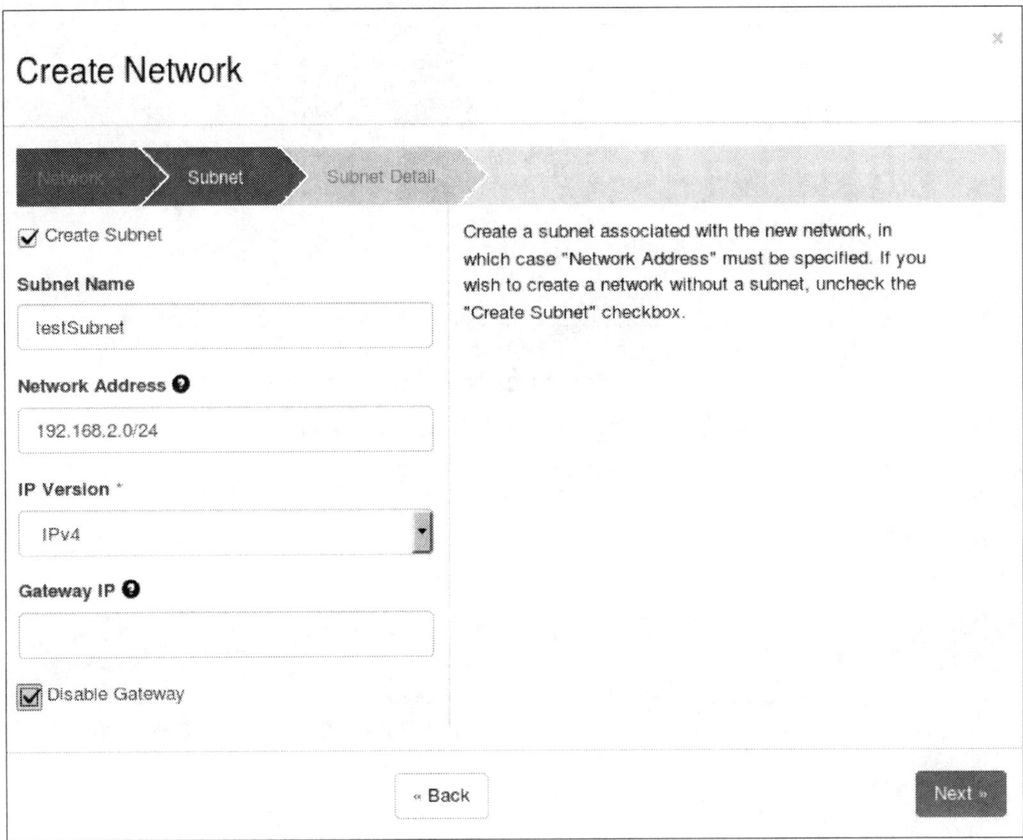

6. After filling in details for our subnet, we select the **Subnet Detail** tab that allows us to configure details such as **Dynamic Host Configuration Protocol** (**DHCP**) range, **Domain Name System** (**DNS**), and any additional routes we want when a user chooses that network:

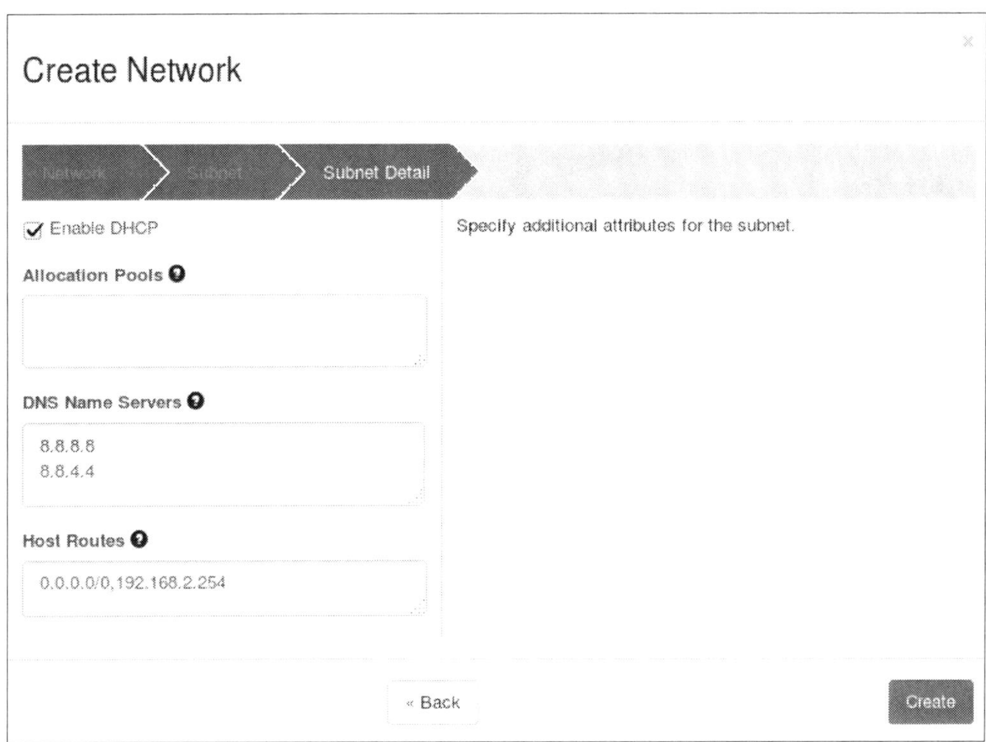

7. After filling in all the details, clicking on the **Create** button makes this network available to users of our tenant and returns us to the list of available networks:

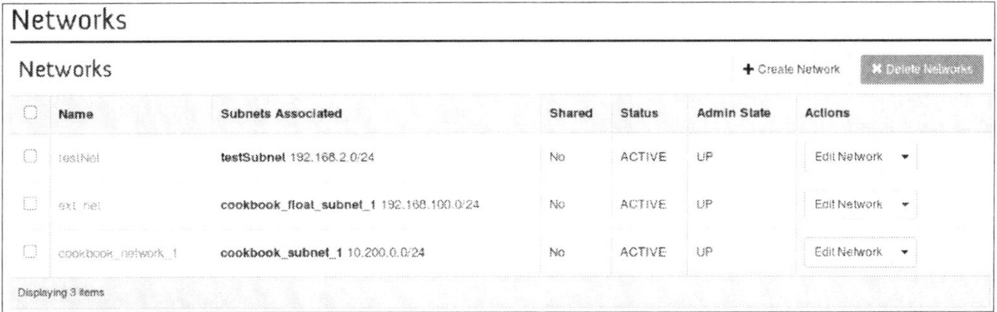

Deleting networks

To delete a private network for a logged in user, carry out the following steps:

1. To manage networks within our OpenStack Dashboard, select the **Network** tab:

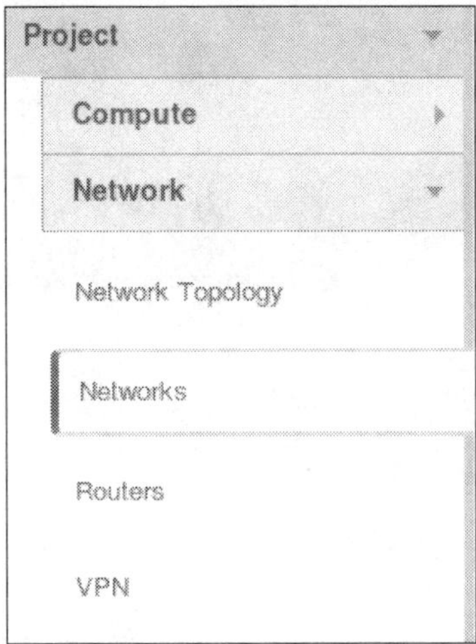

2. When this has been selected, we will be presented with a list of networks that we can assign to our instances:

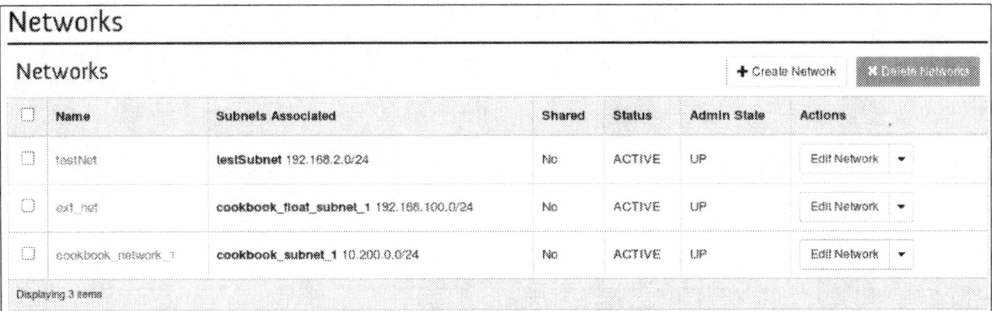

	Name	Subnets Associated	Shared	Status	Admin State	Actions
☐	testNet	**testSubnet** 192.168.2.0/24	No	ACTIVE	UP	Edit Network ▾
☐	ext_net	**cookbook_float_subnet_1** 192.168.100.0/24	No	ACTIVE	UP	Edit Network ▾
☐	cookbook_network_1	**cookbook_subnet_1** 10.200.0.0/24	No	ACTIVE	UP	Edit Network ▾

Displaying 3 items

3. To delete a network, select the checkbox next to the name of the network we want to delete, and then click on the **Delete Networks** button:

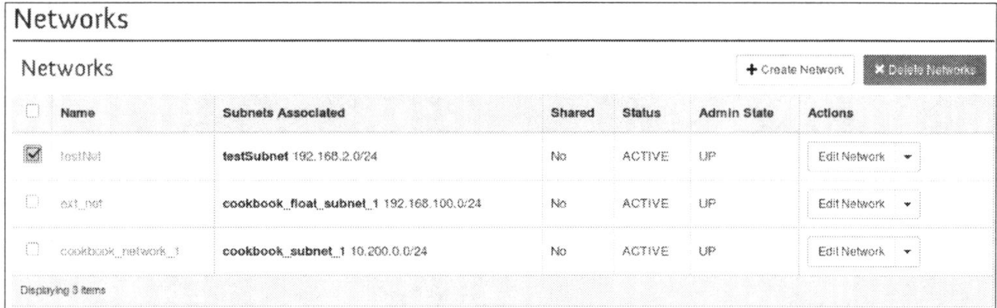

4. We will be presented with a dialog box asking us to confirm the deletion:

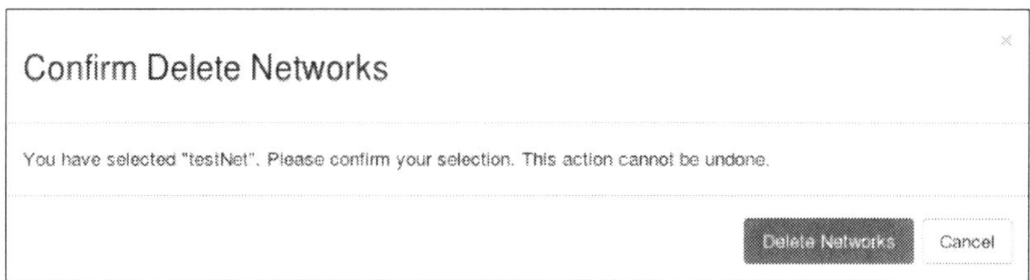

5. Clicking on the **Delete Networks** button will remove that network and return us to the list of available networks.

You can only remove a network that has no instances attached to it. You will be warned that this isn't allowed if there are instances still attached to that network.

Viewing networks

The OpenStack Dashboard gives users and administrators the ability to view the topology of our environment. To view the topology, carry out the following steps:

1. To manage networks within our OpenStack Dashboard, select the **Network** tab:

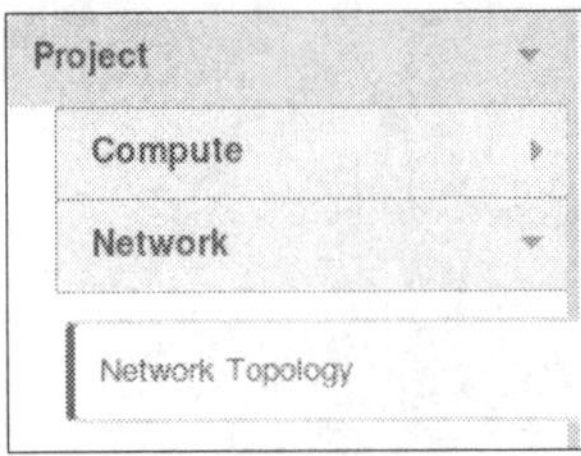

2. Clicking on the **Network Topology** tab launches a rich interface that gives an overview of our networks and instances attached to them:

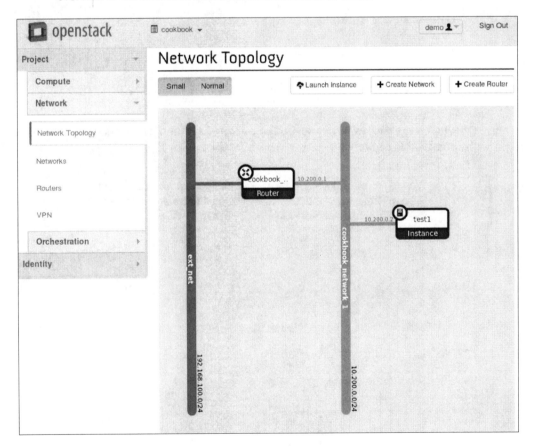

3. From this interface, we can click on various parts of this interface such as the networks (which takes us to the manage network interface) and the instances (which takes us to the instances interface); we can also create new networks and routers, and launch new instances.

How it works...

The ability to view and edit Neutron networks is a feature introduced in the Grizzly release of OpenStack. Managing Neutron networks can be quite complicated, but having a visual aid such as the one provided by the OpenStack Dashboard makes this much easier.

As an administrator (a user with the admin role), you can create shared networks. The same process applies in the preceding recipes, but you are presented with an extra option to allow any created networks to be seen by all tenants.

Using OpenStack Dashboard for security group management

Security groups are network rules that allow instances in one tenant (project) be kept separate from other instances in another. Managing security group rules for our OpenStack instances is done as simply as possible with OpenStack Dashboard.

As described in the *Creating tenants in Keystone* recipe of *Chapter 1, Keystone – OpenStack Identity Service*, projects and tenants are used interchangeably and refer to the same thing. Under the OpenStack Dashboard, tenants are referred to as projects, whereas in Keystone, projects are referred to as tenants.

Getting ready

Load a web browser, point it to our OpenStack Dashboard address at `http://192.168.100.200/`, and log in as a user, such as the `demo` user created in the *Adding users to Keystone* recipe of *Chapter 1, Keystone – OpenStack Identity Service*, with the password `openstack`.

How to do it...

To administer security groups under OpenStack Dashboard, carry out the steps discussed in the following sections.

Creating a security group

To create a security group, perform the following steps:

1. A new security group is added to our system by using the **Access & Security** tab under the **Compute** section, so click on it:

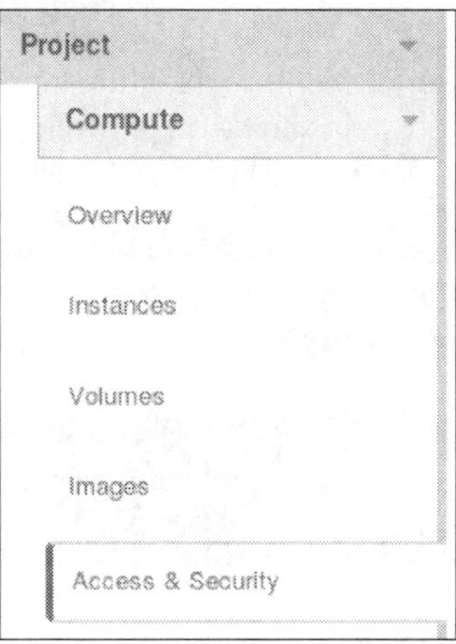

2. Next we see a screen allowing access to security settings and managing key pairs. Under **Security Groups**, there will be a list of security groups that can be used when we launch our instances. To create a new security group, click on the **Create Security Group** button:

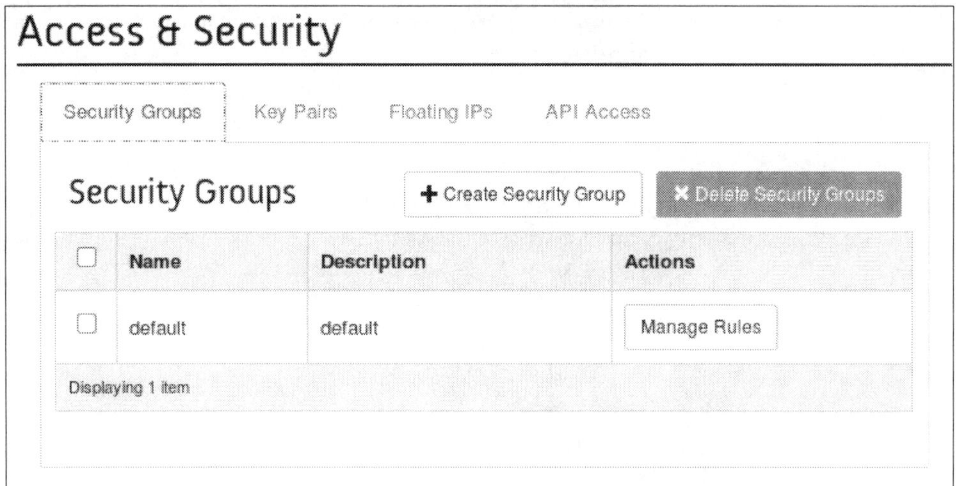

We are asked to name the security group and provide a description. The name cannot contain spaces:

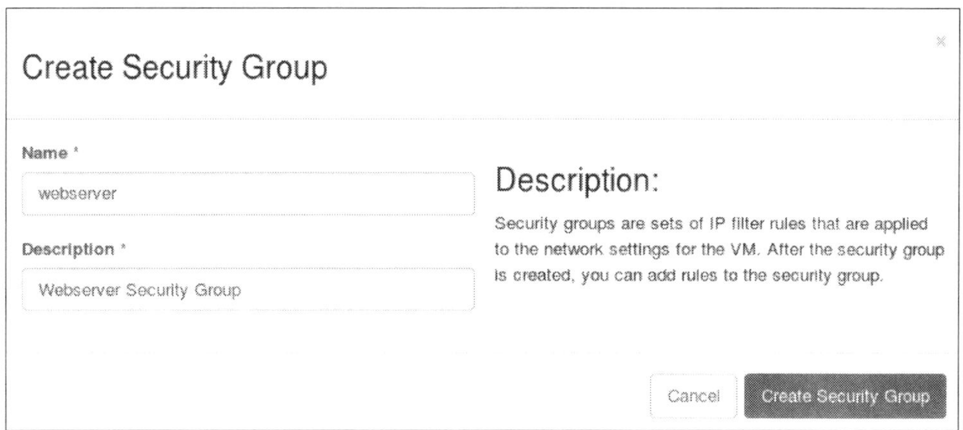

3. Once a new security group is created, the list of available security groups will appear on screen. From here we are able to add new network security rules to the new security group:

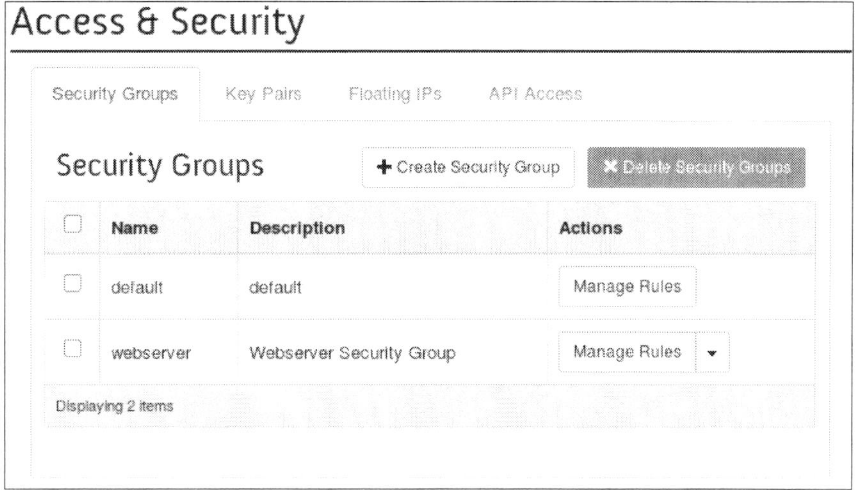

Editing security groups to add and remove rules

To add and remove rules, security groups can be edited by performing the following steps:

1. When we have created a new security group, or wish to modify the rules in an existing security group, we can click on the **Manage Rules** button for that particular security group:

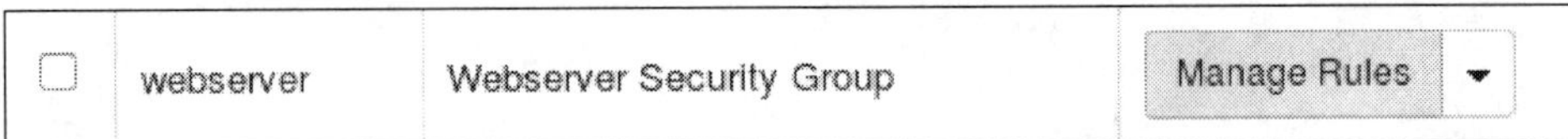

2. After clicking on the **Manage Rules** button, we are taken to a screen that lists any existing rules and enables us to add new rules to this group:

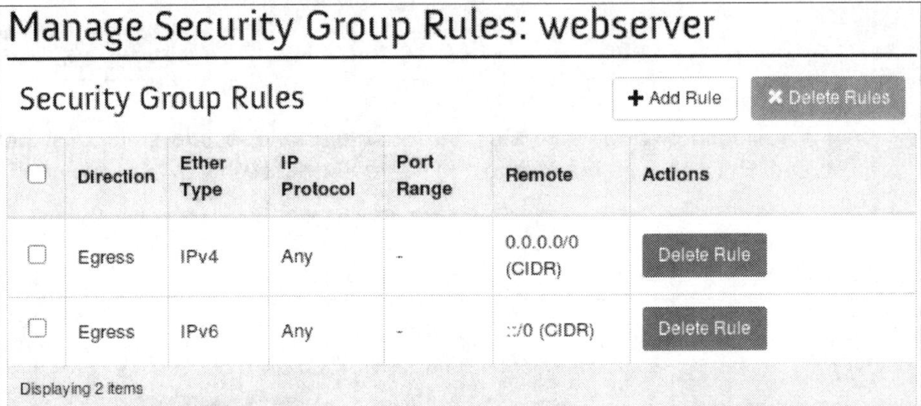

3. To add a rule to our new security group, we click on the **Add Rule** button. This allows us to create rules based on the different protocol types—ICMP, TCP, and UDP. There is also a list of rule templates for commonly added services. As an example, we will add in a security group rule that allows HTTPS access from anywhere. To do this, we choose the following:

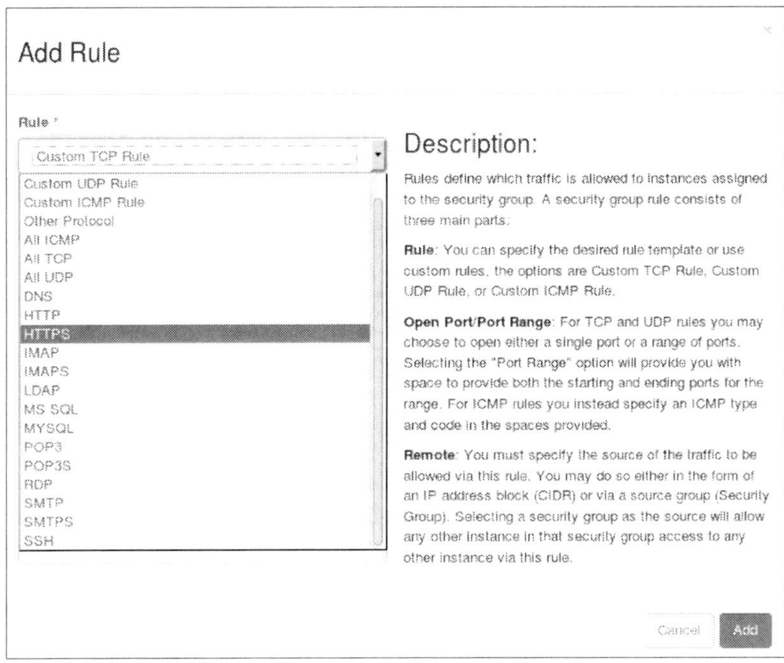

4. We select the **HTTPS** option from the drop-down menu. This returns us to the **Add Rule** menu where we can specify the source of the network traffic:

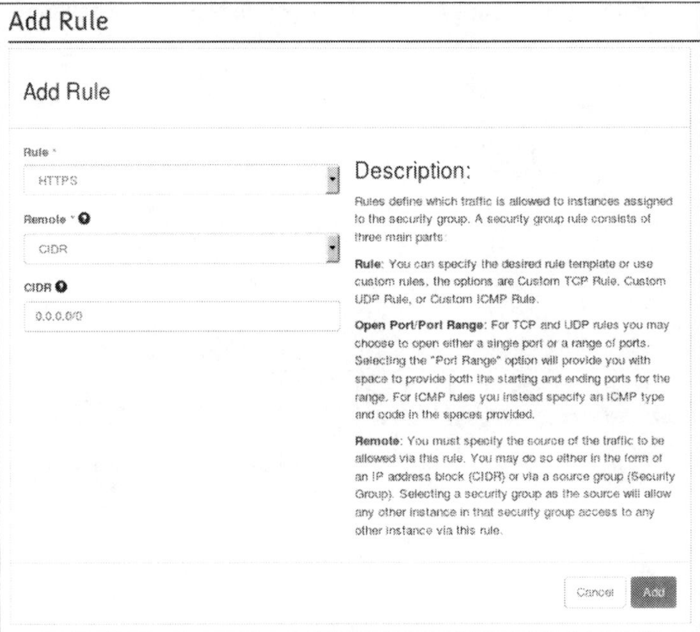

5. When we click on the **Add** button, we are returned to the list of rules now associated with our security group. Repeat the previous steps until all the rules related to our security group have been configured:

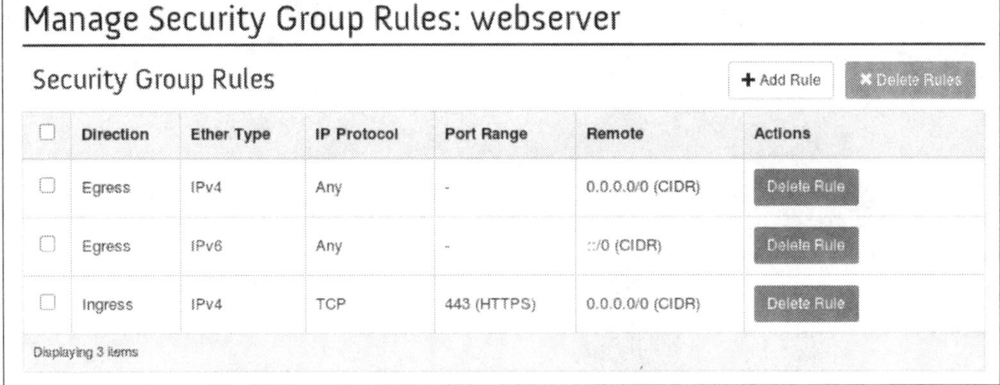

6. We can also add custom security rules for services that do not have built-in rule templates. After we click on the **Add** button, we choose the **Custom TCP Rule** option from the **Rule** drop-down list. Then we select the **Port Range** option from the **Open Port** drop-down list, which presents us with **From Port** and **To Port** fields. We enter a port range and click on the **Add** button:

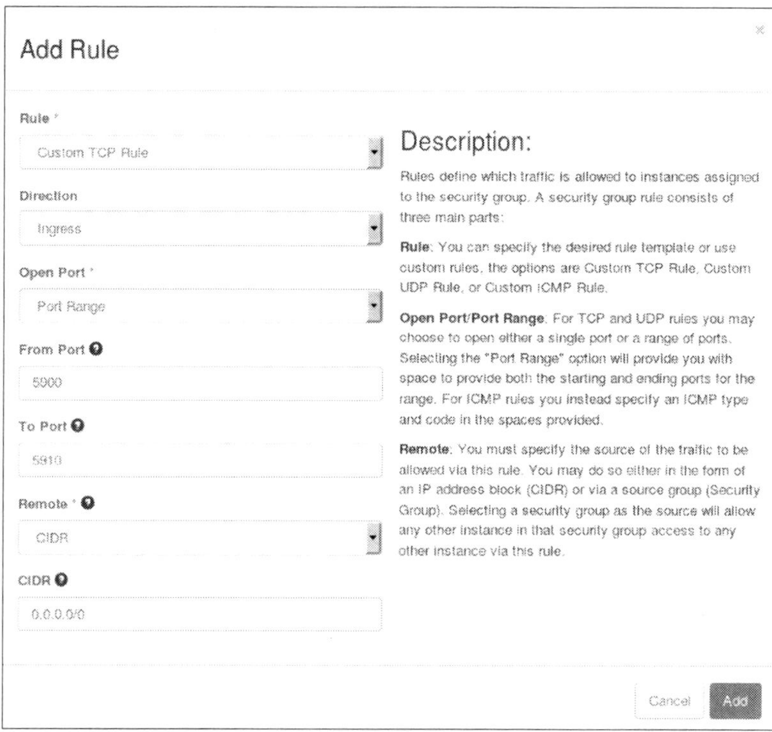

7. Note that we can remove rules from the screen associated with step 5 too. Simply select the rule that we no longer require and click on the **Delete Rule** button. We are asked to confirm this removal.

Deleting security groups

Security groups can be deleted by performing the following steps:

1. Security groups are deleted by selecting the security group that we want to remove and clicking on the **Delete Security Groups** button:

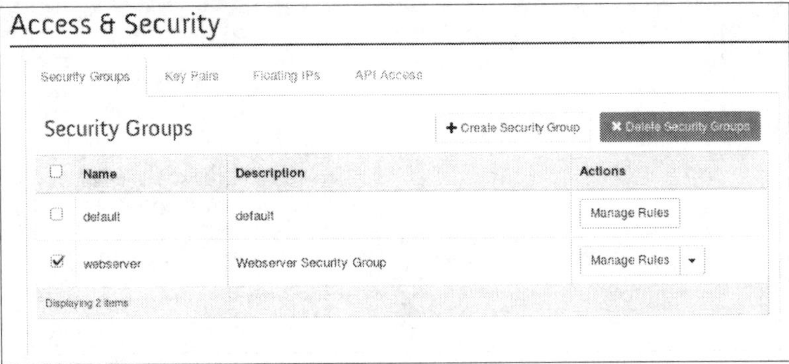

2. You will be asked to confirm this. Clicking on **OK** removes the security group and associated access rules:

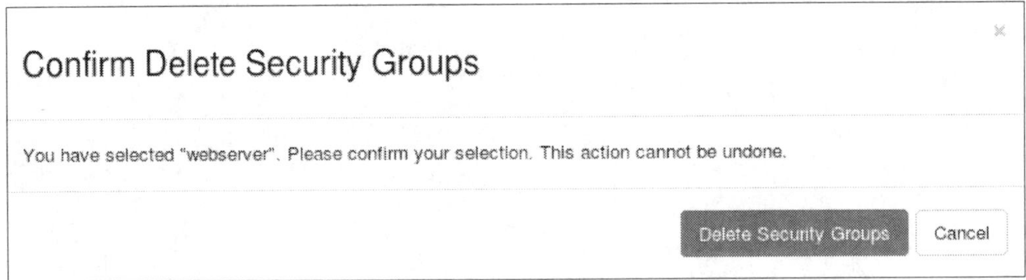

You will not be able to remove a security group while an instance with that assigned security group is running.

How it works...

Security groups are important to our OpenStack environment, as they provide a consistent and secure approach for accessing our running instances. Allowing users to create, delete, and amend security groups to use within their tenants allows them to create secure environments. Rules within a security group are *deny by default*, which means that, if there is no rule for that particular protocol, no traffic for that protocol can access the running instance with that assigned security group.

Security groups are associated with instances on creation, so we can't add a new security group to a running instance. We can, however, modify the rules assigned to a running instance. For example, suppose an instance was launched with only the default security group. The default security group that we have set up has only TCP port 22 accessible and the ability to ping the instance. If we require access to TCP port 80, we either have to add this rule to the default security group or relaunch the instance with a new security assigned to it to allow TCP port 80.

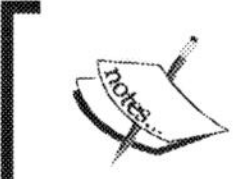

Modifications to security groups take effect immediately, and any instance assigned with that security group will have those new rules associated with it.

Using OpenStack Dashboard to launch instances

Launching instances is easily done using the OpenStack Dashboard. We simply select our chosen image, choose the size of the instance, and then launch it.

Getting ready

Load a web browser, point it to our OpenStack Dashboard address at `http://192.168.100.200/`, and log in as a user, such as the `demo` user created in the *Adding users to Keystone* recipe of *Chapter 1, Keystone – OpenStack Identity Service*, with the password `openstack`.

How to do it...

To launch an instance by using the OpenStack Dashboard interface, carry out the following steps:

1. Navigate to the **Images** tab under the **Compute** section and select an appropriate image to launch—for example, the `trusty-image` server image:

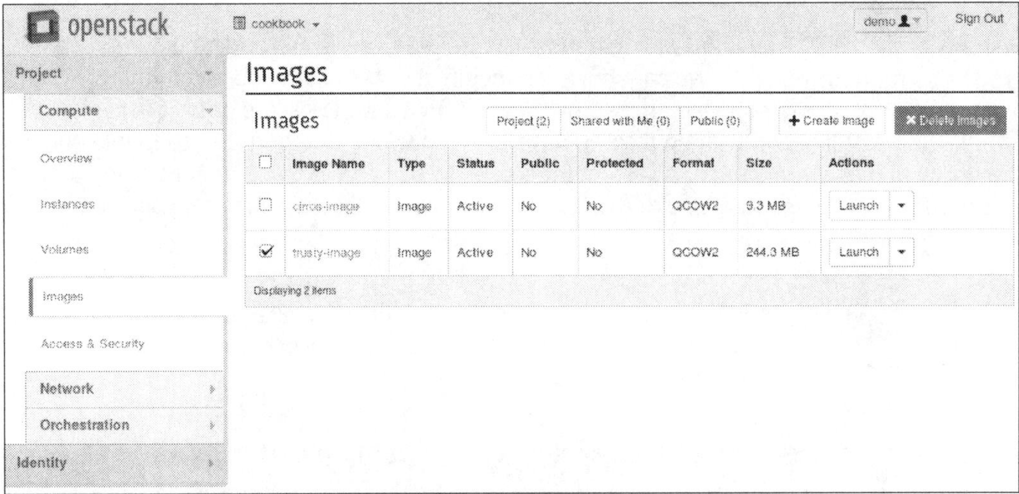

2. Click on the **Launch** button under the **Actions** column applying to the image to be launched.

3. A dialog box appears requesting a name for the instance (for example, `horizon1`). Choose a flavor type of `m1.tiny` for the instance:

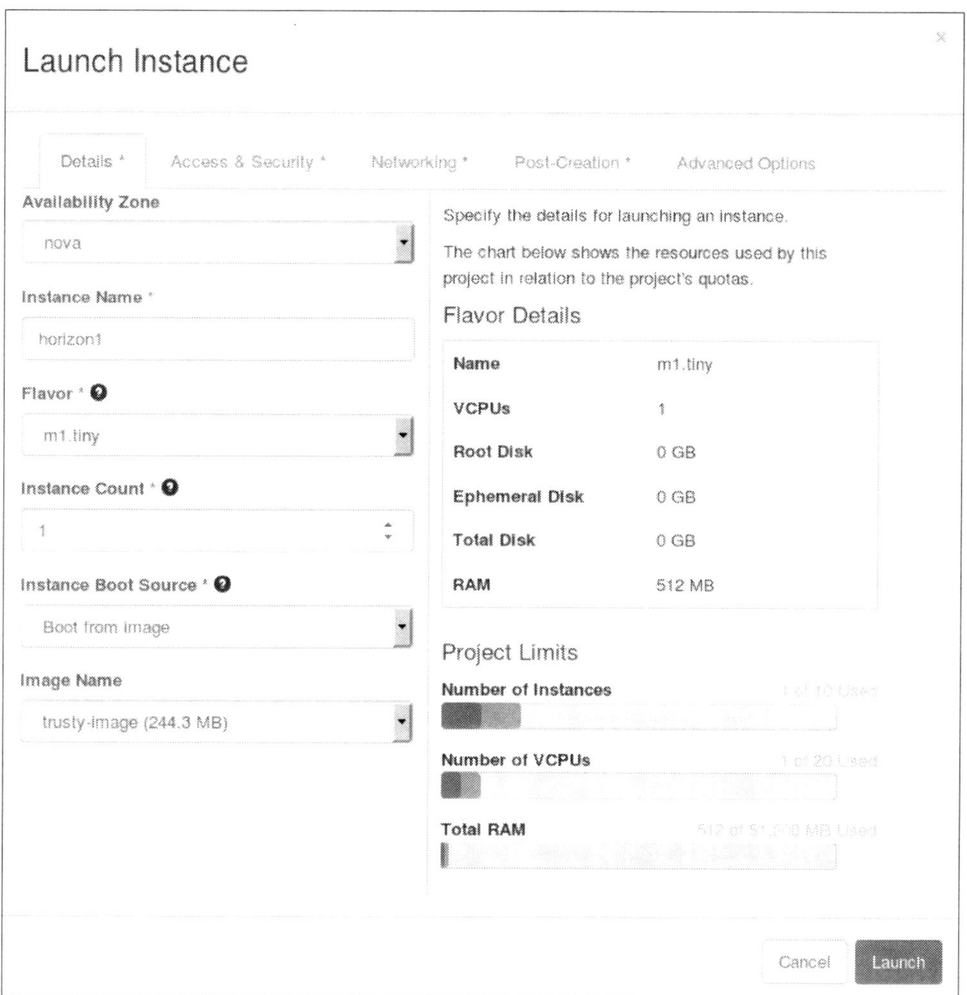

4. Next select the **Access & Security** tab and choose the key pair and security groups for this image:

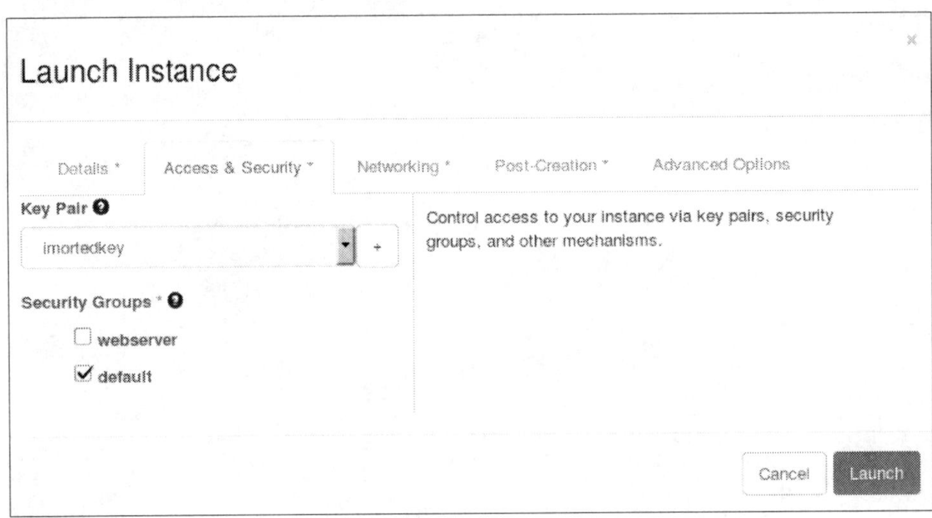

If you haven't created a key pair, you can click on the **+** button and import a key from this dialog box.

5. With Neutron configured in our environment, selecting the **Networking** tab allows us to choose the networks that our instance will be attached to by dragging the networks listed under **Available networks** into the **Selected networks** box:

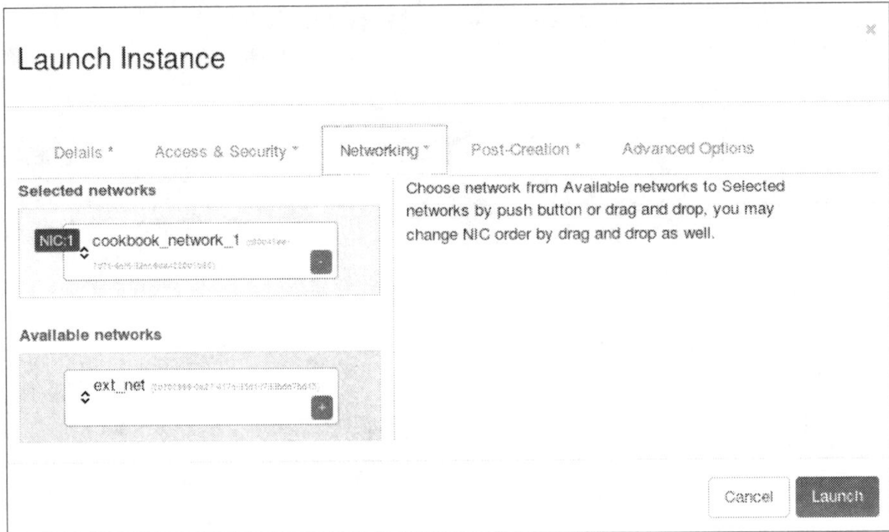

6. Once selected, we can click on the **Launch Instance** button.
7. We will be returned to the **Instances** Tab that shows the instance in a **Build** status, which will eventually change to **Active**:

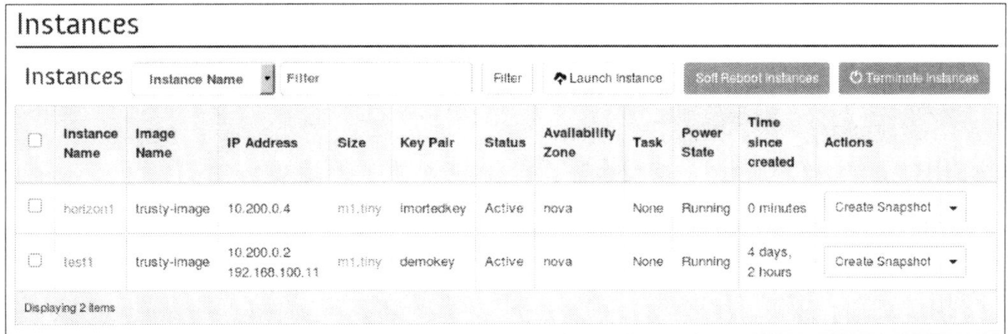

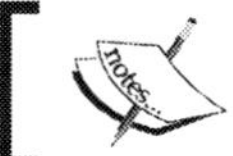

If the display hasn't refreshed, click on the **Instances** tab to refresh the information manually.

How it works...

Launching instances from Horizon—the OpenStack Dashboard—is done in two stages:

1. Selecting the appropriate image from the **Images** tab.
2. Choosing the appropriate values to assign to the instance.

The **Instances** tab shows the running instances under our `cookbook` project.

You can also see an overview of what is running in our environment by clicking on the **Overview** tab.

Using OpenStack Dashboard to terminate instances

Terminating instances is very simple when using OpenStack Dashboard.

Getting ready

Load a web browser, point it to our OpenStack Dashboard address at `http://192.168.100.200/`, and log in as a user, such as the `demo` user created in the *Adding users to Keystone* recipe of *Chapter 1, Keystone – OpenStack Identity Service*, with the password `openstack`.

How to do it...

To terminate instances by using OpenStack Dashboard, carry out the following steps:

1. Select the **Instances** tab and choose the instance to be terminated by selecting the checkbox next to the instance name (or names), and then click on the red **Terminate Instances** button:

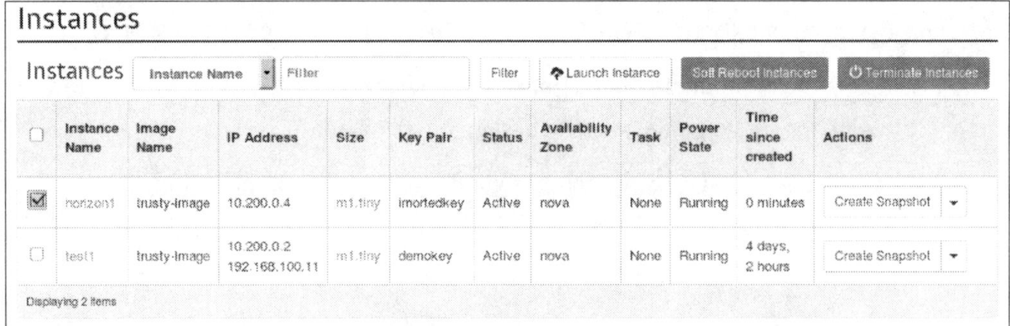

2. We will be presented with a confirmation screen. Click on the **Terminate Instances** button to terminate the selected instance:

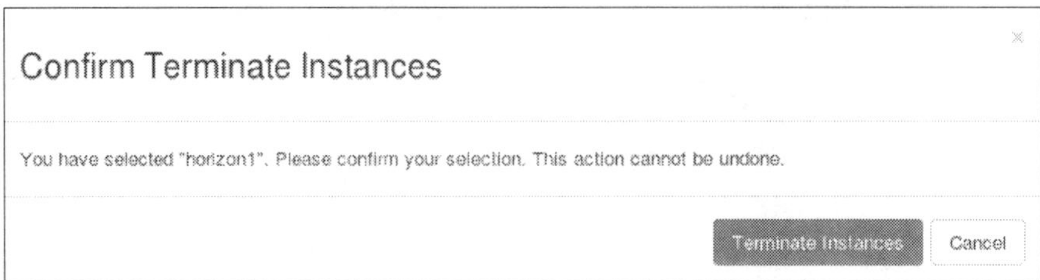

3. We will be presented with the **Instances** screen with a confirmation that the instance has been terminated successfully.

How it works...

Terminating instances by using OpenStack Dashboard is easy. We select our running instance and click on the **Terminate Instances** button, which is highlighted when an instance is selected. After clicking on the **Terminate Instances** button, we are asked to confirm this action to minimize the risk of accidentally terminating an instance.

Using OpenStack Dashboard to connect to instances using a VNC

OpenStack Dashboard has a very handy feature that allows a user to connect to our running instances through a VNC session within our web browser. This gives us the ability to manage our instance through a virtual console window without invoking an SSH session separately and is a great feature for accessing desktop instances such as those running Windows.

Getting ready

Load a web browser, point it to our OpenStack Dashboard address at `http://192.168.100.200/`, and log in as a user, such as the `demo` user created in the *Adding users to Keystone* recipe of *Chapter 1, Keystone – OpenStack Identity Service*, with the password `openstack`.

How to do it...

To connect to a running instance by using VNC through a web browser, carry out the following steps:

1. Click on the **Instances** tab and choose an instance to which you want to connect.

2. Next to the **Create Snapshot** button is a down arrow button, which reveals more options. Click on it:

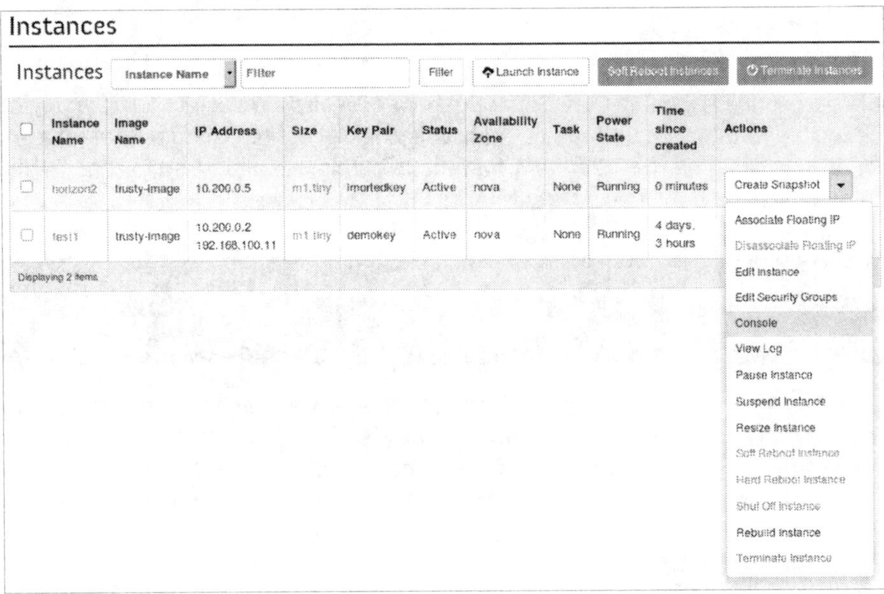

3. Select the **Console** option. This takes you to a console screen, which allows you to log in to your instance:

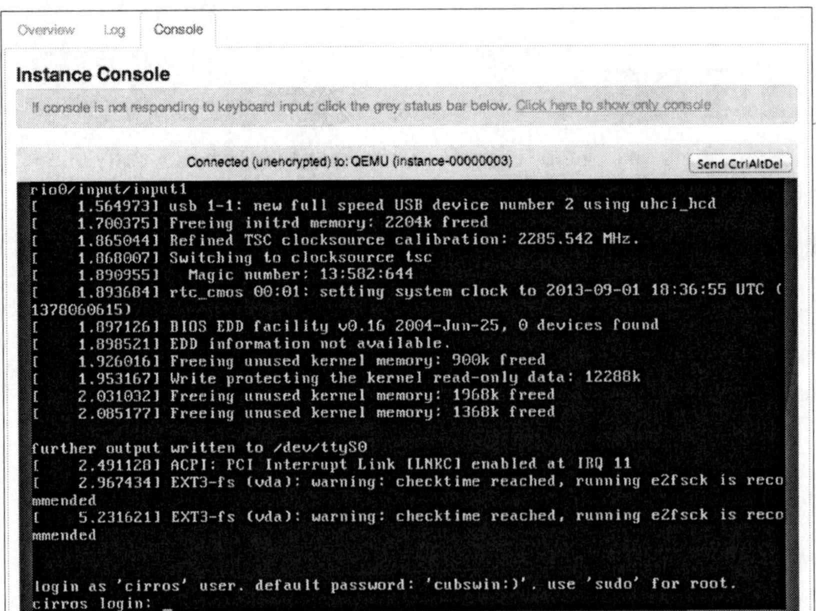

Your instance must support local logins. Many Linux cloud images expect a user to authenticate by using SSH Keys.

How it works...

Connecting through our web browser uses a VNC proxy session, which was configured by using the `novnc`, `nova-consoleauth`, and `nova-console` packages, as described in the installation section. Only browsers that support WebSocket connections are supported. Generally, this can be any modern browser with HTML5 support.

Using OpenStack Dashboard to add new tenants – projects

OpenStack Dashboard is a lot more than just an interface to our instances. It allows an administrator to configure environments, users, and tenants.

Tenants are known as **projects** within the OpenStack Dashboard. Adding new tenants that users can be members of is achieved quite simply in OpenStack Dashboard.

Getting ready

Load a web browser, point it to our OpenStack Dashboard address at `http://192.168.100.200/`, and log in as a user, such as the `admin` user created in the *Adding users to Keystone* recipe of *Chapter 1, Keystone – OpenStack Identity Service*, with the password `openstack`.

How to do it...

To add a new tenant to our OpenStack environment, carry out the following steps:

1. After we login as a user with admin privileges, we get more menu options under the **Identity** tab. One of them is the **Projects** option:

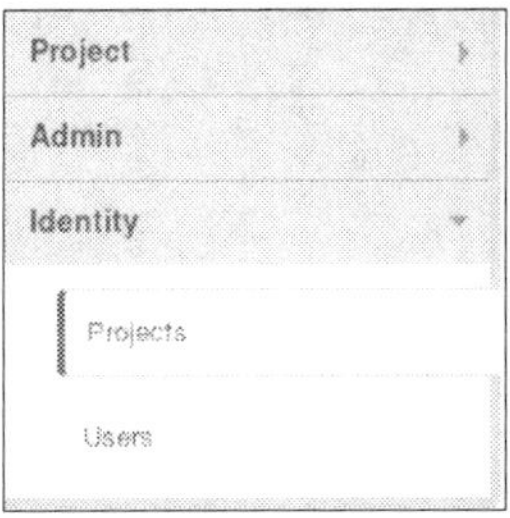

2. To manage tenants, we click on the **Projects** option listed under **Identity**. This will list the available tenants in our environment, as shown in the following screenshot:

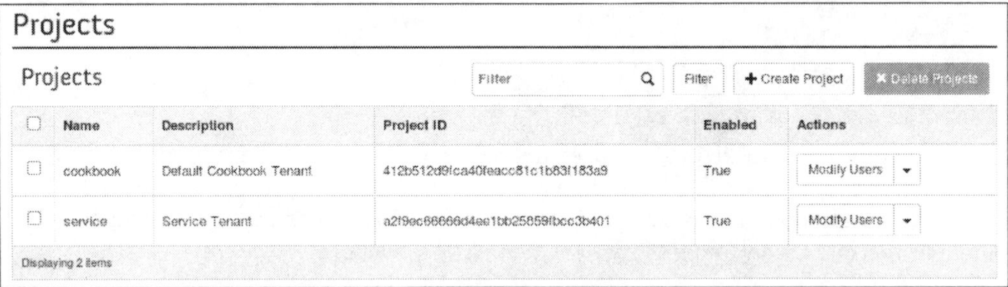

3. To create a new tenant, click on the **Create Project** button.
4. Next, we are presented with a form that asks for the name of the tenant and a description. Enter `horizon` as our tenant name and enter a description:

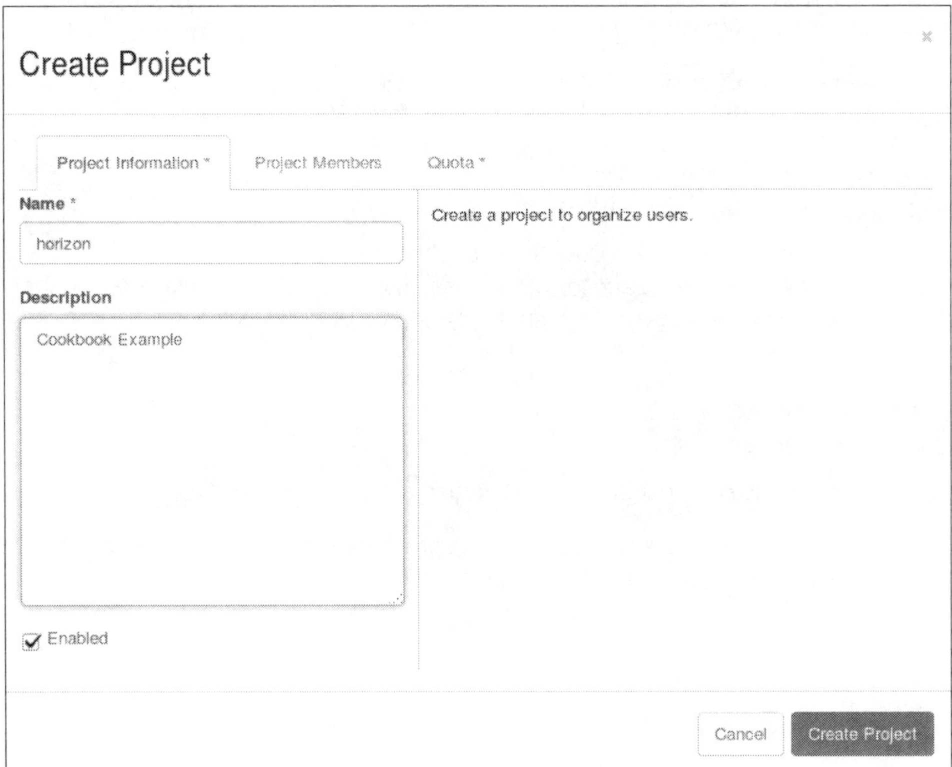

5. We enable the tenant by selecting the **Enabled** checkbox, and then click on the **Create Project** button.

   We will be presented with the list of tenants that are now available and a message saying that the `horizon` tenant was created successfully.

	Name	Description	Project ID	Enabled	Actions
	cookbook	Default Cookbook Tenant	412b512d9fca40feacc81c1b83f183a9	True	Modify Users
	horizon	Cookbook Example	977d0a604660497d81ab7e7a96efa88c	True	Modify Users
	service	Service Tenant	a2f9ec66666d4ee1bb25859fbcc3b401	True	Modify Users

How it works...

OpenStack Dashboard is a feature-rich interface that complements the command-line options available to you when managing your OpenStack environment. This means we can simply create a tenant (Ubuntu's interface refers to this as a project) to which users can belong using OpenStack Dashboard. When creating new tenants, we need to be logged in as a user with admin privileges to get access to the full tenant management interface.

Using OpenStack Dashboard for user management

OpenStack Dashboard gives us the ability to administer users through the web interface. This allows an administrator to easily create and edit users within an OpenStack environment. To manage users, you must log in using an account that is a member of the admin role.

Getting ready

Load a web browser, point it to our OpenStack Dashboard address at `http://192.168.100.200/`, and log in as a user, such as the `admin` user created in the *Adding users to Keystone* recipe of *Chapter 1, Keystone – OpenStack Identity Service*, with the password `openstack`.

How to do it...

User management under OpenStack Dashboard is achieved by carrying out the steps discussed in the following sections.

Adding users

To add users, perform the following steps:

1. Under the **Identity** panel, click on the **Users** option to bring up a list of users set up on the system:

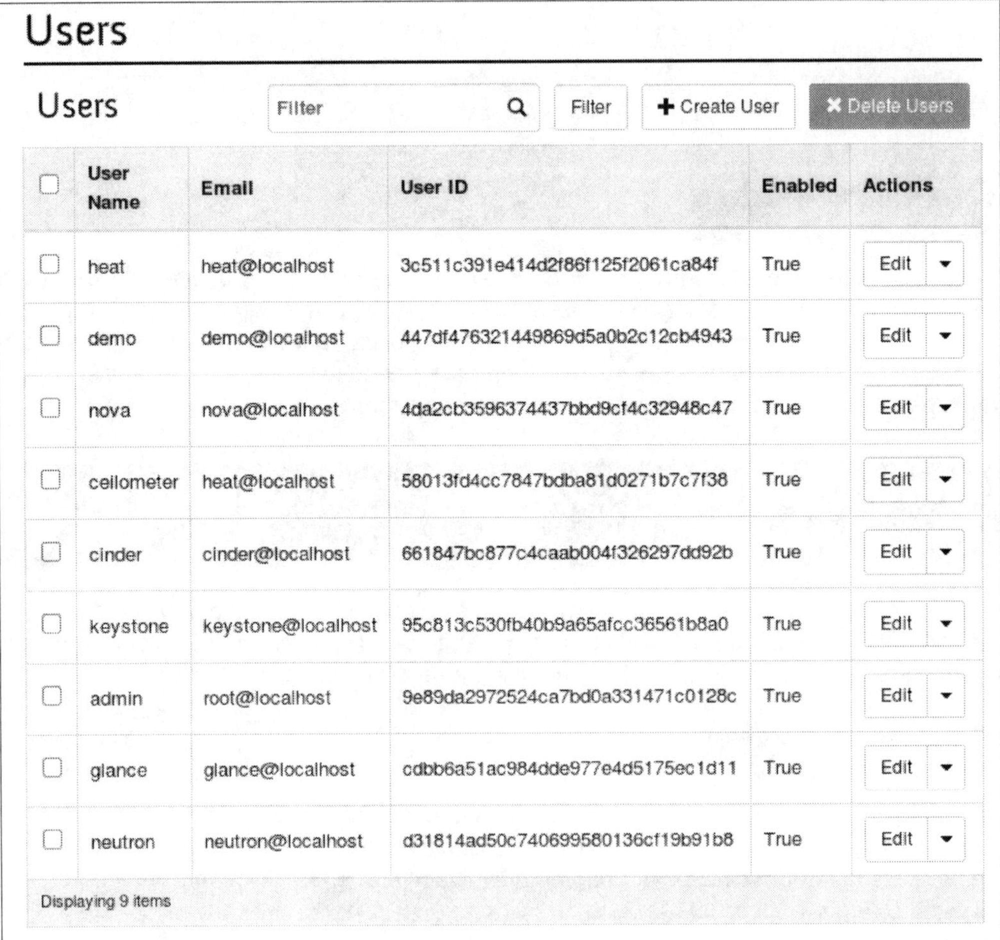

Users

Users — Filter | Filter | + Create User | ✖ Delete Users

	User Name	Email	User ID	Enabled	Actions
☐	heat	heat@localhost	3c511c391e414d2f86f125f2061ca84f	True	Edit ▾
☐	demo	demo@localhost	447df476321449869d5a0b2c12cb4943	True	Edit ▾
☐	nova	nova@localhost	4da2cb3596374437bbd9cf4c32948c47	True	Edit ▾
☐	ceilometer	heat@localhost	58013fd4cc7847bdba81d0271b7c7f38	True	Edit ▾
☐	cinder	cinder@localhost	661847bc877c4caab004f326297dd92b	True	Edit ▾
☐	keystone	keystone@localhost	95c813c530fb40b9a65afcc36561b8a0	True	Edit ▾
☐	admin	root@localhost	9e89da2972524ca7bd0a331471c0128c	True	Edit ▾
☐	glance	glance@localhost	cdbb6a51ac984dde977e4d5175ec1d11	True	Edit ▾
☐	neutron	neutron@localhost	d31814ad50c740699580136cf19b91b8	True	Edit ▾

Displaying 9 items

2. To create a new user, click on the **Create User** button.
3. We will be presented with a form that asks for user name details. Enter the user name, e-mail, and the password for that user. In the example shown in the following screenshot, we create a user named `test`, set `openstack` as the password, and assign that user to the `horizon` tenant with the role of admin:

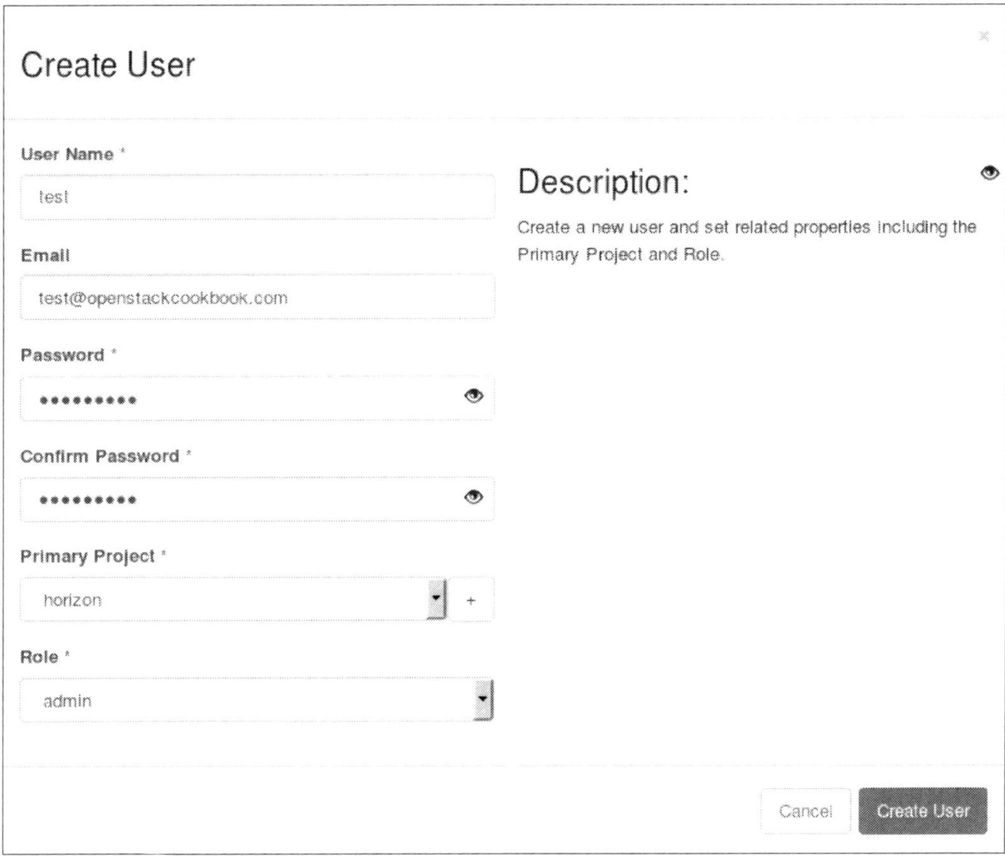

4. We are returned to the screen listing the users of our OpenStack environment with a message stating that our user creation was successful.

Deleting users

To delete users, perform the following steps:

1. Under the **Identity** panel, click on the **Users** option to bring up a list of users on the system.
2. We will be presented with a list of users in our OpenStack environment. To delete a user, click on the appropriate **Edit** button, which will present a drop-down list with the **Delete User** option:

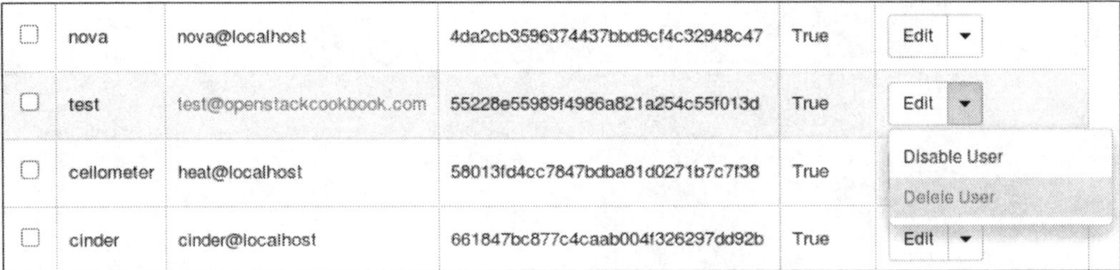

nova
nova@localhost
4da2cb3596374437bbd9cf4c32948c47
True
Edit
test
test@openstackcookbook.com
55228e55989f4986a821a254c55f013d
True
Edit
Disable User
Delete User
ceilometer
heat@localhost
58013fd4cc7847bdba81d0271b7c7f38
True
cinder
cinder@localhost
661847bc877c4caab004f326297dd92b
True
Edit

3. Clicking on the **Delete User** option will bring up a confirmation dialog box. Confirm by clicking on the **Delete User** button to remove the user from the system:

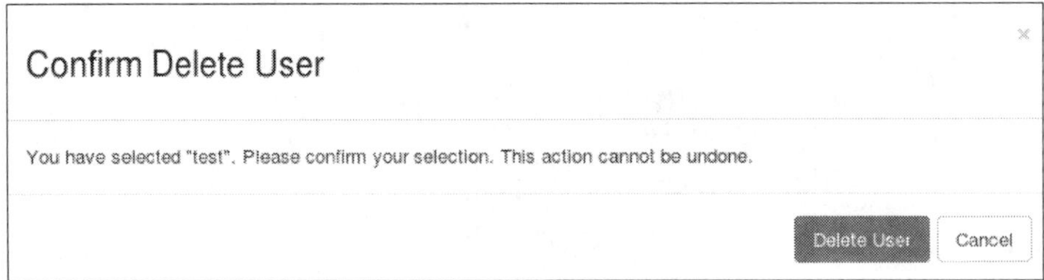

Updating user details and passwords

To update user details and passwords, perform the following steps:

1. Under the **Identity** panel, click on the **Users** option to bring up a list of users on the system.
2. To change a user's password, e-mail address, or primary project (tenant), click on the **Edit** button for that user.

3. This brings up a dialog box asking for the relevant information. When the information has been set as we want it to be, click on the **Update User** button:

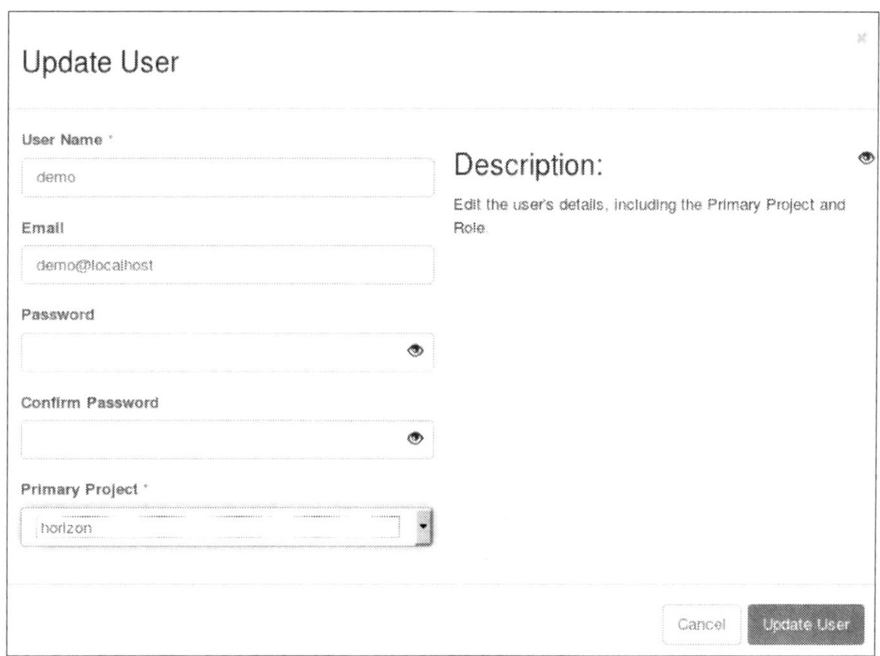

Adding users to tenants

To add users to tenants, perform the following steps:

1. Under the **Identity** panel, click on the **Projects** option to bring up a list of tenants on the system:

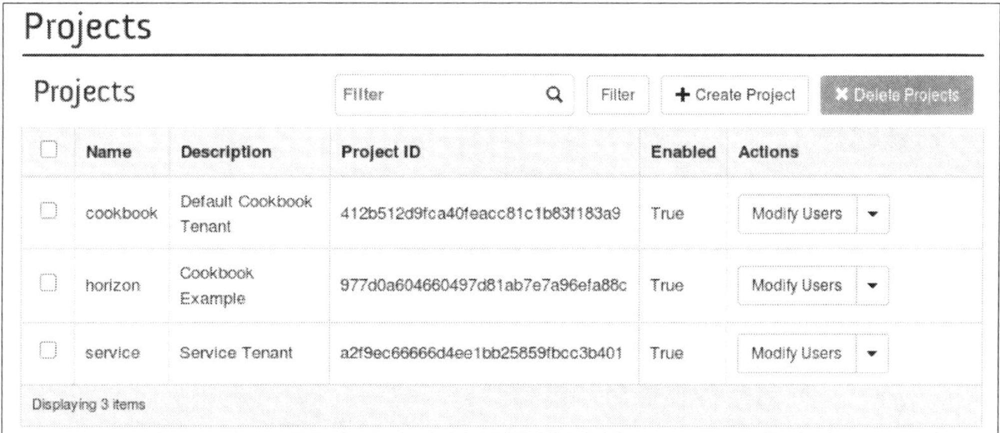

	Name	Description	Project ID	Enabled	Actions
	cookbook	Default Cookbook Tenant	412b512d9fca40feacc81c1b83f183a9	True	Modify Users
	horizon	Cookbook Example	977d0a604660497d81ab7e7a96efa88c	True	Modify Users
	service	Service Tenant	a2f9ec66666d4ee1bb25859fbcc3b401	True	Modify Users

2. Click on the appropriate **Modify Users** option to bring up a list of users associated with a tenant as well as a list of users, which we can add to that tenant:

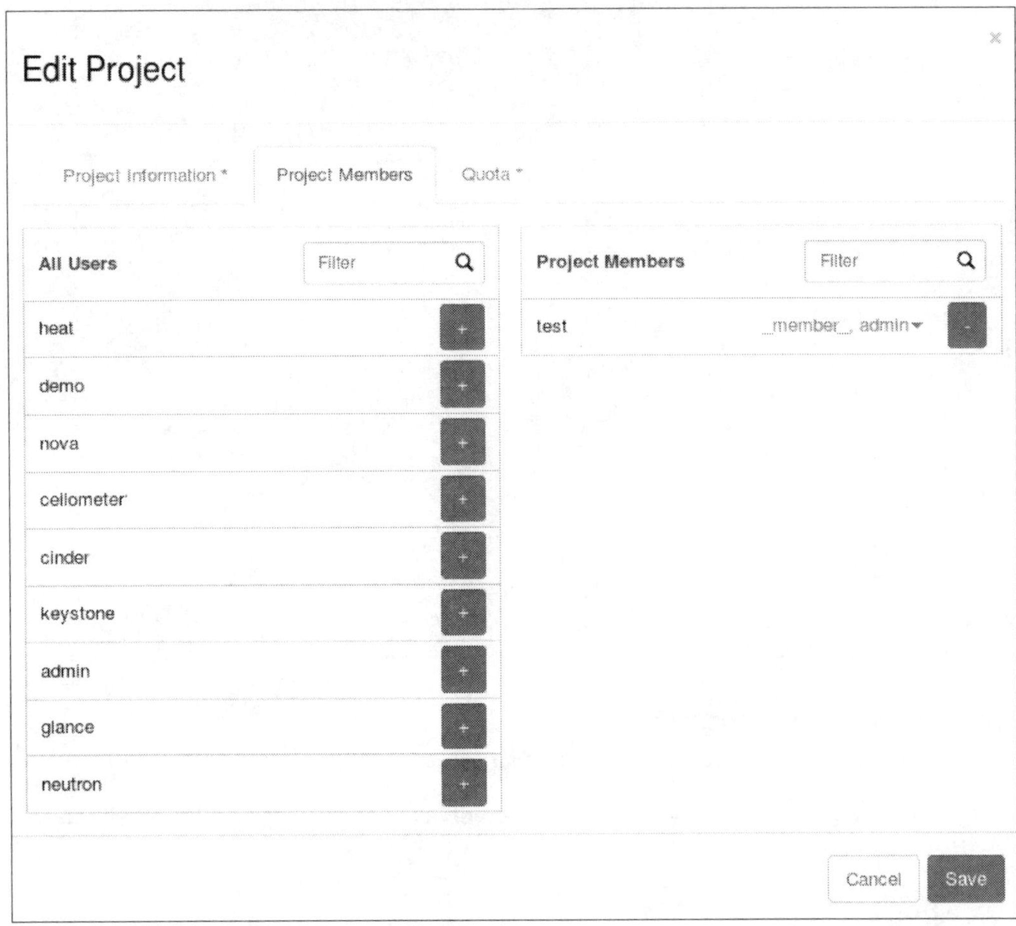

3. To add a new user to the list, simply click on the **+** (plus sign) button next to that user.

4. To change the role of the user within that tenant, select the drop-down arrow next to the username and select a new role:

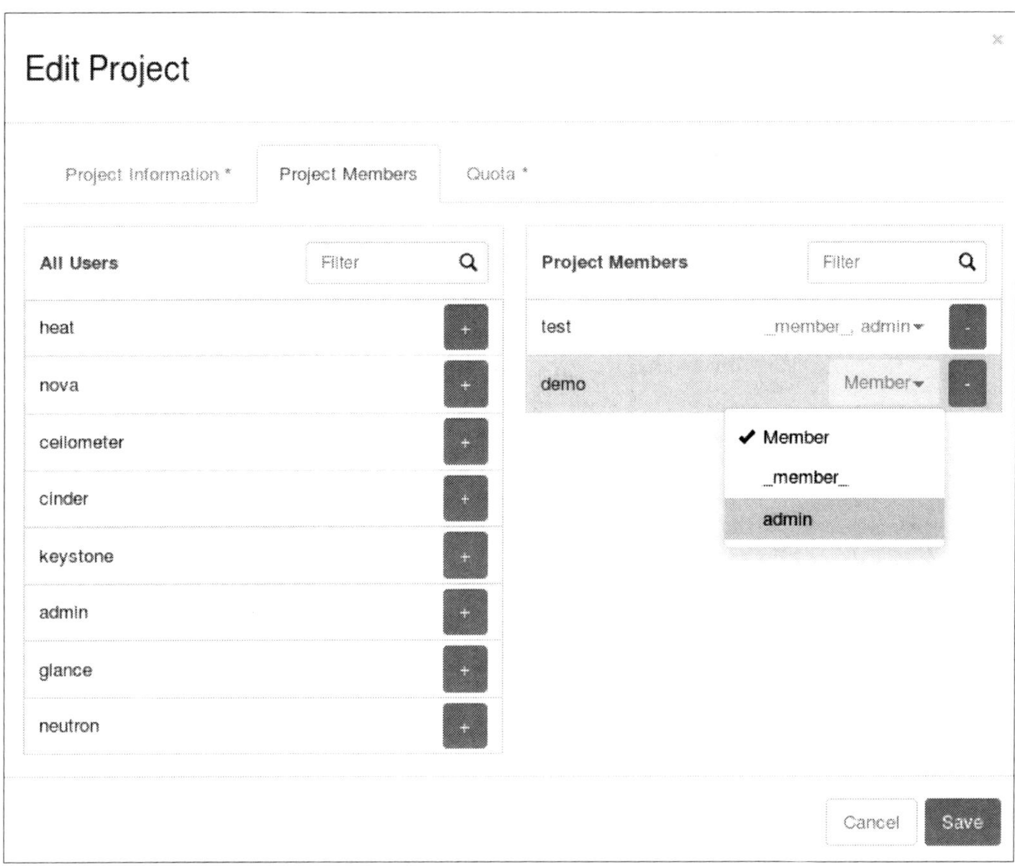

5. After clicking on the **Save** button at the bottom of the dialog box, we see a message saying that our tenant has been updated. This user can now launch instances in different tenants when they log on.

Removing users from tenants

To remove users from tenants, perform the following steps:

1. Under the **Identity** panel, click on the **Projects** option to bring up a list of tenants on the system.
2. To remove a user from a tenant, for example, `horizon`, click on the appropriate **Modify Users** button:

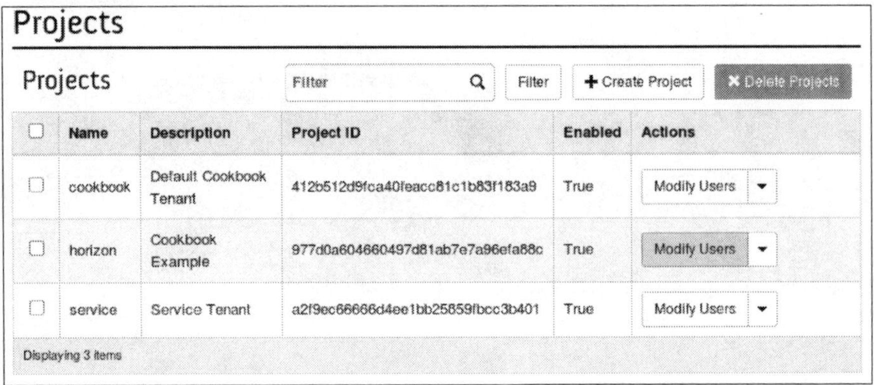

Projects

Projects

	Name	Description	Project ID	Enabled	Actions
	cookbook	Default Cookbook Tenant	412b512d9fca40feacc81c1b83f183a9	True	Modify Users
	horizon	Cookbook Example	977d0a604660497d81ab7e7a96efa88c	True	Modify Users
	service	Service Tenant	a2f9ec66666d4ee1bb25659fbcc3b401	True	Modify Users

Displaying 3 items

3. After clicking on the **Modify Users** button, you will get a modal window with a list of all users as well as project members, which we can remove from that tenant:

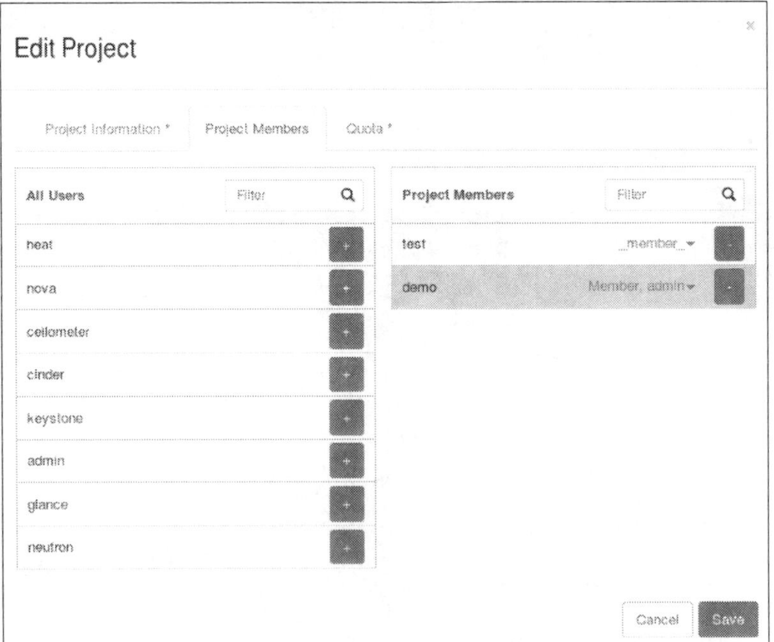

4. To remove a user from this tenant, click on the - (minus sign) button next to that particular user under project members.
5. After clicking on the **Save** button at the bottom of the dialog box, we see a message saying that our tenant has been updated.

How it works...

OpenStack Dashboard is a feature-rich interface that complements the command-line options available to us when managing our cloud environment. The interface has been designed so that the functions available are as intuitive as possible to the administrator. This means that we can easily create users, modify their membership within tenants, update passwords, and remove them from the system altogether.

Using OpenStack Dashboard with LBaaS

The OpenStack Dashboard has the ability to view, create, and edit Load Balancers, add **Virtual IPs** (**VIPs**), and add nodes behind a Load Balancer. Dashboard also provides a user interface for creating HA Proxy server Load Balance services for our instances. We do this first by creating load balancing pools and then adding running instances to those pools.

In this section, we will use two instances running Apache that were created in the previous chapter. We will create an HTTP Load Balance pool, create a VIP, and configure instances to be part of the pool. The result will be the ability to use the HTTP Load Balancer pool address to send traffic to two instances running Apache.

Getting ready

Load a web browser, point it to our OpenStack Dashboard address at `http://192.168.100.200/`, and log in as an admin user, such as the `admin` user created in the *Adding users to Keystone* recipe of *Chapter 1, Keystone – OpenStack Identity Service*, with the password `openstack`.

How to do it...

First we will create an HTTP Load Balance pool.

Creating pools

To create a Load Balancer pool for a logged in user, carry out the following steps:

1. To manage Load Balancers within our OpenStack Dashboard, select the **Load Balancers** tab:

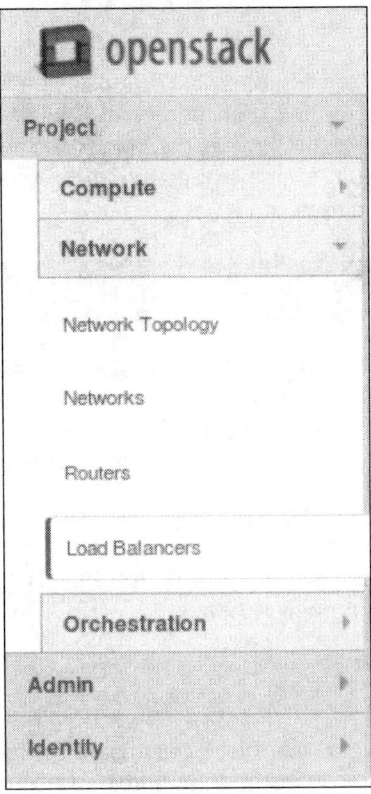

2. This will show available Load Balancer pools. Since we currently do not have any created, click on the **Add Pool** button in the top-right corner to add a pool.

3. After clicking on the **Add Pool** button, we are presented with a modal window. Fill out the details to add a new pool:

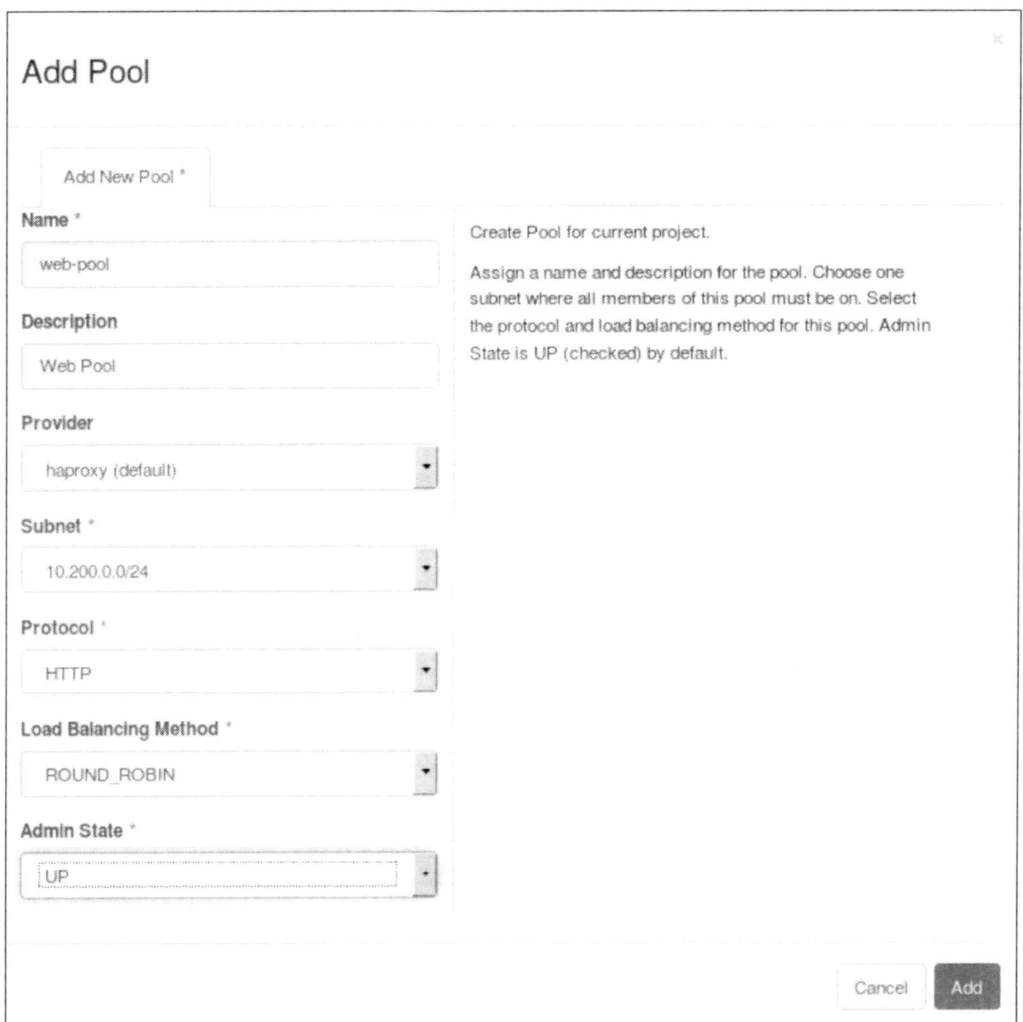

4. Set name, description, and provider in the modal window. We name our pool `web-pool` and give an appropriate description. We choose to go with a default provider since we are creating an HA Proxy.
5. Select a subnet for the pool by clicking on the drop-down menu. All of our instances are attached to the private network, so we select `10.200.0.0/24`.
6. We select the **HTTP** protocol, but **HTTPS** and **TCP** are also available. This selection will depend on what kind of applications you are running.
7. Select your preferred routing algorithm; we choose the **ROUND_ROBIN** balancing method. Other options are **LEAST_CONNECTIONS**, and **SOURCE_IP**.
8. We leave the **Admin State** set to **UP**.
9. Click on the **Add** button to create a new pool. You should see the new pool created in the pool list:

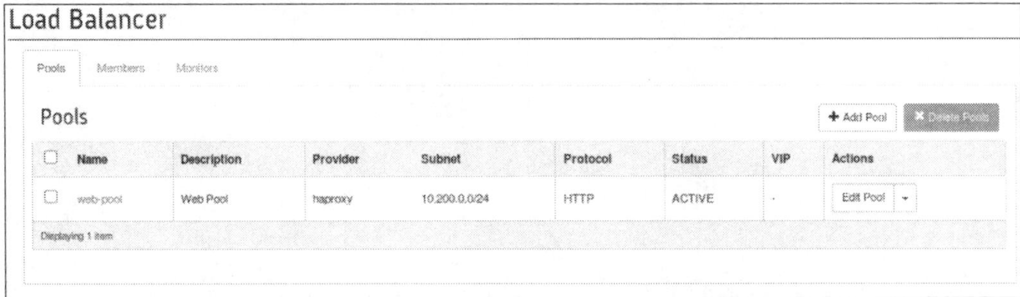

Adding pool members

To add instances to the Load Balancer, follow these steps:

1. After adding a pool, you should still be on the **Load Balancer** page. Click on the **Members** tab. You should see a list of active members, if you have any, or an empty list:

2. On the **Members** tab, click on the **Add Member** button. This will present you with the following menu:

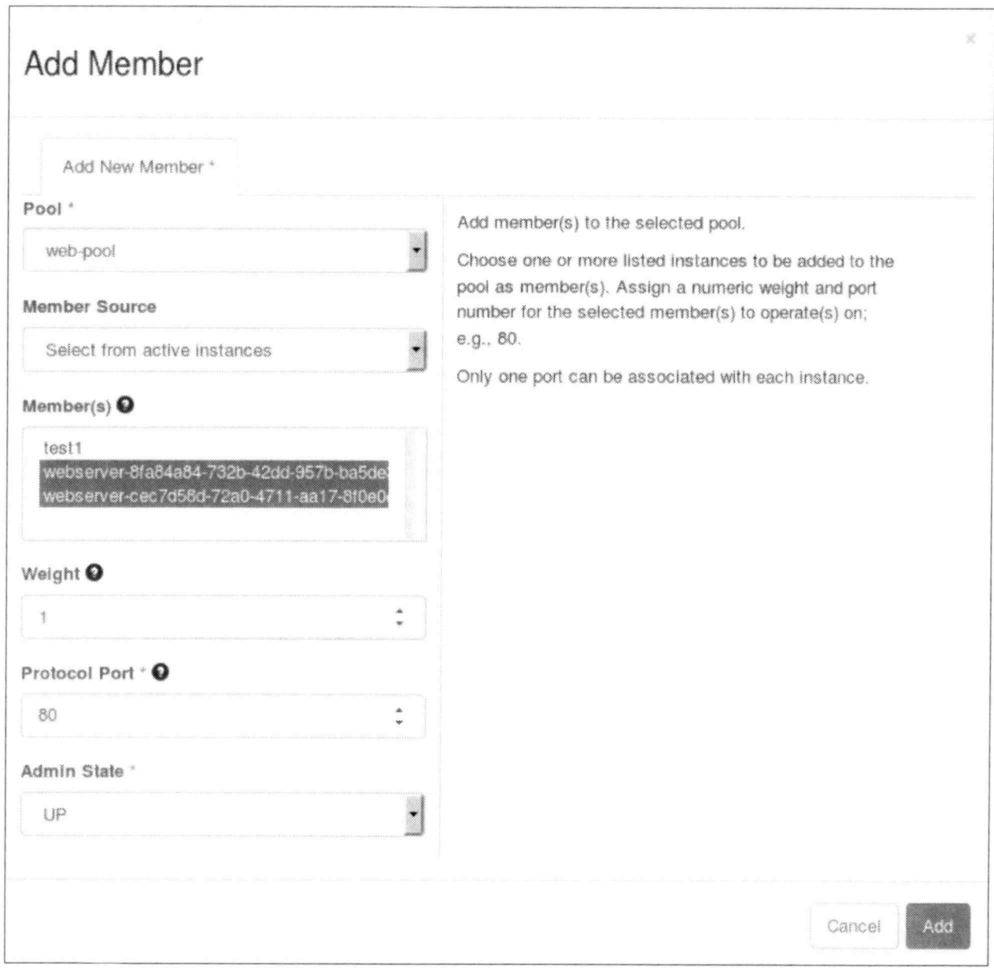

3. We select the pool we just created, **web-pool**, and specify members or instances that will be part of this pool. If you do not have any instances running with Apache installed, refer to the *Using cloud-config to run the post-installation configuration* recipe in *Chapter 9, More OpenStack*, for creating instances with running Apache.
4. Select weights for the members of the pool. In our case, both members of the pool will have equal weights, so we assign the weight as **1**.

5. The selected protocol port will be used to access all members of the pool and, since we are using HTTP, we set the port to 80. We set **Admin State** to **UP**.
6. Click on the **Add** button to add members to the pool.
7. Now the member list should contain two newly added nodes:

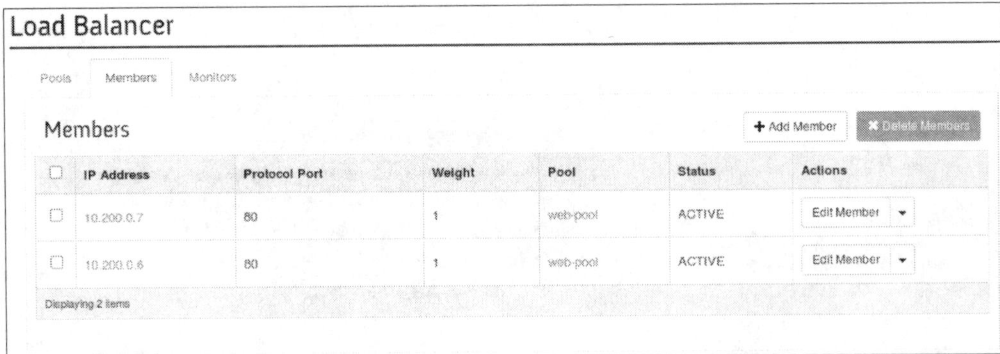

Adding a VIP to the Load Balancer pool

Creating a VIP on the external network will allow access to the Load Balance pool and the instances behind it. To create the VIP, carry out the following steps:

1. From the **Load Balancer** page, select the **Pools** tab and click on the drop-down arrow next to the **Edit Pool** button. This will give you a drop-down menu with an option to add a VIP:

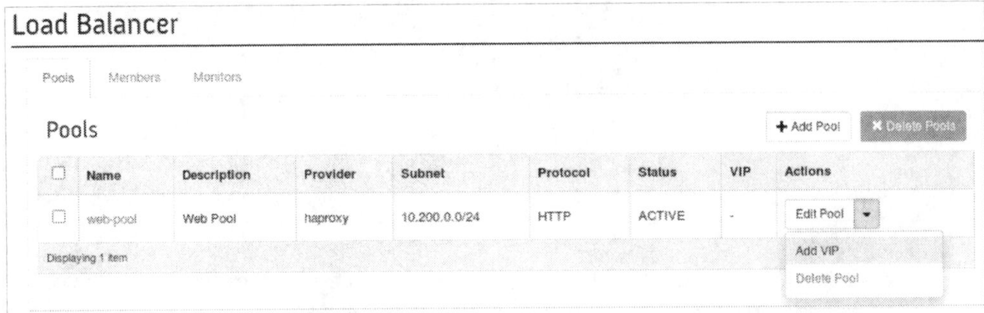

2. Click on the **Add VIP** option. This will present you with the modal window for creating a new VIP:

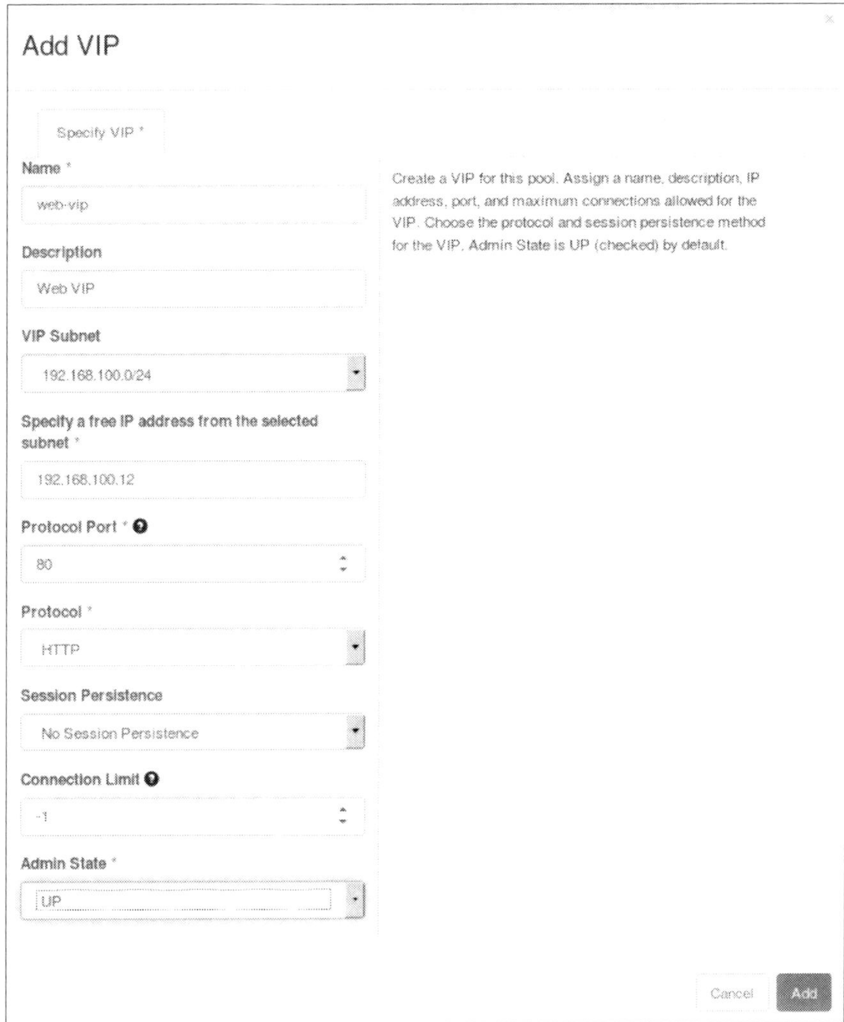

3. We enter a custom name and description for our VIP.
4. For **VIP Subnet**, we pick external subnet `192.168.100.0/24`, followed by an available IP in that subnet. We choose `192.168.100.12`.
5. Enter **80** for **Protocol Port**, followed by selecting **HTTP** for **Protocol**.

6. Set **-1** for **Connection Limit** if you do not wish to have a maximum number of connections for this VIP.
7. Click on the **Add** button to create the VIP. This will create a new VIP and show the current pool list:

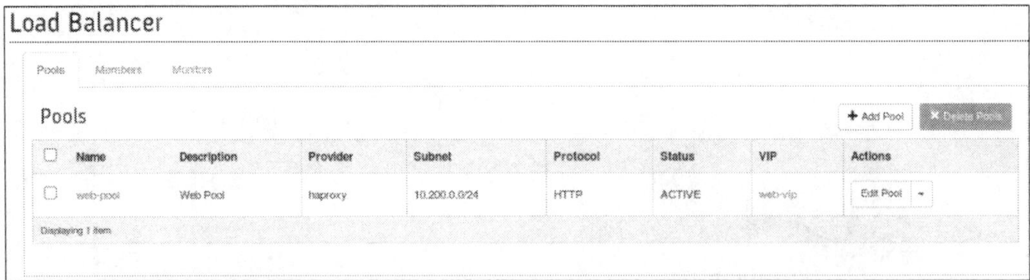

8. Now, when we click on **web-pool**, we will see the following details:

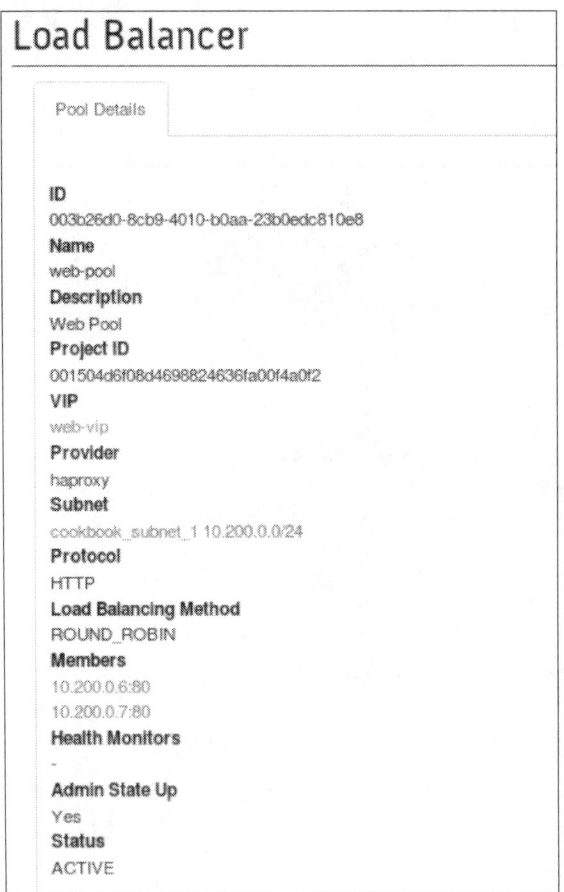

9. Click on the **web-vip** link in the details to view the VIP details:

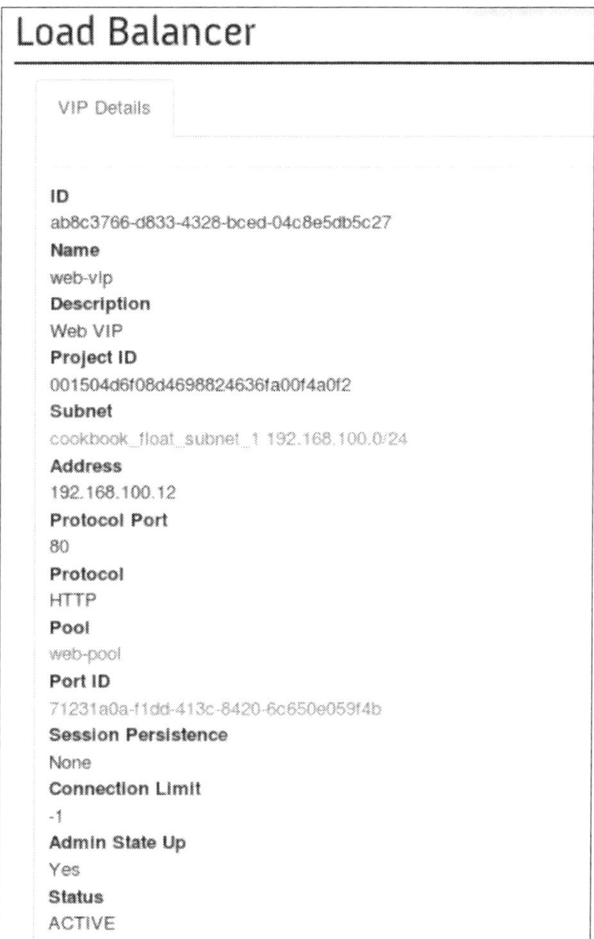

10. You can test this Load Balancer by entering the VIP's IP in a browser. If you selected **ROUND_ROBIN** for your routing algorithm, each time you refresh your browser it should hit a different node.

Deleting the Load Balancer

To delete the Load Balancer, we will first need to delete the attached VIP and then delete the pool.

1. From the **Load Balancer** page, check the **Pools** tab and click on the drop-down arrow next to the **Edit Pool** button. This will give you a drop-down menu with an option to delete a VIP:

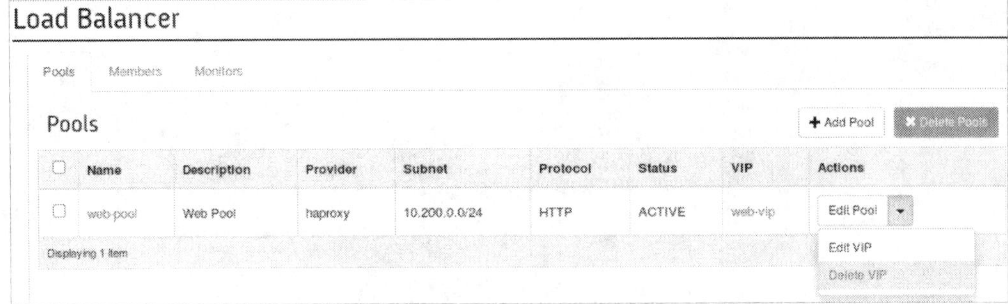

2. Selecting the **Delete VIP** drop-down option will give you a warning and ask you to confirm the deletion of the VIP. Click on the **Delete VIP** button to confirm:

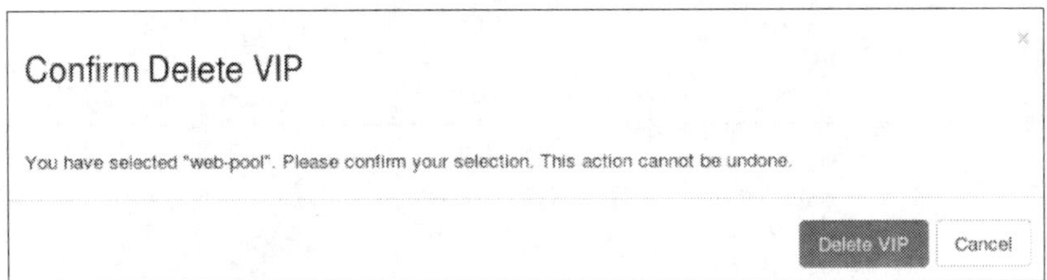

3. After deleting the VIP, now we can delete the pool. From the **Load Balancer** page's **Pools** tab, click on the drop-down arrow next to the appropriate **Edit Pool** button:

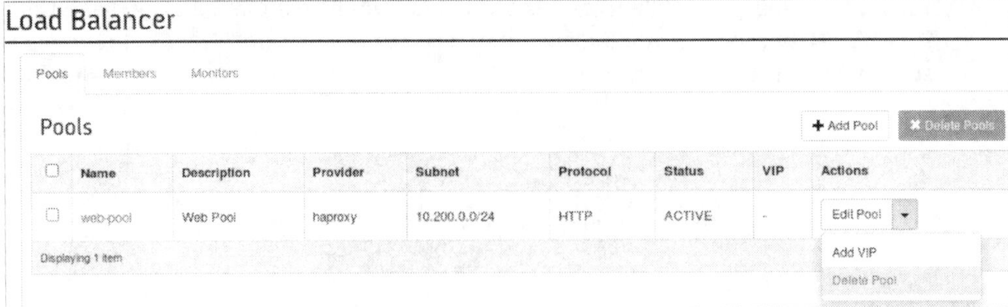

4. Select the **Delete Pool** option from the drop-down list to delete the pool. You will get asked to confirm the deletion. If you are ready to delete the Load Balance pool, click on the **Delete Pool** button:

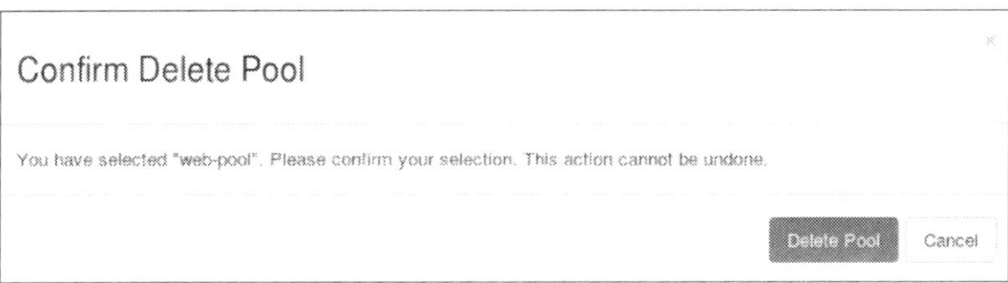

How it works...

We created a Load Balance pool and added two instances with Apache to it. We also created a virtual IP to be used on the external network and assigned it to our pool. To do this, we executed the following steps:

1. Create a pool from the **Load Balancer** page's **Pools** tab.
2. Select the subnet to which all the nodes are attached when creating the pool.
3. Add members to the pool.
4. Create a VIP for the pool.

Both the pool and VIP can be edited after being created. Additional members can also be added to the pool at a later time.

Using OpenStack Dashboard with OpenStack Orchestration

Heat is the OpenStack Orchestration engine that enables users to quickly spin up whole environments using templates. Heat templates, known as **Heat Orchestration Templates** (**HOT**), are **Yet Another Markup Language** (**YAML**) based files. The files describe the resources being used, the type and the size of the instances, the network an instance will be attached to, among other pieces of information required to run that environment.

In the previous chapter, we showed you how to use the Heat command line client. In this section, we will show how to use an existing Heat template file in OpenStack Dashboard to spin up two web servers running Apache, connected to a third instance running HA Proxy.

Getting ready

Load a web browser, point it to our OpenStack Dashboard address at `http://192.168.100.200/` and log in as an admin user, such as the `admin` user created in the *Adding users to Keystone* recipe of *Chapter 1, Keystone – OpenStack Identity Service*, with the password `openstack`.

How to do it...

First, we will launch stack within our OpenStack Dashboard.

Launching stacks

To launch a Heat stack for a logged in user, carry out the following steps:

1. To view available Heat stacks within our OpenStack Dashboard, select the **Stacks** tab under the **Orchestration** menu:

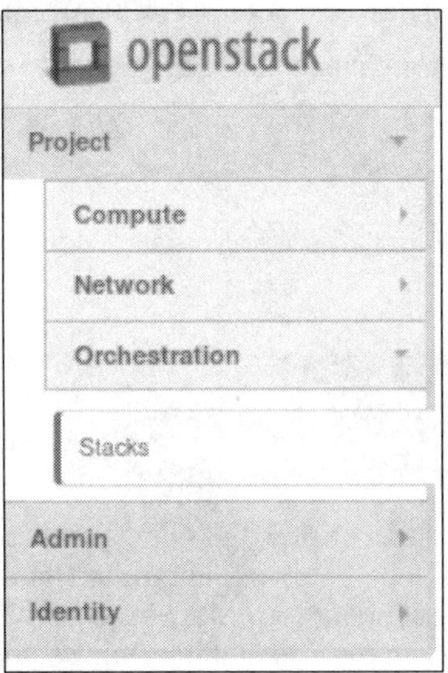

2. After clicking on the **Stacks** tab, you will see all running stacks in your environment. In our case, our list is empty:

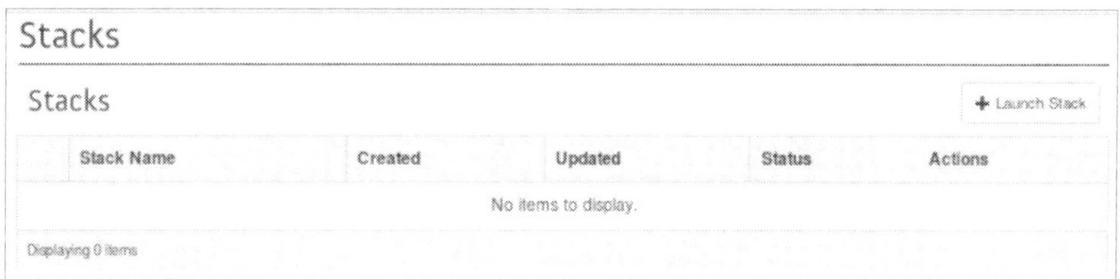

3. Click on the **Launch Stack** button to create a new stack. You will see the following window:

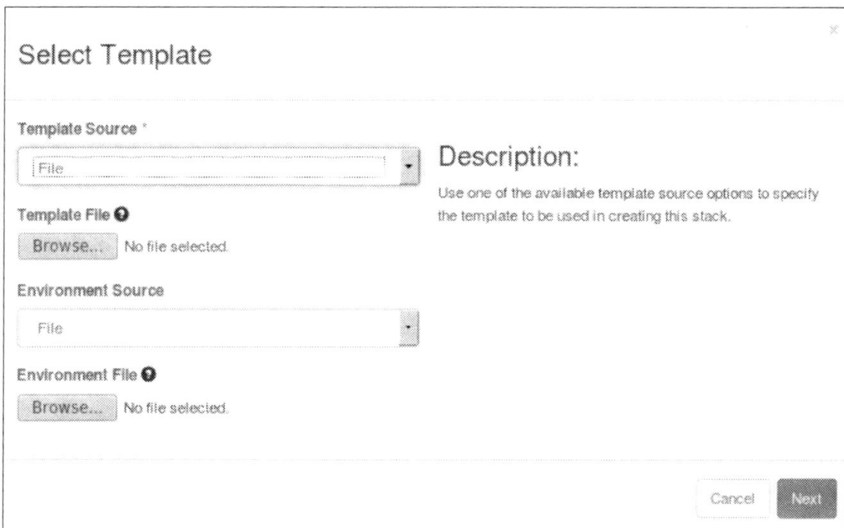

4. There are several ways to specify what template source to use in a stack: **File**, **Direct Input**, or **URL**. Choose which option is the most convenient for you. For our example, you can either use the URL directly or upload a file. The template file can be downloaded from `https://raw.githubusercontent.com/OpenStackCookbook/OpenStackCookbook/master/cookbook.yaml`. We will upload files from our system.

5. Just like we downloaded the `cookbook.yaml` file, we can also download the **Environment Source** file. In this case, we do not have to use the environment source, but it makes it convenient. The environment file stores the values we would have to enter into the browser manually, but instead loads the values for us on the **Launch Stack** screen, as shown in step 8. In our example, we are using the environment file that can be downloaded from `https://raw.githubusercontent.com/OpenStackCookbook/OpenStackCookbook/master/cookbook-env.yaml`. Update the `public_net_id`, `private_net_id`, and `private_subnet_id` fields to match your environment.

> If you are not sure where to find network information, please refer to the *Using OpenStack Dashboard to manage Neutron networks* recipe in this chapter.

6. After selecting the **Template Source** and **Environment Source** files, click on **Next**:

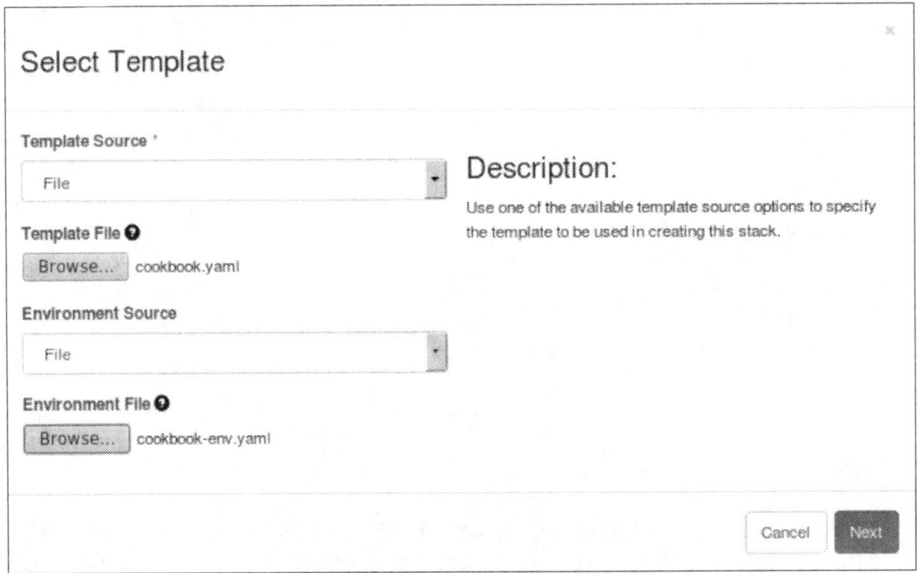

7. Our sample environment file contains the following code:

```
parameters:
  key_name: demokey
  image: trusty-image
  flavor: m1.tiny
  public_net_id: 5e5d24bd-9d1f-4ed1-84b5-0b7e2a9a233b
  private_net_id: 25153759-994f-4835-9b13-bf0ec77fb336
  private_subnet_id: 4cf2c09c-b3d5-40ed-9127-ec40e5e38343
```

8. Clicking on **Next** will give you a **Launch Stack** window with all the inputs:

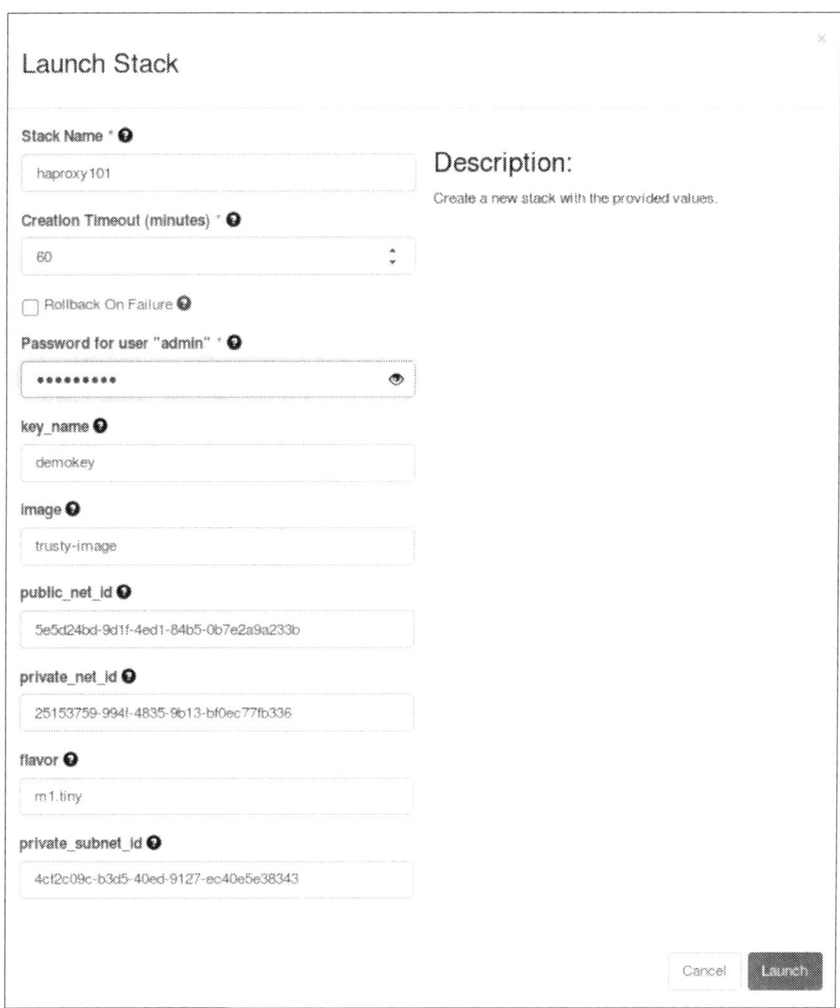

9. Note that most of the inputs in our template are now populated. If you did not specify the environment source file in the previous step, you will need to enter the `key_name`, `image`, `flavor`, `public_net_id`, `private_net_id`, and `private_subnet_id` fields.

These fields are specific to each template used. Your templates may have different fields.

10. Enter the stack name and user password for your user. If you are logged in as `admin` or `demo`, the password is `openstack`.
11. Click on the **Launch** button to start stack creation. If all inputs were correct, you should see your stack being created:

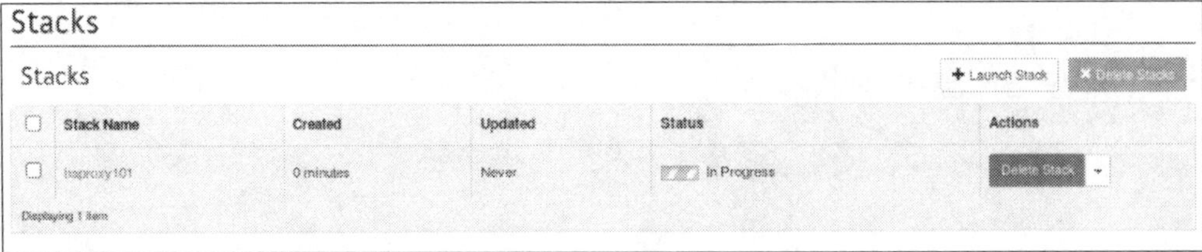

12. After the stack creation finishes and if there were no errors during creation, you will see your stack's status updated to **Complete**:

Viewing stack details

After launching a stack, there is a lot of information associated with it, including inputs, outputs, and, in the case of errors, information about why stack creation failed.

1. To view the details of the stack, click on the stack name from the **Stacks** list. The first available view is **Topology**:

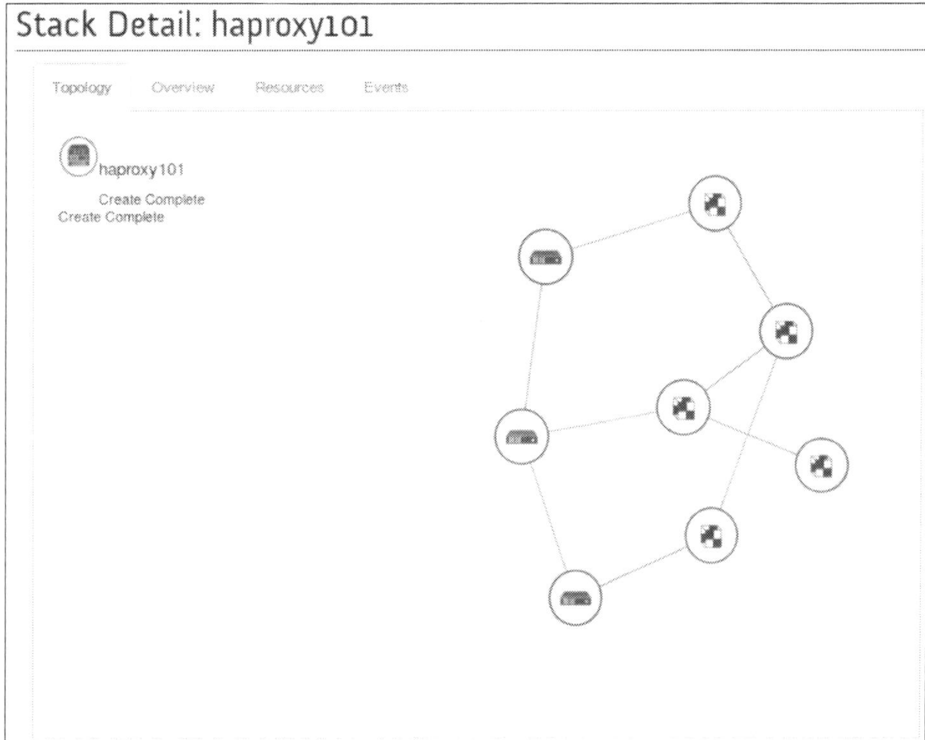

   Explore the topology by clicking on the nodes. If the graph does not fully fit or you would like a different perspective, you can drag the graph around the window.

2. The next tab under **Stack Detail** will provide all of the information that was used in creating the stack:

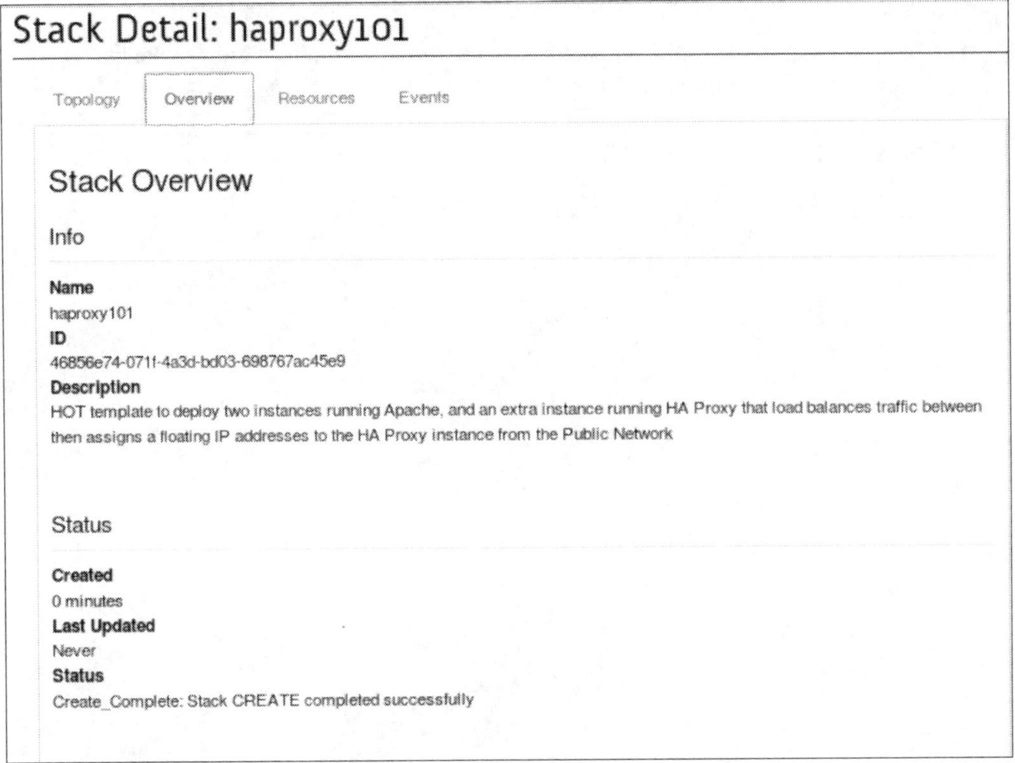

Stack information available in the **Overview** tab is as follows:

- Info
- Status
- Outputs
- Stack parameters
- Launch parameters

3. The **Resources** tab will show all the HEAT resources that were created during stack launch:

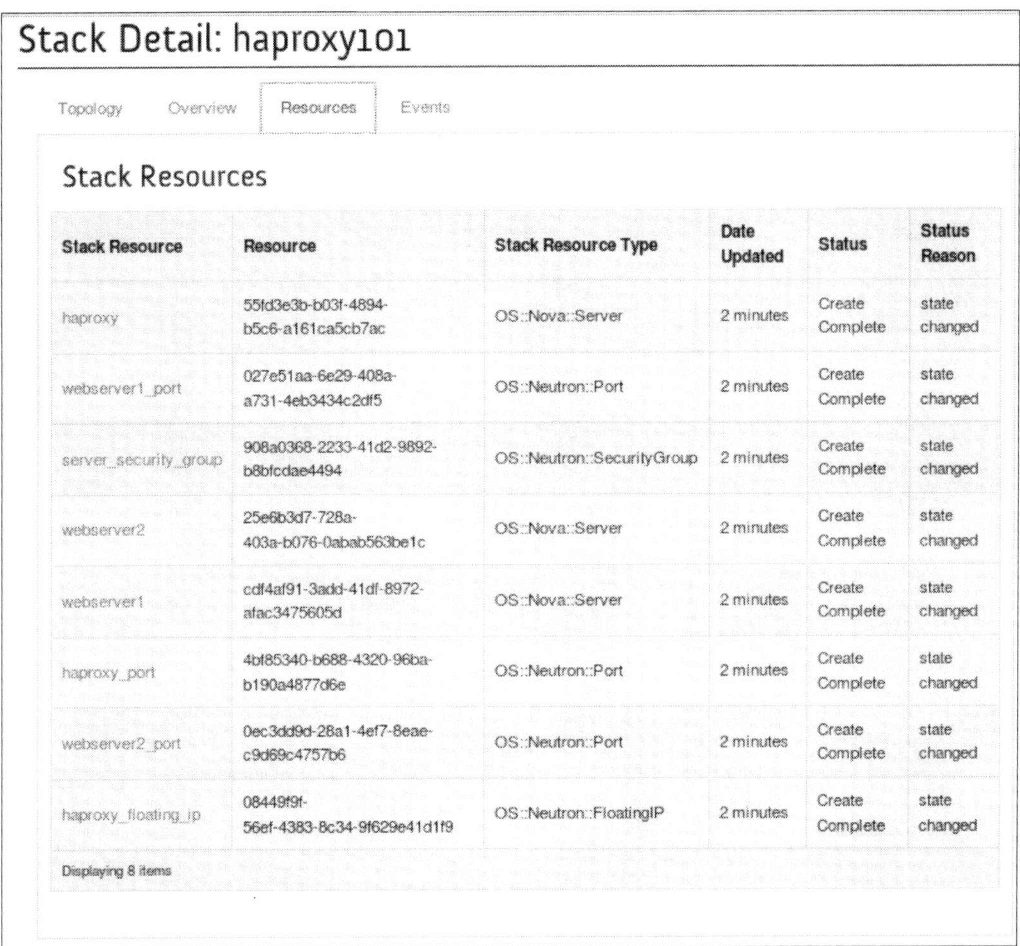

Stack Detail: haproxy101

Topology | Overview | Resources | Events

Stack Resources

Stack Resource	Resource	Stack Resource Type	Date Updated	Status	Status Reason
haproxy	55fd3e3b-b03f-4894-b5c6-a161ca5cb7ac	OS::Nova::Server	2 minutes	Create Complete	state changed
webserver1_port	027e51aa-6e29-408a-a731-4eb3434c2df5	OS::Neutron::Port	2 minutes	Create Complete	state changed
server_security_group	908a0368-2233-41d2-9892-b8bfcdae4494	OS::Neutron::SecurityGroup	2 minutes	Create Complete	state changed
webserver2	25e6b3d7-728a-403a-b076-0abab563be1c	OS::Nova::Server	2 minutes	Create Complete	state changed
webserver1	cdf4af91-3add-41df-8972-afac3475605d	OS::Nova::Server	2 minutes	Create Complete	state changed
haproxy_port	4bf85340-b688-4320-96ba-b190a4877d6e	OS::Neutron::Port	2 minutes	Create Complete	state changed
webserver2_port	0ec3dd9d-28a1-4ef7-8eae-c9d69c4757b6	OS::Neutron::Port	2 minutes	Create Complete	state changed
haproxy_floating_ip	08449f9f-56ef-4383-8c34-9f629e41d1f9	OS::Neutron::FloatingIP	2 minutes	Create Complete	state changed

Displaying 8 items

If there were any errors during stack launch, check this page to see which component's creation failed.

4. The **Events** tab shows all the events that occurred when the stack was created. This page can also be very helpful in troubleshooting Heat templates:

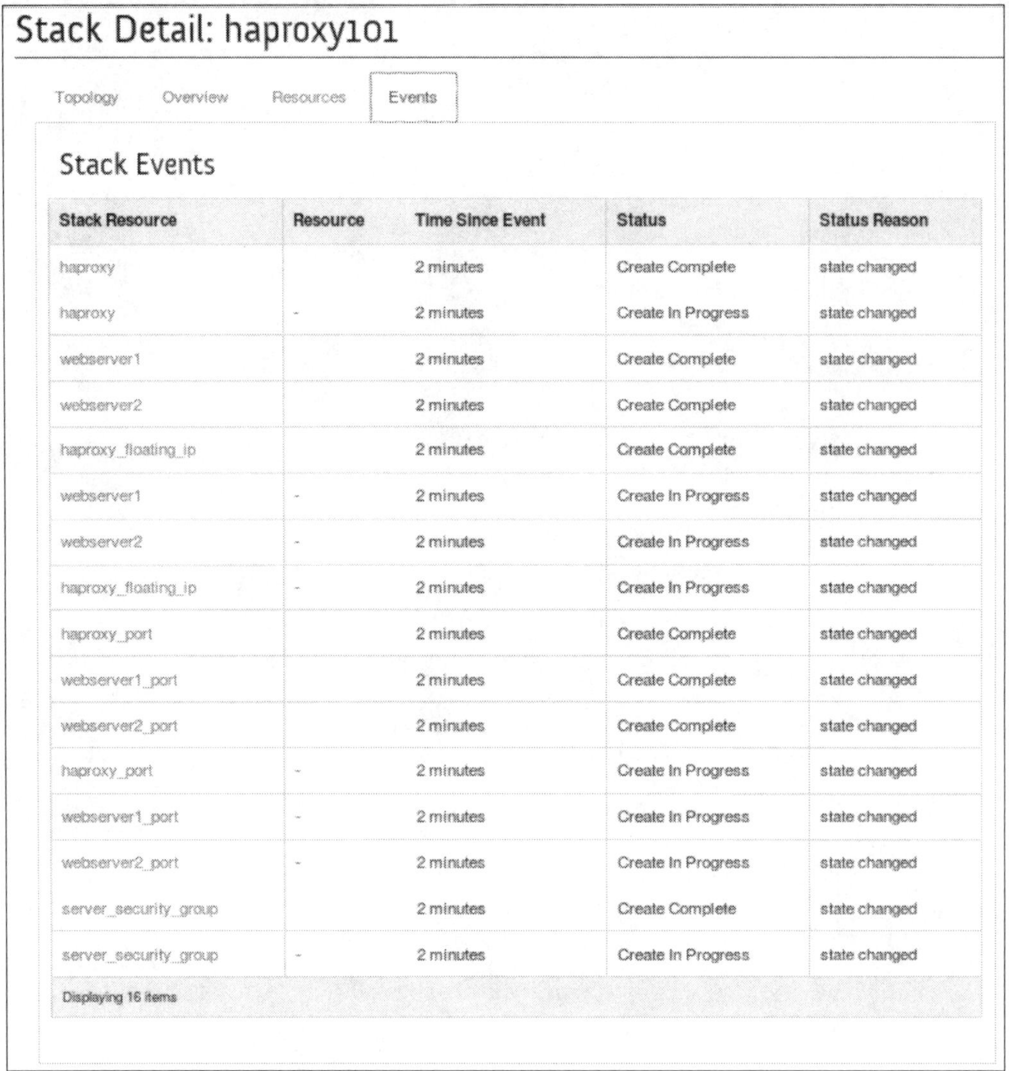

Stack Detail: haproxy101

Topology | Overview | Resources | Events

Stack Events

Stack Resource	Resource	Time Since Event	Status	Status Reason
haproxy		2 minutes	Create Complete	state changed
haproxy	-	2 minutes	Create In Progress	state changed
webserver1		2 minutes	Create Complete	state changed
webserver2		2 minutes	Create Complete	state changed
haproxy_floating_ip		2 minutes	Create Complete	state changed
webserver1	-	2 minutes	Create In Progress	state changed
webserver2	-	2 minutes	Create In Progress	state changed
haproxy_floating_ip	-	2 minutes	Create In Progress	state changed
haproxy_port		2 minutes	Create Complete	state changed
webserver1_port		2 minutes	Create Complete	state changed
webserver2_port		2 minutes	Create Complete	state changed
haproxy_port	-	2 minutes	Create In Progress	state changed
webserver1_port	-	2 minutes	Create In Progress	state changed
webserver2_port	-	2 minutes	Create In Progress	state changed
server_security_group		2 minutes	Create Complete	state changed
server_security_group	-	2 minutes	Create In Progress	state changed

Displaying 16 items

5. While your Heat stack is running, you can also see how many instances it created under the **Compute** tab's **Instance** option. The following is what our instances look like on the **Instances** page:

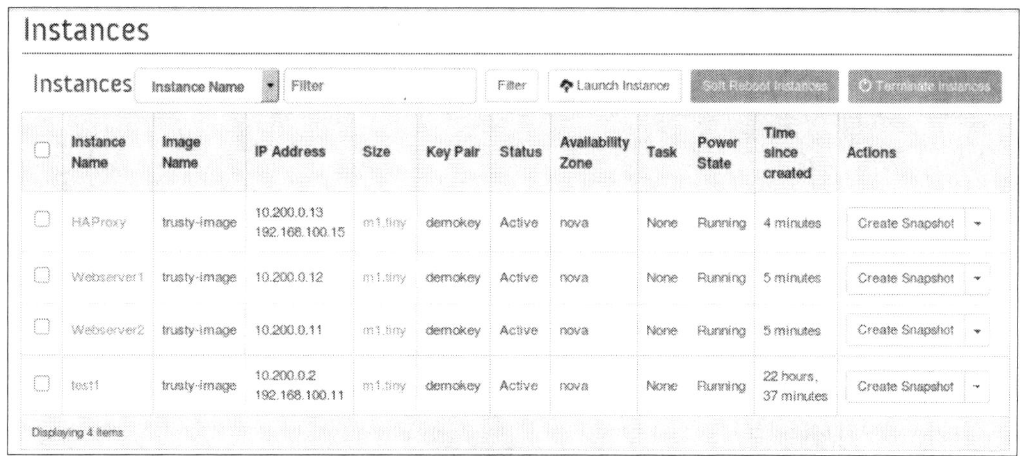

> Note that the **test1** instance was not part of the stack creation. All the other VMs were created during the stack launch.

Deleting stacks

Stack deletion is simple; however, it will delete all resources that were created during stack launch. Follow these steps:

1. To delete a stack, first view the available stacks on the **Stacks** page:

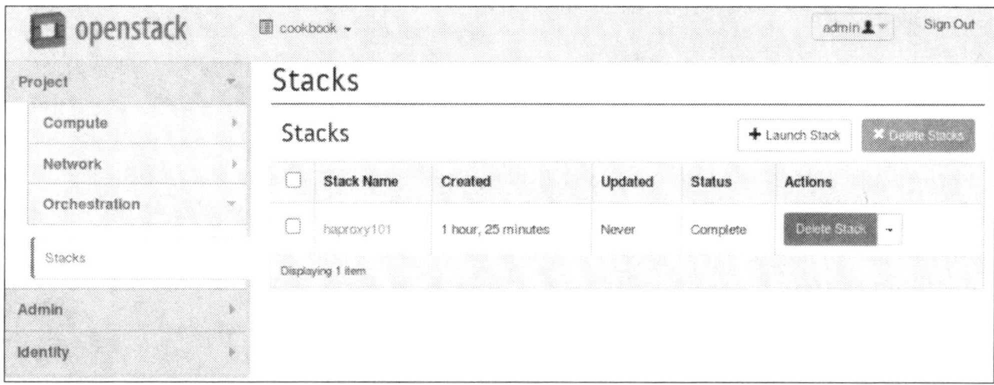

2. Click on the appropriate **Delete Stack** button to delete a stack. You will be asked to confirm the deletion:

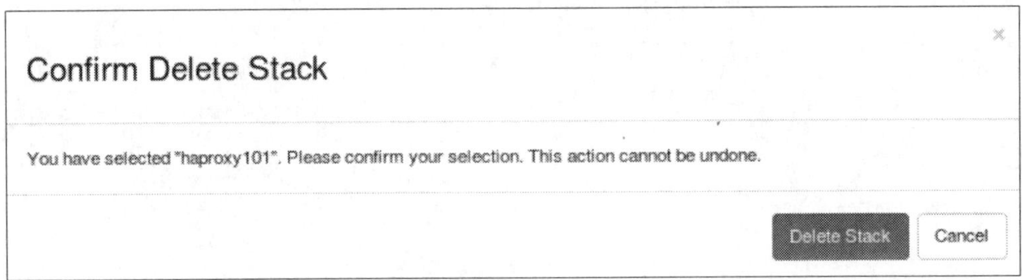
Confirm Delete Stack
You have selected "haproxy101". Please confirm your selection. This action cannot be undone.
Delete Stack
Cancel

3. After confirming deletion, all resources associated with the stack will be deleted.

How it works...

We have used the OpenStack Dashboard to launch, view, and delete Orchestration stacks. We first needed to download a sample HA Proxy Heat Orchestration Template from GitHub. Since we were using an environment file, we also had to modify the appropriate inputs. Your own templates may have different inputs.

After launching our HA Proxy stack, we explored its topology, resources, and events. Resources created during stack launch will also be reflected in the rest of your environment. If you are launching new instances, all of them will also be available on the **Instance** page. Delete and modify resources created during the stack launch only through Orchestration section in the OpenStack dashboard or on the command line. Deleting stacks through the dashboard will delete all associated resources.

11
Production OpenStack

In this chapter, we will cover the following recipes:

- Installing the MariaDB Galera cluster
- Configuring HA Proxy for the MariaDB Galera cluster
- Configuring HA Proxy for high availability
- Installing and configuring Pacemaker with Corosync
- Configuring OpenStack services with Pacemaker and Corosync
- Bonding network interfaces for redundancy
- Automating OpenStack installations using Ansible – host configuration
- Automating OpenStack installations using Ansible – Playbook configuration
- Automating OpenStack installations using Ansible – running Playbooks

Introduction

OpenStack is a suite of software designed to offer scale-out cloud environments, deployed in datacenters around the world. Managing the installation of software in a remote location is different (and sometimes challenging) than installing software locally, and so tools and techniques have been developed to ease this task. Design considerations of how to deal with hardware and software failure must also be taken into consideration in operational environments. Identifying **Single Points Of Failure** (**SPOF**) and adding ways of making them resilient ensures that our OpenStack environment remains available when something goes wrong.

This chapter introduces some methods and software that help manage OpenStack in production datacenters—from making the services highly available to automating installations for consistency and repeatability.

Installing the MariaDB Galera cluster

OpenStack can be backed by a number of database backends, and one of the most common options is MySQL or its other open source fork, MariaDB. There are a number of ways to make MariaDB more resilient and highly available. The following approach uses a Load Balancer to front a multi-read/write master with Galera, taking care of the synchronous replication required in such a setup. Galera is a synchronous multimaster cluster for MariaDB InnoDB databases. Galera clusters allow synchronous data writes across all nodes with any node being able to take that write in a fully active/active topology. It features automatic node management- that is, failed nodes are removed from the cluster and new nodes are automatically registered. The advantage of this is that we are adding resilience in the event of a database node failure, as each node stores a copy of the data. Galera clusters consist of odd-numbered nodes. This is important when a node fails. Galera takes a quorum vote from the remaining nodes to determine the state. Quorum requires a majority, that is, you cannot have automatic failover in a two-node cluster. This is because the failure of one causes the remaining nodes to automatically go into a nonprimary state. Clusters that have an even number of nodes risk split-brain conditions. If should you lose network connectivity somewhere between the partitions in a way that causes the number of nodes to split exactly in half, neither of the partitions can retain quorum and both enter a nonprimary state.

Getting ready

Ensure that you have three servers running Ubuntu 14.04 and at least one interface that will be used to access the machines and be configured for Galera replication. Follow the instructions at `https://github.com/OpenStackCookbook/MariaDB-Galera` to bring up a suitable `vagrant` environment. These steps are also repeated in the following *How to do it...* section.

How to do it...

For this recipe, we will install MariaDB and Galera on three nodes that we will call `Galera1`, `Galera2`, and `Galera3`. They will each have a single IP assigned to them on the `172.16.0.0/16` network and the interface will be referenced as `eth1` on the machines. The IPs used in the following steps are `172.16.0.191`, `172.16.0.192`, and `172.16.0.193`. They will all be running `Ubuntu 14.04 LTS`. The steps are as follows:

1. On the first server, `Galera1`, we configure `apt` to be able to retrieve *MariaDB Cluster 10.0* packages with the following command:

```
apt-get install software-properties-common
sudo apt-key adv --recv-keys --keyserver \
    hkp://keyserver.ubuntu.com:80 0xcbcb082a1bb943db
```

```
sudo add-apt-repository 'deb
http://lon1.mirrors.digitalocean.com/mariadb/repo/10.0/ubuntu
trusty main'
sudo apt-get update
```

2. Install the packages by running the following command:

```
DEBIAN_FRONTEND=noninteractive apt-get install \
    rsync galera mariadb-galera-server
```

3. Ensure that MariaDB isn't running by executing the following command:

```
sudo service mysql stop
```

4. Repeat step 1 to step 3 for `Galera2` and `Galera3`.
5. We then configure MariaDB to use Galera by editing the `/etc/mysql/conf.d/galera.cnf` file to include the following contents:

```
[mysqld]
# mysql settings
binlog_format=ROW
default-storage-engine=innodb
innodb_autoinc_lock_mode=2
query_cache_size=0
query_cache_type=0
bind-address=0.0.0.0
# galera settings
wsrep_provider=/usr/lib/galera/libgalera_smm.so
wsrep_cluster_name="my_wsrep_cluster"
wsrep_cluster_address="gcomm://172.16.0.191,172.16.0.192,17
2.16.0.193"
wsrep_sst_method=rsync
```

6. Log in to `Galera1` and execute the following command to start up a new Galera replication cluster:

```
sudo service mysql start --wsrep-new-cluster
```

7. Log in to `Galera2` and `Galera3` to execute the following command on each node:

```
sudo service mysql start
```

8. Test whether `mysql service` was started by logging into any of the nodes and running the following command:

```
mysql -u root -e 'SELECT VARIABLE_VALUE as "cluster size" \
    FROM INFORMATION_SCHEMA.GLOBAL_STATUS \
    WHERE VARIABLE_NAME="wsrep_cluster_size"'
```

It should return the following output:

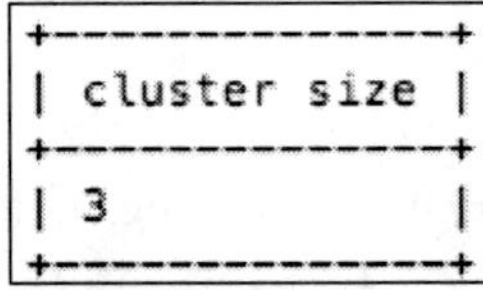

```
+--------------+
| cluster size |
+--------------+
| 3            |
+--------------+
```

How it works...

We configured three servers running Ubuntu 14.04 to be able to install MariaDB and Galera. We do this by adding the MariaDB repository to our `apt` environment and installing the appropriate packages.

Once this has been done on each of the three nodes, we configure MariaDB to use Galera by editing the `/etc/mysql/conf.d/galera.cnf` file. This has a section that describes how Galera is used. We specify a cluster name, the IP addresses used in the cluster, and the method by which the data will be replicated:

```
wsrep_provider=/usr/lib/galera/libgalera_smm.so
wsrep_cluster_name="my_wsrep_cluster"
wsrep_cluster_address="gcomm://172.16.0.191,172.16.0.192,172.16.0.193"
wsrep_sst_method=rsync
```

After this, we start up the cluster. To do this, we choose one of the nodes and execute the following command:

```
service mysql start --wsrep-new-cluster
```

We then start up the remaining nodes as usual using the following command:

```
service mysql start
```

Configuring HA Proxy for the MariaDB Galera cluster

With our MariaDB Galera cluster configured, each node can take traffic, and the writes are seamlessly replicated to other nodes in the cluster. We could use any of the MariaDB node addresses and place them in our configuration files, but if that node failed, we would not have a database to attach to and our OpenStack environment would fail. A possible solution to this is to front the MariaDB cluster using Load Balancing. Given that any of the nodes can take reads and writes, with data consistency, Load Balancing is a great solution. Generally, physical Load Balancers, such as those from F5 or Brocade, are recommended. In the absence of physical Load Balancers, **High Availability** (**HA**) Proxy can be used.

Getting ready

Install two servers, both running Ubuntu 14.04, which are configured on the same management network as our OpenStack environment and the MariaDB Galera cluster. In the following steps, the two nodes will be on the IP addresses `172.16.0.248` and `172.16.0.249`. In the next recipe, we will configure these two nodes with a `FloatingIP` address (that will be set up using `keepalived`) of `172.16.0.251`. This address will be used when we configure the database connections in our OpenStack configuration files.

How to do it...

As we are setting up identical servers to act in a pair, we will configure a single server first *and then repeat the process for the second server*. The first will utilize the IP address `172.16.0.248`. We then repeat the steps utilizing the IP address `172.16.0.249`.

To configure HA Proxy for MariaDB Galera Load Balancing, carry out step 1 to step 5 twice to create two HA Proxy instances—both configured to access our MariaDB Galera nodes.

1. We first install HA Proxy using the usual `apt-get` process, as follows:

   ```
   sudo apt-get update
   sudo apt-get install haproxy
   ```

2. With HA Proxy installed, we'll simply configure this first proxy server appropriately for our MariaDB Galera cluster. To do this, we edit the `/etc/haproxy/haproxy.cfg` file and insert the following contents:

   ```
   global
     log 127.0.0.1   local0
     log 127.0.0.1   local1 notice
     maxconn 4096
     user haproxy
     group haproxy
     daemon

   defaults
     log global
     mode http
     option tcplog
     option dontlognull
     retries 3
     option redispatch
     maxconn 4096
     timeout connect 50000ms
     timeout client 50000ms
   ```

```
    timeout server 50000ms

  # MySQL Load Balance Pool
  listen  mysql 0.0.0.0:3306
    mode tcp
    balance roundrobin
    option tcpka
    option mysql-check user haproxy
    server mysql1 172.16.0.191:3306 weight 1
    server mysql2 172.16.0.192:3306 weight 1
    server mysql3 172.16.0.193:3306 weight 1
```

3. Save and exit the file, and then start up HA Proxy with the following command:

```
sudo sed -i 's/^ENABLED.*/ENABLED=1/' /etc/defaults/haproxy
sudo service haproxy start
```

4. Before we can use this HA Proxy server to access our three MariaDB nodes, we must create the user specified in the `haproxy.cfg` file that is used to do a very simple check to see if MariaDB is up and running. To do this, we add a user into our cluster that is simply able to connect to MariaDB. Using the `mysql` client on any of our Galera nodes, create the user `haproxy` with no password set. This user is allowed access from the IP address of the HA Proxy server. Run the following commands:

```
mysql -u root -h localhost \

    -e "GRANT ALL ON *.* to haproxy@'172.16.0.248';"
```

5. We carry out a similar step to add in a `root` user to our MySQL Galera cluster that has permission to run MySQL commands originating from the HA Proxy servers:

```
mysql -u root -h localhost \
    -e "GRANT ALL ON *.* to root@'172.16.0.248' IDENTIFIED BY
'openstack' WITH GRANT OPTION;"
```

Repeat step 1 to step 5, replacing the IP address `172.16.0.248` with the IP address of our second node, `172.16.0.249`.

How it works...

HA Proxy is a very popular and useful proxy and Load Balancer that makes it ideal for fronting a MariaDB cluster to add load-balancing capabilities. It is simple to set up the service to front MariaDB.

The first requirement is listening on the appropriate port, which for MariaDB is `3306`. The listen line in the configuration files here also specifies that it will listen on all addresses by using `0.0.0.0` as the address, but you can bind this to a particular address by specifying this to add an extra layer of control in our environment.

To use MariaDB, the mode must be set to `tcp` and we set `keepalived` with the `tcpka` option to ensure long-lived connections are not interrupted and closed when a client opens up a connection to our MariaDB servers.

The Load Balance method used is round robin, which is perfectly suitable for a multi-master cluster where any node can perform reads and writes.

We add in a basic check to ensure that our MariaDB servers are marked offline appropriately. Using the inbuilt `mysql-check` option (which requires a user to be set up in MariaDB to log in to the MariaDB nodes and quit), when a MariaDB server fails, the server is ignored and traffic passes to a MariaDB server that is alive. Note that it does not perform any checks for whether a particular table exists—though this can be achieved with more complex configurations using a check script running on each MariaDB server and calling the check script as part of our checks.

The final configuration step for HA Proxy is listing the nodes and the addresses that they listen on, which forms the Load Balance pool of servers.

Configuring HA Proxy for high availability

The steps in the preceding recipe configure a two-node HA Proxy setup that we can use as a MariaDB endpoint to place in our OpenStack configuration files. Having a single HA Proxy acting as a Load Balancer to a highly available multimaster cluster is not recommended, as the Load Balancer then becomes our single point of failure. To overcome this, we can simply install and configure `keepalived`, which gives us the ability to share a `FloatingIP` address between our HA Proxy servers. This allows us to use this `FloatingIP` address as the address to use for our OpenStack services.

Getting ready

Log in to the two HA Proxy servers created in the previous recipe as `root`.

How to do it...

As we have two identical HA Proxy servers running—one on address `172.16.0.248`, and another at `172.16.0.249`—we will assign a floating "virtual IP" address of `172.16.0.251`, which is able to attach itself to one of the servers and switch over to the other in the event of a failure. To do this, follow these steps:

1. Having a single HA Proxy server sitting in front of our multimaster MariaDB cluster makes the HA Proxy server our single point of failure. To overcome this, we use a simple solution provided by `keepalived` for **Virtual Redundant Router Protocol** (**VRRP**) management. To do this, we need to install `keepalived` on both of our HA Proxy servers. As we did before, we will configure one server, and then repeat the steps for our second server. We do this as follows:

   ```
   sudo apt-get update
   sudo apt-get install keepalived
   ```

2. To allow running software to bind to an address that does not physically exist on our server, we add in an option to `sysctl.conf`. Add the following line to `/etc/sysctl.conf`:

   ```
   net.ipv4.ip_nonlocal_bind=1
   ```

3. To pick up the change, issue the following command:

   ```
   sudo sysctl -p
   ```

4. We can now configure `keepalived`. To do this, we create a `/etc/keepalived/keepalived.conf` file with the following contents:

   ```
   vrrp_script chk_haproxy {
     script "killall -0 haproxy" # verify the pid exists or
       not
     interval 2        # check every 2 seconds
     weight 2          # add 2 points if OK
   }

   vrrp_instance VI_1 {
     interface eth1    # interface to monitor
     state MASTER
     virtual_router_id 51  # Assign one ID for this router
     priority 101          # 101 on master, 100 on backup
     virtual_ipaddress {
       172.16.0.251   # the virtual IP
     }
   ```

```
    track_script {
      chk_haproxy
    }
}
```

5. We can now start up `keepalived` on this server by issuing the following command:

   `sudo service keepalived start`

6. With `keepalived` now running on our first HA Proxy server, which we have designated as the master node, we repeat the previous steps for our second HA Proxy server with only two changes to the `keepalived.conf` file (`state` should be set to `BACKUP` and `priority` should be set to `100`) to give the complete file on our second host the following contents:

```
vrrp_script chk_haproxy {
  script "killall -0 haproxy" # verify the pid exists or
not
  interval 2        # check every 2 seconds
  weight 2          # add 2 points if OK
}

vrrp_instance VI_1 {
  interface eth1    # interface to monitor
  state BACKUP
  virtual_router_id 51  # Assign one ID for this router
  priority 100          # 101 on master, 100 on backup
  virtual_ipaddress {
    172.16.0.251  # the virtual IP
  }
  track_script {
    chk_haproxy
  }
}
```

7. Start up `keepalived` on this second node, and they will be acting in coordination with each other. So, if you powered off the first HA Proxy server, the second server will pick up the `FloatingIP` address `172.16.0.251`. After 2 seconds, new connections can be made to our MariaDB cluster without disruption. We can test whether the HA Proxy and MariaDB with Galera setup is working by connecting to the database cluster with the following command:

   `mysql -uroot -popenstack -h 172.16.0.251`

8. To check whether `keepalived` is working correctly, view the messages in `/var/log/syslog` on each of our nodes. Execute the following command:

   `sudo grep VRRP /var/log/syslog`

On the node that currently has the `FloatingIP` address, you will see the following output:

```
Jul  2 16:06:46 packer-vmware-iso Keepalived[3869]: Starting VRRP child process, pid=3873
Jul  2 16:06:46 packer-vmware-iso Keepalived_vrrp[3873]: VRRP_Script(chk_haproxy) succeeded
Jul  2 16:06:47 packer-vmware-iso Keepalived_vrrp[3873]: VRRP_Instance(VI_1) Transition to MASTER STATE
Jul  2 16:06:48 packer-vmware-iso Keepalived_vrrp[3873]: VRRP_Instance(VI_1) Entering MASTER STATE
Jul  2 16:08:53 packer-vmware-iso Keepalived_vrrp[3873]: VRRP_Instance(VI_1) Received lower prio advert, forcing new election
```

On the node that doesn't have the `FloatingIP` assigned, you will see the following output:

```
Jul  2 16:08:52 packer-vmware-iso Keepalived[3886]: Starting VRRP child process, pid=3890
Jul  2 16:08:53 packer-vmware-iso Keepalived_vrrp[3890]: VRRP_Script(chk_haproxy) succeeded
Jul  2 16:08:53 packer-vmware-iso Keepalived_vrrp[3890]: VRRP_Instance(VI_1) Transition to MASTER STATE
Jul  2 16:08:53 packer-vmware-iso Keepalived_vrrp[3890]: VRRP_Instance(VI_1) Received higher prio advert
Jul  2 16:08:53 packer-vmware-iso Keepalived_vrrp[3890]: VRRP_Instance(VI_1) Entering BACKUP STATE
```

OpenStack backend configuration using FloatingIP address

With both HA Proxy servers running the same HA Proxy configuration and both running `keepalived`, we can use the `virtual_ipaddress` address (our `FloatingIP` address) configured as the address that we would then connect to and use in our configuration files. In OpenStack, we would identify each of the configuration files that refer to our database and change the following configuration to use our `FloatingIP` address of `172.16.0.251` where appropriate:

1. First, we must ensure that our new Galera cluster has all the usernames and passwords that we need for our OpenStack environment. In the test `vagrant` environment accompanying the book at `https://github.com/OpenStackCookbook/OpenStackCookbook.git`, we configure our database usernames to be the same as the service name, for example, `neutron`, and password to be `openstack`. To replicate this, execute the following commands to create all users and passwords:

```
USERS="nova
neutron
keystone
glance
cinder
heat"

HAPROXIES="172.16.0.248
```

```
172.16.0.249"

for U in ${USERS}
do
  for H in ${HAPROXIES}
  do
    mysql -u root -h localhost -e "GRANT ALL ON *.* to
${U}@\"${H}\" IDENTIFIED BY \"openstack\";"
  done
done
```

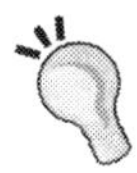

It is recommended that you use stronger, random passwords in production.

2. We can now use these details to replace the SQL connection lines in our configuration files used in OpenStack. Some examples are as follows:

```
# Nova
# /etc/nova/nova.conf
sql_connection = mysql://nova:openstack@172.16.0.251/nova

# Keystone
# /etc/keystone/keystone.conf
connection =
mysql://keystone:openstack@172.16.0.251/keystone

# Glance
# /etc/glance/glance-registry.conf
connection = mysql://glance:openstack@172.16.0.251/glance

# Neutron
# /etc/neutron/neutron.conf
[DATABASE]
connection = mysql://neutron:openstack@172.16.0.251/neutron

# Cinder
# /etc/cinder/cinder.conf
connection = mysql://cinder:openstack@172.16.0.251/cinder
```

How it works...

We install and configure `keepalived`, a service that gives us the ability to have an IP address that can float between each of our HA Proxy servers. In the event of a failure, it will be promoted and attached to the remaining running server.

We configure `keepalived` by editing the `/etc/keepalived/keepalived.conf` file. These look very similar on both nodes but with one difference—we specify the `MASTER` and the slave nodes.

On the `MASTER` node (it can be any nominated instance), we chose the first HA Proxy server. This is illustrated in the following code:

```
vrrp_instance VI_1 {
  interface eth1     # interface to monitor
  state MASTER
  virtual_router_id 51  # Assign one ID for this route
  priority 101          # 101 on master, 100 on backup
  virtual_ipaddress {
    172.16.0.251    # the virtual IP
  }
```

On the slave node, the code is as follows:

```
vrrp_instance VI_1 {
  interface eth1     # interface to monitor
  state BACKUP
  virtual_router_id 51  # Assign one ID for this route
  priority 100          # 101 on master, 100 on backup
  virtual_ipaddress {
    172.16.0.251    # the virtual IP
  }
```

In our example, the IP address we use that can float between our instances is `172.16.0.251`. This is configured as shown in the preceding `virtual_ipaddress` code snippet.

When we start `keepalived` on both servers, the `MASTER` node gets the `172.16.0.251` IP address. If we powered this host off, or it unexpectedly failed, the other HA Proxy server will inherit this IP address. This gives us our HA feature to our HA Proxy servers.

With this in place, we then ensure that our new database has all the relevant usernames and passwords configured and we replace all references to our non-HA configuration to our new MariaDB cluster.

Installing and configuring Pacemaker with Corosync

OpenStack has been designed for highly scalable environments where it is possible to avoid single point of failures (SPOFs), but sometimes you must build this into your own environment. For example, Keystone is a central service underpinning your entire OpenStack environment, so you would build multiple instances into your environment. Glance is another service that is key to the running of your OpenStack environment. By setting up multiple instances running these services, controlled with **Pacemaker** and **Corosync**, we can enjoy an increase in resilience to failure of the nodes running these services. Using Pacemaker and Corosync is one way of providing a highly available solution to OpenStack services. This recipe is designed to give you options for your deployments and allow you to use Pacemaker and Corosync elsewhere in your environment.

Getting ready

For this recipe, we will assume that there are two `controller` nodes available that are running Glance and Keystone. Installation of Keystone and Glance was covered in the first two chapters of this book.

The first `controller1` node will have a host management address of `192.168.100.221`. The second `controller2` node will have a host management address of `192.168.100.222`.

Visit `https://github.com/OpenStackCookbook/Controller-Corosync.git` for a two-node OpenStack Controller example that accompanies this section.

How to do it...

To install Pacemaker and Corosync on the two servers that will be running OpenStack services such as Keystone and Glance, carry out the following steps.

Setting up the first node – controller1

1. Once Keystone and Glance have been installed with an address in our OpenStack environment that our other OpenStack services can communicate with, we can proceed to install Pacemaker and Corosync as follows:

```
sudo apt-get update
sudo apt-get install pacemaker corosync
```

2. It's important that our two nodes know each other by address and hostname, so enter their details in /etc/hosts to avoid DNS lookups:

   ```
   192.168.100.221 controller1.book controller1
   192.168.100.222 controller2.book controller2
   ```

3. Edit the /etc/corosync/corosync.conf file so that the interface section matches the following code:

   ```
   interface {
     # The following values need to be set based on your
   environment
     ringnumber: 0
     bindnetaddr: 192.168.100.0
     mcastaddr: 226.94.1.1
     mcastport: 5405
   }
   ```

Corosync uses multicast. Ensure that the values don't conflict with any other multicast-enabled services on your network.

4. By default, the corosync service isn't set to start. To ensure that it starts, edit the /etc/default/corosync service and set START=yes, as follows:

   ```
   sudo sed -i 's/^START=no/START=yes/g' /etc/default/corosync
   ```

5. We now need to generate an authorization key to secure the communication between our two hosts:

   ```
   sudo corosync-keygen
   ```

6. You will be asked to generate a random entropy by typing using the keyboard. If you are using an SSH session instead of a console connection, you won't be able to generate the entropy using a keyboard. To do this remotely, launch a new SSH session, and in that new session, while the corosync-keygen command is waiting for entropy, run the following command:

   ```
   while /bin/true
   do
       dd if=/dev/urandom of=/tmp/100 bs=1024 count=100000
       for i in {1..10}
       do
           cp /tmp/100 /tmp/tmp_$i_$RANDOM
       done
       rm -f /tmp/tmp_* /tmp/100
   done
   ```

7. When the `corosync-keygen` command has finished running and an `authkey` file has been generated, simply press *Ctrl* + *C* to cancel this random entropy creation loop.

Setting up the second node – controller2

We now need to install Pacemaker and Corosync on our second host, `controller2`.

1. We install the `pacemaker` and `corosync` packages as follows:

```
sudo apt-get update
sudo apt-get install pacemaker corosync
```

2. We also ensure that our `/etc/hosts` file has the same entries for our other host (as before):

```
192.168.100.221 controller1.book controller1
192.168.100.222 controller2.book controller2
```

3. By default, the `corosync` service isn't set to start. To ensure that it starts, edit the `/etc/default/corosync` service and set `START=yes`:

```
sudo sed -i 's/^START=no/START=yes/g' /etc/default/corosync
```

Configuring the first node – controller1

With the `/etc/corosync/corosync.conf` file modified and the `/etc/corosync/authkey` file generated, we copy this to the other node (or nodes) in our cluster:

```
scp /etc/corosync/corosync.conf /etc/corosync/authkey
openstack@192.168.100.222:
```

Configuring the second node – controller2

We can now put the same `corosync.conf` file as used by our first node and the generated `authkey` file into `/etc/corosync`:

```
sudo mv corosync.conf authkey /etc/corosync
```

Starting the Pacemaker and Corosync services

1. We are now ready to start the services. On both nodes, issue the following commands:

```
sudo service pacemaker start
sudo service corosync start
```

2. To check that our services have started fine and our cluster is working, we can use the `crm_mon` command to query the cluster status:

   sudo crm_mon -1

   This will return output similar to the following where the important information includes the number of nodes configured, the expected number of nodes, and a list of our two nodes that are online:

```
Last updated: Sun Mar 29 12:32:45 2015
Last change: Sun Mar 29 12:32:14 2015 via crmd on controller1
Stack: corosync
Current DC: controller1 (739246301) - partition with quorum
Version: 1.1.10-42f2063
2 Nodes configured
0 Resources configured


Online: [ controller1 controller2 ]
```

3. We can validate the configuration using the `crm_verify` command:

   sudo crm_verify -L -V

4. We will get an error mentioning **STONITH** (short for **Shoot The Other Node In The Head**). STONITH is used to maintain quorum when there are at least three nodes configured. It isn't required in a two-node cluster. As we are only configuring a two-node cluster, we disable `stonith`:

   sudo crm configure property stonith-enabled=false

5. Verifying the cluster using `crm_verify` again will now show errors:

   sudo crm_verify -L

6. Again, as this is only a two-node cluster, we disable any notion of `quorum` using the following command:

   sudo crm configure property no-quorum-policy=ignore

7. On the first node, `controller1`, we can now configure our services and set up a floating address that will be shared between the two servers. In the following command, we've chosen `192.168.100.253` as the `FloatingIP` address and a monitoring interval of 5 seconds. To do this, we use the `crm` command again to configure this `FloatingIP` address, which we will call the `FloatingIP` command. The command is as follows:

```
sudo crm configure primitive FloatingIP \
    ocf:heartbeat:IPaddr2 params ip=192.168.100.253 \
    cidr_netmask=32 op monitor interval=5s
```

8. On viewing the status of our cluster using `crm_mon`, we can now see that the `FloatingIP` address has been assigned to our `controller1` host:

   `sudo crm_mon -1`

   The output is similar to the following example that now says we have one resource configured for this setup (our `FloatingIP`):

```
Last updated: Sun Mar 29 15:18:06 2015
Last change: Sun Mar 29 15:13:23 2015 via cibadmin on controller2
Stack: corosync
Current DC: controller1 (1084777693) - partition with quorum
Version: 1.1.10-42f2063
2 Nodes configured
1 Resources configured


Online: [ controller1 controller2 ]

 FloatingIP     (ocf::heartbeat:IPaddr2):       Started controller1
```

9. We can now use this `FloatingIP` address of `192.168.100.253` to connect to our first node. When we power that node off, this address will be sent to our second node after 5 seconds of no response from the first node. We can test this `FloatingIP` address by executing the following commands from either of the controller hosts:

```
export OS_TENANT_NAME=cookbook
export OS_USERNAME=admin
export OS_PASSWORD=openstack
export OS_AUTH_URL=https://192.168.100.253:5000/v2.0/

keystone --insecure endpoint-list
```

   We will get an output similar to this:

```
+----------------------------------+----------+---------+
|                id                |   name   | enabled |
+----------------------------------+----------+---------+
| ee59bfbf11924c90a535a2eb7a9390e1 | cookbook |   True  |
| cd849efa42b7471d819d6c196060b8cb | service  |   True  |
+----------------------------------+----------+---------+
```

Note that we're using the `--insecure` flag on the command line because we're using self-signed certificates generated independently on both controllers. In production, this would not be required.

How it works...

Making OpenStack services highly available is a complex subject, and there are a number of ways to achieve this. Using Pacemaker and Corosync is a very good solution to this problem. It allows us to configure a floating IP address assigned to the cluster that will attach itself to the appropriate node (using Corosync), as well as control services using agents, so the cluster manager can start and stop services as required to provide a highly available experience to the end user.

We install both Keystone and Glance onto two nodes (each configured appropriately with a remote database backend such as MySQL and Galera), having the images available using a shared filesystem or cloud storage solution. Doing this provides us with the advantage of configuring these services with Pacemaker, and allowing Pacemaker to monitor these services. If the required services are unavailable on the active node, Pacemaker can start those services on the passive node.

Configuring OpenStack services with Pacemaker and Corosync

This recipe represents two nodes running both Glance and Keystone, controlled by Pacemaker with Corosync in active/passive mode that allows for a failure of a single node. In a production environment, it is recommended that a cluster consist of at least three nodes to ensure resiliency and consistency in the case of a single node failure.

Getting ready

For this recipe, we will assume the previous recipe, *Installing and configuring Pacemaker with Corosync*, has been followed to give us two controllers called `controller1` and `controller2`, with a `FloatingIP` address `172.16.0.253` provided by Corosync.

How to do it...

To increase the resilience of OpenStack services, carry out the following steps:

1. With Keystone running on `controller1`, we should be able to query Keystone using both its own IP address (`172.16.0.221`) and the `FloatingIP` (`172.16.0.253`) from a client that has access to the OpenStack environment using the following code:

   ```
   # Assigned IP (192.168.100.221)
   export OS_TENANT_NAME=cookbook
   export OS_USERNAME=admin
   export OS_PASSWORD=openstack
   ```

```
export OS_AUTH_URL=https://192.168.100.221:5000/v2.0/
export OS_KEY=/vagrant/cakey-controller1.pem
export OS_CACERT=/vagrant/ca-controller1.pem

keystone user-list

# FloatingIP (Keepalived and HA Proxy)
export OS_AUTH_URL=https://172.16.0.253:5000/v2.0/

keystone user-list
```

2. Copy the `/etc/keystone/keystone.conf` file from the first host, put it in place on the second node, and then restart the `keystone` service. There is no further work required, as the database has already been populated with the endpoints and users when the install was completed on the first node. Restart the service to connect to the database, as follows:

```
sudo stop keystone
sudo start keystone
```

3. We can now interrogate the second `keystone` service on its own IP address.

```
# Second Node
export OS_AUTH_URL=http://172.16.0.112:5000/v2.0/
keystone user-list
```

Glance across two nodes with FloatingIP

For Glance to be able to run across multiple nodes, it must be configured with a shared storage backend (such as Swift) and be backed by a database backend (such as MySQL). On the first host, install and configure Glance, as described in *Chapter 2*, Glance – *OpenStack Image Service*. After that, follow these steps:

1. On the second node, install the required packages to run Glance, which is backed by MySQL and Swift, by running the command:

```
sudo apt-get install glance python-swift
```

2. Copy over the configuration files in `/etc/glance` to the second host, and start the `glance-api` and `glance-registry` services on both nodes:

```
sudo start glance-api
sudo start glance-registry
```

3. We can now use either the Glance server to view our images, as well as the `FloatingIP` address that is assigned to our first node, by using this code:

```
# First node
glance -I admin -K openstack -T cookbook -N
    http://172.16.0.111:5000/v2.0 index
# Second node
glance -I admin -K openstack -T cookbook -N
    http://172.16.0.112:5000/v2.0 index
# FloatingIP
glance -I admin -K openstack -T cookbook -N
    http://172.16.0.253:5000/v2.0 index
```

Configuring Pacemaker for use with Glance and Keystone

With Keystone and Glance running on both nodes, we can now configure Pacemaker to take control of this service so that we can ensure Keystone and Glance are running on the appropriate node when the other node fails. The steps are as follows:

1. To do this, we first disable the upstart jobs for controlling Keystone and Glance services and then create upstart override files for these services (on both nodes). Create `/etc/init/keystone.override`, `/etc/init/glance-api.override` and `/etc/init/glance-registry.override` with just the keyword `manual` in:
2. We now grab the **OCF** (short for **Open Cluster Format**) resource agents that are shell scripts or pieces of code that are able to control our Keystone and Glance services. We must do this on both our nodes. To do so, run the following commands:

```
wget https://raw.github.com/madkiss/keystone/ha/tools/ocf/keystone
wget https://raw.github.com/madkiss/glance/ha/tools/ocf/glance-api
wget https://raw.github.com/madkiss/glance/ha/tools/ocf/glance-
registry
sudo mkdir -p /usr/lib/ocf/resource.d/openstack
sudo cp keystone glance-api glance-registry \
/usr/lib/ocf/resource.d/openstack
sudo chmod 755 /usr/lib/ocf/resource.d/openstack/*
```

3. We should be now be able to query these new OCF agents available to us, which will return the three OCF agents:

```
sudo crm ra list ocf openstack
```

4. We can now configure Pacemaker to use these agents to control our Keystone service. To do this, we run the following set of commands:

```
sudo crm cib new conf-keystone
```

```
sudo crm configure property stonith-enabled=false
sudo crm configure property no-quorum-policy=ignore
sudo crm configure primitive p_keystone
ocf:openstack:keystone \
    params config="/etc/keystone/keystone.conf" \
    os_auth_url="http://localhost:5000/v2.0/" \
    os_password="openstack" \
    os_tenant_name="cookbook" \
    os_username="admin" \
    user="keystone" \
    client_binary="/usr/bin/keystone" \
    op monitor interval="5s" timeout="5s"
sudo crm cib use live
sudo crm cib commit conf-keystone
```

5. We then issue a similar set of commands for the two Glance services, as follows:

```
sudo crm cib new conf-glance-api
sudo crm configure property stonith-enabled=false
sudo crm configure property no-quorum-policy=ignore
sudo crm configure primitive p_glance_api
ocf:openstack:glance-api \
    params config="/etc/glance/glance-api.conf" \
    os_auth_url="http://localhost:5000/v2.0/" \
    os_password="openstack" \
    os_tenant_name="cookbook" \
    os_username="admin" \
    user="glance" \
    client_binary="/usr/bin/glance" \
    op monitor interval="5s" timeout="5s"
sudo crm cib use live
sudo crm cib commit conf-glance-api

sudo crm cib new conf-glance-registry
sudo crm configure property stonith-enabled=false
sudo crm configure property no-quorum-policy=ignore
sudo crm configure primitive p_glance_registry \
ocf:openstack:glance-registry \
```

```
    params config="/etc/glance/glance-registry.conf" \
    os_auth_url="http://localhost:5000/v2.0/" \
    os_password="openstack" \
    os_tenant_name="cookbook" \
    os_username="admin" \
    user="glance" \
    op monitor interval="5s" timeout="5s"
sudo crm cib use live
sudo crm cib commit conf-glance-registry
```

6. We can verify that we have our Pacemaker configured correctly by issuing the following command:

   ```
   sudo crm_mon -1
   ```

   This brings back something similar to the following output:

```
Last updated: Sat Aug 24 22:55:25 2015
Last change: Tue Aug 24 21:06:10 2015 via crmd on
    controller1
Stack: openais
Current DC: controller1 - partition with quorum
Version: 1.1.6-9971ebba4494012a93c03b40a2c58ec0eb60f50c
2 Nodes configured, 2 expected votes
4 Resources configured.
============

Online: [ controller1 controller2 ]

 FloatingIP     (ocf::heartbeat:IPaddr2):       Started controller1
 p_keystone  (ocf::openstack:keystone):
      Started controller1
 p_glance_api  (ocf::openstack:glance_api):
      Started controller1
 p_glance_registry  (ocf::openstack:glance_registry):
      Started controller1
```

Here's what to do if you receive an error similar to the following error:

```
Failed actions:
    p_keystone_monitor_0 (node=controller2, call=3,
rc=5,     status=complete): not installed
```

Issue the following commands to clear the status and then view the status again:

```
sudo crm_resource -P
sudo crm_mon -1
```

7. We can now configure our client so that they use the `FloatingIP` address `172.16.0.253` for both Glance and Keystone services. With this in place, we can bring down the interface on our first node and still have our Keystone and Glance services available on this `FloatingIP` address.

We now have Keystone and Glance running on two separate nodes, where a node can fail and services will still be available.

How it works...

The configuration of Pacemaker is predominantly done with the `crm` tool. This allows us to script the configuration. If invoked on its own, it allows us to invoke an interactive shell that we can use to edit, add, and remove services, as well as query the status of the cluster. This is a very powerful tool to control an equally powerful cluster manager.

With both nodes running Keystone and Glance, and with Pacemaker and Corosync running and accessible on the `FloatingIP` provided by Corosync, we configure Pacemaker to control the running of the Keystone and Glance services by using an **Open Cluster Framework** (**OCF**) agent written specifically for this purpose. The OCF agent uses a number of parameters that will be familiar to us, and they require the same username, password, tenant, and endpoint URL that we would use in a client to access that service.

A timeout of 5 seconds was set up for both the agent and when the `FloatingIP` address moves to another host.

After this configuration, we have a Keystone and Glance active/passive configuration, as shown in the diagram:

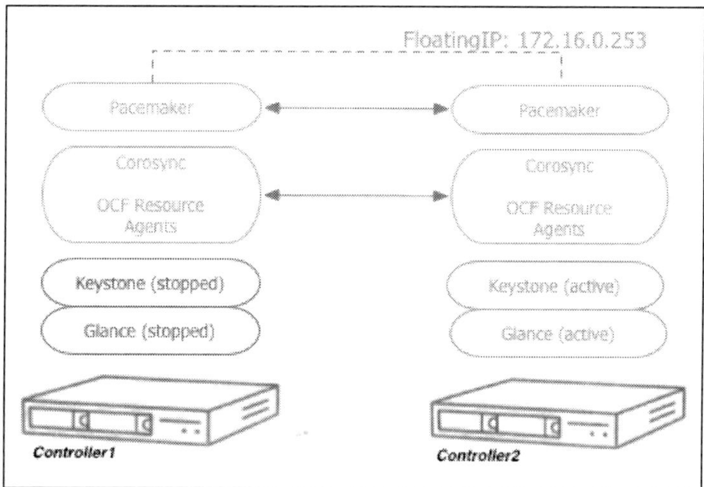

Bonding network interfaces for redundancy

Running multiple services across multiple machines and implementing appropriate HA methods ensure a high degree of tolerance to failure within our environment. But if it's the physical network that fails and not the service, outages will occur if traffic cannot flow to and from that service. Adding in **Network Interface Card** (**NIC**) bonding (also known as teaming or link aggregation) can help alleviate these issues by ensuring traffic flows through diverse routes and switches as appropriate.

Getting ready

NIC bonding requires coordination between system administrators and the network administrators who are responsible for the switches. There are various methods available for NIC bonding. The method presented here is active-passive mode, which describes that traffic will normally flows through a single switch, leaving the other teamed NIC to take no traffic until it is required.

How to do it...

Setting up NIC bonding in Ubuntu 14.04 requires an extra package installation to allow bonding. We set an NIC bond by following these steps:

1. We install the `ifenslave` package in the usual manner, as follows:

   ```
   sudo apt-get update
   sudo apt-get install ifenslave
   ```

2. With the `ifenslave` package installed, we simply configure networking as normal in Ubuntu but add in the required elements for bonding. To do this, we edit the `/etc/network/interfaces` file with the following contents (for active-passive mode bonding). Here, we're bonding `eth1` and `eth2` to give us `bond0` with an address of `172.16.0.111`:

   ```
   auto eth1
   iface eth1 inet manual
     bond-master bond0
     bond-primary eth1 eth2

   auto eth2
   iface eth2 inet manual
     bond-master bond0
     bond-primary eth1 eth2

   auto bond0
   iface bond0 inet static
   ```

```
address 172.16.0.111
netmask 255.255.0.0
network 172.16.0.0
broadcast 172.16.255.255
bond-slaves none
bond-mode 1
bond-miimon 100
```

3. To ensure that the correct bonding mode is used, we add the following contents into `/etc/modprobe.d/bonding.conf`. This describes an active/passive bond (`mode=1`) with a monitoring interval of 100 milliseconds:

   ```
   alias bond0 bonding
   options bonding mode=1 miimon=100
   ```

4. We can now restart our networking, which in turn will bring up our bonded interface with the required IP address:

   ```
   sudo service networking restart
   ```

How it works...

Bonding network interfaces in Ubuntu to cater to a switch failure is relatively straightforward. This is achieved by providing the coordination with how the switches are set up and configured. With different paths to different switches configured and each network interface going to separate switches, a high level of fault tolerance to network-level events, such as a switch failure, can be achieved.

To do this, we configure our bonding in the traditional `/etc/network/interfaces` file under Ubuntu, but we specify which NICs are teamed with which bonded interface. Each bonded interface configured has at least a unique pair of interfaces assigned to it, and then we configure that bonded interface, `bond0`, with the usual IP address, netmask, and so on. We tag a few options specifically to notify Ubuntu that this is a bonded interface of a particular mode.

To ensure the bonding module that gets loaded as part of the kernel has the right mode assigned to it, we configure the module in `/etc/modprobe.d/bonding.conf`. When the bonding module loads along with te network interface, we end up with a server that is able to withstand isolated switch failures.

See also

- For more information on the different bonding modes that Ubuntu Linux supports, see `https://help.ubuntu.com/community/LinkAggregation`

Automating OpenStack installations using Ansible – host configuration

There are a number of ways to automate an installation of OpenStack. These methods predominantly make use of configuration management tools such as Chef, Puppet, and Ansible. In this recipe, we will see how to use **Ansible** for the installation of OpenStack and how the Playbooks make use of **LXC containers**, in which isolate resources and filesystems to the service are running in the container. At the time of writing, the Ansible Playbooks that are used for installing OpenStack are hosted on Stackforge. These will soon move to the OpenStack GitHub branch as an official project.

Getting ready

The environment that we will be using in this recipe will consist of seven physical servers:

- Three Controller nodes make up a cluster of nodes running the OpenStack API services, such as Glance, Keystone, and Horizon, as well as MariaDB and RabbitMQ.
- One Storage node is used for Cinder LVM volumes.
- Two (or more) nodes will be the Compute nodes. With this infrastructure, we can scale out the Compute to meet demand in our environment, as well as separate our Controller services across a larger set of nodes and scale as required.
- One HA Proxy node will be the host we will install our environment from, as well as provide HA Proxy services to Load Balance the APIs of the services.

In production environments, it is highly recommended that a pair of physical Load Balancers are used instead of HA Proxy.

- All of the machines will need to have Ubuntu 14.04 LTS release freshly installed as used in the rest of the book.
- All of the machines will have access to the Internet.

Each server will have at least two network cards installed and utilize VLANs (a total of four distinct networks are created for the installation). In production, it is assumed you will have at least four network cards so that you create two bonded pair of interfaces and appropriately cable them to different HA switches for resilience.

To better understand the networking, refer to the following diagram:

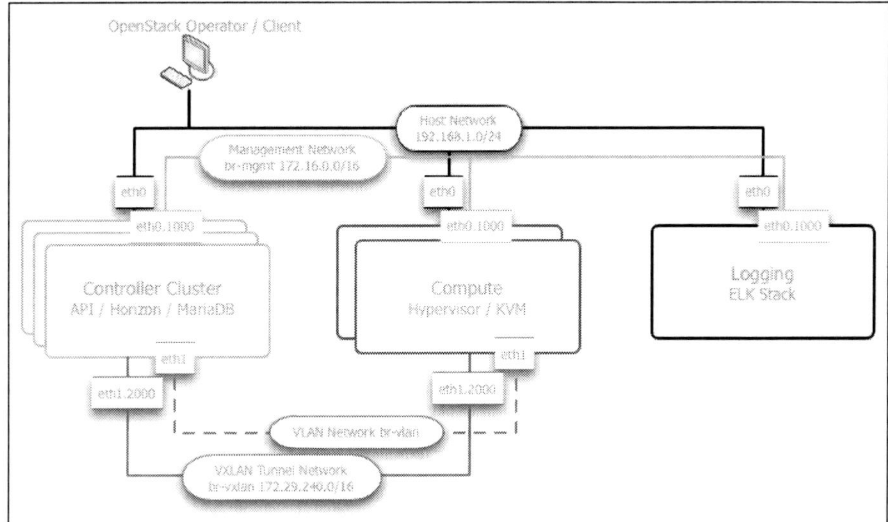

The following networks will be used for our OpenStack installation using Ansible:

- `eth0`: This will be used for accessing the host itself (untagged VLAN). This interface will have an IP assigned on the host subnet. This will also be used for storage traffic. An optional `br-storage` bridge and interface can be used for dedicated storage traffic. This isn't used in this section.
- `eth0.1000`: This will be the VLAN (tag 1000) interface that the container bridge (`br-mgmt`) will be created on. The `eth0.1000` interface will not have an IP assigned to it directly; this IP will be assigned to the bridge (`br-mgmt`) as described here.
    - `br-mgmt`: This will be the bridge created that connects to `eth0.1000` and is a network utilized solely for container to container network traffic. This network carries the communication between OpenStack services, such as Glance requiring access to Keystone. This `br-mgmt` bridge will have an IP address on the management network (also called the container network) so our hosts can access the containers.
- `eth1`: This will be the network interface that all VLAN based Neutron traffic will traverse. The controllers and computes will need this interface configured. The storage nodes and HA Proxy node do not need this configuring.
    - `br-vlan`: This will be a bridge that connects to `eth1`. Neither `br-vlan` nor `eth1` will have an IP assigned as OpenStack Neutron controls these on the fly when networks of type VLAN are created.

- `eth1.2000`: This will be the VLAN (tag `2000`) interface that a VXLAN network will be created on. OpenStack Neutron has the ability to create private tenant networks of type VXLAN. This will be created over this interface.
    - `br-vxlan`: This will be a bridge that includes `eth1.2000` to carry the data created in a VXLAN tunnel network. For our OpenStack environment, this network will allow a user to create Neutron networks of type VXLAN that will be overlaid over this network. This bridge will have an IP assigned to it in the *tunnel network*.

How to do it...

The first stage is to ensure that the seven hosts described in this section are configured and ready for installation of OpenStack using the Ansible Playbooks; to do so, follow these steps.

1. Configure the network on all seven hosts by editing the `/etc/network/interfaces` file with the following contents (consider using bonded interfaces for production, and edit to suit your network details):

```
# Host Interface
auto eth0
  iface eth0
  inet static
  address 192.168.1.101
  netmask 255.255.255.0
  gateway 192.168.1.1
  dns-nameservers 192.168.1.1

# Neutron Interface, no IP assigned
auto eth1
  iface eth1
  inet manual

# Container management VLAN interface
iface eth0.1000
  inet manual
  vlan-raw-device eth0

# OpenStack VXLAN (tunnel/overlay) VLAN interface
iface eth1.2000
  inet manual
  vlan-raw-device eth1
```

2. We continue editing the same `/etc/network/interfaces` file to add in the matching bridge information, as follows:

```
# Bridge for Container network
auto br-mgmt
  iface br-mgmt inet static
  bridge_stp off
  bridge_waitport 0
  bridge_fd 0
  # Bridge port references tagged interface
  bridge_ports eth1.1000
  address 172.16.0.101
  netmask 255.255.0.0
  dns-nameservers 192.168.1.1

# Bridge for vlan network
auto br-vlan
  iface br-vlan inet manual
  bridge_stp off
  bridge_waitport 0
  bridge_fd 0
  # Notice this bridge port is an Untagged interface
  bridge_ports eth1

# Bridge for vxlan network
auto br-vxlan
  iface br-vxlan inet static
  bridge_stp off
  bridge_waitport 0
  bridge_fd 0
  # Bridge port references tagged interface
  bridge_ports eth1.2000
  address 172.29.240.101
  netmask 255.255.252.0
  dns-nameservers 192.168.1.1
```

3. We can now restart our networking, which, in turn, will bring up our host interfaces and bridges with the required IP addresses:

```
sudo service networking restart
```

4. Repeat step 1 to step 3 for each host on your network that will have OpenStack installed, adjusting the IP addresses accordingly.

5. Ensure that all seven nodes in the environment are reachable on all networks created. This can be achieved using `fping`, as shown here:

```
# host network (eth0)
fping -g 192.168.1.101 192.168.1.107

# container network (br-mgmt)
fping -g 172.16.0.101 172.16.0.107

# For Computes and Controllers Only
# tunnel network (br-vxlan)
fping -g 172.29.240.101 172.29.240.105
```

How it works...

Setting up the networking correctly is important. Retrospectively, altering the network once an installation of OpenStack has occurred can be tricky.

We used two physical interfaces (if using bonding, it is a total of four but is referred to as two), allocating appropriate VLANs and dropping the created interfaces into specific bridges. These bridged interfaces, `br-mgmt`, `br-vxlan` and `br-vlan`, are referenced directly in the Ansible Playbook configurations, so do not change these names.

The host network on `eth0` is the network that will have the default gateway of your LAN, and this network will be used to access the Internet to pull down the required packages as part of the OpenStack installation.

We create a VLAN tagged interface `eth0.1000` on `eth0`, which will be used for container-to-container traffic. The Ansible Playbooks install the OpenStack services in LXC containers, and these containers must be able to communicate with each other. This network is not routable and is only used for inter-container communication. This VLAN tagged interface is dropped into the bridge, `br-mgmt`. The `br-mgmt` bridge is given an IP address on this management (container) network so that the hosts can communicate with the containers when they eventually get created in the next two recipes.

The second interface (or second bonded interface) carries the traffic for Neutron, so only the controllers and computes need this interface. As we are configuring our environment to carry both VLAN Neutron tenant networks and VXLAN tenant networks, we first create a VLAN tagged interface `eth1.2000` and drop this into the bridge `br-vxlan`. As this is for VXLAN traffic, we assign an IP to this bridge. Now, tunnels can be created over this network. This network doesn't have any routes associated with it. We then create a `br-vlan` bridge and drop the untagged interface `eth1` into this. This is because when we eventually come to create Neutron tenant networks of type VLAN, Neutron adds the tags to this untagged interface.

Automating OpenStack installations using Ansible – Playbook configuration

Now that the hosts have been configured correctly and all of the network interfaces are set up correctly, we can begin editing the configuration files that will be used when the Ansible Playbooks are run. In this recipe, we use Git to check the **OpenStack Ansible Deployment** (**OSAD**) Playbooks, the same ones originally developed by Rackspace and used by them to deploy OpenStack for its customers. We will be using the latest release at the time of writing: Git Tag 11.0.3 that refers to the Kilo release (Kilo refers to the letter K, which is the 11th letter in the alphabet).

The environment we will configure is shown in the following diagram:

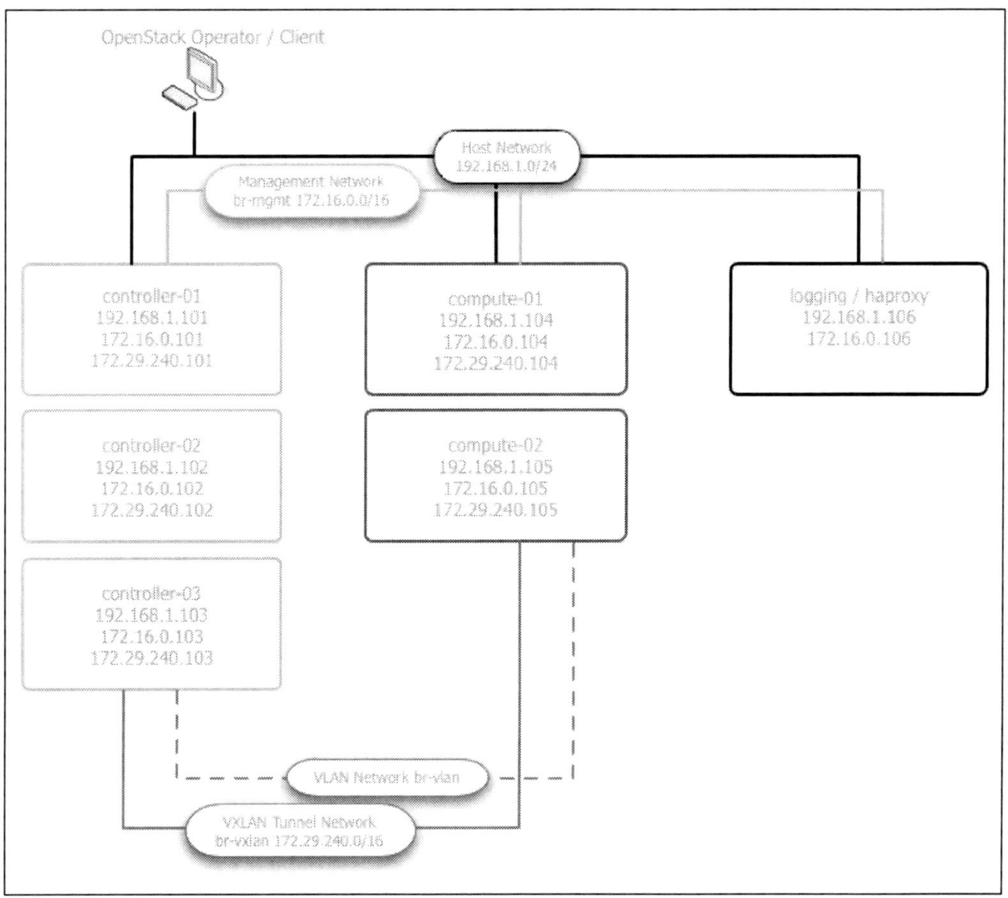

Getting ready

It is important that the previous recipe, *Automating OpenStack installations using Ansible – host configuration*, has been followed and that all the configured networks are working as expected.

The environment will consist of three Controller nodes, one Storage node, one HA Proxy node, and two Compute nodes. Identify which of these will be the HA Proxy server and log into it as the *root* user. Out of convenience, this server will also be used to install OpenStack.

How to do it...

In this recipe, we are configuring the YAML configuration files that are used by the Playbooks. There are three files that we will be configuring: `openstack_user_config.yml`, `user_variables.yml`, and `user_secrets.yml`. The three of these files combined describe our entire installation, from what server in our datacenter is running which OpenStack function to passwords and features to enable in OpenStack.

1. We first need to get the Ansible Playbooks from GitHub and place them into `/opt/os-ansible-deployment`. This is achieved with the following command:

   ```
   cd /opt
   git clone -b 11.0.3 \
       https://github.com/stackforge/os-ansible-deployment.git
   ```

2. We then proceed to configure the installation by first copying the example and empty configuration files from the cloned GitHub repository to `/etc/openstack_deploy`, as shown here:

   ```
   cp -R /opt/os-ansible/etc/openstack_deploy /etc
   ```

3. The first file we configure is a large file located at `/etc/openstack_deploy/openstack_user_config.yml`, which describes our physical environment. The information here is very specific to our installation describing network ranges, interfaces used, and the nodes that are running each service. The first section refers to the CIDRs used in our environment:

   ```
   ---
   cidr_networks:
     management: 172.16.0.0/16
     tunnel: 172.29.240.0/22

   used_ips:
     - 172.16.0.101,172.16.0.107
     - 172.29.240.101,172.29.240.107
   ```

This file can be found online at `https://github.com/OpenStackCookbook/OpenStackCookbook/blob/master/ansible-openstack/openstack_user_config.yml`.

4. In the same file, we have the `global_overrides` section. The `global_overrides` section describes our Load Balance VIP addresses, our network bridges, and details of the Neutron networking. This a longer section that has the following in our environment. Note that we are pre-empting how things will be installed. Here, we set the IP addresses needed for a Load Balancer that does not yet exist in our environment. We will be using HA Proxy (installed in the next recipe) that will use these addresses:

```
global_overrides:
  internal_lb_vip_address: 172.16.0.107
  external_lb_vip_address: 192.168.1.107
  lb_name: haproxy
  tunnel_bridge: "br-vxlan"
  management_bridge: "br-mgmt"
  provider_networks:
    - network:
        group_binds:
          - all_containers
          - hosts
        type: "raw"
        container_bridge: "br-mgmt"
        container_interface: "eth1"
        container_type: "veth"
        ip_from_q: "management"
        is_container_address: true
        is_ssh_address: true
    - network:
        group_binds:
          - neutron_linuxbridge_agent
        container_bridge: "br-vxlan"
        container_type: "veth"
        container_interface: "eth10"
        ip_from_q: "tunnel"
        type: "vxlan"
        range: "1:1000"
        net_name: "vxlan"
    - network:
        group_binds:
          - neutron_linuxbridge_agent
```

```
            container_bridge: "br-vlan"
            container_type: "veth"
            container_interface: "eth11"
            type: "vlan"
            range: "1:1"
            net_name: "vlan"
        - network:
            group_binds:
              - neutron_linuxbridge_agent
            container_bridge: "br-vlan"
            container_type: "veth"
            container_interface: "eth12"
            host_bind_override: "eth12"
            type: "flat"
            net_name: "flat"
```

5. After this section, we get to describe what servers make up our OpenStack installation. In the same file, next, add these, details which will refer to our infrastructure hosts (or the controller nodes). Each section has the three servers listed we allocated as our controller nodes. This section is about the shared services such as MariaDB and RabbitMQ:

```
# Shared infrastructure parts
shared-infra_hosts:
  controller-01:
    ip: 172.16.0.101
  controller-02:
    ip: 172.16.0.102
  controller-03:
    ip: 172.16.0.103
```

6. This section is where our OpenStack Compute services, such as the Nova API, will get installed:

```
# OpenStack infrastructure parts
os-infra_hosts:
  controller-01:
    ip: 172.16.0.101
  controller-02:
    ip: 172.16.0.102
  controller-03:
    ip: 172.16.0.103
```

7. The `storage-infra` section is where the Cinder storage API will be found:

```
# OpenStack Storage infrastructure parts
storage-infra_hosts:
  controller-01:
    ip: 172.16.0.101
  controller-02:
    ip: 172.16.0.102
  controller-03:
    ip: 172.16.0.103
```

8. This describes where we will find the Keystone API:

```
# Keystone Identity infrastructure parts
identity_hosts:
  controller-01:
    ip: 172.16.0.101
  controller-02:
    ip: 172.16.0.102
  controller-03:
    ip: 172.16.0.103
```

9. Next, we describe the servers that will be used for our Compute nodes (the hypervisor nodes). In the same file, add these details that refer to our Compute hosts:

```
# Compute Hosts
compute_hosts:
  compute-01:
    ip: 172.16.0.104
  compute-02:
    ip: 172.16.0.105
```

10. Next, we configure any Cinder storage nodes. We enter the information about how this is configured (such as the backend type such as NFS with NetApp or LVM) here:

```
storage_hosts:
  storage:
    ip: 172.16.0.106
    container_vars:
      cinder_backends:
        limit_container_types: cinder_volume
        lvm:
          volume_group: cinder-volumes
          volume_driver:
cinder.volume.drivers.lvm.LVMISCSIDriver
          volume_backend_name: LVM_iSCSI
```

11. As part of the Playbooks, we can install the Neutron services on a number of infrastructure nodes. We tell Ansible to deploy this software at these addresses:

```
network_hosts:
  controller-01:
    ip: 172.16.0.101
  controller-02:
    ip: 172.16.0.102
  controller-03:
    ip: 172.16.0.103
```

12. Define the repository hosts that are used for installation of the packages within the environment:

```
# User defined Repository Hosts
repo-infra_hosts:
  controller-01:
    ip: 172.16.0.101
  controller-02:
    ip: 172.16.0.102
  controller-03:
    ip: 172.16.0.103
```

13. Finally, we add in the following section so that when we install HA Proxy (to wrap our cluster behind), the Playbooks know where to install the service:

```
haproxy_hosts:
  haproxy:
    ip: 172.16.0.107
```

14. The next file that we need to edit is the `/etc/openstack_deploy/user_variables.yml` file. This file is a much smaller file that describes OpenStack configuration options. For example, we specify in here what the backend filesystem is used for Glance, options for Nova, as well as options for Apache (which sits in front of Keystone):

```
## Glance Options
# Set default_store to "swift" if using Cloud Files
# or swift backend or file to use NFS or local filesystem
glance_default_store: file
glance_notification_driver: noop

## Nova options
nova_virt_type: kvm
nova_cpu_allocation_ratio: 2.0
nova_ram_allocation_ratio: 1.0

## Apache SSL Settings
```

```
# These do not need to be configured unless you're creating
# certificates for
# services running behind Apache (currently, Horizon and
# Keystone).
ssl_protocol: "ALL -SSLv2 -SSLv3"
# Cipher suite string from
https://hynek.me/articles/hardening-your-web-servers-ssl-
ciphers/
ssl_cipher_suite:
"ECDH+AESGCM:DH+AESGCM:ECDH+AES256:DH+AES256:ECDH+AES128:DH
+AES:ECDH+3DES:DH+3DES:RSA+AESGCM:RSA+AES:RSA+3DES:!aNULL:!
MD5:!DSS"
```

This file can be found online at `https://github.com/OpenStackCookbook/OpenStackCookbook/ansible-openstack/user_variables.yml`.

15. The last file that we need to configure is the `/etc/openstack_deploy/user_secrets.yml` file, which holds the passphrases the services use within OpenStack. To configure this securely for our environment, and to provide randomly generated strings, execute the following command:

```
cd /opt/os-ansible-deployment
scripts/pw-token-gen.py --file
  /etc/openstack_deploy/user_secrets.yml
```

Congratulations! We're now ready to use the Ansible Playbooks to install OpenStack.

How it works...

All configuration management and automated system installations require a lot of effort in the first few stages, which reduces a lot of time later on. Installing something as complex as OpenStack is no different.

After we fetched the Playbooks from GitHub, we configured the following files:

- `/etc/openstack_deploy/openstack_user_config.yml`: This file describes our physical environment (which includes networking, the hosts that are being used, and what services those hosts will run)
- `/etc/openstack_deploy/user_variables.yml`: This file describes the configuration of OpenStack services, such as the CPU contention ratio for KVM
- `/etc/openstack_deploy/user_secrets.yml`: This file has the service passphrases, such as the MariaDB root user passphrase for use with MariaDB, and the Nova service passphrase when the service gets created in Keystone

Once these files have been edited to suit the environment, the Playbooks in the next recipe, *Automating OpenStack installations using Ansible – running Playbooks*, can be executed. Then, we can run through a hands-free installation of OpenStack.

See also

- More information on configuring and running the OpenStack Ansible Deployment can be found in the Rackspace documentation at `http://docs.rackspace.com/`

Automating OpenStack installations using Ansible – running Playbooks

In this recipe, we simply run a series of Ansible Playbooks that lay down the infrastructure needed on top of our six Ubuntu 14.04 LTS hosts, and then install all of the software required to run a highly available OpenStack installation.

Ansible uses SSH and Python to execute the Playbooks that describe how to install and configure software on distributed systems. Its lightweight design with very few dependencies makes it perfect to install OpenStack across our many Ubuntu hosts.

Getting ready

It is important that the previous two recipes, *Automating OpenStack installations using Ansible – host configuration* and *Automating OpenStack installations using Ansible – Playbook configuration*, have been followed, that all the configured networks are working as expected, and that the relevant configuration files are edited to suit the upcoming installation. If not, please log in to the Logging host where the Ansible OpenStack Deployment has been configured.

How to do it...

Now that we have a set of configuration files in `/etc/openstack_deploy` that our Ansible Playbooks will look for and understand, we can begin the installation of OpenStack by following these steps:

1. First, we need to ensure that Ansible is installed on our host that we're using to run the installation from. In this case, this is the Logging host. This can be achieved by running the following command:

   ```
   cd /opt/os-ansible-deployment
   scripts/bootstrap-ansible.sh
   ```

2. Once the installation has finished, it will have produced a wrapper script called `openstack-ansible` that we will use to run the Playbooks. The first Playbook to run is the `setup-hosts.yml` file. This is run by executing the following commands:

   ```
   cd /opt/os-ansible-deployment/playbooks
   openstack-ansible setup-hosts.yml
   ```

   We will get an output that will be familiar to anyone running Ansible and give verbose information during the running of the Playbooks.

If the Playbook fails, as denoted by the final message with the states of the changes, we can re-run the Playbooks and target only the failed portions by executing the following commands:

```
openstack-ansible setup-hosts.yml \
    --limit @/root/setup-hosts.retry
```

3. If the output shows all OK messages in green, with no failed or unreachable hosts, then we can proceed to run the next set of Playbooks. As we're running HA Proxy in this recipe, we run this next by executing the following. Note that if you are installing OpenStack sitting behind a Load Balancer such as an F5, this must be configured separately at this stage:

   ```
   openstack-ansible haproxy-install.yml
   ```

If the Playbook fails as denoted by the final message with the states of the changes, we can re-run the Playbook and targeting only the failed portions by executing the following commands:

```
openstack-ansible haproxy-install.yml \
    --limit @/root/haproxy-install.retry
```

4. If the output shows all OK messages in green, with no failed or unreachable hosts, then we can proceed to run the next set of Playbooks that runs the infrastructure services required to support OpenStack. This Playbook configures the many LXC containers used in this installation and the Galera and RabbitMQ services that support OpenStack. To execute this Playbook, run the following command. Note that this usually takes quite a bit of time to run, so be patient:

   ```
   openstack-ansible setup-infrastructure.yml
   ```

If the Playbook fails, as denoted by the final message with the states of the changes, we can re-run the Playbook and target only the failed portions by executing the following command:

```
openstack-ansible setup-infrastructure.yml \
    --limit @/root/setup-infrastructure.retry
```

5. If the output is all green and OK, we can now carry on and install all of the OpenStack services by simply executing the following command. This step takes a while:

   ```
   openstack-ansible setup-openstack.yml
   ```

If the Playbook fails, as denoted by the final message with the states of the changes, we can re-run the Playbook and target only the failed portions by executing the following command:

```
openstack-ansible setup-openstack.yml \
    --limit @/root/setup-openstack.retry
```

6. Congratulations! We have completed the installation of OpenStack using Ansible. To log in to the environment either use Horizon, by pointing the browser to the Load Balancer address, or use `ssh` command to connect to a utility container as follows:

   ```
   grep utility /etc/hosts
   ```

   Identify one of them to connect using the `ssh` command to the following:

   ```
   ssh controller-01_utility_container-88105269
   ```

   Source in the OpenStack credentials and use the environment as usual:

   ```
   . openrc
   ```

How it works...

Ansible is a very powerful yet lightweight system that runs Playbooks over SSH to install and configure software. It is perfect for installing OpenStack that lays down software across the many number of nodes.

A number of Playbooks are run, and they are listed as follows:

- `setup-hosts.yml`: This installs and configures the LXC containers across our nodes, which will be the targets for the installation of the various OpenStack services in the environment.

- `haproxy-install.yml`: This allows us to use HA Proxy for our installation. As we are running a set of three controllers, we need a Load Balancer to allow the services to communicate correctly in our environment.
- `setup-infrastructure.yml`: This installs all the ancillary services such, as MariaDB, Galera, memcached, and RabbitMQ.
- `setup-openstack.yml`: This installs all the OpenStack services required to give a complete, production-ready installation on our environment.

Should any of the Playbooks fail, a shortcut to fix just the necessary parts can be achieved by specifying `--limit @/root/{playbook}.retry` (omitting the `.yml` extension). Ansible is very verbose in its output and will inform you when this is possible, as shown here:

```
PLAY RECAP ***********************************************************************
        to retry, use: --limit @/root/setup-openstack.retry

controller-02_glance_container-05d84ae8 : ok=0    changed=0    unreachable=1    failed=0
controller-03_glance_container-f3ad477d : ok=58   changed=43   unreachable=0    failed=0
```

This environment has been configured so that Glance uses the local filesystem for the uploaded images to be used in OpenStack. As we have installed a cluster of three Glance image servers, it is assumed that images will be uploaded to Glance using the `--location <IMAGE_URL>` flag. This flag tells Glance to fetch the image from the `IMAGE_URL` provided rather than store the image locally. Adjust the `/etc/openstack_deploy/user_variables.yml` file as described in the previous recipe to choose a different storage option for Glance to suit your environment.

There's more...

This installation involved a number of Playbooks that configured our host, installed extra services, and then installed OpenStack. There is a wrapper script that can be used that covers all of these steps in one command. This can be achieved by running the following command instead:

```
cd /opt/os-ansible-deployment
scripts/run-playbooks.sh
```

Note that by splitting up the installation, we can fix specific Playbook issues as well as having a chance for HA Proxy to be configured correctly. It is therefore prudent to use the preceding Playbook when setting up a test environment on a single host.

See also

- More information on configuring and running the OpenStack Ansible Deployment can be found at the Rackspace documentation site at `http://docs.rackspace.com/`
- Further information can also be found by reading the README at `https://github.com/stackforge/os-ansible-deployment`

Index

F

G

H

I

J

K

T

U

V

W

Y

Z

Thank you for buying
OpenStack Cloud Computing Cookbook
Third Edition

About Packt Publishing

Packt, pronounced 'packed', published its first book, *Mastering phpMyAdmin for Effective MySQL Management*, in April 2004, and subsequently continued to specialize in publishing highly focused books on specific technologies and solutions.

Our books and publications share the experiences of your fellow IT professionals in adapting and customizing today's systems, applications, and frameworks. Our solution-based books give you the knowledge and power to customize the software and technologies you're using to get the job done. Packt books are more specific and less general than the IT books you have seen in the past. Our unique business model allows us to bring you more focused information, giving you more of what you need to know, and less of what you don't.

Packt is a modern yet unique publishing company that focuses on producing quality, cutting-edge books for communities of developers, administrators, and newbies alike. For more information, please visit our website at `www.packtpub.com`.

About Packt Open Source

In 2010, Packt launched two new brands, Packt Open Source and Packt Enterprise, in order to continue its focus on specialization. This book is part of the Packt open source brand, home to books published on software built around open source licenses, and offering information to anybody from advanced developers to budding web designers. The Open Source brand also runs Packt's open source Royalty Scheme, by which Packt gives a royalty to each open source project about whose software a book is sold.

Writing for Packt

We welcome all inquiries from people who are interested in authoring. Book proposals should be sent to `author@packtpub.com`. If your book idea is still at an early stage and you would like to discuss it first before writing a formal book proposal, then please contact us; one of our commissioning editors will get in touch with you.

We're not just looking for published authors; if you have strong technical skills but no writing experience, our experienced editors can help you develop a writing career, or simply get some additional reward for your expertise.

Learning OpenStack Networking (Neutron)

ISBN: 978-1-78398-330-8 Paperback: 300 pages

Architect and build a network infrastructure for your cloud using OpenStack Neutron networking

1. Build a virtual switching infrastructure for virtual machines using the Open vSwitch or Linux Bridge plugins.
2. Create networks and software routers that connect virtual machines to the Internet using built-in Linux networking features.
3. Scale your application using Neutron's load-balancing-as-a-service feature using the haproxy plugin.

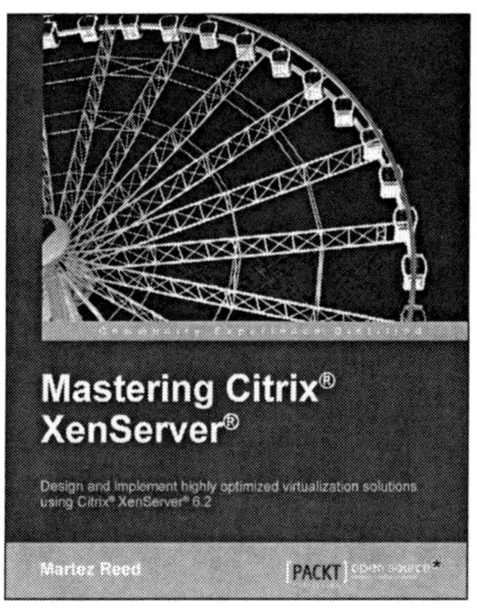

Mastering Citrix® XenServer®

ISBN: 978-1-78328-739-0 Paperback: 300 pages

Design and implement highly optimized virtualization solutions using Citrix® XenServer® 6.2

1. Master mission-critical aspects of virtualization to develop, deploy, and administer virtual infrastructures.
2. Integrate Citrix XenServer with OpenStack and CloudStack to create a private cloud.
3. Implement automation with command-line Windows PowerShell scripting.

Please check **www.PacktPub.com** for information on our titles

CPSIA information can be obtained
at www.ICGtesting.com
Printed in the USA
FSOW01n0034230316
18304FS

9 781782 174783